CHURCHILL'S CRUSADE

Churchill's Crusade

The British Invasion of Russia, 1918–1920

Clifford Kinvig

hambledon
continuum

Hambledon Continuum, a Continuum imprint
The Tower Building, 11 York Road, London SE1 7NX, UK
80 Maiden Lane, Suite 704, New York, NY 10038, USA

First Published 2006

ISBN 1 85285 477 4

A description of this book is available from the
British Library and from the Library of Congress.

Typeset by Egan Reid Ltd, Auckland, New Zealand.
Printed in Great Britain by MPG Books Ltd, Cornwall.

Contents

Illustrations

Plates

Between Pages 76 and 77

Between Pages 172 and 173

Maps and Text Illustrations

Illustration Acknowledgements

The author and publisher are grateful to the Imperial War Museum for permission to reproduce plates 1, 3, 5, 6, 9–14, 16–19, 22, 23; to Lucy Sheppard for plate 15; and to the Royal Hampshire for plates 20 and 21.

Acknowledgements

In *Churchill's Crusade* I have tried to let the participants in the intervention in Russia speak for themselves. I must consequently first acknowledge my debt to the many copyright holders of the letters, diaries, photographs and other personal accounts which I have used in writing it. I have tried to contact them all and apologise to any who, despite my best efforts, may have been missed. My thanks go also to those who maintain the archives in which these records are preserved, especially to the staff of the Churchill Archives Centre, Churchill College, Cambridge; the Department of Documents at the Imperial War Museum, and particularly to its Keeper, Roderick Suddaby; to Kate O'Brien, Military Archivist, and the staff of the Liddell Hart Centre for Military Archives, King's College, London; and to Alastair Massie and the archival and library staff of the National Army Museum. Those in charge of regimental collections have also been most helpful, in particular Lieutenant Colonel John Darroch, Honorary Archivist of the Royal Hampshire Regiment; Lieutenant Colonel Neil McIntosh MBE, at the Regimental Headquarters, the Green Howards; Simon Jones, sometime Curator of the King's Regiment Collection, Museum of Liverpool Life; and Paul Evans, Librarian of the James Clavell Library, Firepower, Woolwich. Dr Peter Hartley kindly lent me and allowed me to quote from family letters in his care.

I would also like to express my gratitude to the relatively small band of historians who have worked at unravelling the political and diplomatic complexities of Britain's relations with its allies and with Russia during the period of the Russian Civil War. I am particularly grateful to Richard H. Ullman and Michael Kettle, authors, respectively, of the muti-volume histories published under the general titles of *Anglo-Soviet Relations, 1917–1921* and *Russia and the Allies, 1917–1920*. No author examining any aspect of the long and distinguished career of Winston Churchill can do other than acknowledge a great debt to his biographer Sir Martin Gilbert, in my case particularly for volume four of his monumental biography and its two invaluable companion volumes of documents.

Several libraries have given me generous assistance. I should like to thank Tim Ward and the staff of the Prince Consort's Library, Aldershot; the staff of the Departments of Printed Books and of Photographs at the Imperial War Museum; Jackie Willcox, Librarian of the Russian and Eurasian Studies Centre, St Antony's College, Oxford; the Bentley Historical Library, University of Michigan; and the

Bodleian Library, Oxford. I am also grateful to the Cirencester Bingham Library, part of the Gloucestershire Library Service, whose staff have been most helpful in accessing books from beyond their local collections.

Copyright material drawn from collections for which they are responsible appears by permission of the Master and Fellows of Churchill College, Cambridge, the Museum of the Hampshire Regiment and the Trustees of the Imperial War Museum, the Liddell Hart Centre for Military Archives, the National Army Museum and the Royal Artillery Historical Trust. Quotations from Crown Copyright material appear by permission of the Controller of Her Majesty's Stationery Office.

Dr Geoffrey Best and Dr Peter Hartley were kind enough to discuss aspects of this study with me, and Major Alan Baker, Dr Best and Major General Tony Trythall generously read and commented on parts of the draft manuscript.

My publishers, Hambledon Continuum, deserve my sincere thanks: Tony Morris for his interest in the project from an early stage and encouragement throughout, and Martin Sheppard for his many helpful suggestions, his meticulous editing and his patience.

Finally, my thanks go to my wife, Shirley, who has borne my preoccupation with this bizarre episode in Churchill's life and Britain's military history with her customary patience and good humour. It goes without saying that neither she, nor any of the others who have assisted me with the book, bear responsibility for any errors and imperfections it still contains.

IN MEMORY OF
COLONEL ARCHIE WHITE VC, MC
1891–1971

Soldier and Educator

He fought at Gallipoli, the Somme and Archangel

I wonder whether it is any use my making one last effort to induce you to throw off this obsession which, if you will forgive me for saying so, is upsetting your balance. I again ask you to let Russia be, at any rate for a few days, and to concentrate your mind on the quite unjustifiable expenditure in France, at home and in the East, incurred by both the War Office and the Air Department. Some of the items could not possibly have been tolerated by you if you had given one-fifth of the thought to these matters which you have devoted to Russia.

David Lloyd George to Winston Churchill
22 September 1919

Introduction

On 27 June 1919 final preparations were being made at the palace of Versailles for a decisive moment in the life of Europe: the following day the Peace Treaty with Germany was to be signed after four bitter years of war. The ceremony was to take place in the magnificent Hall of Mirrors, at last bringing formal settlement to the most destructive conflict in human history. Meanwhile, in the unpretentious Cabinet Room in London, events of a much less pacific character were being planned. Winston Churchill was endeavouring to persuade his government colleagues to allow General Ironside's strongly reinforced troops in north Russia to take the offensive against the Bolsheviks. This was the third occasion in as many weeks on which he had argued for the operation to go ahead. Churchill had occupied the post of Secretary of State for War and Air in Lloyd George's coalition government for almost six months. From the moment he took charge at the War Office he had expressed his violent opposition to Russia's new rulers in the most vivid and extravagant language. He had also been the most vigorous proponent of expanded action in Russia, aimed at toppling the Bolshevik regime which had betrayed the Allies by making peace with the Germans at Brest-Litovsk in March 1918.

At this point, British forces were deployed at Archangel and Murmansk in north Russia. Military Missions and huge quantities of armaments and military supplies, together with volunteer units, had also been despatched there and to the other theatres where the Russian Civil War was raging. Churchill's enthusiastic espousal of the cause of the White Russians, and the notion of putting together a great coalition to fight Lenin and his confederates, not only distanced him from the war-shocked nation, still grieving the loss of three-quarters of a million men in the conflict just ended, but also from the views of the Prime Minister. Lloyd George was keenly sensitive to public opinion and increasingly fearful that Churchill's crusade against the Bolsheviks would merely stimulate domestic Russian backing for their regime, besides costing Britain huge sums it could ill afford and disturbing its newly enlarged electorate.

In arguing for, and then masterminding, Britain's enlarged intervention, Churchill joined the select band of leaders who have led invasions of Russia. The results of his efforts, of course, are hardly to be compared with those of Napoleon's *Grande Armée* of 600,000, which had crossed into Russia in 1812, or indeed with the 148 divisions with which in 1941 Hitler launched Operation Barbarossa against the Soviet state. Yet Churchill's aims were no less total than theirs: he was fighting for a complete regime change in Russia, and he was as sanguine as they were of success.* While his own land forces were small, he had substantial naval and air support, the latest weaponry, and what appeared to be powerful allies in the White armies he was training, supporting and supplying. His Bolshevik opponents, moreover, seemed to have only a tenuous hold on power and their armies were poorly trained and irresolute. While at times there seemed every chance of success, in the end Churchill's crusade failed. But while Napoleon's and Hitler's invasions of Russia sealed their fates, Churchill emerged from his invasion with his political position intact, if by no means unshaken.

The Russian campaign brought Churchill a number of short-term political costs. It opened up a gulf with his Liberal Party colleagues, exasperated the Prime Minister and soured his reputation inside his own constituency. Of greater long-term significance, his Russian adventure underscored doubts about his judgement, particularly on military matters. It reinforced the reputation he had acquired from Antwerp and Gallipoli for impulsive military adventurism. Those on the left of British politics used a stronger term for it: they accused him of being a warmonger. This reputation, and the mistrust it generated in the main political parties, contributed significantly to Churchill's political isolation for long periods during the subsequent decade and a half. The invasion as a whole, apparently on the cusp of success at one moment, ultimately ended in a failure which at time verged on fiasco. Yet, despite its historical significance, and indeed its resonance with the current invasion and occupation of Iraq, Churchill's Russian policy during the twenty-five months he spent at the War Office has received little attention from most of his biographers.[1]

When the Peace Treaty with Germany was signed, Britain had been fighting the Bolsheviks for almost a year. While small beer compared with its role in the mammoth conflict concluded at Versailles, Britain was again involved in a war. Its principal allies were an assortment of Russian forces under the collective title of the 'Whites'. In the far north of Russia, British forces had penetrated hundreds of miles into Russian territory and, in cooperation with Russian units which Britain had raised, trained and armed, were battling against the Bolshevik Sixth and Seventh Armies. Thousands of miles to the south, General Denikin's White armies, also equipped and advised by Britain, supported by British-manned aircraft and tanks, and by a strong Military Mission, were advancing on Moscow and were about to capture Tsaritsyn (later Stalingrad). In the Far Eastern

---

* Unlike Napoleon and Hitler, Churchill never went to Russia during his 'invasion', despite his fondness for visiting battlefields. Although very widely travelled, he had also never visited Russia before or during the First World War.

theatre, where the White Russian Supreme Commander Admiral Kolchak was based, Britain's forces on the ground were few, but its contribution, in weapons, equipment, advice and training, to the White drive along the Trans-Siberian Railway was immense. A Military Mission under Lieutenant General Sir Hubert Gough was also in place in the Baltic States, preparing to support the White General Yudenitch in an offensive to take the old Russian capital, Petrograd. The Royal Navy was blockading the ports of Russia's new regime at each of its limited points of access to the open sea and attacking its navies wherever it could, while ships of the Merchant Navy were pouring supplies to the White Russian forces in their widely scattered theatres of resistance.

In Britain itself, the centre of the opposition to the Bolsheviks, Churchill was doing his best to stiffen Lloyd George's wavering resolve and allay the Cabinet's doubts about the advisability of the projected, but secret, offensive from Archangel by which he set such store. These British operations involved an impoverished and war-weary nation, beset by serious financial, social and industrial problems rooted in the previous great conflict, in an undeclared war being waged over vast swathes of Russian territory. It was a situation which cried out for explanation. As a friend put it in a letter to Churchill in March 1919: 'That with your gifts you should start again this crazy game of war, when for years every country will be hanging on by its eyelids to mere existence, is more than I can understand.'[2]

The military intervention in Russia by the Allies at the end of the Great War, a complex and confusing affair for the participants at the time, is scarcely less so now for those who attempt to make sense of it. George F. Kennan, a leading scholar of the period, likened its study to entering 'one of the most impenetrable thickets of confusion and perplexity to be found anywhere in the forests of recent history'.[3] This is largely because so many different national forces were involved in what became, in conjunction with the efforts of the White Russian armies themselves, a substantial and at times critical assault on the fledgling Bolshevik state. In north Russia alone, besides the British themselves, there were American, Canadian, Chinese, Czech, French, Italian, Polish, and Serb national contingents, assorted 'Red Finns', Karelian nationalists and various soldiers of fortune. In the south, where General Denikin's Volunteer Army posed for a time a much greater threat to the Bolsheviks, France and Italy, as well as Britain, had at one stage considerable forces deployed. On the distant Siberian front, where Admiral Kolchak's White armies were operating, Britain's modest manpower contribution – a Military Mission, two battalions and a naval detachment – was entirely dwarfed by the American and especially by the Japanese contingents. Even in the nearer Baltic theatre, where General Yudenitch's campaign took his White Russian troops momentarily to the gates of Petrograd, others besides the

British were deployed in support of what was in the event, as in every theatre of the intervention, a despairing effort. Then there were the 70,000 troops of the Czech Legion in the heart of Russia itself, whose possible redeployment to the Western Front in France was the inspiration for some of the first plans and early moves by the intervening powers.

To the great assortment of national contingents must be added the differing policies of the nations that supplied them, though all theoretically operated under the direction of the Supreme War Council at Versailles, which attempted to coordinate all the Allies' operations via the Commanders-in-Chief whom it appointed to lead the various multinational forces. Furthermore, in the initial months of peace following the Armistice, Britain's intervention policy, or rather the maddening slowness in developing any policy at all, stemmed not simply from the impulses and prevarications of Westminster but also from the confused deliberations in Paris and Versailles. Added to this, the internal dynamics of the Civil War itself were even more baffling in their complexity than were the motives and actions of the intervening powers.

Whilst it is true that the Japanese deployed many more troops on Russian soil than did Britain or indeed any other power, their intervention was a strictly localised affair designed solely to extend their developing empire and influence in east Asia. The French also put considerable effort into their campaign against Lenin's regime, with a major deployment at Odessa, representation in the other theatres and at least theoretical leadership of the Czech Legion in Siberia. But, despite its leaders' virulent anti-Bolshevism, France lacked the staying power and even the dependable military forces with which to prosecute it. For its part, the United States had an ailing and preoccupied President whose domestic support was steadily evaporating. Around him counsels were divided, but in any case America had only limited interventionist aims. The Czech Legion, pivotal to the intervention planning as a whole, was a large, professional and initially well-disciplined force, but it was struggling for national independence rather than against Bolshevism. Its efforts were restricted, for the most part, to Siberia.

Britain, by contrast, with some support from the Empire, had troops in every theatre where there was major opposition to Russia's new rulers. It appointed large Military Missions to the key areas of resistance, helped train the White Russian forces in the north, the south and the east, supplied gigantic quantities of military stores and weaponry to the Whites, and deployed the lion's share of the naval forces which attempted to blockade the Bolshevik state and support the armies assailing it. Britain provided the commanding generals at Murmansk and Archangel and sent to the inhospitable northern regions a force approaching three divisions in strength.

Whilst American support for the intervention, never more than lukewarm, quickly cooled, and the efforts of all the other Allies, save Japan, rapidly faded once the Armistice came into operation, Britain's comprehensive involvement continued unabated. Two months after the Great War had concluded, as many as six British major generals were holding separate appointments on Russian soil.[4] Paradoxically, although the initial rationale for the intervention derived from the Great War itself, it was only after the Armistice that Britain's effort really got into its stride. It was then that Churchill provided the inspiration and sustaining force for the intervention's prolongation and for the only worthwhile attempt at uniting the separate and very varied national efforts. Churchill maintained this impetus in the face of an increasingly unsympathetic Prime Minister, a lukewarm Cabinet, a broadly hostile population and a rapidly disintegrating international coalition. He it was who most regularly and most vehemently articulated anti-Bolshevik policy. He was to continue to do so long after the last British contingent had left Russian soil and the final efforts of the Whites had been extinguished. Under his leadership Britain played by far the greatest external role in sustaining and supporting the Whites.

The account which follows deals essentially with the military operations at the heart of Britain's intervention, the activities of the servicemen who implemented them, and the military direction which, once the war in the west was over, Churchill gave to the venture. In its treatment of these operational aspects it may claim to have broken new ground. There is, of course, no official British history of these campaigns, as the nation was never officially at war with Russia; nor have its military historians taken much interest in them.

When the intervention began, with the war on the Western Front in its most critical phase, men and materials could ill be spared for peripheral ventures. Consequently, low category units were hastily cobbled together, generally from medically downgraded men unfit for active service on the Western Front, only to be sent to parts of Russia which made even greater demands on their courage and physical resources. After the Armistice, the military difficulties were no easier to overcome. With a citizen army to be demobilised, an occupation force to be maintained in Europe, a general peace settlement to be policed, Ireland to be pacified and an Empire sustained, there were scant forces available for the Russian operations. Besides, the intervention was unpopular with the general public and the war-weary rank and file; only volunteers could be justified to the nation at large for service in the remote and uninviting Russian theatres. There were excellent, willing, professional soldiers among those who served against the Bolsheviks, but also many who volunteered merely to escape a humdrum existence in an impoverished post-war society, or to pocket the attractive pay and bounties which the postings to Russia brought. Others fought because they believed their comrades on Russian soil were in grave danger. Many others, in contrast, had in fact not volunteered at all. Some saw no great national purpose

in their service and were rapidly demoralised by the absence of a cause with
which they could identify or allies whom they could respect, and by the profound
social dislocation, squalor and misery which surrounded them and which
their own actions at times exacerbated. Campaigning in these circumstances
provided a stern test of leadership. Not all placed in positions of authority were
able to survive it. The study of soldiering in such circumstances is nevertheless
a compelling one.

Many participants, both commanders and commanded, kept diaries or
wrote contemporary accounts of the campaigns. Among them were a surprising
number of junior officers who were later to rise to high military positions, giving
their accounts a particular resonance.[5] There were also mature and articulate
soldiers in the ranks who kept similar records. The recollections of both groups
provide a fascinating insight into the strains to which they were subjected by these
distant and little understood campaigns. They have a freshness and immediacy
which admirably complement the somewhat bland narratives produced long
after the event by the leading figures of the intervention. General Maynard,
the Murmansk commander, wrote his elegant but overlong account nine years
after the invasion. The shorter, more sketchy memoir by General Ironside, his
Archangel-based compatriot, did not appear until thirty-three years and another
world war had supervened. Both are highly sanitised accounts which omit, brush
aside or reinterpret many uncomfortable episodes. Churchill's own account,
in *The Aftermath*, appeared in 1927 as the final part of his very successful,
multi-volume *The World Crisis*; but it must rank among the more fanciful of his
historical writings, while its partisanship is evident from its opening dedication
to 'Our Faithful Colleagues and Comrades in the Russian Imperial Army'. One
is reminded of Churchill's concern, as he wrote his 'memoir-histories',[6] to
justify the part he himself played in the events he recorded. Of greater value
is Churchill's voluminous correspondence with the Prime Minister, with Sir
Henry Wilson, the Chief of the Imperial General Staff (CIGS), and with the
various military commanders on Russian soil – with whom, characteristically,
he often communicated directly. Wilson's own diary is passionately penned and
revealing. The Cabinet papers, war diaries and official military correspondence
and reports of the time complete the record. Altogether it is a rich and
revealing vein.

It is partly because the intervention in Russia's internal affairs had such limited
popular support that so little information about it was publicly available at the
time. The contrast with the abundance of the documentary record at hand today
is stark. For the most part the intervention proceeded under an even thicker
cloak of censorship than had applied to the Great War itself. Nor did the new
Parliament of 1919 do much to disturb the government's conduct of this aspect
of its international policy. Lloyd George's post-war coalition had a huge majority.

The government benches were filled, as Baldwin famously put it, with 'hard-faced men who had done well out of the war' and who, according to one disapproving Opposition MP, rapidly emptied the parliamentary cellars of their stocks of wines and spirits.[7] Such limited checks and questioning as there were of the intervention policy came mostly not from the ranks of the inexperienced Labour MPs who formed the official Opposition, but from an unusual trio of political mavericks who, though by no means an effective brake on policy, nevertheless wielded an influence greatly beyond their numbers. They were Colonel Josiah Wedgwood, Commander J.M. Kenworthy and (preferring to discard his military rank) Cecil Malone. All had commendable war records but were resolutely opposed to this latest military venture.

As for the press, the brother barons, Rothermere and Northcliffe, dominated the Fourth Estate and determined much of what was printed and read: Lord Northcliffe alone controlled half the daily papers sold in London. Their ability to influence policy had already been demonstrated in the Great War. During the intervention they tended dutifully to follow the government line for much of the time. Predictably, it was the *Manchester Guardian* and the newly-established *Daily Herald* which led the opposition to the Russian policy, joined, more surprisingly, by Lord Beaverbrook's by no means left-wing *Daily* and *Sunday Express*. These latter proved particularly sharp thorns in the government's side, and particularly in Churchill's, for Beaverbrook had a tendency to personalise his political campaigns.

Although the topic of Russia seldom left Beaverbrook's front pages for more than a few days, it was not until September 1919, as Britain's north Russian venture was drawing to a close, that his campaign against it reached its cimax. On Saturday 6 September, the *Daily Express* published a sensational front-page story. Beneath banner headlines announcing 'ARCHANGEL SCANDAL EXPOSED: FAMOUS VC APPEALS TO THE NATION', appeared a long open letter from an apparently unimpeachable source, the four-times wounded war hero Lieutenant Colonel Sherwood Kelly VC, CMG, DSO. Submitting the letter was itself a serious military offence for which its author was later court martialled. What made it the more grave was that Kelly deliberately challenged the government's account of its involvement in Russia's civil war and pointed the finger specifically at Winston Churchill as the author of the deception.

Churchill did not produce a response for several days but then defended himself with his customary vigour. Challenging Sherwood Kelly's bona fides, he claimed that Britain's Russian policy had been determined by the government long before he had come to office. It was, in all conscience, something less that the whole truth. The dispute rumbled on, with further disquieting revelations and growing popular support for Kelly. Churchill was forced by the publicity to promise to publish a White Paper, once the campaign was over, giving a full account of the entire north Russian episode. The affair was eloquent of the extent to which the intervention had divided the nation.

A remarkable feature of the Great War in Europe was the willingness of British infantrymen to go 'over the top' when the odds against survival were so great. It was a test from which the sorely-tried French armies ultimately flinched and against which the Imperial Russian armies finally rebelled. Remarkably, the British held firm. In the intervention in Russia, however, the challenge was of a different kind. Were men prepared to take any risks at all when no obvious national purpose seemed to demand the military gamble? To this question was returned a range of answers, reflecting the conditions, leadership, allies and opponents the men encountered, as well as their own social backgrounds and experiences.

As for the performance of Churchill himself, his biographers generally acknowledge, if cursorily, that his role in the intervention did little to enhance his reputation. One recently judged his time in Lloyd George's peacetime coalition, of which his spell at the War Office occupied the larger part, to be among the least creditable episodes in his long and distinguished career.[8] His attempt to destroy the Bolshevik government almost at its birth forced the Bolshevik leaders, Lenin, Trotsky and Stalin, to extreme measures to frustrate it. The suffering of the Russian people, already horrendous as a result of the main war, was consequently prolonged by the invasion and the death, disease and starvation it brought with it. Nor were the Bolshevik leaders under any illusions about Churchill being the architect and driving force behind the external opposition to their rule. How significant this bitter remembrance was when the Soviet Union and Britain became uneasy allies in the Second World War is difficult to determine. Certainly little evident gratitude attended Stalin's acceptance of Churchill's instant offer of aid (aid which could ill be spared by Britain) when the Russians again faced a German invasion in June 1941.

The Eastern Front

At the outbreak of war in 1914 the Imperial Russian Army faced its German and Austro-Hungarian adversaries with one very considerable advantage – manpower. With a population at least as great as that of Germany, Austria-Hungary and its own ally France combined, Russia had the potential to put an almost inexhaustible supply of stoically brave peasant conscripts into the field. Unfortunately, the defects of the Russian military system were so considerable as largely to negate this priceless asset. Russia had a number of able commanders. The Commander-in-Chief himself, the Grand Duke Nicholas, was a man of strong character and considerable strategical ability. Supporting him were some respected and capable generals. There were others, however, whose ineptitude and carelessness beggared belief. Furthermore, the commanders were served by a poor staff: too many unsuitable and untrained young aristocrats thronged its ranks, whilst many staff-trained officers had little or no regimental experience. Weaponry and equipment were also much behind western standards. The scale of issue of field artillery to the armies was about half that in the German service, and heavy artillery was very scarce. Reserves of rifles and ammunition for the inadequately trained conscripts were insufficient and the Russian munitions industry was poorly developed. Corruption pervaded the army's administrative services. Compounding these handicaps was interference from the Court: from the resentful and unstable Tsarina, and from the Tsar himself, who was only with difficulty dissuaded from taking personal command of his armies. In the light of these disadvantages, it is not surprising that the Russian high command had difficulty in concentrating its substantial armies to advantage on the battlefield and enabling them to fight effectively once there.[1]

In the campaign of 1914 Russia advanced westwards from its Polish salient. In the north, at the urging of the French, it advanced into East Prussia with comparative ease, only to be overwhelmingly defeated when Germany reacted with reinforcements. Russia lost over 300,000 men, about a quarter of its troops then mobilised, as well some 650 of its precious guns. In the south, however, the Russian armies were able to drive the Austrians out of eastern Galicia and advance to the Carpathians. When the Germans came to the aid of their Austrian allies, the Russians were saved from another decisive defeat only by the Grand Duke's decision to abandon western Poland and concentrate immense forces behind the Vistula. Nevertheless, fierce battles raged in Poland and huge casualties were again sustained by the Russians, who suffered severely from their shortage of munitions.

The enormous losses of weapons and equipment and the dearth of reserve stocks left the Russian armies in a poor condition for the conduct of a major campaign in 1915. Theoretically they had six and a quarter million men under arms, but over a third of them were without rifles, while others were armed with an assortment of imported foreign weapons. Artillery ammunition was still insufficient and many sections of the front had yet to be fortified. The armies were, nevertheless, sufficiently large for the Grand Duke to make an attempt, in February and March, to launch attacks on both his major fronts. Russia's evident durability, and the parlous state to which Austria-Hungary's forces were being reduced, determined the German War Minister, Falkenhayn, to make his country's principal effort of 1915 on the Eastern Front. When a German army of eight divisions was transferred east for this purpose the results were again decisive. The Rusians were driven out of Galicia in May and in a summer campaign were forced out of eastern Poland. The Russian retreat, long, bloody and costly, was accompanied by a huge exodus of refugees. Warsaw fell and Poland was lost. Russia was left defending an almost straight line running from Riga on the Baltic to the borders of Rumania in the south. Its army was still in being, but it lacked many of its best fighting divisions and was desperately short of munitions. Recruits were now being sent to the front after only four weeks' training armed simply with clubs. Over two million men had been lost, half of them as prisoners, in defeats on a scale never experienced on the Western Front. Desertion from the ranks was already serious. Yet this desperate blow to Russia perhaps saved Britain. If Mackensen's great spring offensive in Poland had been directed instead against the British line on the Western Front, it would have met an exhausted army, short of men and at the height of a munition shortage. It could have been a disaster for the British Army.

By the following year, however, Russia's munitions situation had actually improved. Britain and France, desperate to keep Russia in the fight, were now despatching supplies to the White sea ports of Archangel and Murmansk, and to Vladivostok in Siberia. Despite its gigantic manpower losses, Russia had yet to mobilise as large a proportion of its available manpower as any of the other great powers, except Britain. Indeed, during the winter lull it created and trained a reserve of another million men and, with Allied help, largely overcame the rifle shortage, though artillery was still in short supply. But the collosal battlefield losses were now having a serious political impact.. In September 1915, the Tsar dismissed the able Grand Duke Nicholas and took personal command himself. Unsuitable and reactionary appointments as Premier and Minister of War soon followed, increasing the isolation and unpopularity of the Court and heightening opposition to the war.

The 1916 campaign began early with another gallant, costly and unsuccessful offensive in the north, launched to take the pressure off France. It cost the Russians a further 120,000 men without significantly affecting German dispositions. Yet another appeal, this time from hard-pressed Italy, forced a change of direction to the south, where General Brusilov's four armies of the south-western front achieved a substantial enough initial success against the Austrians to force the switching of fifteen German divisions from the west. It was this emergency reaction alone which redeemed a substantial Austrian defeat. In the long, bloody and increasingly punishing campaign which followed, lasting from June to early October, Russia lost a further million men. This bitter fighting finally broke the spirit of the army. By the onset of winter 1916 a further million had deserted the ranks and returned to their homes. 'For the last time', wrote Basil Liddell Hart, 'Russia had sacrificed herself for her Allies, and it is not just that subsequent events should obscure the debt.'[2]

The Tsar's regime did not last long. The succession of colossal military defeats, the worsening food supply situation in Petrograd, growing indiscipline in the armies and seething political discontent were at the heart of its failure. The reaction of the Tsar and the corrupt clique around him was to tighten their control, which served only to heighten their unpopularity, complete the alienation of the liberal middle classes and finally break the loyalty of the army. In the capital food was scarce and strikes by the workers became general; rioters ransacked the bakers' shops; the police were overpowered in parts of the city; and Cossack and Guards regiments sent to deal with the strikers chose instead to support them. Finding themselves powerless, the government ministers went into hiding. Tsar Nicholas abdicated on 15 March 1917. The rule of the Romanov dynasty, which had held autocratic sway in Russia for over three hundred years, was at an end.

The liberal leaders of the Provisional Government which followed tried to restore order and prepare for the election of a democratic national body, the Constituent Assembly. Their mistake was to believe that this process could be combined with continued prosecution of the war at the side of France and Britain, for the revolution had been as much against the war itself as against the Romanov autocracy. Furthermore, the government faced a parallel hierarchy of workers, peasants and soldiers soviets (councils) which had quite different aims, among them the destruction of the existing disciplinary system in the armies, an end to the war itself and, increasingly, the Bolsheviks' seductive programme of bread, peace and the partition of the land. These ideas festered in the Russian trenches at the front, which the Germans wisely left alone.

These profound political unheavals could not have come at a worse time for the Western Allies. Nivelle's spring offensive of 1917 had failed and widespread mutinies had weakened sixteen of the French army corps. For the remainder of the year the weight of the war in the west fell for the first time on Britain. As the political crisis in Russia deepened, Britain's offensive at Passchendaele was grinding to an indecisive conclusion. It had been horrendously expensive in manpower. There was a 'wastage rate' – to use an inhuman term – of 76,000 men a month in France and Flanders in the autumn of 1917. This was twice the rate of enlistment and quite unsustainable. Help from the Russian Front was still desperately needed.

Whilst the Bolshevik leaders, Lenin and Trotsky, were systematically preparing for their revolution, Kerensky, the Minister of War, was touring the military units at the front haranguing the troops for a further disciplined effort in support of Russia's allies. Two hundred thousand men, many Czechs among them, were collected in Galicia for another attack on the Austrian front. This, the final Russian effort of the war, and one which the Allied missions urged on them, was, ironically, better supported with artillery than any of its predecessors, but it ended in similar failure, for the Germans were forewarned of a Bolshevik rising in Petrograd and timed their counter-attack to coincide with it. The counter-attack succeeded, but the rising failed. In consequence Kerensky's government (for he was now Prime Minister) enjoyed 'a transient flicker of deceptive revival'.[3] The flicker died, however, when Ludendorff seized Riga in an attempt to force Russia out of the war. Yet the Provisional Government managed to survive even this and to defeat a further coup: an ill-considered attempt to seize power by its own Commander-in-Chief, General Kornilov.[4] This, however, was to be its last success.

Anger at the lenient treatment accorded to Kornilov, coupled with the imminent danger posed to Petrograd itself and its naval base at Kronstadt by the loss of Riga, increased the support enjoyed by the revolutionaries of the far left, the Bolsheviks. The city soviets of both Petrograd and Moscow became dominated by the extremists, while the promise of peace, bread and land for the peasants drew widespread support. The imprisoned Bolsheviks were set free and Lenin emerged from hiding to finalise his plans. With Trotsky now president of the key Petrograd Soviet and the assurance that the men of the capital's garrison would take their orders from it rather than the government, the revolutionaries made their move. They struck on 7 November, capturing first the banks, post offices, telephone exchanges, railway stations and bridges, in a speedy and almost bloodless coup. The Provisional Government, immured with a few defenders in the Winter Palace, was quickly subdued by shells from the Bolshevik-manned cruiser *Aurore*, which steamed up from Kronstadt for the purpose. The struggle for Moscow was a little more protracted, but the city fell after eight days. At the time of the revolution there were said to be more than 100,000 officers in the two cities of Moscow and Petrograd, but they offered virtually no opposition.[5] The

Bolsheviks now held the levers of power. They quickly set about consolidating their position, whilst refusing to continue the war.

It was some months before the Russian military collapse and the Bolshevik accession to power resulted in a formal peace treaty with the German victors. The Germans were harsh negotiators and it required Lenin to exert his full authority before his colleagues accepted their terms. The treaty of Brest-Litovsk represented one of the most savage settlements imposed by one state upon another in modern times. Russia was stripped of the Ukraine, the Baltic states and the Caucasus, lost a third of its population and most of its coal, oil, railways and iron. Following the treaty's conclusion, using one pretext or another, Germany occupied an area of Russia almost as large as its conquests a quarter of a century later. The access which Germany now gained to the wheatfields and cattle of the Ukraine, the coal of the Donetz basin and, via the Black Sea and the Caspian, the vast oil deposits of the Caspian littoral, threatened to negate the entire effect of the Allied blockade, which had been maintained at great cost. Strictly speaking, the territories lost by the Bolsheviks were actually non-Russian, the lands of its extensive empire. Their peoples were encouraged by Germany to declare their independence, though Germany lost no time in extending its own political and especially its economic influence over the successor states. Thus, to Britain's initial concern at the collapse of the Eastern Front was now added the graver worry that Russia might become a supply store and puppet of the Germans. The fact that German exactions from Russia, though considerable, were often so brutally applied that they rapidly alienated the local populations gave little comfort, other than a modicum of hope, to the Allies.

The British had considerable difficulty in determining how to deal with the new Russian regime. Information from Petrograd and Moscow was patchy, often unreliable and ever changing. It was very clear how important the contribution of Russia on the Eastern Front was to the battlefield fortunes of the French and British on the Western one. Despite widespread dislike of its new rulers, there was no certainty that the Bolsheviks would remain in power for very long. What was clearest of all in the confusion of the revolution was that the manpower problems on the Western Front were no nearer resolution. In the first three months of 1918 the British Expeditionary Force had to reduce the infantry battalion content of forty-eight of its divisions from twelve to nine. Later in the year ten more divisions suffered the same dilution. Five divisions were also diverted to the Italian front, where Italy was still reeling from the disaster of Caporetto and demanding weapons and munitions from its allies. Haig's armies were also being asked to take over more of the front from the French.

Throughout the first two and a half years of the Great War, Russia had fought loyally and steadfastly in support of the Allied cause, its apparently inexhaustible

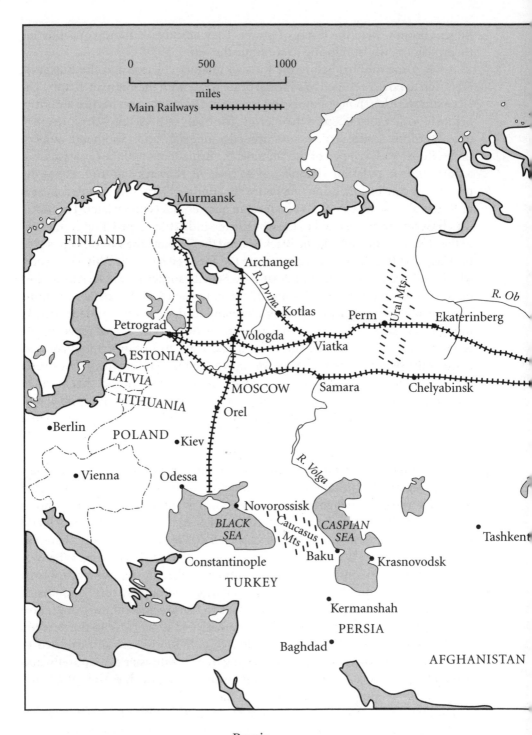

Russia

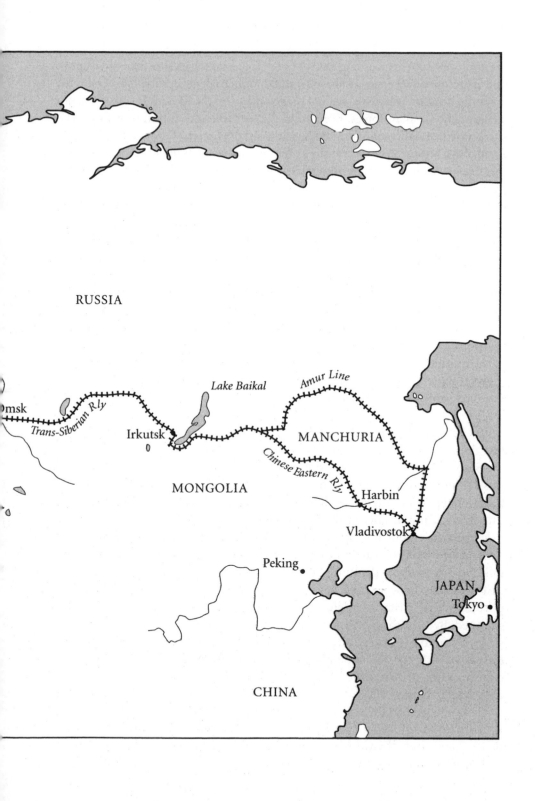

manpower resources seeming always to compensate for its shortage of weapons and its frequent reverses. However limited and costly its combat successes, the Imperial Russian Army had ensured the retention on the Eastern Front of a major share of the German forces. Even amid the turmoil and mutinies of July 1917, there were still eighty-one German divisions on the Eastern Front, with 154 facing France and Britain. When Kerensky's offensive achieved its opening successes that month, Germany was forced immediately to transfer eight divisions to restore the threatened sector. Between August and November 1917 it never had fewer than eighty-five infantry divisions facing Russia; in September the figure actually rose to eighty-nine infantry and seven cavalry divisions, the highest ever fielded there by the *Ostheer*, the German Eastern Army. Not until October was it possible for these reinforcements to return to the west. When the Bolsheviks seized power and the Eastern Front became inactive, the crowded German troop trains began rattling westwards, carrying, by March 1918, a total of fifty-one divisions to the Western Front to assist in the major offensive which it was hoped would finally break the lines of the Entente powers. 'It was no longer a case of replacing tired divisions in the West by fresh ones', Ludendorff recorded, 'but of really adding to the number of combatants in the West.'[6] A means had to be found to end and then reverse this flow of German manpower. A re-establishment of the Eastern Front by some means seemed the obvious solution.

It was because Russia was so vital to the Allied cause that Britain and France had done all they could to keep its armies in the fight. As it was to do again in the Second World War, Britain shipped huge quantities of military *matériel* to Russia's northern ports, to Archangel during the summer months, when that traditional port for English trade was ice-free, and all year round to Murmansk. The strategic importance of the Kola Inlet, which was permanently ice-free, led to Murmansk's rapid development and the hurried construction, by German and Austrian prisoners of war and Chinese labour, of an all-important if ramshackle railroad driven across the tundra to link it with Petrograd and the main Russian east–west line. To Murmansk and Archangel, and also to Vladivostok, the Pacific port for Siberia, Britain despatched the wherewithal to keep the Russia divisions supplied. By 1917 the British Navy was delivering three million tons of military stores a year to her eastern ally. In the months following the Russian revolution, the fate of such stores as remained in the coastal dumps was a matter of growing concern to the British as they watched the Germans encroach on the territory of their hapless former ally.

So developed had Britain's relations become with the Arctic ports that a naval squadron under Admiral T.W. Kemp was based at Murmansk during the winter of 1917 and strengthened when the Bolsheviks began their peace negotiations with Germany. It was not a large force, consisting of the old battleship *Glory* (some of whose guns had been removed to provide extra accommodation for an enlarged detachment of Royal Marines), a depot ship, an armed boarding vessel and a dozen trawlers or drifters, armed and converted for minesweeping. Its main task had been to keep the sea lanes to north Russia free from German U-boats and minelayers; but its presence now reflected Britain's determination not to allow its military stores to fall into the hands of the Bolsheviks, still less of the Germans. In fact, during the time of the Kerensky Provisional Government, Admiral Kemp had been advising a reduction in the flow of supplies since they were merely piling up at the ports where there was no real effort to get them to where they were needed. The Russians were not even in a position to keep open the sea lanes during the winter months: in 1917 only two of the dozen Archangel ice-breakers were fit for service and those badly needed a refit.[7]

There were powerful reasons for Britain to disapprove of the new revolutionary regime in Russia. For a start, the Bolsheviks' *coup d'état* was plainly not endorsed by the population at large. Ten days after Moscow had fallen to them, elections for the Constituent Assembly gave them only 25 per cent of the popular vote, with almost 60 per cent going to the Social Revolutionaries. But the Bolsheviks soon dispensed with the assembly in favour of its own Soviet Congress. Russia then became, in Robert Conquest's phrase, 'a country precariously in the grip of a determined minority'. The British leadership was further antagonised by the extreme social and economic policies which the Bolsheviks advocated, as well as by their evident anti-imperialism. It is perhaps unsurprising that, as early as 10 November 1917, the Conservative *Morning Post* should have been calling for direct intervention in Russia to supplant the Bolsheviks and replace them with a more complaisant regime.

Winston Churchill was quick to give his views, though these were to change as the months went by. His first reacton was to regard the Bolsheviks' usurpation of power as an act of treachery by an ally. In a speech in December 1917, when he was still Minister of Munitions, he declared that 'It is this melancholy event which has prolonged the war, that has robbed the French, the British and the Italian armies of the prize that was perhaps almost within their reach this summer'. Attending a December meeting of the War Cabinet by invitation, he spoke of the number of Russian officers who remained loyal to the Entente and wished to be kept together as a rallying point for the future. Churchill regarded them as a valuable political asset. Meantime, in the light of the new situation, he was damping down the production of war materials destined for the support of the Russians, but keeping a skeleton system going so that full production could restored 'in the event of a change in the situation'.[8] This belief that a substantial body of Russians was ready to resume the fight against the Central Powers was not confined to Churchill.

British policy remained for some time one of keeping in touch with both the *de facto* government of Russia and the opposition parties. The Bolsheviks' hold on power seemed tenuous in the extreme and their 'decree of peace' a world away from the actual conclusion of a peace treaty with Germany. R.H. Bruce Lockhart, once the British acting Consul-General in Moscow and well known to the leading members of the Provisional Government, was sent back to Russia early in 1918 as 'British Agent', head of the unofficial mission to the Bolsheviks, with whom there were no formal diplomatic relations, both Ambassador Sir George Buchanan and Military Attaché Major General Alfred Knox having returned to London. The Bolshevik government had moved to the security of Moscow, while the remaining Allied ambassadors had decamped to Vologda, a provincial northern town, hundreds of miles distant. In Moscow, however, Bruce Lockhart, a fluent Russian speaker, developed close personal relations with Foreign Minister Chicherin and War Minister Trotsky and had several interviews with the emotionless Lenin himself. Lockhart was a valuable conduit for Bolshevik views and policies to a largely uncomprehending British government; but he was not the only channel. The Military Missions which earlier had been responsible for providing aid and advice to their Russian ally were still on Russian soil, sending back to London their own interpretations of the confused events around them. With the departure of General Knox, the senior military representative in Russia was Major General Frederick Poole, in charge of the Military Supply Mission. Immediately after the Bolshevik coup he wrote to his Foreign Office contact, 'Disabuse your mind and that of all others in London as to the idea of any "war party" existing. A few stalwarts talk big about wishing to go to war, but it's all talk and no chance of action. The people are tired and will never fight again.'[9]

In February 1918, however, the British military representatives were heartened when the peace negotiations at Brest-Litovsk broke down and fighting resumed between Russia and Germany. Both British and French chargés d'affaires let it be known to the Bolsheviks that aid would be readily forthcoming if they requested it. General Poole wired the Director of Military Operations (DMO) at the War Office that, if the Allies once recognised the Bolsheviks, they would turn anti-German and join the Allies.[10] Trotsky, it seemed, was coming around to the British view that it would be impossible to satisfy German imperialism, since Germany's proposed peace terms threatened to emasculate Russia totally. He told Lockhart that the Russians would go on fighting even if they had to retreat to the Urals. Some Allied officers from the Military Missions even joined the retreating Russians as demolition experts in an effort to impede the German advance.[11] For a time it seems that even Churchill supported Poole's revised view. As late as April 1918, Churchill went so far as to propose that Britain and the United States should offer the Bolsheviks a formula for 'safeguarding the permanent fruits of the revolution' in return for Russia's re-entering the war. Lenin and Trotsky were fighting with ropes round their necks, he declared. 'Show them any real chance of consolidating their power, of getting some kind of protection against the vengeance of a counter-revolution and they would be non-human not to embrace it.'[12] This idea came too late. Brest-Litovsk had already been signed in early March and Churchill's virulent anti Bolshevism soon reasserted itself. He was later to advise the War Cabinet, even as the war with Germany continued, that 'we might have to build up the German Army, as it was important to get Germany on its legs again for fear of the spread of Bolshevism'.[13]

The overriding concern of Lloyd George and his War Cabinet was less the character of the new Russian regime, which he personally had been prepared to recognise, but the effect its defection from the alliance and the enforced peace were having on the war with Germany, 'There can be no doubt', he was later to write, 'that throughout 1918 the Germans looked to Russia, not merely to supply them with substantial territorial gains to reward them for their war effort, but still more as a vitally important source of foodstuffs and fodder, of oil and minerals.'[14] Then there was the matter of the military stores at the Russian ports. Those at the Arctic ports have already been mentioned. Similar concerns applied to the stores which had been supplied by Britain and the United States to Russia's Far-Eastern port of Vladivostok. The possible use of these by Germany might appear an exaggerated fear in view of the many thousands of miles to the nearest German lines, but other factors entered the increasingly complex strategic calculations. Russia held large numbers of German and Austrian prisoners of war in Siberia and reports began to circulate that the authorities were losing control of the camps in which the men were incarcerated and that the prisoners were fleeing to the railway towns to make their way west. There had been reports that the Bolsheviks were organising and arming large groups of them. The concern was about the purposes which the new units might serve and the possibility of the Allied weapon stocks being taken over by them. This, and other reports, led to the fear that the Germans might be attempting to turn the region into an armed economic dependency.

One gleam of hope emanating from the otherwise forbidding situation in Siberia lay in the presence there of a substantial military force committed to the cause of the Western Allies. This was part of the Czech Legion, which was destined to play an instrumental role in the intervention as a whole. In the early months of the Great War men from the Czech and Slovak communities in Russia had been used for reconnaissance duties with the Russian formations, where their ability to speak the language of Russia's opponents was a great asset. Subsequently the Russians captured large numbers of other Czechs who had been conscripted into the Imperial Austrian Army.[15] The Czech units were expanded into an army corps. They fought on the Russian side during Kerensky's offensive and gained a glowing tribute from Brusilov himself.[16] These troops subsequently became an instrument in the larger political campaign of the statesmen Thomas Masaryk and Eduard Beneš for the independence of the Czech and Slovak lands. These leaders found common cause with the manpower-hungry French authorities for the recruitment of the Czech Legion, as it became called, to fight alongside the French on the Western Front. The Bolshevik leadership initially supported the plan for the Czech troops, under French leadership, to make their way by rail to Vladivostok, where they were to embark on Britsh ships for their voyage to the Western Front. From July 1917 the Czechs began to benefit from substantial funding from France and a little from Britain They started their journey without any animosity towards, or from, the Bolsheviks. It took a series of developments, some predictable, others quite unexpected, to turn this valuable anti-German manpower asset into a central feature of the intervention against the Bolsheviks themselves.

Perhaps the most auspicious, but at the same time most exasperating, development in the search for a way to rebuild the Eastern Front came not from north Russia, nor from eastern Siberia, where there was much disorganisation, even chaos, but from the south where the bulk of Russia's agricultural and mineral resources lay. Here German influence was strong, but at the same time the region contained the nucleus of a genuine Russian opposition to the Bolsheviks and to the domination of the region by Germany. General Kaledin, the Ataman, or elected leader, of the Don Cossacks, made an offer of sanctuary in the Don lands to any of his military comrades who opposed the Bolsheviks. General Alexeiev, former Chief of Staff to Tsar Nicholas, took up the offer and headed south, inviting all officers who wished to reject Bolshevism to join him. Those who responded became the nucleus of a new force, the so-called 'Volunteer Army', which became the most effective fighting force on the White side throughout the subsequent civil war. Alexeiev's army, initially a tiny force with a nucleus of a few hundred officers serving as ordinary rankers in officers' battalions, and with little financial backing, was later joined by General Kornilov, the failed coup leader, General Romanovsky, sometime Chief of Staff at the Imperial General Headquarters, and General Denikin, who had been Commander-in-Chief of the Imperial Army's South Western Front. This group of very senior commanders now took charge of the resistance in the south and in a series of desperate little campaigns managed to draw support for their cause and finally to take and hold territory. In January 1918 the group issued a joint declaration announcing the formation of an anti-Bolshevik movement in the south as the means of liberating 'Great Russia', pledging loyalty to the Constituent Assembly and committing themselves to the Allied cause in the war against Germany. For the Allies this seemed a valuable development. The difficulty was that the Volunteer Army was landlocked and largely beyond their assistance; Germany and its ally Turkey dominated the approaches to the Black Sea and the Don lands. Its struggle was also against the Bolsheviks rather than the Germans, though the two had become closely intertwined in the minds of many on the British side.

Although the main British effort was to be in the north of Russia, at much the same time as this was being prepared, there was a remarkable intervention even further south than the beleaguered enclave of General Alexiev and his comrades. This resulted in the British garrisoning the port of Baku, sending troops into Russian Central Asia, and the Royal Navy establishing a flotilla on the Caspian Sea. These hurried, scratch deployments, and the bizarre campaigns associated with them, resulted partly from Britain's traditional concern to protect 'the tranquillity of India', but they were all directed against the Central Powers. Nevertheless, each drew the British into the invasion of Russian territory and action against the Bolsheviks who were struggling to protect it. General Knox, now the Cabinet's principal military adviser on Russian affairs, had written a paper in early 1918 warning of the danger of a German and Turkish advance into the Caucasus, Transcaspia and Turkestan, following the withdrawal of Russian troops from the region. Overstretched militarily, and sensitive to its local weakness after the failure at Gallipoli, Britain hardly had the troops to protect this vast area but, after the early abandonment of an absurd plan to induce Japan to do the job, it did make some moves for its defence against enemy invasion.

The first of these was to summon Major General Lionel Dunsterville from India and give him the task of making his way, via Baghdad, to Tiflis in Georgia. There he was to organise, train and lead native troops drawn from the tribes of Asia Minor and Mesopotamia to resist Turko-German penetration into the territories of Transcaucasia, which now considered themselves independent of Russia's Bolshevik regime. The scheme was based on the largely mistaken belief that the Transcaucasian tribesmen would fight to defend their homes against the Turks.

General Dunsterville, an experienced eastern soldier with a commanding personality and a knowledge of numerous eastern languages including Persian and Russian, seemed ideally suited to lead this early intervention. His initial force, 150 officers and 300 men, mostly with the ranks of captain and sergeant appropriate to their training role, together with five squadrons of armoured cars, was gathered with some difficulty from the Australian, Canadian and South African forces as well as those of Britain itself. By the end of the mission, Dunsterforce, as it was officially titled, or the 'Hush Hush Army' as it was more colloquially known, was to grow to brigade-group size as its difficuties mounted and its objectives were changed. Dunsterville's men encountered a host of military challenges and did as much fighting as training as they made their 600-mile journey across the mountains to the coastal port of Enzeli. Local tribespeople had already been raised by the Turks and Germans to support their cause, while Enzeli itself was held by the Bolsheviks until Dunsterville and his local allies removed them. Dunsterville's final objective became Baku rather than Tiflis, since the Turks were reported already to be advancing against this centre of the Russian oil industry on the Caspian coast. Dunsterville sent ahead his intelligence chief, Lieutenant Colonel C.B. Stokes, to see if the new imperative of 'denying the oil of Baku to the enemy' was practicable.

'It always seemed to me', Stokes wrote later, 'that someone at the War Office had a picture in his mind of an officer landing secretly from a boat with a box of matches and setting fire to the oilfields in several places and hastily rowing away leaving them in flames.'[17] Baku, in fact, was a substantial, ethnically-mixed, industrial city. The oilfields embraced wells, derricks, pipelines, refineries and piers covering several square miles, giving employment to 120,000 men and supplying the peacetime needs of most of central and south Russia. A box of matches seemed inappropriate. Armed with the knowledge that the Bolshevik government of Baku had recently been overturned and jailed, that the new regime had twenty small battalions of mainly Armenian troops and some Russians at its disposal, and that all the oil workers were armed with rifles and would presumably fight for their livelihoods, Dunsterville accepted the locals' invitation to defend the place. A modest Turkish attack was beaten off by the Armenians the day before the first substantial body of his troops arrived.

After this the British garrison was increased and the defences were organised and developed. Liaison officers were appointed to all the local battalions; some even, at the invitation of the troops, took command of them. The local garrison, however, remained remarkably casual despite the Turkish attacks, quitting the lines to wander off into town to attend political gatherings or meet their girlfriends for tea. 'In one case', marvelled Stokes, 'a whole machine gun section just walked in with its machine guns without asking anyone's leave.' When the Turks struck in strength on 26 August, the British bore the brunt of the attacks with the local Armenians and Russians doing little to support them. Captain Harrison, a Canadian commanding the 24th Armenian battalion, 'found that his unit ceased to exist on occasions through the predisposition of his men to scamper off at the first appearance of the enemy'.[18] On 14 September a heavy Turkish attack broke straight through a strong sector of the defences held by an Armenian battalion. A stand by the British troops prevented a complete rout and forced the Turks to dig in after they had suffered heavy losses. Vastly outnumbered, and with casualties mounting, Dunsterville decided to withdraw. Before he did so he released the imprisoned Bolshevik commissars of the previous Baku administration, who escaped by sea, hoping to make for Astrakhan, which their comrades held. The British slipped away that night to Enzeli in four ships bearing the troops, the wounded and the bulk of the ammunition. Dunsterforce was disbanded soon afterwards. It had achieved a great deal. Getting to Baku at all had been a considerable feat; holding the Russian oil city for six weeks against a much stronger enemy had been a greater one. This remarkable little campaign in Russian territory had involved significant anti-Bolshevik action, but only as part of the larger war against the Central Powers. Indeed, if a Bolshevik-held Baku had asked for British aid against the Turks, it would surely have been given. The Turks' occupation of the oilfields, however, was brief and without benefit. By the end of the following month they were out of the war and no oil had flowed to their erstwhile allies. Turkey's armistice with Britain provided for the Allied reoccupation of the oil city.[19]

At much the same time, efforts were being made to establish a naval presence on the Caspian. If the Turks were making for the coast at Baku, they had to be prevented, at all costs, from crossing the Caspian Sea to Russian Central Asia. Commodore D.T. Norris and a small naval detachment of twenty-two men from the gunboats *Mantis* and *Moth*, both later to serve in north Russia, left Baghdad by lorry, laboriously transporting naval guns and ammunition across to Enzeli, with instructions to capture merchant ships, mount guns on them and establish a Caspian patrol. These early parties supported Dunsterville's operations at Enzeli and Baku, but with reinforcements, including coastal motor boats (CMBs), again transported overland, they began to build up a British Caspian flotilla, establishing naval bases at Enzeli and Krasnovodsk. Lieutenant C.N.H. Bilney, a naval aviator, explained that the procedure was to find a merchantman flying the red flag and present the ultimatum, 'Surrender or you will be torpedoed'. The CMBs would then do a couple of quick circuits around the merchantman with the commander of the lead boat firing his pistol at the bridge. Shortly after, the red flag would be lowered and the surrender negotiated. In fact the ships could not have been torpedoed – the CMBs had no compressors fitted.[20] In this way a Caspian flotilla of armed merchantmen was established, commanded by British officers and crewed by Russians watched carefully by Royal Marine guards. After its precautionary role against the Turks' advance, the flotilla began to play a more active part against the Bolsheviks. It was the first time in history that the Royal Navy had been afloat on the Caspian Sea.

The Foreign Office's concerns about the threat to Russian Central Asia and possibly India brought further action beyond the Caspian Sea in Transcaspia itself. With German forces already at Tiflis and the Turks making for Baku, there seemed a serious risk of them managing to cross the Caspian to Krasnovodsk. There they would have had access to the Central Asian Railway, to the two or three year stock of cotton, a commodity desperately needed by the German munitions industry, and to the forty thousand German and Austrian prisoners who had been released in the region. The Central Asian Railway traversed a largely desert territory the size of Europe, connecting sparsely populated but exotically named towns including Bokhara, Samarkand and Tashkent. Tashkent was the base for the regional Bolshevik administration which was struggling to reassert its control over the western end of the line from which, much as at Baku, a rival anti-Bolshevik administration, composed largely of local railwaymen, had recently ejected it. The 'Ashkhabad Committee', as this group was called, was based on the railway town of that name and had extended its authority westward to the eastern Caspian port of Krasnovodsk. The security of this port and the railway running east from it was the focus of British concern.

Another Indian Army officer, Major General Wilfred Malleson, a soldier with a strong Intelligence background, was despatched to Meshed in north-west Persia to watch developments. Very soon after his arrival the Ashkhabad Committee appealed to Malleson for help against the Bolsheviks, who had driven back the committee's ragbag army almost to its base. With no more authority than that of General Munro, his chief in India, 'to act as he thought best', Malleson concluded, in August 1918, a formal treaty with the Ashkhabad administration on behalf of the British government. This compromised the neutrality of Persia, where he was based, at the same time. In return for British aid in troops, munitions and possibly cash to oppose the Tashkent Bolsheviks, Malleson was given extensive powers over the defence of Krasnovodsk and the railway running east from it against possible attack by the Central Powers. With the fall of Baku to the Turks, Malleson also became involved with the fate of its erstwhile government of commissars, a matter which became a *cause célèbre* for the Bolsheviks.* Very soon Malleson was able to put together a small force, initially a machine gun detachment, then some Punjabi troops and a field battery, and finally an Indian cavalry regiment. The Bolshevik advance along the railway was first halted and then, in some very heavy fighting in November, driven back beyond the Merv Oasis. The threat from the Central Powers never developed and, with the coming of the Armistice, evaporated altogether. For eight months, therefore, until replaced by some of General Denikin's White Russians in April 1919, General Malleson's small force was engaged solely in the Transcaspian variant of the Russian Civil War, doing most of the fighting on the anti-Bolshevik side and suffering disproportionately heavily in consequence, but gaining much land and inflicting severe losses on the Red forces opposing it.[21]

---

* The affair of the Twenty-Six Commissars is summarised in Appendix 1, pp. 327–29 below.

2

Arctic Danger

In the early months of 1918, fears were growing among the Bolshevik leaders for the security of Murmansk in the far north west of Russia. Nearby, Finland was in the grip of a civil war between the 'White Finns', who formed the official government under Marshal Mannerheim with strong German support, and the 'Red Finns', the Bolsheviks' brother revolutionaries. The Finnish border ran roughly parallel with the new Murman railway, which linked the Arctic port of Murmansk with the Russian capital Petrograd, at a distance of only some hundred miles. If the Bolsheviks' intransigence at the peace talks at Brest-Litovsk caused a resumption of the German advance, they might well move via Murmansk and the railway to take Petrograd. Of more concern to Britain's naval chiefs was the possibility of the capture of Murmansk itself by the Germans and its development as a naval base, enabling Germany to break the stranglehold of the Allied blockade and send submarines to threaten the vital north Atlantic traffic of supplies and troop convoys. It seemed a credible threat, despite the distance to the main Allied shipping lanes. Even nearer the Finnish border was the tiny fishing village of Pechenga, less than ideal for German naval purposes since it was not ice-free all year and had difficult landward access, but still a potential submarine base for at least part of the year. Admiral Kemp, commander of the British Northern Squadron, had already complained at the difficulty of protecting the military stores at Archangel without landing a military force there. Now he had the security of Murmansk, where some Russian ships were also based, added to his concerns. He asked London for six thousand men to defend the port. In early March the Admiralty, perhaps suspecting that the peppery Kemp was overstating his difficulties, replied that no troops would be sent but that he could use the crews of his ships to resist any overland German advance upon Murmansk, though he was not to commit himself to operations inland of the port itself. His main tasks were to keep the Russian ships at Murmansk out of German hands, to help with refugee evacuation, and to safeguard the stores there and at Archangel, where some British staff and diplomatic officials were based. A little later, under arrangements of the Allied Supreme War Council, Kemp's northern squadron was strengthened by the cruiser HMS *Cochrane*, detached from the Grand Fleet, and by the French heavy cruiser *Amiral Aube*, with the promise of a similar reinforcement from the United States to whom Britain had appealed for help.[1]

Relations between Kemp and the Murmansk authorities were good. He was in regular contact with the small town soviet and its leader, an independent-minded ex-ship's stoker and long-term Socialist by the name of Yuryev. In early March, fearful of the White Finns across the border, Yuryev telegraphed Petrograd for instructions, noting that his soviet was setting up a local defence force, and reporting that the Allied missions at Murmansk 'continue to show themselves inalterably well-inclined towards us and prepared to render us assistance, running all the way from food supply to armed aid'. In Petrograd, Trotsky was poorly informed about the progress of the peace negotiations with Germany and the precise state of the threat from Finland. Fearing the worst on both counts,[2] he telegraphed back to Yuryev: 'The peace negotiations have apparently broken off. It is your duty to do everything to protect the Murman Railway ... You must accept any and all assistance from the Allied missions and use every means to obstruct the advance of the plunderers'.[3] Admiral Kemp, the British Consul and a French official soon reached an agreement with the soviet and on 6 March 1918 a company of 130 Royal Marines went ashore, marched to the drab huts which passed for a barracks in Murmansk, mounted some naval guns outside them and prepared to repel the Finns. Completing this display of concord and amity, the old battleship *Glory* and the Russian battleship *Chesma* exchanged salutes. An embryonic Eastern Front had apparently been reopened; British troops were on Russian soil, apparently with the full agreement of the Bolshevik authorities. In mid April the Foreign Office issued a statement designed to make Kemp's position easier: 'You are authorised to state officially that Great Britain has no intention of annexing any part of Russian territory and will continue to assist in defence of district against outside aggression with such forces as can be spared and will maintain friendly relations on basis of mutual advantage.'[4] It was a claim soon to be belied by actions on the ground.

Present-day Murmansk, the largest city in the world north of the Arctic Circle, is the capital and economic centre of the region around it and one of Russia's biggest seaports. In 1914 it barely existed and lacked all developed communications with the Russian hinterland. Yet its location, thirty miles inland from the Barents Sea along the Kola Inlet and ice-free all year, made it ideally suited for development as a port. Kola itself, a fishing village six miles further south along the inlet, and Alexandrovsk, a tiny settlement nearer the inlet's coastal extremity where the telegraph cable from Scotland later came ashore, were the only other inhabited settlements. That a working port and landward communications were so rapidly constructed at Murmansk was largely the result of Britain's need for year-round facilities through which to supply the vast quantities of stores required to sustain the war effort of her Russian ally. South east of Murmansk across the White Sea was the well-developed port of Archangel; but this presented a longer journey for British ships, and it was ice-bound for half the year and could not cope with the quantities needed. The construction work at Murmansk employed Chinese and Korean labourers and Austrian and German prisoners of war working under Canadian engineers loaned to Russia for the purpose. It began in September 1915 and by the end of the following year a primitive port had been built and a single-track railway laid to connect it with the Petrograd. Like its Second World War equivalent, the Burma–Thailand railway, the Murman line bore all the signs of hurried and gimcrack construction, and its building exacted a great human toll: at least 40,000 prisoners of war died in its construction. The irony was that this lifeline to the embattled Russians came into use just as the first cracks in their will to resist were appearing.

Murmansk was not an attractive billet for the marines who landed there. The Murman coastline was vast and hilly but otherwise featureless, land and sea merging in a grey blur unbroken by the outline of any significant buildings or trees. The settlement itself was little more than a collection of unattractive, dark, wooden huts, storage sheds and primitive port facilities, with a few slightly more impressive buildings and a large, ornate church. The buildings were linked by unmade roads which became a morass of mud in the short summer months when the warmth thawed the surface layers of the Arctic tundra. Movement on foot was by duck-board pavements with a few roads 'corduroyed' with laid logs. One officer, arriving after winter had set in, described the town as presenting 'a bleak and desolate spectacle, enough to damp the ardour of the most enthusiastic: long stretches of barren land, fir trees, a handful of log huts, a small landing stage and snow'.[5] The flat hinterland, relieved only by stunted birches, low-growing ling and in the distance an endless vista of pine and fir, was frozen solid in winter. In summer it became a boggy expanse barely sustaining the railway track along which the British-supplied engines pulled their trains of military stores, swaying alarmingly on the yielding tundra and crossing hundreds of bridges that spanned the small rivers which quickly developed once the thaw began. Murmansk had few of the facilities normally found in a town of its size with which to greet the incoming troops. Yet it already hosted an extraordinarily diverse, largely male, international population as it swelled with refugees from the fighting and turmoil further south as well as with the British newcomers. Accommodation was already desperately short.

The day after the marines from *Glory* marched ashore, *Cochrane* arrived at Murmansk and landed a party of its own marines. These were reinforced by men from the recently-arrived French Military Mission from Roumania and were quickly sent south by makeshift armoured train hastily fitted out with naval guns. Their destination was the small but important coastal town of Kandalaksha, eighty miles away, which was reported to be threatened by a force of White Finns. Kandalaksha lay at the southern end of the Murman peninsula on an inlet in the White Sea. The Finns were easily scattered by the sight of the armoured train's guns, and the marines steamed back to Murmansk. The threat from the Finns, however, was real enough: further south along the line they did manage to capture the White Sea port of Kem before being driven off by Bolshevik Red Guards, at this stage still the allies of Kemp's marines. These incursions and the threat of worse to come brought a fresh urgency to the situation. In April the Admiralty, already heavily committed in the larger naval war, decided to press for the War Office to assume responsibility for the defence of the Murman coast. At the same time, the Supreme War Council in Paris decided on a policy of 'effective intervention', whilst recognising that the critical situation on the Western Front would allow the transfer of only a modest number of troops.

Meanwhile, the Murmansk soviet reported to Admiral Kemp that the German-supported White Finns had advanced on Pechenga. This seemed to confirm the Admiralty's worst fears. HMS *Cochrane* re-embarked her marines together with a party of Red Guards and steamed off to face this latest challenge thirty miles away along the coast. About a hundred seamen were landed with the marines and Red Guards and began a series of running fights with the Finns. A few days later *Glory* brought reinforcements with Lewis guns and a 12-pounder which was manhandled across the ice from *Cochrane.* By 10 May the marines were established around an imposing stone-built monastery at the head of the harbour overlooking the small cluster of village buildings. The main monastery of Saint Zosimus, a place of pilgrimage, was about six miles inland. The 'lower monastery' at Pechenga was actually a sort of coastal reception centre for pilgrims and had several large, weatherproof, wooden rest-houses clustered around the main building and belfry. These provided excellent accommodation for the tiny garrison in an area lacking most other amenities. Two days later they beat off a determined attack by over 150 Finns who fought skilfully and with some determination. The marines had few casualties, but among them was the detachment commander, Captain Browne of the Royal Marine Artillery, who received a shoulder wound and was later awarded the DSO for his conduct of the defence. Although alarming reports continued to be received of further threats to the tiny port, this proved to be the last attempt by the White Finns to take it. Its security continued to be assured by the guns of the *Cochrane* moored in the small harbour.

The apparent threat posed to the Russian Murman coast was underscored when a U-boat appeared off Pechenga and sank a number of small Russian steamers and Norwegian fishing craft. It did not stay long and never returned, whilst the spring thaw soon rendered a landward attack on the small port unlikely without huge resources being devoted to it. But this was not how the matter appeared to the Allies, who continued to plan against a major advance by the Finns and their German supporters. General Rüdiger von der Goltz was believed to have 50,000 troops ready to support a Finnish attack. Plans to reinforce the

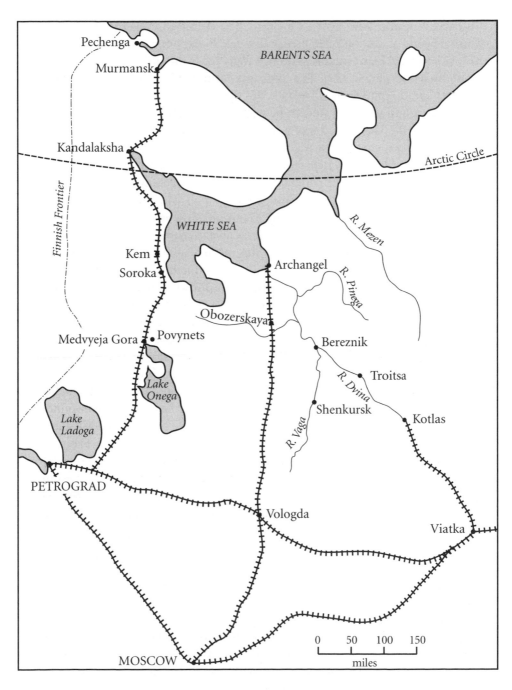

Murmansk and Archangel Commands

Murmansk region were hurried forward. The Admiralty put together a Royal Marine Field Force of over 300 men with a field battery of naval guns, a company of Royal Marine Light Infantry cobbled together from different stations, and a strong machine gun section. The force was equipped for a long stay with both summer clothing and Arctic winter kit. But the marines were no longer to operate under the Admiralty; they were to be part of the North Russian Expeditionary Force which the War Office was now assembling for its new responsibility of defending the Murman coast and railway.

In the light of the threat it imagined it was to face, the army element of the new force was pitifully small – a company of infantry, a machine gun company and most of an engineer field company – 600 men in all. The force was codenamed 'Syren' and was to be commanded by Major General Sir Charles Maynard, an officer with plenty of operational experience in a variety of campaigns, but none at all of Russia and the Russians. What was more disquieting was that Maynard had been invalided home from Salonika, and the medical board summoned to clear him for the new post declared him still unfit for general service. When a high-level intervention from the War Office assured the board that Maynard's undisclosed appointment 'was of a purely sedentary nature', but had to be assumed immediately, the board washed its hands of the matter and Maynard was appointed. 'There was a spirit of adventure about the whole enterprise that made a strong appeal to me', Maynard later recalled; but he was to find the command at Murmansk anything but sedentary. His men were similarly doubtful medical material, mainly category 'B' soldiers who had been evacuated wounded from France; mostly now fit only for indoor duties or work at the Murmansk base. Most wore at least one wound stripe. One officer enrolled for 'Syren' was a sixty-three-year-old 'dugout' who had retired from the Indian Army in 1913. One of the younger members of Syren called him 'a dear old duffer who was quite useless', but some of his comments on the campaign were quite perceptive. The dire situation on the Western Front coupled with the much tighter coordination of mobilised manpower between army and industry meant that these were the only men available. Indeed there was an air of haste and incomplete preparation about the whole enterprise, with questions of transport, local conditions and even finance hardly being considered. When Maynard approached the Treasury for a sterling grant to cover local purchases at Murmansk, the officials at first demurred, offering Maynard instead 'an immense number of barrels of salted herrings stored at Vardo in Norway' for payment in kind! 'I had a strong objection to adding the running of a glorified fish-shop to my other duties', was the general's comment. The Treasury later relented; but Maynard was to find the lack of cash a continuing problem during his time at Murmansk. As for the herrings, they were finally landed weeks later on the quays at Archangel, stinking in the hot sun and quite unfit for consumption.[6]

The War Office also raised a training mission codenamed 'Elope'. This, under Brigadier General Finlayson, was to sail to Murmansk with Syren and then cross the White Sea to Archangel as soon as the ice broke up. There it was to take charge of the military stores lodged at the docks and then equip and train a force of Czech troops who had fought alongside the Russians against Germany. The latest idea for the Czechs was that they would make their way across from Central Russia to Archangel before moving on as a reinforcement for the Western Front. It was planned that both Syren and Elope forces would also recruit and train local Russians to take the field against the Germans in the reconstituted Eastern Front. Manpower for Elope was equally difficult to find and both Australia and Canada were asked to provide men. From the volunteers who came forward eight officers and eleven sergeants were selected. They were to prove among the best fighting men in the force. The Supreme War Council formally authorised the expedition under British command and the other Allied nations agreed to make a contribution, though they were as pressed for manpower as were the British. Much was expected of the promised American contribution to the new front. While the two forces had their separate commanders, in overall charge of the Allied effort in north Russia was Major General Frederick Poole.

Most authorities write of General Poole's distinguished early military career, apparently unaware that he had retired from the Army in the spring of 1914 after twenty-five years' service with the relatively modest rank of major. He rejoined the service when the war broke out and thereafter, like many experienced regular officers, levitated very rapidly through the ranks. By 1917 he was a major general, chief of the British Artillery and Aviation Mission supplying the Russians. He was familiar with the old Tsarist Army and knew something of the local conditions of Archangel through which so much military *matériel* from Britain had passed. Poole travelled to Murmansk ahead of his twin task forces aboard the US cruiser *Olympia*, a belated American contribution to Kemp's naval squadron. He arrived at Murmansk on 24 May, only a couple of months after he had quit his previous post in Petrograd, and just as the War Office was beginning to mobilise his troops. The importance of their timely despatch was emphasised five days later when Poole telegraphed to say that an attack by the Finns on Pechenga and Murmansk was expected at the end of June or in early July.

A shroud of secrecy cloaked the assembly of the expeditionary force for North Russia. The two task forces, known only by their codenames, were assembled at the Tower of London 'as the mobilisation of a unit there causes no comment'.[7] There was absolute secrecy as to their destination, though the men were allowed to hint at America where the weather extremes were similar to Russia's and which would explain the extra kit taken on the march to King's Cross station. Only Maynard, Finlayson and the captain of the heavily camouflaged *City of Marseilles*, which was to carry them to the Arctic Circle, had any idea where they were bound.

Not until the ship put out from Newcastle on 18 June with its destroyer escort did Maynard call the officers together and explain their destination and mission. No sooner were they out of danger of U-boat attack than influenza broke out among the crew. The Lascar stokers were the first to succumb. Their symptoms were exacerbated by the men being Muslims and the voyage taking place during Ramadan: they were not allowed to eat before dusk but the sun never really set at all. Numbers of them died during the voyage. During this crisis the vessel had to proceed at half speed, a disquieting necessity since there was a precise date at which the Murmansk end of the operation was to take over escort duties. The stoker problem was solved by borrowing crew from the oil-burning destroyers and taking volunteers from among the soldiers. Even some officers volunteered for stoking: none liked the idea of being a half-speed target for submarines. Eventually most of the force fell victim to the infuenza pandemic which was sweeping the world. Despite these difficulties, the soldiers seemed to regard the venture on which they were bound as something of a picnic.

With the task forces on the high seas, a wire arrived at the War Office from General Poole expressing the view that it was very unlikely that any of the Czechs would ever materialise in North Russia. A couple of days later came the confirmation that the Czech 1st Division had given up all hope of getting to the Archangel–Vologda railway and was following its comrades of the 2nd Division east to Vladivostok. Nevertheless the government persisted in the view that a junction with the Czechs was still possible and planning proceeded on that basis as the task forces ploughed across the Barents Sea to Murmansk. The generals and their diminutive forces of second-rate soldiers arrived at the port on 23 June, giving Maynard the first chance to survey his command and assess the threats he faced.

The Murmansk command was potentially vast and its boundaries indeterminate. The critical territory, however, was the corridor of land varying in width from 50 to 140 miles which lay between Finland's eastern frontier and the Murman railway. In theory the railway was vulnerable to attack from any section of this corridor by a Finnish-German force of up to 100,000 strong. To defend it Maynard had a motley, second-rate, international force of about 2500 – Royal Marines, French gunners and a Serb battalion, together with his own task force. The odds seemed overwhelming. It appeared preposterous that this minute army could do anything significant to resurrect the Eastern Front which had once held down so many German divisions. Its own security would surely absorb all the force's energies. In fact the difficult conditions of the swampy tundra during the summer months reduced the perceived imbalance to more manageable proportions, for they prevented the movement of all but small bodies of troops. There were only two serviceable routes from the Finnish frontier, and these debouched at the White Sea ports of Kandalaksha and Kem, whose garrisons could be reinforced, or at worst evacuated, by sea. The ports lay respectively 150 and 300 miles from Murmansk, to which any landward threat would come up the railway from one of these places. There were also tortuous river routes from Finnish territory, but they ran through difficult, inhospitable country and were most unlikely to be used. The railway itself crossed innumerable small streams whose wooden bridges were easily destroyed or defended, while the enemy's supply lines would be precariously extended and exposed as they tried to move north. With the two White Sea ports 'held and strengthened', Maynard reasoned, 'as I hoped they shortly would be by the arrival of Allied contingents, we should have a reasonable chance of preventing Murmansk falling into German hands, so long as summer conditions prevailed'.[8]

As for Pechenga, a visit to the tiny village quickly convinced the Murmansk commander that 'von der Goltz would not waste men and material in a real effort to establish himself there': the Finnish railhead was 250 miles away and there were no roads capable of taking more than the lightest transport. In Maynard's view Pechenga's attraction as a German submarine base was much exaggerated. 'It was inconceivable', he later wrote, 'that such a base could have been established ... without years of toil and concentrated labour, which must include the construction of 250 miles of railway.' He left the defence of the diminutive port to the *Cochrane* and the detachment of marines and Serbs marooned at the desolate monastery.[9]

The Finnish-German threat to the coastal ports was, however, not the only factor for consideration. Maynard already had the support of the 'Red Finns', or Finnish Legion as they became called, composed of Bolshevik Finns driven from their homeland by the Whites. But a reconstructed Eastern Front meant recruiting Russians willing to take the field against the Germans. That in turn required the occupation of territory from which they might be recruited. What if the agreement with the Murmansk authorities turned sour or was actively opposed by Petrograd? As Lieutenant-Colonel Burn, the Indian Army veteran of the Elope force, reflected on the problem, he was plainly aware of the contradictions which lay at the heart of the intervention policy:

> We have come over here to form and train a Russian Army with which we can threaten Germany and compel her to withdraw troops from the Western Front, and to do this we have landed in a country whose de facto government is at peace with Germany, but which is threatened by counter-revolutionary forces whom we favour and intend to assist; at the same time we expect Moscow not to interfere with our plans.[10]

The Bolshevik authorities were already angered by the turn of events in Siberia, where the Czechs, apparently under Allied guidance, were now fighting their former Bolshevik comrades. This coloured the regime's view of the fresh landings at Murmansk. Lenin himself despatched two peremptory telegrams to Yuryev's soviet ordering it to break off relations with the Allies. Yuryev was a Socialist though not a Boshevik. His little regime operated under the shadow of a strong Allied squadron in Murmansk harbour whose guns could have blown the small town to matchwood. He defended his position with sturdy independence. 'It is all very well for you to talk that way, sitting there in Moscow', he challenged Lenin, knowing that his little community depended on the Allies for virtually all their provisions. When Chicherin, the Commissar of Foreign Affairs, later repeated the orders to throw out the imperialists, Yuryev again queried their practicability: 'Can you supply the region with food, which we are now lacking, and send us a force to carry out your instructions? If not there is no need to lecture us.'[11] It was all getting rather messy in Murmansk.

The changed attitudes of the Bolshevik authorities became clear when Maynard, accompanied by a small escort, took the train south for his first tour of inspection. At Kandalaksha he found a trainload of Bolsheviks about to leave for the north. After a brief argument, and despite being vastly outnumbered, Maynard managed to bluff their commander into inaction until Serb reinforcements arrived from the town and took over the train. With a stronger escort he journeyed further south to Kem, which was crowded with Red Guards from two recently arrived trains. With the aid of the larger garrison in the town, he had no difficulty in getting them all to detrain. He told his local commander not to allow any Bolshevik troops to move further north. On return to Murmansk he learnt that that the Reds he had encountered were only the advance guard of a much larger force whose orders were to attack the Allies and drive them from Murmansk. Maynard promptly ordered all the Red Guards as far south as Kem to be disarmed and all the villages along the line to be searched for arms. The search yielded 10,000 rifles, sixty machine guns and much ammunition. He also reinforced the Kem garrison, where several Bolsheviks were killed during the search. The Red Guards responded by withdrawing to Soroka, a small port on the railway at the southern end of the White Sea, destroying bridges as they went and dealing with any residents whom they suspected of having Allied leanings. HMS *Attentive* was sent down from Kem with a detachment of Red Finns. By the time Maynard followed by train the Bolsheviks had headed further south still. He decided to hold the town and arranged for another small force to garrison it. The brief honeymoon with the Bolshevik central government was clearly at an end.

Maynard's small international force now held Pechenga, Murmansk and over 300 miles of railway stretching to the southern end of the White Sea. The dilemma of the Murmansk intervention was starkly exposed. The polyglot little army was in charge of a great swathe of Russian territory and faced, as potential opponents, Germans, White Finns and Bolsheviks. Substantial territory had to be held from which 'loyal' Russians might be recruited; yet the sight of such an inadequate garrison was unlikely to give many local men sufficient confidence to throw in their lot with the Allies. For how long would the Red Finns of the Finnish Legion remain loyal when opposing fellow-Bolshevik Red Guards? Could Yuryev's regime remain unaffected by the growing pressure from Moscow to oppose the Allied intervention? Maynard inevitably took the view that he needed a larger British contingent and soon made his views known to the War Office. 'Mission creep', as the Americans call it, was beginning to exert its insidious influence on the campaign.

On Midsummer Day 1918, Lieutenant Colonel P.J. Woods arrived in Murmansk with a party of reinforcements for Maynard's garrison. He was soon sent south to Kem, which was part of the Russian province of Karelia, a tract of country lying between the railway and the Finnish border, stretching from Kandalaksha in the north to Lake Onega in the south. It was an area historically contested between the Russians and the local Finns, the Karelians, who had developed their own sense of nationality over the centuries. Now it was menaced by the infiltration of White Finns along its many rivers and lakes. General Maynard arrived at the Kem garrison post and addressed the newly-arrived colonel: 'Woods, these fearsome-looking fellows outside are Karelians. They want arms, a little food and an officer to lead them. Their object is to clear the Finns, who are being led by German officers, out of their county. They won't take any oath of allegiance to the Allies, so that we shall have to take them largely on trust, would you take them on?' Woods agreed to the task and so began his valuable relationship with this fiercely independent people. Active recruiting began and within a month a 500-strong regiment had been created. All the men had experience in the Imperial Russian Army and they proved, at least in the view of their commander, to be a well-disciplined force, free of insubordination, drunkenness or complaints. The regiment's strength ultimately rose to 4000. Using a transport force of small boats manned by brightly-dressed village women and basing its movements on excellent intelligence from the local population, the regiment steadily cleared Karelia of the German and Finnish invaders in a summer and autumn campaign of small engagements. As each fresh village was cleared so fresh recruits were obtained and the regiment was expanded. Soon the province was entirely free of the invaders; border posts were established and fontier guards appointed to man them. The Karelian Regiment's headquarters was located at Kem, where Woods organised a fur-trading company whose profits provided short-term pensions for the widows and orphans of the those killed in the campaign, until the War Office finally assumed financial responsibility for this unusual force. Woods's little campaign was eminently successful, but at the cost of adding a fresh political dimension to Maynard's command.[12]

Meanwhile, General Poole was making his plans for the expansion of the intervention. Maynard was later to describe his chief as 'the most confirmed optimist it has ever been my fortune to meet', adding, in the politest of understatements, that Poole had 'perhaps no great liking for the study of detail' and was at times prone to 'the occasional departure from the letter of King's Regulations'. He might have added that Poole (despite what he had earlier advised the government in regard to them) had complete disdain for the fighting abilities of the Bolsheviks and the most profound distaste for their regime. In fact, his unjustified optimism was certainly a factor in the expansion of the intervention as a whole.

Soon after the departure of the expeditionary forces from home waters, the War Cabinet became concerned at the conflicting reports it was receiving from Russia. Admiral Kemp, on the one hand (whose 'violent temper and very strong opinions' might necessitate replacing him, admitted the First Sea Lord), and Bruce Lockhart, the unofficial consul in Moscow, on the other, held totally different views on Russian policy. General Poole and the consuls in North Russian were similarly divided. The Cabinet decided to send the First Lord of the Admiralty, Sir Eric Geddes, to Murmansk to confer with Admiral Kemp and General Poole and to make a personal investigation. Geddes's important and influential report bears all the signs of infection with Poole's optimism. He claimed to find 'an extraordinary element of comic opera' in the situation in north Russia where 'there is really no Government; there is no organisation; and there is no authority'. He was assured (more than likely by Poole) that this was 'typical of what is going on under the Lenin–Trotsky Government in all parts of Russia'. He reported Poole's view that, with modest additions to the reinforcements promised, he could advance down the Murman railway and recruit 10,000 Russians to the anti-German cause, whilst, with 5000 men added to his Elope force, he might proceed along the Archangel–Vologda railway and the River Dvina and draw 'say 100,000 anti-German Russians to his forces'. It was a sublimely over-sanguine projection, but given the large element of *opéra bouffe* which Geddes detected in the government of Russia, which reminded him more of a minor South American republic, he recommended that Poole's plan, despite the risks it involved, should be accepted. Much early planning seemed to proceed on the assumption that the Bolshevik regime rested on the flimsiest foundations, was widely detested by the Russian people, and could easily be toppled.[13]

Poole's immediate difficulty was that, even with his combination of optimism and disdain for the opposition, the Elope force was hardly sufficient to make what was certain to be an opposed landing at the substantial town of Archangel. He was committed to making his attempt as soon as the ice had broken up sufficiently to allow passage down the White Sea from Murmansk. Moreover, there was considerable urgency. Unlike Murmansk, Archangel had loyal Bolsheviks forming the local administation and they were known to be busily removing the war stores supplied by the British and sending them south, where it was feared they would fall into German hands. The news of the clash at Kem and the death of local Bolsheviks during the search for arms had already inflamed local relations with the British officials. Admiral Kemp had been in the town when the news broke. He had gone so far as to offer to transport representatives of the Archangel soviet on his yacht to investigate the incident, but they chose to make the voyage under their own arrangements and were treated very suspiciously on arrival. If the Kem incident was the moment when the intervention at Murmansk changed from being a collaborative venture with the Bolsheviks into an operation as much against them as the Germans, the expedition to Archangel was an opposed, anti-Bolshevik invasion from the very start.

A *coup d'état* to topple the Bolshevik soviet at Archangel simultaneous with his landing at the town was a key feature of Poole's plan from the outset. It was to be undertaken by Captain Georgi Chaplin, a young Tsarist naval officer with profound anti-Bolshevik sentiments who had served with the Royal Navy and spoke good English. He was provided with a British passport and a false identity as 'Commander Thompson of the British Naval Mission' for the purpose. Since the Bolsheviks' accession he had been recruiting for the White Volunteer Army in the south before coming into contact with the British at Murmansk, to whom he claimed to have suggested the operation for the liberation of Archangel. The coup arrangements were agreed with Poole during July and were well coordinated with the Allied diplomats at Vologda, where Chaplin had turned up in his British naval officer's uniform.[14] In mid-July Poole warned them to be ready for an early departure from Bolshevik territory as he was planning to land at Archangel at the end of the month or early in August. Special trains were arranged with the authorities for their journey and they arrived in Archangel on 26 July. From there the local Bolsheviks laid on two ships to take them across the White Sea to Kandalaksha, little knowing that in return for their services they were about to be deposed.

The diplomats were joined at Archangel at the last minute by the members of a British economic mission that had been sent to Moscow to discover, in Lord Balfour's words, 'the best means of restoring and developing British trade relations and interests in Russia and of countering enemy schemes of commercial penetration'.[15] It was a priceless example of the left hand not knowing what the right was doing. In view of the advanced state of the coup's preparations it is scarcely surprising that the mission stayed only two days and achieved nothing, or that Bruce Lockhart, the British representative who conducted it around Moscow, was afterwards accused by the Bolsheviks of 'machiavellian duplicity'. In fact Lockhart had been 'staggered' at the arrival of the trade mission, knowing that the Archangel intervention was imminent. He called it 'one more comedy before the final tragedy'.[16] The mission members arrived at the Archangel quayside in great haste and with evident relief at the prospect of quitting Bolshevik soil. They joined the diplomats aboard the little steamers just as they were about to weigh anchor. A disinterested onlooker might have detected *opéra bouffe* on the British side as well.

Once across the White Sea the diplomats hurriedly contacted Poole at Murmansk and warned him that the Soviet secret police were hard on Chaplin's heels; some of his accomplices had already been arrested: the coup could not be delayed much longer. Whilst at Archangel, they had made it clear to Chaplin that the new regime had to be left of centre and that they had already persuaded a veteran revolutionary socialist, Nikolai Chaikovsky, a tall, lean seventy-year-old with a flowing white beard and great revolutionary prestige who had spent most of his life in exile, to join the escapade and head the new administration. Chaplin disliked Socialists of every hue and agreed to the arrangement with pronounced reluctance. Poole was urged to put his plan into operation without delay. He had hoped to await further reinforcements but decided to manage with the sole addition of the French 21st Colonial Infantry, an 870-strong battalion which had just arrived to join his force, following the Supreme War Council's approval of the venture. The success of the coup was vital to Poole's undertaking since his force was not strong enough to deal with Archangel's seaward defences and take on resistance in the inland town itself. It was agreed that Poole's attack on the sea defences would take place on 31 July and Chaplin's rising the following day.

Rumours continued during August and September of German-Finnish plans for operations against the Syren forces. General Maynard was already reporting a serious food shortage in Murmansk; after the break with the Bolsheviks, supplies were not coming up from the south and the population was expanding as the garrison increased. In early September Maynard put in his demand for substantial reinforcements: a brigade of infantry, two machine gun companies and some artillery support. It was a substantial shopping list given the needs of other theatres. By the end of the month the first instalment arrived – most of the requested artillery but only one battalion, the 11th Royal Sussex. The battalion had come from barracks in Aldershot whence they had been expecting to return to France. The first indication that they were not bound for the Flanders trenches had come when a large consignment of ankle-length, fur-lined ulsters was issued to the puzzled men, together with extra-long rifles with permanently-fixed bayonets and a Cyrillic inscription on the breech metalwork, which made their destination a little clearer. To ease the supply problems, all the intervention forces were being issued with Russian-pattern rifles. The men were rushed north by train and then had a stormy passage to Murmansk. Within a few days they were absorbing their first, demoralising sight of the place, whose appearance produced its customary depressing effect. 'Hardly the class of port that a great sea-faring people was entitled to expect', wrote one of their number. 'True, there were some timber jetties and a variety of nondescript shipping, but, ashore, no recognizable town, no buildings of the slightest distinction, just rows of drab log huts.'[17]

Maynard's intelligence staff had reported that Pechenga was about to be raided, so two companies of the freshly disembarked battalion, together with a machine gun company, were bundled directly into a collier that had just discharged its cargo and sent straightaway to the threatened village. No threats materialised. Nevertheless, with the prospect of the swampy, summer hinterland giving place to a surer footing for an invader as the temperature began to drop to its sub-zero winter level, the garrison prepared for a long stay and set about fortifying the beachhead of the lower monastery with an outer perimeter of wooded blockhouses on the low hills that ringed the Pechenga fjord. They also built a substantial observation post on an outlying crag to guide the gunfire of *Cochrane* if any worthwhile targets should appear.[18]

Towards the end of October Maynard took delivery of another reinforcement, this time a less than welcome one: it was the polar explorer and popular hero Ernest Shackleton, now a temporary major on the active list despite a suspected heart condition. 'I've heard about this man Shackleton', the general grumbled. 'He's an impossible person. He likes to run everything in his own way ... I'm not going to have him.' Shackleton had been badgering various government departments for employment with the Russians since the summer of 1917. 'I am anxious to leave at the earliest possible moment', he had written, 'and I may add that the higher the rank given me temporarily here the better it will be for me in dealing with the Russians.' Later he wrote again, 'I can inspire the Russians, *I know it*'; but the ambassador and the military attaché advised against employing him. Instead Shackleton was first sent to Buenos Aires to investigate ways of improving Britain's war propaganda in the neutral states of South America, and then appointed leader of a bizarre undercover operation which was part of an attempt to stake Britain's claim to the disputed territory of Spitsbergen; but in August 1918 he was abruptly recalled from Tromsø. The Murmansk venture was then in train and a winter campaign in Arctic conditions lay ahead. The War Office wanted an expert to organise the transport and equipment for the troops in the Arctic and Shackleton seemed the man. One of the early results of Shackleton's War Office labours was the fur-lined overcoats which so puzzled the men of the Royal Sussex. By early October, Shackleton was sailing to Murmansk where some of his old comrades from the *Endurance* and *Nimrod* expeditions were already based, as indeed were some of those of his rival polar explorer, Scott. One of Shackleton's men reported to him that General Maynard was a 'rather disgruntled, unsmiling, bad-tempered customer',[19] but the explorer was confident he could cope with him and did his best to make himself agreeable to his chief. He seems to have succeeded, for, despite his initial frosty reaction, the general found Shackleton a cheerful and amusing companion who kept the little headquarters from gloom and depression with his fund of adventure stories.[20]

'A Little War Coming in the East': a cartoon by Strube, *Daily Express*,
23 January 1920.

3

Archangel

In the late evening of 27 July 1918 the Elope expeditionary force steamed down the Kola Inlet and headed east for the still ice-pocked White Sea and the descent upon Archangel. It sailed with no assurance of success. 'We were given to understand that it was a matter of life and death whether we got there in 24 hours', wrote Captain Altham of HMS *Attentive*. 'To do this meant taking considerable risks, for the opposition we were likely to encounter was unknown.' Having earlier scouted the entrance to the channel of the River Dvina that led to Archangel, Altham's light cruiser took the lead. Behind her sailed the seaplane-carrier HMS *Nairana* and the French cruiser *Amiral Aube*. *Attentive* carried 100 French infantry, *Nairana* 200 and *Amiral Aube* another 200 and 100 Royal Marines. Behind them were two former Russian destroyers now crewed by the Royal Navy, followed by Admiral Kemp's force of trawler-minesweepers bearing the men of Poole's training mission together with some Poles, the rest of the French battalion, a detachment of US marines from *Olympia* and a section of machine gunners, all but the French borrowed from a reluctant Maynard. The admiral's yacht, HMS *Salvator*, with General Poole aboard, completed the armada. Whilst the ships were numerous and not unimpressive, the land force which Poole had scraped together scarcely amounted to 1500 men, of whom 600 in the first three ships constituted the assault landing force. The various elements had never trained together and were ill-prepared for their venture. To make matters worse a dense fog caused the ships to part company and within twenty-four hours the French cruiser, carrying the most substantial force, reported that she had run aground. The assault element was now reduced to little more than three hundred men. It is true that the coup in the town was expected to be successful, but Archangel lay twenty-five miles up the tortuous and island-strewn Dvina estuary whose entrance was dominated by the island fortress of Modyuski, close to which ran the only navigable channel for the deep-draught warships leading the expedition. Modyuski island's 6-inch gun batteries were the town's main defences and the channel it commanded was reported to be mined.[1]

Undaunted by the unexpected depletion of their force, Kemp and Finlayson, the operational commander under Poole, decided to push on with their plan unchanged. At the estuary entrance *Attentive* sent a boarding party to the lightship from which it was hoped to communicate with the commander of the formidable Modyuski batteries and demand the garrison's surrender. Eight pilots and a commissar were quickly rounded up and the ultimatum was passed by telephone to the Modyuski commandant. After some procrastination, and under threat from the ship's guns, he finally agreed to surrender and to lead his garrison from the forts. This message was immediately contradicted by another from the lightship landing party to the effect that they had learnt that the fortress commander was under orders to resist the Allied advance so as to give the Archangel authorities time to withdraw up river with all the goods, vessels and war *matériel* they could take with them. *Attentive* immediately withdrew. There began what should have been a very unequal fire-fight between the guns of the light cruiser and the fortress. Much of the Boshevik fire was wide, but one well-handled 6-inch gun soon had the range and took out one of *Attentive's* four funnels and the two boilers beneath. Fortunately, by this time the cruiser's fire was beginning to tell, assisted by some effective bombing from *Nairana's* seaplanes. Modyuski's four batteries, 'which ought to have blown us out of the water', Captain Altham later admitted, soon fell silent. Part of the ship's assault force was landed on the island as the seaplanes circled overhead. It was one of the first air-supported sea landings in military history. 'By sheer affrontery, by nightfall, the whole of the effective defences of Archangel were in our hands and the Bolshevik garrison had fled up harbour.' Two wounded Frenchmen had been the only Allied casualties.[2]

From then onwards the occupation of Archangel became little more than a formality. By the following morning Chaplin's coup had been executed, with moral support from the seaplanes flying above the town. The old Russian national flag was soon fluttering once again over the town hall. Viewed from the town, the great river was an extraordinary sight, one resident recalled, 'all the paddle-steamers, every type of craft the Bolsheviks could lay their hands on, were hurrying up the river to the south. The Bolsheviks were fleeing'.[3] The Allied armada steamed up the estuary in triumphal procession, led by the slightly damaged cruiser, the threat of mines and blockships being easily avoided by the experienced pilots now captive on the vessels. The sawmills and shipyards of the strangely silent northern industrial suburb of Solombola hove into view first and then, rounding a bend in the river, the anchorage of the port itself appeared. 'The whole waterside of the town was black with cheering people, greeting us in a frenzy of acclamation. For many our arrival meant literally deliverance from imminent death' was the somewhat overheated conclusion of the cruiser's captain. An Archangel schoolgirl saw the force's arrival in similar dramatic terms:

> As if entering the stage from the wings of a theatre, the first ships of the flotilla came into view. The others followed. They were all there – Russian, British, French, American.

They sailed serenely, majestically, one after the other, in perfect formation, against the pink glow of the setting sun. There was breathless hush followed by tremendous cheering, growing louder as each ship passed before our eyes ... Never before had the banks of our river seen such a glorious armada. I have never forgotten that stirring sight, nor yet the old lady beside me, tears streaming down her face, crossing herself and repeating over and over again, 'Slava Tyebye Gospodi' ... 'The Lord be praised.'[4]

The spectators were not to know how inadequate the task force which the ships were bearing was. Russia was being invaded by 1500 men.

As the news of the successful operation reached Moscow on 4 August, the day Dunsterville's men landed at Baku, the city was wild with fevered rumour. It was said that the Allies had landed in considerable strength; some stories put the figure at 100,000 men. When something approaching the actual number got through to Bruce Lockhart he was dismayed: 'We had committed the unbelievable folly of landing at Archangel with fewer than twelve hundred men. It was a blunder comparable with the worst mistakes of the Crimean War.'[5] Archangel-based diplomats had similar misgivings. Two months earlier the British Consul at Archangel had warned the Foreign Secretary that military operations without the consent of the rulers of Russia could not lead to permanent advantage and would commit the government to ever-increasing obligations from which they would be unable to free themselves without discredit and great loss of prestige. As Generals Poole and Finlayson were being greeted with the traditional Russian welcome of bread and salt, the US Consul, Felix Cole, who was opposed to the intervention, was remarking with disquiet that the large and enthusiastic crowd which greeted it was composed only of the bourgeoisie and richer peasants who had suffered most during the brief reign of the Bolsheviks. 'The working class was patently absent', he noted, a feature of the welcome which became even more apparent as the Allied officers marched through the streets to the government buildings, underscoring the earlier silence of the workers as the ships steamed past Solombola.[6]

The Archangel which Poole and Chaplin had now seized presented a welcome contrast to the bare, dark huts of Murmansk. It was the oldest seaport in Russia, with a thriving timber industry and several dozen sawmills in its substantial industrial area. It has long-established trade relations with Britain, which took the lion's share of its timber – about a million and three-quarter tons a year before the war began – and also provided Archangel's main imports. The town boasted a large stone-built cathedral with five gilded domes, wood-paved streets, a theatre, a tram service, street lighting and a main shopping street – Troitsky Prospect. It was also soon to have, a tramcar's journey away at the other end of town, a brothel established for the incoming garrison, known euphemistically simply as 'the house with the green roof'. As in every other settlement in this forested region, wooden buildings predominated. Unlike Murmansk, Archangel also had a substantial middle class. With the accession of the Bolsheviks, one citizen recalled, 'the bourgeoisie had suffered a quiet subservience to the new regime; commissars were overbearing, servants were truculent, shortages of basic commodities were widespread, but there were few of the class outrages that afflicted other regions'.[7] Conditions nevertheless deteriorated as the normal population of about 70,000 swelled in the turmoil of war and revolution. There were many shortages. The place became thronged with refugees of all kinds, among them many Tsarist officers and members of the Petrograd and Moscow nobility. In May a prominent Bolshevik, Mikail Kedrov, had arrived in Archangel in an impressive armoured train as head of a mission to reinforce Bolshevism. He had appointed an experienced and willing ex-Tsarist general as his army commander and together they had set about disciplining the local population and recruiting a local contingent for the Red Army. Poole's descent had interrupted this process and they had made their escape with their Red Army troops up the Dvina, nearer to the safety of the base at Kotlas.

The rivers of the region dictated much of the pattern of life around Archangel. Aside from the railway running south to Vologda, the rivers were the main communication links with the south during the summer months when the great thaw made the tracks and the few roads boggy and often impassable, and the railway slow and unreliable as it lurched over the pliant roadbed. The only significant settlements lay in the clearings along the river banks which the few tracks tended to follow. Over the rest of the land great coniferous forests stretched to the horizon. The River Dvina, a mile and a half wide in places, was nevertheless relatively shallow, with shifting sandbanks. With Archangel situated on its northern bank, the river dominated the region. It followed a course south east from the port and was joined after about 100 miles by its first major tributary, the Emptsa, and after some 200 miles by a larger tributary, the Vaga. In the late autumn of 1918, the rivers were wide and full. All three had significant settlements along their banks. On the Emptsa lay Seletskoe, important as a staging post on a rough road that linked the railway with the Dvina. At the junction of the Vaga and the Dvina was Bereznik, where Poole's forward tactical base was to be located. The major town of Shenkursk lay further south on the Vaga, and further south still was Kotlas on the Dvina. Kotlas, too, was an important town and a railway terminus for another line joining the major east–west Russian system. War in north Russia – and outright war, if limited in scale, was what the intervention was already becoming – would be fought for the domination of these railway and river communication routes.

As he planned his advance south, Poole was presented with two problems. The further south he pushed, the more widely separated became his tiny forces as the routes diverged. It was the perennial problem for the invader of Russia, whose vast territory ultimately swallowed up hostile forces of whatever size. The second

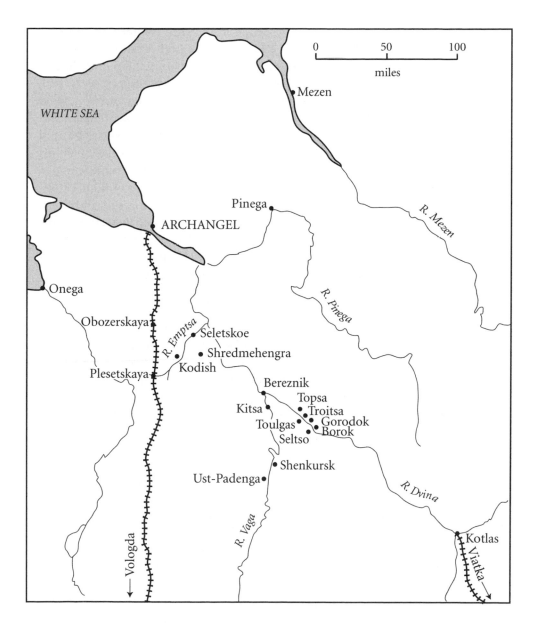

Archangel and the Dvina

difficulty was the climate's dramatic variation between winter and summer. When winter descended the Dvina at Archangel froze over with ice a yard thick, strong enough to bear the rails of a tram service across to its island suburb. Beaten snow created the main tracks, but off them movement was difficult except by sled, ski or snowshoe. The hours of darkness extended dramatically and all activity was restricted to the few hours of twilight each day. The melting of the ice and snow in spring produced boggy conditions almost everywhere which lasted until the first frosts. During the short summer the temperature could rise to almost tropical levels with daylight lasting almost the entire twenty-four hours. Summer, when the rivers were the only sure and swift means of travel, also brought clouds of maddening mosquitoes. Seasonal change gave the Allied force an additional tactical difficulty. As they were based north of their enemy, their section of the rivers thawed later in the spring and froze over earlier in the winter than did their enemy's. Since all supplies had to be got forward from Archangel by river or frozen tracks, depending on the season, this time difference was critical and gave the Bolsheviks a brief but clear advantage. Their river-based artillery, mounted on shallow-draught craft, could remain in support of forward troops later at the end of the summer and return earlier in the late spring, when the river at Archangel was still choked with ice. Adding to General Poole's difficulties was his lack of boat-based artillery which could rival the Bolsheviks'. The guns of *Attentive* and *Cochrane* were fine for threatening Russian ports from the deep seas but the ships could not venture into the shallow waters of the north Russian rivers. These impediments, even had he been aware of them, were not such as to weaken the determination or dampen the optimism of the Allied Commander-in-Chief as he made his first moves in August 1918.

Although the 'Supreme Government of North Russia' was now in the hands of Nikolai Chaikovsky, to all intents and purposes General Poole ran Archangel. Poole's instructions had enjoined him to operate 'under the authority of the coordinating diplomatic official in Russia appointed by HM Government'. Prior to the latter officer's appointment he was to liaise directly with Bruce Lockhart in Moscow. He had been enjoined to 'be careful not to intervene in diplomatic affairs without prior consultation'.[8] Poole, however, took charge of Archangel as though it were a colonial territory and he its governor, an arrangement to which his years of colonial campaigning perhaps inclined him. 'One of General Poole's first acts', Consul Young complained to the Foreign Office, 'was to requisition for himself and his personal staff the largest and finest residence in town.' The owner's wife, very much of the bourgeoisie, declared him to be 'worse than the Bolsheviks'. 'Whole school buildings were requisitioned', explained Young, 'and in large rooms capable of holding four or five people might be seen one officer and one table.'[9] Poole appointed a French colonel as military governor, placed the district under martial law and decreed that any attempts to spread 'false rumours calculated to provoke unrest or disturbance among the troops and population would be punishable by death'. He even decided which flags the Russian community were permitted to fly, which did not include the red flag of socialism which Chaikovsky's government, composed of six Socialist members of the old Constituent Assembly, had resolved to display alongside the national flag.

Under pressure from Poole, the local government restored conscription on 20 August, while delaying the call-up until after the harvest. This was a mistake, the British Consul believed; conscription was virtually unenforceable and the odium of introducing it would inevitably fall on the Allies. In regard to Russian personnel who might volunteer to join his force, Poole had been instructed to ensure that 'they are to be administered as near as possible on Russian and not English lines and no departure from this should be made without reference to the War Office'.[10] It is unclear whether this instruction was ever varied, but at both Murmansk and Archangel Poole established units of what became called the Slavo-British Legion (SBL), initially composed of Tsarist officers unacceptable to the Archangel government for its own embryonic forces, from which the SBL was kept quite separate. This force was uniformed and officered by the British and trained along British lines.

Poole was, however, operating on the basis of extremely vague instructions from the War Office. The main justification for the intervention, the threat of a German advance from Finland, was already disappearing. A week after the Archangel landing, the British Consul at Helsingfors (Helsinki) told the Foreign Office that the German forces were rapidly quitting Finland, reacting to the Allied successes on the Western Front. The military supplies stored at Archangel, for the security of which so much concern had been expressed, had been largely spirited away by the Bolsheviks before the expedition landed; whilst the third important purpose of the landing, the reception and training of the Czechs, now seemed highly unlikely: events in central Russia determined this. Fresh orders from the War Office enjoined Poole to 'cooperate in restoring Russia with the object of resisting German influence and penetration' and 'to help the Russians to take the field side by side with their Allies'. This language was vague in the extreme, but, since the Bolsheviks had long since made peace with Germany, it clearly implied opposing them, an objective which Poole was already pursuing with alacrity. The new instructions, however, still gave him the immediate aim of establishing contact with the Czechs in central Russia and required an advance along the main rail and river axes to join up with them.[11]

Poole's operation order of 5 August declared his intention 'to proceed up the River Dvina, making good and reassuring the chief centres of population, and eventually to occupy and hold Kotlas'. But Kotlas, the nearest Bolshevik base, was some 250 miles to the south and Poole was intending to advance on it with a force of 150 French, roughly fifty British and a similar number of Russians and Poles whom Chaplin (now Chaikovsky's Commander-in-Chief) was to supply. This Dvina force was but one of four which Poole sent along river, railway and track in pursuit of the fleeing Bolsheviks. The second was along the Vologda railway, while the final two were little more than strong fighting patrols. The Dvina party was to advance by bounds of about 60 miles, travelling in three river boats escorted by two tugs. One boat was to mount a 75-mm gun, 'if personnel can be found to man it'. Every effort was to be made to obtain recruits *en route*, against which possibility a hundred extra sets of clothing and equipment were to be carried. It seemed a remarkably ambitious undertaking.[12]

The tiny expeditionary force was soon augmented by the reinforcement for which Poole had been badgering London. On 26 August the 2/10th Royal Scots, Poole's first sizeable force of British infantry, disembarked at Archangel, marched ceremonially through the town and were immediately re-embarked aboard barges and hurried to the front. Like their predecessors, they were by no means a first-class fighting battalion, but war-weary soldiers recovered from wounds, unfit for service in France and frankly of limited value in Russia. The Royal Scots' shrunken ranks had been filled out by drafts from most of the other Scottish regiments. They arrived not a moment too soon, for the panicky Bolshevik evacuation soon came to a halt and resistance began to stiffen against each of Poole's thrusts. Then on 4 September the promised American contingent arrived: three battalions of 339 Infantry Regiment, supported by engineers, a field hospital and an ambulance company; in all about 4500 men under their commander Colonel George Stewart. Expecting to dock at Murmansk, they had been diverted en route direct to Archangel by instructions from Poole. The Americans were now the largest and most important contingent in North Russia; but, while they were fresh, they were only partially trained, and that for trench warfare. They were quite unprepared for the situation they were to face at the front. Their ranks were already being thinned by the influenza outbreak.

The day following its arrival, the regiment's 3rd Battalion was hurriedly packed into box cars and sent down the Vologda railway to Obozerskaya, where the Bolsheviks had now halted the Allied advance, while the 2nd Battalion was given the job of patrolling Archangel itself. The 1st Battalion was sent off in a string of barges to reinforce the Dvina front, where most of the Royal Scots had gone. Further cases of influenza were reported in all three battalions; by 16 September the regiment had suffered thirty deaths. This rapid deployment not only split up the regiment, which was organised, and had expected to operate, as a single unit, it was also a serious breach of President Wilson's *aide mémoire* on the employment of US troops in Russia, which restricted them to guarding military stores and 'rendering such aid as may be acceptable to the Russians in the organisation of their own self defence'.[13] These instructions were even more delphic that Poole's from London. Furthermore Colonel Stewart had not even seen them, but only the simple order 'report to General Poole'. The US Ambassador also seems to have been unaware of his President's wishes until after the regiment had been split up and sent forward to operate under British commanders, a deployment which he also discovered after the event.[14]

At this juncture a fresh crisis enveloped Archangel's affairs. Captain Chaplin, the coup leader, had found Chaikovsky's socialist government irksome from the very start. He had now become totally exasperated by what he saw as the otherworldly approach of Chaikovsky and his Socialist ministers to the problem of the struggle with the Bolsheviks. Aided by some of the Tsarist officers whom the government had studiously ignored, he decided to engineer another coup. When the British Consul got wind of the plan he spoke to Poole of the grave diplomatic consequences it would have. Instead of taking firm personal action to prevent it, Poole merely had one of his aides write to Chaplin advising against the step. But that very night some thirty Russian officers dressed as soldiers arrested Chaikovsky and his colleagues and deported them to Solovetski Island in the White Sea. The extent of Poole's, or his staff's, complicity in Chaplin's coup is uncertain. Suffice it to say that Chaikovsky's house was directly opposite that occupied by Poole's intelligence headquarters, that his senior intelligence officer, Colonel Thornhill, was a personal friend of Chaplin, and that all military guards were absent from the surrounding streets on the night of the seizure. At a military review the following morning, Poole calmly told the astonished US Ambassador Francis that Chaplin had deposed the government. The Russian admitted his role in the affair, explaining that 'The ministers were in General Poole's way. I see no use for any government here anyway'. A young French diplomat at Archangel, by no means in sympathy with the Chaikovsky regime, noted that the coup had been 'carried off with great cunning' by Chaplin, and wrote that 'The heads of the diplomatic missions whom I saw at the palace are furious ... the military on the contrary, and in particular General Poole and his headquarters staff, had radiant faces ... and even if they took no part in last night's little operation, they cannot have done much to prevent it'.[15] The *chefs de mission* condemned the coup and ordered the deposed government to be rescued and returned to the town. The British Consul urged that Chaplin and his accomplices be arrested, but Poole refused and was supported by the French Ambassador Noulens. The working-class people of Archangel, supported Chaikovsky while the industrial workers, believing correctly that a right-wing coup had taken place, launched a series of strikes. Poole replied with a decree threatening to hand the ringleaders over to military courts. The strikers took no notice and all routine activity in the town came to a standstill. Poole's headquarters reacted by using troops to supply basic services and the American battalion to man the trams. The American Ambassador was furious: neither he nor the men's regimental commander had been consulted.[16]

Explaining the affair in a letter to the War Office, Poole wrote that the coup had been 'carried out by Chaplin – who is a really good man – and about twenty of his officers. Personally they have my entire sympathy ... Our diplomats – I am not a great admirer of their prowess – did the rest'.[17] In fact the coup was a disaster which only strengthened the hand of the extremists in the re-established Chaikovsky government. It was also a calamity for General Poole. Hitherto the American and French Ambassadors had keenly supported the intervention; only the British Consul, Lindley, had complained continually to the Foreign Office of Poole's high-handedness. But now US Ambassador Francis coordinated the chorus of condemnation from the diplomats and reported unfavourably on Poole. Finally, the US President made it clear that, unless Poole changed his entire attitude to the local government at Archangel, all American forces would be withdrawn from his command. On 10 and 17 September criticisms of Poole were even being made in Cabinet. His days in north Russia were clearly numbered.[18]

On the purely military front things were also not going well. Early in September Poole had been explaining his plans to take Plesetskaya, about 130 miles down the Vologda railway, and 'give a knockout blow to the forces which are opposing me', whilst on the river front he was preparing for another 'knockout blow to the defenders of Kotlas' which he hoped to take by the 20th. 'I am anxious to bring off the big thing if I can', he wrote, 'as it makes me so much nearer the Czechs if I can push down to Viatka. Now that you are sending me some more troops I hope it will come off.'[19] It was all something of a pipe dream. In mid-September his troops were driven out of Seletskoe on the Emptsa river and it took them three days to regain it. The following month, on the Dvina, heavy shelling by the Bolsheviks forced a withdrawal from Seltso and Borok on opposite banks of the river, back to Tulgas and Troitsa. Four field guns and many Maxims were lost to the enemy. By 16 October the GHQ war diary was recording rather ominously 'offensive operations on railway abandoned owing to attitude of French and American troops'.[20] This was a far cry from the optimism which had so recently infused Poole's reports. The fact was that the Bolsheviks were much more numerous than Poole's men on every sector of the front, they were able to outgun their opponents with their river flotilla, and they were beginning to show improved organisation and the first faint flicker of determination. All these minor successes, however, were coming at the cost of heavy casualties.

By early October Poole was also becoming much less confident about the development of the new Russian army. 'Recruiting is now in a bad way', he wrote on the 11th, 'chiefly owing to the fact that this [the volunteer] method of enlistment is foreign to the nature of the Russian who does little on his own initiative.' Only two thousand had volunteered. In this, his last significant report from Archangel, Poole argued for the transfer of four battalions and three artillery batteries from Murmansk, which had been considerably reinforced by this time. He also asked for three more foreign battalions, preferring Americans if they were allowed to fight, and no fewer than four more brigadiers to command his dispersed forces. He wanted men who were 'good fighting soldiers who must be physically sound and not worn out by campaigning in France'. This substantial shopping list concluded with a request for twenty-five officer and fifty NCO interpreters, a substantial requirement for his operational and training tasks which he might have anticipated long before the campaign began. Finally, he argued against Maynard's proposal for a campaign south from Kem to Petrograd, believing, sensibly, that the capture of the old capital, long deserted by the Bolshevik leadership, would achieve nothing but the responsibility for feeding its starving population. Whereas, he concluded, 'If we are driven out of Archangel our prestige in Russia is gone for ever'.[21] This issue of 'prestige' was to reappear frequently in the arguments as the intervention developed. Three days later Major General Poole, accompanied by his intelligence chief, Colonel Thornhill, was sailing back to Britain aboard HMS *Attentive*, apparently on leave. He was not to return.

Brigadier General Edmund Ironside had arrived in Archangel on 30 September as Poole's new Chief of Staff. With him came Brigadier General Henry Needham who was to be Chief Administrative Officer in the headquarters. Both were welcome additions to the small and inexperienced staff, though Poole jokingly declared that he could not think why the War Office had sent them. With the two senior officers came an assortment of reinforcements for the American, British, French and Russian contingents, together with two batteries of Canadian field artillery – experienced and well-disciplined men who were to provide sorely needed support for the outgunned front-line troops of the Allied force. Even with these additions to the British complement, the Americans still formed the largest national contingent in the whole force and provided the greatest total of infantry soldiers. Ironside was surprised at Poole's explanation that he was taking a 'short leave'. The Commander-in-Chief informed the *chefs de mission* in Archangel that he would be away for thirty days, hardly a brief absence; but he clearly feared that a permanent recall was planned for him since he had the presumption, in the light of all that had passed between them, to call on President Chaikovsky and ask his old adversary to write to London requesting his return to Archangel. For the first few weeks of his acting command Ironside operated in the belief that his predecessor would soon return to his post; it was not until 19 November that the War Office told Ironside officially that Poole was not returning and that he was appointed Commander-in-Chief in his stead and had already been gazetted as a major general. Most of the headquarters staff had made that assumption a few days earlier when Poole had telegraphed for his aide-de-camp and his kit to be sent home. 'So he has not yet left England and is presumably not returning', concluded the war diary.[22] It was hardly a satisfactory way to arrange the command of an isolated international headquarters in what were decisive weeks of a campaign. It has to be said, however, that Ironside's initial subordination to Poole and subsequent temporary status did little to diminish the energy and decisiveness with which he tackled his new responsibilities.

There could hardly have been a greater contrast between the two commanders. The departed Poole, fiftyish, stocky and somewhat portly, with no staff experience and little of senior command prior to his appointment in north Russia, was very much a 'broad brush' general who left the running of the military operations to Brigadier General Finlayson while he stayed at the Archangel base, whose social life he much enjoyed and from which he seldom ventured.[23] Ironside was only thirty-eight; he stood six foot four and weighed almost twenty stone and had extensive staff as well as command experience.* His friend, the novelist John Buchan, had already used him as the main model for Richard Hannay, the hero of his adventure stories.[24] Ironside had abounding energy and was eager to immerse himself in the detail and meet all the personalities of his first truly independent command. In most respects he was well suited even for the complications of this muddled campaign with its international, polyglot force, for he spoke several European languages, including Russian, and had served with the Canadians before. If there was one lacuna in his military make-up it was the lack of politico-military experience, such as an appointment on the General Staff in the War Office might have given him. In fact he was never to serve on the central General Staff until, in 1939, he was briefly in charge of it as CIGS, when his political naivety was all too evident. At his pre-appointment interview with Sir Henry Wilson, the CIGS had given him a very simple instruction: 'Your business in North Russia is to hold the fort until the local Russians can take the field. You are to prepare for a winter campaign. No joke that!'[25] No joke indeed. Within a month of Ironside's arrival there was a mutiny among the Russian trainees in Archangel. The problem of the loyalty of the new Russian army he was charged with building was already beginning to assert itself.

In the closing months of 1918, as the cool of autumn started to colour the trees and the late rains to swell the rivers of north Russia, Ironside began to assess the problems of his command. It would not be long before the first frosts would start their transformation of the tactical situation and give the Bolsheviks their brief advantage of free movement on the upper Dvina while their opponents to the north were denied it, as the sea froze and the ice backed-up behind them. Then there would be the winter campaign of which the CIGS had warned him, with

---

* One sergeant in the force recalled that Ironside was 'built on such generous lines that he required two ordinary sleeping bags sewn up to make one which would accommodate him. I can recall the difficulty we had in stowing him into it, preparatory to his taking a fifty mile sledge drive to visit another force on the River Dvina'.[26]

all its difficulties of supplying the forces spread out in a wide arc, some 180 miles from the Archangel base. Supply problems would be transformed in character and complexity as communications switched from river to snow track and from boat and barge to sleigh and *droshky*, the Russian pony-sled. Then there was the basic business of staying alive in the desperate cold of North Russia, with the winter temperature often dropping at night to forty degrees below zero. Fighting in the open for any length of time would be impossible in such conditions. The forward troops would have to operate from blockhouses of which many more would need to be constructed. Soldiers wounded in the open would die quickly if they were not rapidly given shelter and warmth. Finally, there was the problem of morale in the small isolated detachments of which the Archangel command largely consisted. The perpetual cold, the featureless landscape, the basic living conditions, the monotonous diet, the brief hours of daylight and the ever-present threat from the Bolsheviks, whose units were composed of men inured to the cold and hardships of the north, all this presented great challenges to the spirit of the troops and the generalship of Ironside. The Bosheviks' attacks on the Allied positions, inexpertly conducted as they often were, would always come in far greater strength than the defenders could muster. Furthermore the enemy would become more skilful as time went on. It was not an encouraging prospect.

Ironside went forward to Finlayson's headquarters and discussed the situation with him. As the Dvina and railway fronts were widely separated and each contained numerous subordinate, isolated positions, Ironside decided to divide the command into two, leaving Finlayson to manage the more important Dvina river front. He offered the command of the railway front to the US regimental commander, Colonel Stewart, but the American surprisingly declined, preferring to remain at Archangel without the direct command of any troops, even his own, most of whom he seldom saw. Perhaps the delicacy of the political situation of his regiment, operating far beyond the guidelines of his President, weighed more heavily on his shoulders than it did on those of his forthright and determined ambassador. Ultimately a French officer, Commandant Lucas, took the railway command. The sudden withdrawal of the small flotilla of Allied gunboats back to Archangel as the ice took a brief hold brought the first crisis of the campaign, for while the Bolshevik gunboats were able quickly to return to support their forward troops, when a rapid thaw unexpectedly followed, Ironside's were not. The Archangel anchorages and the river above them were already blocked by ice. A few longer-range guns had been dismantled from the gunboats before their withdrawal and mounted ashore, and a couple more were later riskily brought forward from the base, but Poole's headquarters had made no general artillery plan for the inevitable freeze-up and for the dangerous days before the ice took a firm hold upriver, negating the Bolsheviks's decisive gunnery advantage. It was an unfortunate oversight since both Poole and Finlayson were experienced gunners. Furthermore, the forward land commanders received no warning from the navy of the river batteries' departure. Ironside spoke of this lack of artillery planning being 'perhaps the worst mistake of the early campaign ... and the fault lay entirely with the Army'. Numerous casualties and the loss of much front-line accommodation were the result. Ultimately the hardening frost, some hasty rebuilding and the arrival of the Canadian batteries did something to restore the balance.[27]

Leadership within the command was also a factor with which Ironside had to grapple. Many of the British officers he inherited from Poole were of poor quality, worn out from service in France, unimaginative and untalented. This was a particular disadvantage since the British were generally in command of mixed detachments in which the Americans predominated. Being under the command of British officers was particularly resented by the Americans, who nevertheless had some duds among their own leaders and whose regimental commander, Colonel Stewart, was an uninspiring and almost anonymous figure who had become the target of intense criticism even before the campaign in north Russia was fully into its stride. Too often his solution to any military problem was to look the other way. What made matters worse was that large quantities of whisky had been sent out from England and many officers, and not simply those at headquarters, had taken to it too readily. One American orderly reported that the initial response of a British commander on the railway front to discovering he had given a faulty artillery order was to telephone 'for another quart of whisky', even before he had summoned his artillery adviser.[28] Another abuse was the selling of whisky to the Russians at inflated prices.

Ironside also found a disturbing number of his British officers openly sympathetic with the most reactionary monarchists among their Russian counterparts. This seems to have been a tendency to which Poole himself and Colonel Thornhill had given an unfortunate lead. Poole's sympathies were well known, while Thornhill, long a 'rabid interventionist' in the words of Bruce Lockhart, was overconcerned with intrigue rather than hard military information. Ironside had earlier complained to Thornhill, 'it is much more interesting for me to know when the frost will begin than what Trotsky is saying in Moscow'.[29] The Commander-in-Chief moved rapidly to end these abuses and within a week of his arrival had called all the officers at the base together and warned them against criticism of the Chaikovsky regime and meddling in local political affairs. In particular there was to be 'no further espousing of the Tsarist cause', he told them. He asked the War Office for fresh, young lieutenant colonels to replace some of his less satisfactory commanders.

Despite the enthusiastic crowds which had lined the Archangel riverside when the intervention first began, the local population showed little enthusiasm for volunteering for the new Russian army. The Archangel bourgeoisie were unlikely to furnish recruits, while the Tsarist refugees were unwilling to serve in the Socialist government's army. The Solombola dock workers were not willing to join what they regarded as the forces of reaction. Among the peasants of the occupied villages and hamlets further south, Finlayson told Ironside, there was no desire to serve in the new army. It was a problem which Ironside had rapidly to address since Poole had placed great reliance on being able to recruit many thousands. He tackled the issue with President Chaikovsky; but he found the old revolutionary quite uninterested in all military matters, despite his regime's existence depending on them. He referred Ironside to his Governor-General, Colonel Douroff, a nervous officer with no command experience who had risen to eminence as one of Kerensky's military advisers. After a discussion with him and his Chief of Staff, General Samarine, Ironside came to a depressing conclusion: 'The stark fact was that they had done exactly nothing during the two and a half months they had been in office. They were terrified of the men with whom they had to deal.' This was a reference to the 1500 soldiers occupying the town barracks and the 300 ex-Tsarist officers in the town whose suitability for employment in the new army had not even begun to be investigated. As for fresh recruitment, the Governor-General averred that volunteering was totally alien to the Russian mind, while conscription was undemocratic. The exasperated Ironside told them to restore discipline to everyone wearing uniform and to dismiss those who were clearly unsuitable. He ordered the Russian commander to form a model company, drawn from the occupants of the barracks, which he would inspect in a week's time. He left with the determination to have these supine Russians officers replaced as soon as possible.

Ironside's disenchantment was completed by his interview with each of the ambassadors in Archangel. Almost without exception he found that they had no instructions regarding the future policy to be pursued towards the Bolsheviks. Although Ironside's forces were preparing for a winter campaign against them, the general opinion among the diplomats was that there would be a tacit ceasefire as soon as the Germans were out of the struggle. The sole exception to this view came from the Serbian representative, who believed the Bolsheviks would continue to fight against the interventionists and that they were in better touch with the people than Chaikovsky's government, which lacked firm leadership. He also echoed Finlayson's view that the Provisional Government would get little support from the North Russian peasants: 'All peasants were the same', he said, 'They were already Communistic in their attitude towards the ownership of land, and would be faithful to Lenin'. When Colonel Douroff's model company mutinied and refused to parade for the Allied Commander-in-Chief or respond to the comradely entreaties of Chief of Staff Samarine himself, the latter promptly resigned, as did his chief. In desperation, Ironside turned to one Russian colonel whom he knew in Archangel and asked him to take over, but the officer politely refused to serve the Provisional Government. Finally, he found two Russian officers serving on the Dvina front who agreed to take charge until he could arrange for more senior ones from elsewhere. An urgent request to London followed. The enormity of the task which confronted Ironside was now dawning upon him: 'I was slowly beginning to realise what we were up against in fighting the Bolsheviks', he wrote. Ironside was still at the headquarters wrestling with the problems of creating the new Russian army and supporting his own, when, on the afternoon of 11 November, the news came in of the signing of the Armistice with Germany.

The Bolsheviks were, in fact, already a rather better force than their early showing at Murmansk and Archangel had led General Poole to suppose. Though far from the equal of their professional opponents in the north, they were nevertheless improving in purely military terms and, in their underground work in both towns, showing themselves to be masters of propaganda with their night-time leafleting. In March 1918, Trotsky had become Commissar for Military Affairs and Chairman of the Supreme War Council of the new republic. His zeal, popularity and talent for exhorting the masses were already producing results. Trotsky was the chief proponent of the policy of using 'military specialists' – Tsarist officers – in the struggle against the Whites and their capitalist backers. The reliability of the military specialists was ensured by a 'dual control' system by which commanding officers were monitored by political commissars, 'the direct representatives of the Soviet regime in the Army', Trotsky called them. The commissars had two important sanctions: the regime's knowledge of the whereabouts of the Tsarist officers' families, who became, in effect, hostages for the latters' good behaviour, and 'the commissar's right of the revolver'. If any specialist officer were to behave suspiciously, declared Trotsky, 'then it stands to reason, the accused – there can be no argument about it, the question is open and shut – must be shot'. By such utter ruthlessness, 'the severity of the proletarian dictatorship' he called it, and improved training and supply systems, Trotsky was moulding his Red Army.[30]

It was some time before his methods took effect. 'Some of our troops are not yet much good', admitted another senior Bolshevik, 'One day they fight, and the next day they would rather not. So that our best troops, those in which there are most workmen, have to be flung in all directions'. Furthermore, although the Bolshevik regime was cut off from supplies from the West, they claimed to have ample munitions for a long fight. Heavy artillery was of little use in the kind of fighting done in Russia, claimed the Commissar for Trade and Industry who was also President of the Committee for supplying the needs of the army. In light artillery they were 'making and mending their own'. As to artillery shells, the old regime 'had left scattered about Russia supplies of 3-inch shells sufficient to last them several years'. They had dynamite in enormous quantities and were manufacturing gunpowder, while cartridge output had trebled since August 1918. Even as things were (this was early spring 1919) the Commissar thought they could certainly fight for a year.[31] By November 1918, they had already regrouped in north Russia. At much the same time as Ironside heard news of the Armistice, messages were reaching his headquarters of heavy fighting on the Dvina. The Bolsheviks were launching a major attack. The winter trial of the tiny Allied army at Archangel was about to begin.

4

Siberia

Even before the company of Royal Marines went ashore at Murmansk to the relief and welcome of the town soviet, Britain was already taking anti-Bolshevik initiatives in the Far East. In the Manchurian town of Manchuli, a small but strategically significant settlement just inside Manchuria but under Russian control, a twenty-eight-year-old Cossack leader, Captain Grigori Semenov, seemed to be developing the very kind of resistance to the Bolshevik appeasers of Germany for which Britain was looking. There, Semenov had outfaced and then disarmed the pro-Bolshevik garrison, beaten up the members of the local soviet and sent both groups packing up the railway into Russia. Manchuli lay on the Chinese Eastern Railway, not far from its junction with the Trans-Siberian line, and provided the most direct route from the west to the important Russian port of Vladivostok. Operating from this relatively secure base, Semenov recruited a mixed, but largely Chinese and Mongol, force of desperadoes and began to set about the small, isolated and dispirited Red Army garrisons spread along this important line, succeeding initially in driving them back as far as the main Russian railway in the province of Trans-Baikalia. The British Assistant Military Attaché in Peking, Captain Denny, who visited Semenov's base, was very favourably impressed by his exploits, and reported back in encouraging terms. Not all were so sanguine. Colonel Josiah Wedgwood MP had been sent east to act as military adviser to the Kerenskyite local government believed to be in control at Tomsk. His parting advice from Churchill had been, 'Get on to a locomotive at Vladivostok, go as far west as you can, and then retire blowing up every bridge behind you'. The information on which Wedgwood's mission was based proved as unreliable as much else upon which Britain's intervention in Russia's Civil War was founded. Finding Tomsk already in Bolshevik hands, Wedgwood made his way back to Vladivostok and reported to the War Office, in one of the first of his many objections to the less reputable aspects of the intervention policy, that it would be 'stupid and criminal to spend money bribing a robber chief like Semianov [sic] and his Cossacks to fight the Bolsheviks'.[1]

The War Office disregarded this advice and Wedgwood was promptly recalled; minds in Whitehall had been made up even before Denny's report was received. In early February 1918 the government began to allot the surprisingly large monthly sum of £10,000 to Semenov without, even more extraordinarily, attaching any conditions to its use. The French authorities soon followed suit, as did the Japanese, who supplied not only cash and weapons but, more ominously, 'volunteers' and an energetic staff officer whose activity soon ensured that Semenov became a Japanese puppet. Prime Minister Lloyd George, little appreciating the true nature of the multi-national band of brigands, mercenaries and adventurers who made up Semenov's 'army', tried to persuade the Americans to support him as a 'purely Russian movement in Siberia'. President Wilson demurred, believing that any involvement of the United States would unleash the Japanese in strength on the mainland. Although Britain halted its misguided support of the half-Mongol freebooter in June, the consequences of its initial subsidy were wholly deleterious to British policy in Siberia and to its intervention purposes as a whole.

Britain alone could do little to reopen the Eastern Front via Vladivostok and its initial, and for quite some time its main, proposals were to encourage intervention by its Japanese ally, whose limited and self-interested motives in Siberia were not yet clearly understood. By January 1918 Britain, France and Italy were asking Japan to intervene and advance at least to Omsk and possibly to Chelyabinsk in the foothills of the Urals, though these were distant from Vladivostok by some thousands of miles. Nevertheless, in June 1918 a detailed War Office appreciation put the case for substantial intervention via Vladivostok with the Japanese taking the lead. This British proposal was based on the belief that the war against the Central Powers would stretch on into 1919, when the substantial forces which Germany still deployed in Russia might extend their depredations from the grainfields of the Ukraine and the Donetz coalmines into the Baku and Grosni oilfields and the Caucasian manganese deposits, in support of their war effort. A bleak future was held out for the Entente Powers, who faced an overwhelming German superiority on the Western Front with no chance of the Americans balancing it with their fresh divisions until 1919 was well advanced. Whether the projected advance by Japanese divisions along the Trans-Siberian Railway, which the Supreme War Council subsequently endorsed, would have achieved the British purposes is very doubtful: the nearest German forces were still a thousand miles further west than Omsk. Besides, the scheme was of doubtful practicability. In the view of the Japanese General Staff, intervention on the scale which the Allies were proposing would have involved all Japan's permanent divisions and some reserves as well. Moving just one division along the railway would have required fifty trains.[2] Nor did the idea of Japanese intervention appeal to the Americans, who saw Japan as their principal commercial rival in Russia's Asian provinces. The Japanese army was content enough to intervene but the government would only do so if agreement were first reached with the USA, its rival for influence in the Far East.

The Americans had no greater relish for the British suggestion that the USA should send troops to Vladivostok to safeguard the 600,000 tons of stores and ammunition, with an estimated value of $1000 million, lying in a series of warehouses and indeed on the open hillsides around the port, despite some of it being American-supplied and none of it being paid for. As a result of the war-time emergency, the port had become little more than a huge supply dump of small arms, ammunition, high explosives, food, clothing and raw materials sent to assist the Russian war effort. Although the Bolsheviks were not yet in full control in Russia's premier Asian port, the situation there was chaotic and dangerous for the Allies, who feared that the invaluable war *matériel* might fall into the hands of the hordes of Austrian and German prisoners whom they believed were held in the area and could soon find their way to the fighting line in the west. There were indeed as many as 800,000 enemy prisoners east of the Urals, technically free men once the Brest-Litovsk treaty had been signed; but only a small proportion were German and a smaller number still had been armed by the Bolsheviks. It was, however, rumour rather than fact which dominated Britain's reading of the situation.[3] At the end of December the British Ambassador in Tokyo voiced his concerns to the Foreign Office and the cruiser *Suffolk* was despatched from Hong Kong to Vladivostok. The Japanese promptly responded by sending two cruisers. The United States, displaying the dilatoriness and reluctance to get involved that was to characterise its role throughout the intervention, did not act until late February, when the cruiser *Brooklyn* joined the monitoring force in Vladivostok waters. By the middle of March 1918, the captain of the *Suffolk* was reporting that Bolshevik elements were trying to move the stores and ammunition westwards and recommended that they be put under Allied military protection. Early in April the murder of some Japanese citizens in Vladivostok brought the growing crisis to a head. The Japanese landed five hundred marines and sailors to restore order and the *Suffolk* put ashore a smaller number to guard the British consulate. By the end of the month the incident was over and both forces had withdrawn to their ships; but by then the Bolsheviks had taken control of the port and the intervention of the Allied squadron, whilst apparently solving the local problem, had done much larger diplomatic damage.

The Bolsheviks' relations with the Czech Corps, withdrawing in sixty-odd trains along the railway to Vladivostok, had been anomalous from the start. The Czechs were, after all, travelling to join the fight against the Germans with whom the Russians had, since early March, been at peace. The Bolshevik authorities inevitably came under pressure from the German Ambassador in Moscow to have the Czechs disarmed. They had been given arms by the Russians in the first place and were actually carrying far larger quantities than were stipulated in the agreement with their hosts and one-time allies. The Czechs were annoyed by the restrictions being imposed on the increasingly disorganised railway along which they were making their snail-like progress eastwards; their journey seemed to be given a maddeningly lower priority than that of the trains of prisoners travelling west. The searches of their wagons for unauthorised arms were irksome in the extreme. Further frustration developed when the first Czech contingents arrived in Vladivostok in April and found no British transports waiting to carry them across the seas to the Western Front. For their part, the Bolshevik authorites were incensed at the Allied landings at Vladivostok, which confirmed their worst fears of Japanese intentions. The landings also negated the continuing efforts of Bruce Lockhart in Moscow to have any intervention in Russia take place on an agreed basis with the Bolsheviks.

In mid-May one of the rearmost echelons of the Czech force, whose trains were now strung out irregularly along the five thousand miles of line between the Volga and the Pacific, was at a standstill in the station at Chelyabinsk, an insignificant town on the eastern foothills of the Urals. It was joined there by a trainload of Austrian and Hungarian ex-prisoners of war travelling in the opposite direction. The natural animosity between the two groups culminated in a Czech soldier being injured by one of the ex-prisoners. The Czechs lynched the culprit and when the local Bolshevik officials tardily intervened, and arrested some of their men, the Czechs' patience finally snapped. Two battalions took over Chelyabinsk, its railway station and the surrounding area. By 25 May the situation had escalated to the point where Trotsky, the Bolshevik War Commissar, ordered the halting of all the Czech trains and the shooting of any Czech found with a weapon in his hands. Alas for Trotsky, he could will the ends, but he could not will the means. The Czechs intercepted his message and other peremptory orders from Moscow which passed along the sections of railway telegraph which they now controlled. After a hurriedly-convened council of war, the young Czech leaders (the ethnic Russian generals who were nominally in command played no part in the decision-making) took the historic decision to fight their way out from the heart of Russia to the Pacific.

This decision by the Czechs also involved contravening the Supreme War Council's recent decision, of which the Czechs themselves were not all aware, that all their troops still to the west of Omsk should be directed to France overland via Archangel and Murmansk in the far north, where Allied landings had already taken place, rather than via Vladivostok. This Anglo-French decision, known as the Abbeville Resolution, had been taken partly as a result of the shipping shortage and likely delay if the Czechs were all to travel by sea, and partly because of the British wish to see Czech participation in the revived Eastern Front. Of course, the move via Archangel and Murmansk would have required Trotsky's agreement, unlikely at any stage and out of the question now that open conflict had begun. The Abbeville Resolution formally established the attractive but elusive connection between the intervention in the far north at Archangel and the venture from Vladivostok which was about to take shape. The Czech decision to fight was carried by the railway telegraph to all the Czech echelons along the line. By the end of the first week of June many of the important stations between Omsk and the Manchurian frontier were in the hands of the Legion, as the Czech force was now being called. Reasonably well armed and admirably disciplined as the Czechs were at this stage, they had little difficulty in overcoming the Bolshevik garrisons at some stations, though at others there was hard fighting and some initial reverses before their battalions took control. Trotsky's peremptory intervention, following the restrictions on the Czechs imposed by Joseph Stalin, the Bolshevik Commissar for Nationalities, had been speedily followed by the overthrow of much of Bolshevik authority in Siberia and the Urals. This created the circumstances for intervention in the region for which Britain and France had long been pressing.[4]

The communications between the crisis centres in the Far East and the capitals of the Western Powers were not good and the latter tended to fear the worst. The gallant Czechs were precariously split, it seemed, between the group holding all the railway between the Urals and the outskirts of Irkutsk and the other group now turning back from Vladivostok to aid their comrades inland. Between the two, in the Irkutsk area, lay the principal Bolshevik military centre in Siberia with a large concentration of troops and ex-prisoners, as well as the great strategic barrier of Lake Baikal itself. At the very least, a major defeat of the western group of Czechs was feared, even their annihilation, although their resistance drew admiring comments in the local reports sent back to London. 'I have never seen finer spirit than that which prevails among the Czechs', wrote the captain of the *Suffolk*, 'their pluck is indomitable and their discipline perfection.' In the light of the Czechs' apparent plight, US President Wilson, who had opposed Japanese intervention for so long and declined to allow his own troops to get involved, at last relented. On 6 July he appealed to Japan for a joint intervention to help the Czechs and suggested a limit of 7000 men on the force which each might deploy and that the Japanese might 'have the high command'. Japan readily accepted, though her ambassador in Washington made it clear to the American Secretary of State that 'his Government for political reasons could not bind itself to limit the force to 7000 ...' This US action, however, specifically discounted the practicability or desirability of establishing a new Eastern Front against Germany. US troops were merely going to the aid of the Czechs, who were menaced by 'German and Austrian prisoners'. There was no consideration in the American position of action against Russians, either Bolshevik or White. In the light of Japan's subsequent actions in Siberia it is instructive to quote at greater length its declaration of 3 August 1918 affirming the principles of its intervention:

In adopting this course, the Japanese Government remain constant in their desire to promote relations of enduring friendship, and they reaffirm their avowed policy of respecting the territorial integrity of Russia, and of abstaining from all interference in its internal politics. They further declare that upon the realisation of the objects above indicated [the relief of the Czechs] they will immediately withdraw all Japanese troops from Russian territory, and will leave wholly unimpaired the sovereignty of Russia in all its phases, whether political or military.[5]

Four days later, partly to stimulate American action, Britain decided to intervene. The force selected for this token action made all too clear the grave shortage of manpower which hobbled all British actions away from the decisive Western Front. The 25th (Garrison) Battalion of the Middlesex Regiment was a low-grade unit composed of men unfit for service in an active theatre of war and commanded by fifty-two-year-old Lieutenant Colonel John Ward MP, a trade union leader. In June 1918 the battalion was on garrison duties, split between Hong Kong and Singapore, when the order came for it to concentrate at Hong Kong and sail to Vladivostok. Ward was a remarkable man. He had started work as a navvy at the age of twelve and founded the Navvies' Union when he was only twenty-four. He won the constituency of Stoke-on-Trent for Labour in the 1906 election, and continued to represent it under a variety of political labels for the next twenty-nine years until defeated by the Labour-supporting Lady Cynthia Mosley, Sir Oswald's first wife, in 1929. Although by no means a professional soldier, he had seen previous military service at the age of nineteen at the relief of Khartoum and more recently on the Western Front. As leader of the Navvies' Union he had raised five labour battalions for the war; the 25th Middlesex was also a unit he had founded. The performance of the unschooled Ward was to draw some mocking comments from more expensively educated observers. One young regular captain (later a lieutenant general), a desk officer in the Military Mission later established at Vladivostok, was to describe Ward as 'a pompous old ass, without an "H" to his vocabulary, but his sojourn among the Russians has modified his views as regards Socialism and Labour'. The author Peter Fleming noted that in Ward's 'bluff but valuable' account of the Siberian intervention 'Omsk is almost the only proper name spelled correctly'. Both comments had some justification, but Ward was a more substantial figure on the local scene than either suggests. Although his Middlesex battalion was derided by other soldiers as the 'hernia battalion' composed of 'poor old men' who 'ought never to have been sent here' and Ward himself as 'a gas bag', both were destined to play a significant role in the events of the region, as Ward did subsequently in the House of Commons, defending the government's more controversial intervention policies with the credibility which his operational experience conferred.[6]

The 25th Middlesex, the first Allied infantrymen to reach Siberia, landed at Vladivostok on 3 August. They were quickly followed by another token force, a 500-strong French colonial regiment from Indo-China. Then came the big battalions. On 8th the Japanese began landing troops on a large scale and continuously, watched with growing concern by the local Americans. Before the end of the month 18,000 Japanese troops had disembarked at Vladivostok while a further six thousand moved up through Manchuria to Semenov's base at Manchuli, taking control of the whole of the Chinese Eastern Railway. This latter move, the Japanese explained, not entirely persuasively, was a precautionary measure allowed for by its military agreement with China and quite different from the joint intervention at Vladivostok. By the beginning of November the Japanese had 72,400 troops in Siberia and northern Manchuria, the bulk of them front-line soldiers. The Americans sent their 27th Infantry Regiment from the Philippines on 16 August and then, in early September, the 31st Regiment arrived from San Francisco together with the overall American force commander, Major General William Graves. The US force finally totalled 8763 men.[7] The only briefing which Graves received came in a hurried interview with Secretary of War Newton Baker at Kansas City railway station, at which Baker handed him a copy of the President's *aide mémoire* with the celebrated words: 'This contains the policy of the United States in Russia which you are to follow. Watch your step; you will be walking on eggs loaded with dynamite.' The *aide mémoire*, the same ambiguous document applied to Colonel Stewart at Archangel, dealing with the USA's Russian policy as a whole, was hardly a prescription for forthright military action; but if ever there was a commander who regarded his instructions as a cage rather than a springboard it was General Graves. By general agreement (though one which Graves never accepted) on 18 August the Japanese General Otani Kikuzo assumed command of all the Allied forces. These soon included detachments of Italians, Poles, Serbs and Roumanians. John Ward's 25th Middlesex were totally dwarfed by this multi-national army.

Ward's men were, nevertheless, the first local manifestation of Allied support and their arrival at Vladivostok aboard the *Ping Suie* was greeted with appropriate ceremony, their ship even being escorted to the wharf by two Japanese destroyers. Ashore a guard of honour from HMS *Suffolk* awaited and a rousing public reception from the townspeople. 'As I descended the gangway', Ward recorded, 'the Czech band struck up the National Anthem, and a petty officer of the *Suffolk* unfurled the Union Jack, while some of the armed forces came to the present and others saluted. It made quite a pretty, interesting and immensely impressive scene.' The Middlesex battalion marched through the crowds to their quarters in the old Siberian Barracks, not expecting that they would soon be in action. Since the battalion was not intended for front-line service, it lacked even basic field equipment. In Hong Kong Ward had suggested that tents might be useful, but the proposal was turned down. When he asked about mosquito nets, the Chief of Staff had scornfully replied, 'Who ever heard of mosquitoes in Siberia?' Keen to exploit its position as the first Allied unit ashore, the War Office accepted the recommendation of Colonel Robertson, the military representative in Vladivostok, that half the battalion should go to the front on the Ussuri river to help the Czechs and Cossacks hold the line there until the Japanese arrived in strength. It was agreed that the five hundred infantrymen and forty-three machine gunners whom Ward took forward would be used 'defensively and in reserve'. Within a week the men were on their way to the front, where they took over from a front-line Cossack unit destined for the coming offensive. They were soon digging trenches in the swampy ground near the river, maddened by mosquitoes and under shell fire from enemy guns and armoured trains. The men were 'working all night under terrible difficulties', one recorded in his diary, as they held part of the threatened right flank at Kraevesk. Ward later advanced his troops in defiance of instructions from Vladivostok in order to enable the hard-pressed Czechs to retire safely over the river bridges. Outnumbered and outgunned in this early engagement, the scratch forces of which Ward's battalion was a part were forced to withdraw. Ward cabled the *Suffolk*'s captain to ask for any available artillery support. Captain Payne responded quickly, fitting out an armoured train with two 12-pounder naval guns and two machine guns, with a second train following. This welcome reinforcement became an invaluable element in Britain's tiny intervention force.

Subsequently, operating under the Japanese commander, the Middlesex Battalion played a small but important part in the main battle of Dukhovskaya, where Ward was in command of French, Czech, Cossack and Japanese detachments as well as his own men. General Otani's orders to Ward called for an unrealistic night advance of four miles in fifteen minutes with scant notice. Ward believed Otani had arranged these timings in the expectation that his force would take no part in the action. Indeed his Czech, Cossack and Japanese detachments made no effort to comply. Ward, however, got his battalion alerted and, moving forward over ground he already knew, and cleverly using a railway cutting obscured from enemy view, was able to get his men close enough to an armoured train to rake it with machine gun and rifle fire and force its retirement. The battle as a whole was an extraordinary engagement in which the main Bolshevik force of five armoured trains was courageously attacked over open ground and in extended order by the Japanese, who suffered over 600 casualties despite the artillery support which included the 12-pounders served by the Royal Marine Light Infantry detachment from HMS *Suffolk*. This limited but decisive engagement entirely eliminated organised Bolshevik resistance on the Ussuri front, with many defeated Reds scattering into the surrounding countryside. The men of the 'hernia battalion' had not acquitted themselves at all badly. 'Ward seems to have done very well', judged the War Office, 'he is evidently a man of initiative and character.' His first contact with the Japanese was instructive: Ward found them 'overbearing and duplicitous' and very disrespectful of the British and French. 'I found it to be the general policy of the Japanese Army to treat everybody as inferior to themselves', he declared. At this stage in the intervention the Japanese were plainly expecting a German victory in the wider war.[8]

If the American General Graves arrived in Vladivostok badly briefed and ignorant of the Russians, the man appointed on 16 July to represent British interests in Siberia knew them well, in some respects too well for his own good. Major General Alfred Knox had served as Military Attaché in St Petersburg from 1911 to 1918, operating with the Russian forces proper from 1914 to 1917. He may even have played a minor role in support of Kornilov's attempted *coup d'état*, for Locker Lampson would hardly have got involved without his authority. Knox was said to have provided the Russian uniforms for the armoured car squadron's part in the venture. He spoke Russian, was direct in manner and on paper, and, from his personal knowledge of some of their brutal excesses, detested the Bolsheviks and had no time at all for their more democratic colleagues, the Social Revolutionaries. On his return to London with the ambassador when the Bolsheviks first took power, he had acted as military adviser to the War Office on Russian affairs and was very much the architect of Britain's Russian policy during this early period. Knox was a bitter opponent of the unofficial British agent Bruce Lockhart and could see no point in having him in communication with the hated Bolsheviks. In a paper written for the CIGS, he declared that Lockhart's telegrams to the Foreign Office were 'in a political sense unsound' and 'in a military sense criminally misleading'. By the time of Knox's involvement in the Siberian crisis, Lockhart was already in a Soviet jail. Knox enjoyed the firm support of Lloyd George, who believed that 'There is no man in the British Army who knows Russia as Knox does'. When Lord Reading, the British Ambassador in Washington reported that the Americans regarded Knox as a reactionary and monarchist in his Russian leanings, Lloyd George held to his determination to send him to Siberia as head of the Military Mission 'because he is much the best man for dealing with the military aspect of the Russian problem'.[9] Knox was advised to travel unobtrusively across America to his Far Eastern destination. His task there was expressed to the War Cabinet by Lord Robert Cecil: 'What we wanted was that friendly elements among the Russian troops should be collected and formed into an army'. Knox was sufficiently a realist to appreciate that this would not be a simple task. He had witnessed the deplorable collapse of the imperial armies where, in his words at the time, 'units have turned into political debating societies; the infantry refuses to allow the guns to shoot at the enemy; parleying in betrayal of the Allies and of the best interests of Russia takes place daily with the enemy'. Knox travelled first to Tokyo, where he met the distinguished Russian Vice Admiral Aleksandr Kolchak whom he already knew slightly and respected and for whom the British Government were seeking an appropriate appointment in support of the Allied cause. The Japanese raised no

objectons to the use of Kolchak in Siberia, but Knox advised him to remain in
Japan until he himself had assessed the situation. The British emissary stepped
ashore in Vladivostok a few days after General Graves.

The apparently grave situation of the Czech Legion, which finally brought
about American and Japanese intervention in Siberia, proved illusory. Just as the
Czech units in European Russia had managed to fight their way through to join
up with those east of the Urals at Chelyabinsk by early July, so this combined
western group made light of a much more formidable barrier, the huge detour
around Lake Baikal with its rocky shores and mountainous environs, which
separated them from their colleagues in eastern Siberia. The key to this obstacle
zone was the area between the towns of Baikal and Kultuk on the southern tip of
the lake, where the railway ran along a mountain ledge and through thirty-nine
tunnels before emerging onto the eastern plains. The Czechs managed to drive
the Bolsheviks through the tunnels until they approached the final one which the
Reds managed to blow. Further advance seemed impossible, for the tunnel would
take weeks to clear and all movement across this vast territory depended upon
control of the railway. To bypass the position via the lake was out of the question,
since every ferry and river boat had been taken by the Bolsheviks. The apparent
impasse was broken by a daring plan of the young Czech leader, Colonel Gaida,
which resulted in the ambush of the Bolshevik forces at the eastern side of the
blocked tunnel. The Czechs managed to defeat and scatter them after two days
of fighting. They captured the entire Bolshevik rolling stock of three armoured
trains, two hospital trains, two supply trains and nine empty troop trains – an
invaluable haul. The exhausted but exultant Czechs were soon able to join hands
with their comrades from Vladivostok. Before long the railway was operating
again throughout Siberia and up to the most advanced Czech positions at the
cities of Samara and Kazan on the banks of the Volga, far to the west beyond
the Urals, in European Russia. 'The whole of Russia from the Volga River to the
Pacific Ocean, a region almost as large as the continent of Africa, had passed as
if by magic into the control of the Allies', Winston Churchill later declared. It
was a sweetly beguiling but very dangerous description. Nearer to the truth was
General Denikin's observation that the area 'became the arena of continuous
political strife between numberless Soviets, committees, governments and rulers,
all hating and overthrowing one another'.[10]

Japan and Britain were technically still allies under their 1902 treaty and
relations between London and Tokyo continued to be conducted with appropriate
diplomatic amity. On the ground in Siberia, however, their policies were
discordant and relations between them anything but friendly. Japan's refusal to
move further west than Irkutsk was a disappointment to the British government,
which had hoped, against all the diplomatic evidence and military practicalities,
for a leading role from its Asian ally in reconstructing the Eastern Front. It rapidly

became clear that Japan was intent on pursuing its own agenda in Manchuria and Russia's Maritime Province. Whilst Britain and France appointed High Commissioners to manage their political relations in the region, Japan declined to do so, leaving such matters in the hands of a special department of their army's general staff at Vladivostok. Its intervention in Manchuria, ostensibly 'precautionary' and under the terms of the agreement with China, was carried out without China being consulted and against its strenuous objections. Japan persisted in supporting Semenov and a lesser Ussuri Cossak leader, Ataman Kalmykov, who had a reputation for even greater brutality. Both sacked villages, looted on a widespread scale, robbed trains and gunned down their prisoners indiscriminately. Kalmykov was reputed to beat and kill with his own hands. General Knox reported angrily to London that General Otani had offered Semenov command of all Cossacks east of Lake Baikal. Both leaders were financed entirely by Japan. Otani's forces also behaved with arrogance, duplicity and occasionally with a savagery more characteristic of their performance in the Second World War than in the more recent Russo-Japanese conflict, when they had scrupulously observed western norms and gained much credit thereby. Many reports recorded the total disregard of the Japanese for the ordinary Russian. Knox telegraphed London that they treated all Russians 'as swine'. Even their ostensible British allies became victims of their imperious swagger. In mid-October, when Ward's Middlesex Battalion was ordered forward to Omsk, the Japanese detained their train and similarly held up one in which General Knox was travelling west and tried to arrest him. Ward was later to write, 'During the first three months I was in Siberia their arrogance was simply sublime'. The depressing evaluation of Japanese policy in Siberia was aptly summarised in a Foreign Office paper circulated to the Cabinet at the end of the year which concluded: 'The immediate impression created was that they were endeavouring by every means in their power to prevent the establishment of a strong Central Government with a single army, and their behaviour was generally described as that of a people who intended to annex what they have occupied.'[11]

The other important ally included in Churchill's seductive summary of the situation was the United States. In fact the Americans proved no more amenable to the establishment of a strong, unified anti-Bolshevik government in Siberia than the Japanese, though for quite different reasons. Like Japan, the United States refused to appoint a high commissioner in Siberia, believing that this would smack of political interference. When the Czechs' positions at Samara came under severe pressure, President Wilson refused them any aid, stipulating that they would receive no more American support 'unless they retired east of the Urals'. He regarded the idea of developing a fresh Eastern Front from the Czech position on the Volga as not 'based upon sound reason or good military judgement'. Given the circumstances, there was some truth in this. As for the US military commander on the ground, General Graves was not the man for independent military initiatives. One of his subordinates, Colonel Styer, having been told, quite correctly, by the Japanese that he was operating under their overall command, committed his regiment to two joint actions with them against a force of largely ex-POW Austro-Hungarians at Khabarovsk and Blagoveshchensk on the Amur river. Graves abruptly ended this cooperation as soon as he learnt of it and thereafter rigidly obeyed his orders as contained in the President Wilson's *aide mémoire*, the only guide to action that he had. He acted only when his orders were clear; when they required an interpretation based on his own initiative, Graves did nothing. As to the stated policy of extending aid to the 'Russian people' for their own defence, Graves resolved to do nothing until an accepted Russian government had come into being and requested help. The role of the eight thousand US troops in Siberia henceforth became one of merely guarding the stretch of the Trans-Siberian Railroad between Khabarovsk and Vladivostok and the military stores around the port. Even these were now less significant: Ward had noted as early as June 1919 that 'huge stores of iron were being collected and some of it has already been shipped to Japan'.[12]

The United States and Japan, though nominally on a collaborative venture in Siberia, were nevertheless bitter rivals for the Siberian trade. Much of Russian railway development, of which the Trans-Siberian was a major element, had depended upon US steel manufacturers and Amercan expertise. US investment in Siberia was considerable. The International Harvester Company, for example, had its own plants in Russia and over two hundred branches in Siberia. The Japanese were now attempting to challenge this domination and looking for opportunities to develop their own trade. Far from supporting the Czechs in the westward drive that lay at the heart of Anglo-French policy, the Japanese interests lay in the commercial domination of the Russian and Chinese territory nearest to their own home islands, and the development of their trade beyond.

The railways were the key arteries in the vastness of Siberia both for peacetime commerce and for war. Because of their operational value, military formations tended to retain the trains they used for their operations, as the Japanese did the fifty which took their division initially to Irkutsk, and the Czechs the ones they used for all but the most local tactical movements. This reduced the numbers available for other purposes and limited the flexibility of all movements along the line. It disrupted commerce, produced scarcities and irregular prices, and encouraged brigandage and theft from the trains as the service became more erratic. Dislocation of rail services was a main factor in the falling value of the rouble and, as this declined, peasants chose to retain their agricultural surpluses rather than sell them. Surpluses on one area were matched by scarcities in another, with hardship and chaos the inevitable result. Soon the Siberian section of the line ceased to be a through route allowing for the free exchange of goods. The Japanese had rejected an American proposal that its Advisory Railway Commission should operate the route. As Ward made his way through the Maritime Province to Omsk in October 1918, he noted that hundreds of miles of unharvested grain had been left in the fields to rot. The situation was exacerbated by the control of the line between Lake Baikal and Khabarovsk by the Japanese, who used the protection afforded by their military forces to flood Siberia with businessmen and merchants in an attempt to control local commerce. The movement of Japanese goods was smoothed by its control while that of her competitors, the Americans, was disrupted by the delays, confiscations and thefts in which Japan's agents, Semenov and Kalmikov, played a major part. Japan's trade with Siberia mushroomed in 1919 at the same time as disorder and distress developed among the communities along the line.

Conscious of its inability to provide more than a symbolic military presence in the Siberian theatre, Britain had approached Canada for support as soon as American intervention was agreed. The Canadian Prime Minister, Sir Robert Borden, reacted favourably, believing that trade benefits would flow from the establishment of a friendly Russian regime. His Minister of Militia quickly put together a proposal for a Canadian Siberian Expeditionary Force of about brigade size. This arrangement had the added attraction of being the first British Empire military venture over which a Canadian was to exercise the command, with the already-deployed Middlesex Regiment becoming an operational component of it. Major General Emsley, an experienced Western Front brigade commander, was appointed to the post. Although the organisation was quickly agreed, it was a month before its despatch was formally authorised by the Privy Council and longer still before conscripts were allocated to the force, a prior attempt to recruit sufficient volunteers having failed.[13] Emsley and his advance party did not sail from Vancouver until 11 October. They arrived in Vladivostok on the 26th to find the best accommodation already taken by the Japanese and Americans, and having therefore to settle for barracks some distance from the main port which required considerable refurbishment before the main body arrived. Late perhaps, but a most important reinforcement nonetheless. The self-contained Canadian brigade, 6000-strong with the Middlesex Battalion added, was working to War Office directives with the immediate aim of supporting the Czechs and then of restoring order and reconstituting the Eastern Front against Germany.

When Emsley arrived at Vladivostok, the British component of his force was already 3500 miles away at Omsk, detraining after their remarkable month-long journey from Vladivostok during which interference from the Japanese had been only one of Colonel Ward's problems. Supplies had been difficult to obtain and the local contractors whom he engaged had proved very unreliable. Omsk was to be the main base for the battalion throughout the next six months of the glacial Siberian winter.

The last of the Allied commanders to arrive at Vladivostok was in theory the most important of them all. General Maurice Janin was commander of the French Military Mission and had been appointed by Clemenceau as Commander-in-Chief of all Allied forces in Russia, a particularly grandiloquent title and an appointment which seemed in conflict with Otani's. In addition, Janin was titular commander of the Czechoslovak Legion, an appointment conferred on him by the Czech National Council. Janin was stout, neat, ambitious and self-important. He claimed to have twenty-six years' experience of Russia, against General Knox's ten, and was not averse to pointing this out. Like Knox, he had spent much of the war in Russia. Janin did not arrive in Siberia until a month after Knox, long after his appointment was announced. He broke his journey in Washington to see President Wilson, and in Tokyo for an audience with the Japanese Emperor. His aim in both cases was to urge the Americans and Japanese to move west to the assistance of the Czechs and to recreate the second front against Germany. In this he was no more successful than the British. The support from the Allies on which the Czechs at the front were depending was turning out to be as mythical as the supposed cooperation among them.

If the Allies were deeply divided over the purposes of their intervention at Vladivostok, the Russians in Siberia was equally disunited. Inhabiting this vast and richly-resourced region were fewer than ten million Russians, of whom the Bolsheviks never amounted to more than a minute fraction. Even in 1922, when the Communists emerged victorious from the civil war, they represented only half of one per cent of the population of the more industrialised and politically active western Siberia. But the anti-Bolsheviks were by no means united. One historian has identified as many as nineteen separate 'governments' between the Volga and the Pacific, each raising forces to support its cause and aiming to establish local control. The regimes of the Cossack Atamans Semenov and Kalmykov have already been mentioned. There were others like Russian General Horvat who, with Chinese and subsequently lukewarm Japanese support, exercised a precarious and transient authority over the Chinese Eastern Railway and parts of eastern Siberia from a base at Harbin. Another was Peter Derber, a Socialist-Revolutionary who set up a non-Bolshevik 'Provisional Government of Autonomous Siberia' from his base at Vladivostok. His regime proved too left-wing to gain support even from the trouble-making Japanese. Other smaller local regimes clamoured for attention. The main centres of anti-Bolshevik political authority lay in two cities far to the west of Japanese influence in the prosperous plains which lay on each side of the Ural mountains. The first was at the river port of Samara on the Volga, an important agricultural and industrial centre, where a group of seventy Socialist Revolutionary members of the old Constituent Assembly led by Peter Chernov, its one-time President, regarded themselves as the temporary rulers of all Russia until the full Assembly was able to meet again.

Because of its socialist orientation, the Samara government inevitably forfeited the support of the more prosperous grain farmers in the region; but it probably represented the nearest thing to non-Bolshevik legitimacy that contemporary Russia had to offer. By August 1918 it had managed to build up a People's Army of 10,000 which was the main support for the Czechs on the Volga front. The second regime was the five-man Siberian Provisional Government at Omsk, far to the east across the Urals, which initially derived its authority from the Siberian Regional Duma which the Bolsheviks had dissolved and these men had revived. But the five-man regime soon tired of the Duma's Socialist Revolutionary pretentions to genuine power and dissolved it again with violence. This bourgeois government had the support of the more prosperous peasants and also attracted many former Tsarist officers. In political terms the two governments were worlds apart, but, largely as a result of the efforts of the Czechs to have a united regime of which they could approve supporting them, the two met near the front line at Ufa to resolve their differences. Their deliberations were given added urgency by renewed Boshevik attacks not far away. The outcome was an All-Russian Provisional Government headed by a five-member Directorate.

It had been hoped to include Chaikovsky from Archangel and General Alexiev from the Don lands to give the new Directorate a genuine all-Russian authority, but the former could not leave his precarious administration and the latter died in post. The Directorate contained two Socialist Revolutionary members as well as the premier of the Omsk Siberian Government and General Boldyrev, a liberal-minded professional officer. It established itself at Omsk, where the Siberian Provisional Government also operated. Attempting to straddle the right- and left-wing administrations which it purported to represent, devoid of any executive authority and accommodated in railway carriages in an Omsk siding, the Directorate did not give the impression of permanence or power. A little later it was agreed that the two competing governments would themselves amalgamate, with the Council of Ministers of the Siberian government becoming the new All-Russian Provisional Government, leaving the Directorate as little more than a figurehead. The Socialist Revolutionaries were very dissatisfied with both the composition of the Directorate and its location. Its leaders made little effort to disguise their discontent. Meanwhile the exhausted Czech units in the front line were beginning to withdraw, the French Commander-in-Chief was still in Japan and the right-leaning Siberian government was looking for a firmer administration to control the front and withstand the stresses of the civil war. Omsk was ripe for a *coup d'état*.

As this political crisis developed, three men who were to play important roles in its resolution were travelling to Omsk. The first to arrive was Admiral Kolchak from Japan. He was hoping to make his way to the Don country to offer his services to General Alexiev, but within days General Boldyrev, the local

Commander-in-Chief and Directorate member, had persuaded him to become Minister of War and Navy in the new All-Russia administration. Kolchak had no political experience and, as a sailor, knew little of land warfare; the 'navy' element in his title giving him control only of some river craft. He appointed General Ivanov-Rivov to represent him in the area east of Lake Baikal and to command all the Russian troops in the Russian Far East; but although Ivanov-Rivov imposed martial law and assumed dictatorial powers, he soon fell under Japanese influence and was of little use to Kolchak and the Provisional Government.

Next to arrive in Omsk, on 21 October, was General Knox. He was in a difficult position. Although Britain's senior and most knowledgeable representative, he was still technically subordinate to Otani, a Japanese full general, and he had only the Middlesex Battalion and the rest of Emsley's incomplete Canadian contingent with which to influence affairs, though he actually commanded neither. At Omsk he found a disturbing situation. There was no planned mobilisation for the new Russian army, though one was badly needed to augment the weary Czechs. Instead the traditional Russian practice was being followed of rushing men to the colours and then to the front, before equipment was available, training schools were established or proper discipline could be imposed. Omsk was thronged with Russian officers clad in uniforms bearing Tsarist epaulettes but showing no inclination to participate in the fighting. Knox suggested that General Boldyrev, the Commander-in-Chief as well as a Liberal member of the Directorate, should reduce by half the 200,000 men who had been quickly mobilised so that a realistic number could be equipped and trained; that those at the front should receive any new equipment before those at the rear; that officers be formally called up and that those not fit to serve be deprived of their uniforms; and that wide powers be given to Admiral Kolchak as Minister of War. Although these suggestions seemed necessary and practical, he received only the lukewarm reply that such things would be done in time.[14] General Boldyrev agreed to sign over his Supreme Command to French General Janin, who technically became Commander-in-Chief of all Allied and Russian Forces. In return the Allies promised the Whites material and technical aid and advice on the formation of the new Russian army. This seemed a significant political advance; but Janin's was an empty title and he was not to arrive in the theatre for a further three weeks, though his Military Mission was already assembling. His authority was to be resisted by the Russian headquarters (the Stavka), by the White commanders themselves and, of course, by the Japanese and their puppets.

On the day of Boldyrev's announcement came the third notable arrival in Omsk: that of Colonel Ward with his Middlesex Battalion, who detrained to a resounding reception from the populace, which perhaps fondly imagined that this was the first contingent of the great Allied force which would save them from the anarchy of the civil war. 'The one thing wanting is tangible Allied force at the front', Knox wrote disconsolately to Emsley; but all that had been so far provided, he noted, was 'a few British sailors, one British garrison battalion, one French battalion, and a battery and a couple of Italian battalions'. Little more in the way of combat troops was to come from the French and the British, though both were now setting up substantial military missions to advise the Russians and Czechs and channel such material support for the growing White forces as they were able to provide. General Knox was to retain his base at Vladivostok, where the British High Commissioner Sir Charles Eliot was also located. At Omsk, as his local representatives, he had Lieutenant Colonel J. F. Neilson and Captain Leo Steveni, who were quartered in a railway carriage in the square outside the Russian headquarters building. A branch line from the main station had been built to the square which had become a sort of railway dormitory to ease the local accommodation problem. Colonel Neilson, a cavalry officer, was a talented water-colourist and trainer of polo ponies. He was married to a daughter of William Cazalet, a wealthy English trader in Moscow. He spoke Russian and had served on General Knox's staff in Petrograd from the start of the main war. Captain Steveni, who spoke Russian fluently, came from an old British Petrograd family. He had been given the job of liaising with various anti-Bolshevik groups since the early summer and was, in the words of one historian, 'a thorough-going reactionary who desired a complete restoration of the Tsarist regime'.[15] Colonel Ward of the Middlesex spoke no Russian but had a good interpreter, a Russian officer called Colonel Frank. No doubt believing that his position as a British Labour MP and trade-union leader gave him greater responsibilities than merely commanding his battalion as the garrison for Omsk, he soon busied himself in meeting the Siberian political and military leaders.

General Knox's discussions with Boldyrev and Kolchak, the new Minister of War, took place before the 5 November merger of the Directorate and the Siberian Government. By the time he left Omsk for Vladivostok to welcome the arriving French Commander-in-Chief, General Janin, Knox had secured a formal agreement with them. In return for doing all he could to assist their government in organising a Russian army, they would ensure that full control was in the hands of the officers with 'no committees or commissars of any kind among the rank and file'; that neither officers nor men were 'to mix in politics'; that the Omsk government was to demand that the Allies (this included the Japanese) were to give all aid through the Omsk administration and none to Kalmykov and Semenov; that all promotions and appointments were to be made only from Omsk (again directed against the Japanese); and that Horvat's troops in Manchuria were to be disbanded. Knox was looking to reinforce the authority of Omsk so far as he was able; but it was very clear which part of the Omsk administration he supported. He plainly favoured the Siberian Government. During his visit he conspicuously paid no official call on Avksentiev, the Socialist

Revolutionary chairman of the Directorate. Boldyrev's diary recorded that at tea Knox jocularly warned him that, if the Directorate did not come to terms with the Siberian Government, he would organise a gang and overthrow them. This was the very day that the Political Intelligence Department of the Foreign Office was strongly recommending the recognition of the Directorate to the British Cabinet.[16]

On 18 November 1918, a week after the Armistice with the Central Powers, there was a *coup d'état* in Omsk which overthrew the Directorate and installed Admiral Kolchak, the War Minister, as Supreme Ruler in its place. The circumstances of the coup were such as to raise suspicions in the minds of the French and Japanese commanders of a significant degree of British involvement. Ten days earlier, on 8 November, Colonel Ward and a strong detachment of his battalion, which had been despatched to Omsk largely 'to show the flag' (as a second-class garrison battalion it could not have been expected to do much else), went forward to the front itself. It did so, taking the regimental band with it, at General Knox's request, as a guard for Admiral Kolchak, the new War Minister, who was visiting the forward units to hearten the troops and attending a ceremony for the inauguration of the Czech National Army and the presentation of new colours and decorations. This, at least, is Ward's account; General Knox claimed that it was sent forward merely to attend the Czech presentation. The party was given an enthusiastic reception at all the stations along the route. Everything appeared to go according to plan, though Kolchak seemed already to have taken against the Czechs. Their front-line units were tired and Kolchak believed they had shot their bolt. He also thought they were given to politicking; they had not been slow to express their views on the Siberian Government, and certainly believed they had been let down by not being reinforced by the Allies or the Russians. After the ceremonies Ward and his men went to the front line itself at Konguyr, intent on raising spirits, and marched with their band to an outpost near the railway. There the band struck up, but hardly with the desired effect. 'Band playing upset enemy gunners', declared Ward in his report of the incident, 'who began shelling us, the projectiles dropped harmlessly in our rear, no damage.' The Czechs defending this sector saw things rather differently, as one of their officers recalled:

> Smartly the British detachment marched back to the station, smartly they entrained, and as smartly the engine whistled and drew them out of the danger zone, leaving the Bolsheviks in a thoroughly nasty frame of mind which they proceeded to vent upon us.[17]

Ward and his men returned to Omsk, still formally as Kolchak's guard, the train stopping *en route* at Petropavlovsk to enable Kolchak to confer with General

Boldyrev, the Commander-in-Chief, who was on his way to the front. They spoke at great length, raising Ward's suspicions that something was afoot. Back at Omsk, Colonel Neilson had long been aware that a coup was being planned. He seems to have done his best to keep out of it, but, when asked directly for his views by the military plotters, he 'could not help agreeing that the existing state of affairs was most unsatisfactory, and that Admiral Kolchak was the only man capable of saving the country'. When asked if he thought the British government would support Admiral Kolchak when he had assumed power, he claimed to have replied, 'We are not concerned with individuals, or the composition of governments, but we desire to see, and support, a government capable of restoring order and carrying on the war'. He made it clear that Britain would take no part in the coup, but that it would be logical for it to support Kolchak, whose policy would further the aims of the Allies. The main war, of course, though still being fought, was then in its final days. The day after Kolchak's return from visiting the front he was approached by the plotters, and asked to take power, but refused.[18]

The coup was carried out by a squad of Cossacks led by Lieutenant Colonel Krasilnikov, a Cossack ataman and something of a firebrand. They arrested the two Socialist-Revolutionary members of the Directorate and some of their party colleagues and took them off. A third Directorate member resigned when he heard the news. With the fourth, General Boldyrev, away at the front, the negotiations with the plotters and the Council of Ministers were conducted by the sole remaining member. After some discussion, the decision was taken to invite Kolchak to assume full control. Since the overthrow of the Directorate was now an accomplished fact, Kolchak agreed to take over, becoming the 'Supreme Ruler' of Russia, or as much of it as the Whites controlled, for the other White leaders subsequently recognised his overlordship. In the early evening, Kolchak sent for Neilson who, realising that the deed was done, decided that it was his duty to support the new ruler. He obeyed the summons and was given Kolchak's account of events. The admiral then decided to make his personal declaration to the senior French and British representatives right away and asked Neilsen to accompany him to the French High Commissioner's train. Thus the French representative had his first sight of the new Supreme Ruler as he arrived in the company of the senior British staff officer in Omsk. The fact that Colonel Ward, as soon as he heard the news of the coup and acting on his own authority, sent his battalion out into the streets of Omsk, where they set up their machine guns to dominate all approaches to the place where the plotters and ministers were holding their meetings, no doubt heightened suspicions that the British were complicit in the takeover. The Czech forces strongly disapproved of the coup, but would have had to pass the Middlesex's machine guns to have intervened. They made no attempt to do so. The impression of British collusion was strengthened when Kolchak next called on Ward himself, apparently in the mistaken belief that

Ward was the senior British representative in Omsk, an impression which Ward's interpreter, and perhaps the colonel himself, liked to foster. Ward had indeed spent considerable time with the White Russian ministers and with Kolchak. Indeed, Neilson had warned him against mixing with the Russian ministers, since Ward spoke no Russian, and Neilsen did not trust his interpreter. Ward certainly seemed to see himself as some sort of general British emissary, as well as a battalion commander. He was greatly attracted to Kolchak. It seems to have been Ward's intervention which kept the coup bloodless: his soldiers conducted the deposed Directorate members in safety to Vladivostok, completing the picture of apparent British abetment of the takeover. But the French were not alone in believing that the British military had overstepped the mark. When it received the news, the Foreign Office had similar suspicions which the War Office General Staff may well have shared.[19]

Ward sent General Knox a report of his role in the events of 18 November, explaining how the Russian leader, 'in full dress of a Russian Admiral', had called on him 'as the Senior British Officer holding official position at Omsk' and explained the circumstances of his appointment. Ward had argued for the safety of the imprisoned members of the now defunct Directorate in the interests, he said, 'of the establishment of free political institutions as understood by the democracy of England'. Kolchak gave him a guarantee of their safety and hoped that Russia might soon 'enjoy the blessing of equally free institutions'. Ward seems to have been something of a confident and industrious innocent abroad. General Knox's comment on Ward's report was: 'I am afraid that the old leaven of politics has burst through Ward's temporary dress of khaki, but I am sure he has done no harm. I have told Neilson to warn him.' When these reports arrived, very belatedly, at the War Office, the General Staff disagreed with Knox's comment and with the idea of Neilson doing any warning, since he was 'hot-headed and irresponsible'. It was even suggested that Ward's account of his meeting with Kolchak, and a special report he had written at the request of the CIGS, should be used for publicity purposes. Churchill, who was now in post, did not like the idea. 'Colonel Ward is doing admirably', he commented, 'but I do not think the publication necessary at this moment. Our policy in Siberia is too nebulous and our prospects too gloomy for special attention to be invited.'[20] The policy was indeed nebulous: the government had been discussing *de facto* recognition of the Omsk government with the French when news of the *coup d'état* came in. Now the whole question of recognition would have to start over again.

The extent to which Lieutenant Colonel Neilson may have compromised his position and that of the government by his words and actions at the time of the *coup d'état* at Omsk exercised minds at Vladivostok and in Whitehall, with Neilson having finally to write a full report of his activities over the period. The British High Commissioner, Sir Charles Eliot, criticised Knox for leaving

Neilson at Omsk without consulting him. He said he had thought Neilson was concerned exclusively with such matters as equipment and training, 'but he has lately manifested a most indiscreet political activity', for which he thought he should be removed from Omsk and allocated purely military duties elsewhere. General Knox did not agree, though he did believe his subordinate had been indiscreet. Lord Balfour advised that the Director of Military Operations should send a formal warning to Neilson. 'But we must also ask Sir Charles Eliot whether he thinks it sufficient', he wrote, 'Remember General Poole!' The sensitivity over Poole's association with the Archangel *coup d'état* a few months previously still lingered. Neilson received a formal rebuke for his 'recent activities in political matters', which General Knox was instructed to pass on to him. In doing so, Knox explained, not quite correctly, 'This is not the result of any representation made by the High Commissioner or me. In fact you would have got it in the neck if your messages had not been expurgated'. Neilson deserves some sympathy. One wonders why both the High Commissioner and the Head of the Military Mission chose to be based at Vladivostok when all the political and military decisions of any consequence were taking place at Omsk.[21]

The forty-five-year-old Admiral Aleksandr Kolchak, who had won distinction at sea in the Russo-Japanese War and the global conflict just ended, and was held in high regard in naval circles in both Britain and the United States, now found himself in command of armies which held great expanses of land, but of very little in the way of ships or sea. He was generally agreed to be a man of the highest character and a true patriot. General Knox, who knew Kolchak well, said that he had 'two characteristics uncommon in a Russian – a quick temper which inspired a useful awe among his subordinates, and a disinclination to talk merely for talking's sake'. He found the White ruler 'deficient in real stength of character', however, so that he easily fell under the influence of his principal subordinates. 'Kolchak', he declared, 'wasted time by imagining he was directing operations of which he knew nothing and neglected the civil administration in rear.' That Knox should have concluded, despite this critical evaluation with which none of his mission staff would have disagreed, that Kolchak 'was and is the best man in Siberia', suggests a very poor field of competitors. Colonel Ward, another who saw Kolchak at close quarters, confirmed this by writing, 'the pigmies by whom he is surrounded are so many drags on the wheels of state. There is not one that I would trust to manage a whelk-stall'.[22]

5

Armistice

The German delegates finally agreed the terms for an Armistice with the Allies in a French railway carriage at Compiègne at 5 a.m. on 11 November 1918. The agreement came into effect at 11 a.m. when the 'Cease Fire' sounded along the entire Western Front. As the guns fell silent, the Allied armies held fast along the line they had gained. They had retaken almost all the conquered territory of France and had won back a third of Belgium. In the last minutes of the war Canadian troops retook Mons, and paused to let through the 5th Royal Irish Lancers who had fought their first action of the war there over four years earlier. In a series of victories since June the Allies had taken 385,000 prisoners and 6600 guns. In the war as a whole the British Empire had suffered over three million casualties, with almost a million dead; three quarters of a million were mourned in Britain itself. The losses suffered by Russia will probably never be accurately computed, but they certainly totalled more than nine million: about two million dead, five million wounded, and two and a half million prisoners – more than any other belligerent and greater than all the Allies combined. The civil war and the accompanying intervention were to add significantly to that figure and to bring many more civilians into the count. Among its other conditions, the terms of the Armistice required the tearing up of the crippling Treaty of Brest-Litovsk and the withdrawal of all German troops from Russian territory, though the manner in which this was finally achieved was complex and by no means rapid. When the House of Commons met in the afternoon of the 11th, the Prime Minister read out the Armistice terms to his assembled colleagues. Lloyd George's speech concluded with the sentence, 'I hope we may say that thus, this fateful morning, came to an end all wars'. This noble aspiration overlooked, of course, the small matter of the undeclared war with Russia that was flickering and smouldering at that vast empire's accessible extremities.

In the fighting lines across the Channel the cease-fire was greeted with relief rather than elation, relief tinged with bewilderment – bewilderment that the immense and unrelenting engine of war which European civilisation had created was at last being brought to a halt. Among the fighting troops there was little fraternisation and scant rejoicing: rather an overpowering sense of deliverance from the horrors of the conflict. In the home islands, however, joy was unrestrained. Church bells rang out, the Union flag was run up everywhere, shops, offices and factories closed as the news spread, and delirious crowds surged through the streets. In London there was triumphant pandemonium. The celebrations and increasingly wild revelry continued for three days until the police finally tired of the excesses and intervened to restore some semblance of order. The jubilation penetrated to every corner of the British Isles. In the small city of Kirkwall, the capital of the Orkney Islands, the bells of the ancient cathedral of St Magnus rang out and all the ships in the crowded harbour and standing out to sea sounded a deafening salute to the end of the conflict. In less than half an hour flags were flying all over the town as the little community of farmers and fisherfolk shared in the nation's elation. There were also large numbers of temporary and rather shaken visitors to Kirkwall that day who greeted the news with something less than the relief of their Western Front comrades or the joy of the islanders around them. These visitors were a shipload of almost 3000 officers and men on their way to Russia as reinforcements for the garrison at Murmansk.

Aside from the staff for two brigade headquarters being despatched to General Maynard's command and some reinforcements for the King's Regiment on the Archangel front, the main body of reinforcements enjoying the hospitality of the Kirkwallers were the men of the 6th and 13th battalions the Yorkshire Regiment. In truth, they were now 'Yorkshire Regiment' in name only; both battalions had been formed and reformed in the course of the war as heavy losses took their toll. The 6th, for example, had begun its latest re-formation in early July with a small cadre from the 3rd and 4th battalions. It had drawn the rest of its complement from thirty different regiments and all parts of the country, only reaching full strength after 385 men provisionally allocated to it were declared unfit by a medical board and replaced by others. Its officers came from eight different regiments. The 13th battalion was no more homogeneous; indeed it did not get a commanding officer until it had served in Russia for over two months. Thus was the barrel being scraped and rescraped to reinforce General Poole's command.

The journey of the two battalions had begun with a march from their camp in Mychett to Aldershot station and then a long but uneventful train journey to Dundee, where they were to embark for Murmansk. The men had some days kicking their heels in the Scottish port while their ship was got ready. According to one of their number, they had 'a real rollicking time' whilst waiting. They embarked in the morning of 16 October on the dirty, insanitary and frankly unserviceable *Tras-os-Montes*, an ex-Norddeutscher-Lloyd liner commandeered by the Portuguese early in the war. When it was announced that the voyage would not start until nightfall the men were looking forward to another day on land. 'We expect to be let off to go ashore again, which is refused us', wrote one later; 'well then the trouble starts'. About 150 of the men pushed their way ashore and were only halted when confronted by military police and sentries at the dock gates. They then returned to the ship to encourage their comrades to join them in rushing the gates by main force. Private Hirst of 6th Yorkshires takes up the story: 'The officers are asking the men to play the game and be quiet, but they are told that it is our turn now. The Colonel draws his revolver and says that the next man to go over the side of the ship will be fired upon, he is told if he does fire that rifles will soon be fetched out and so he has to put his revolver away ... In another place the Brigadier-General has a crowd around him and the lads are just telling him what they think of him'. The near mutiny was not finally quelled until the ship was towed into midstream and all hopes of a run ashore were dashed.

The *Tras-os-Montes* did not start its voyage until the following day and soon developed a pronounced list as well as steering problems. A day later, following the bursting of a boiler, the ship began to drift helplessly towards a minefield. In desperation one of the accompanying destroyers tried to take the wallowing liner in tow but proved unequal to the task. Finally, tugs appeared and towed it to an anchorage in the Shetlands where it remained for three weeks while temporary repairs were made. By this time the ship's victuals were running low and the sorely-tried troops were put on short rations and had their days filled with route marches and fishing expeditions.

Once able to proceed under her own steam, the troopship set out for the Invergordon naval base, where it was hoped to effect more permanent repairs. Conditions on board proved no less precarious than before. The troops were ordered to stay on the port side to try to correct the list as the ship got under way. 'We are nearly walking on our hands and knees, the list of the ship is now worse than ever', recorded Private Hirst. During the night one of the crew was washed overboard and lost. Within hours the steering gear failed again and the captain was forced to take refuge in Inganess Firth on the Orkneys, anchoring with only auxiliary anchors since the main ones had failed. Even then the trials of the Yorkshires were not at an end, for a storm blew up and steadily pushed the poorly-anchored ship towards the cliffs. In what appeared a life-threatening emergency, some men were precariously taken off in ship's boats guided by landline as rescue craft rushed to the firth in answer to the distress rockets and SOS which the ship put out. It was to universal relief that the rudderless and anchorless *Tras-os-Montes* was finally towed from the gale-lashed sea to the protection of Kirkwall's excellent harbour. 'After what we had been through this was a grand respite', wrote one corporal of 6th Yorkshires.

At Kirkwall the authorities finally gave up their struggle to make the vessel fit to sail to Murmansk and sent the troops north to the Arctic Circle aboard a sister vessel, the *Huntsend*. This voyage proved uneventful. The Yorkshires arrived at Murmansk on 27 November, six weeks after they had first embarked at Dundee and over a fortnight after the war had apparently ended. They were no

more impressed with the primitive Russian port than the first arrivals had been
months earlier. 'I have not seen a stone or brick building here, all wood', noted
Private Hirst, 'and some would not do for pig sties for us.' It had all been a most
dispiriting prelude to an operational tour of duty whose purpose, now that the
Armistice was in effect, remained a mystery to many in the ranks.[1]

The Armistice with Germany removed at a stroke the primary justification for
the intervention in Russia. The plan to ease the pressure on the Western Front
by reopening the Eastern, never a serious requirement once the succession
of Allied victories was clearly under way in July, was now quite irrelevant to
Britain's concerns. Even the need to consider reopening hostilities if Germany's
peacemakers proved intransigent was not a factor likely to involve the small forces
on distant Russian soil. With the imperatives of war at an end, the Armistice also
removed the primacy of the General Staff in Britain's Russian policy-making,
which now returned firmly to the hands of the politicians. What then was
their future policy towards the Bolshevik regime to be? What was to happen to
Ironside's little army, shortly to be immured by ice and snow in its Archangel
blockhouses? Since Maynard's men no longer needed to watch the long frontier
with Finland, or protect Murmansk, could they not go home? What of Ward's
Middlesex Battalion in Siberia and the Hampshires who would shortly arrive
from India to join it? Could they now begin the long journey back to Britain?
The end of the war also meant that other areas of Russian territory, the Baltic
States, the Black Sea coast and Transcaucasia were now accessible to British
influence. The Baltic states were struggling for independence, whilst beyond the
Black Sea General Denikin's Volunteer Army was still holding its own against the
Bolsheviks. Numerous other communities north and south of the Caucasus were
fighting for at least local sovereignty. Would Britain now lend them assistance
and what form might this take?

The mainspring of Britain's intervention policy had indeed disappeared, but
it was being replaced by two other perceived threats which formed an important
part of the development of the post-war Russian policy. The first was the fear
of the spread of Bolshevism, with its class war doctrines, to western Europe
and Britain itself. The new Russian regime had already appealed to the citizens
of the West to overthrow their governments and had put some finance behind
these urgings. Anti-Bolshevism had never been entirely absent from Britain's
motivation for intervention; with a more fervent championing it was soon to
move to the foreground. The contrary fear was that, if Germany survived the war
relatively intact and were to take the leading role in 'restoring Russia to order'
(the euphemistic shorthand for the defeat of Bolshevism), it might be Germany,
ideally situated geographically and with thousands of troops still on Russian soil,
that would gain paramount influence in the Russian state. Both arguments had

1. Churchill as Secretary of State for War and Air in 1919. CIGS Sir Henry Wilson
on far right. (*IWM, Q 34664*)

2. Murmansk from the sea, 1919.

3. Murmansk, March 1919: 'a handful of log huts, a landing stage and snow'.
(*IWM, Q 16631*)

4. General Maynard (left) with his Chief of Staff Colonel Lewin at the entrance to GHQ Murmansk.

5. General Frederick Poole (left) with one of his staff on the quayside at Archangel.
(*IWM, GSA 048/Q 17007*)

6. General Edmund Ironside (third left) towers over the Archangel staff.
(*IWM, Q 16349*)

7. The colour party of Dyer's battalion of the Slavo-British Legion. The standard bearer was reputed to be a former Bolshevik commissar.

8. Ironside's social work: members of the junior unit of the
Archangel Slavo-British Legion.

9. Troops of the Slavo-British Legion encamped with their British officers.
(*IWM, Q 16222*)

10. Military transport: dog teams in north Russia. (*IWM,Q 17022*)

11. Machine gun training for the White Russians in north Lapland.
(*IWM, Q 81046*)

their place in the thinking of the men who were planning Britain's Russian policy as the Great War drew to a close.

Robert Bruce Lockhart, the unofficial but well-connected British link with the Bolsheviks, had now been returned to Britain as part of an exchange of diplomatic personnel with the Russian regime. He has passed an anxious and disagreeable spell imprisoned in the Loubianka headquarters of the Moscow Cheka (secret police) following the intervention at Archangel and an assassination attempt on Lenin in which the Cheka believed the British were complicit. After a month's confinement, he was set free to travel back to Britain via Petrograd's Finland Station, where he spent further uncomfortable days in an unheated train whilst the ever-suspicious Bolsheviks ensured the British kept their part of the bargain by releasing Maxim Litvinov and his staff in England. Once he was safely home, Lockhart produced, at the request of the Foreign Office, a lengthy memorandum on possible future Allied policy towards Russia. He considered three options: withdrawing all forces and coming to terms with the Bolshevik regime; launching a full-scale intervention designed to crush it once and for all; and adopting a middle course of merely aiding the Whites and creating a protective chain of small states along Russia's western border. Whilst he had earlier argued earnestly for intervention to take place only on an agreed basis with the Bolsheviks, he now plumped for massive intervention. In this action he proposed that the Americans should play the leading role. The futility, at this stage, of expecting the Americans to do any such thing was probably the reason why Lockhart's otherwise cogent and well-regarded paper was not at first sent to the War Cabinet. There was, nevertheless, one very sound element in his impractical proposal. This was the judgement that by the end of 1918 the Bolshevik regime was strong – stronger than at any time in its brief history and much more powerful than all its domestic opponents combined – and that any support which ordinary Russians might give to the Whites' cause would be in direct proportion to the scale of Allied intervention in support of them.[2]

The Chief of the Imperial General Staff, Sir Henry Wilson, was similarly giving much thought to the Russian situation. It is difficult to believe that Wilson, the professional head of the armies of the British Empire, had once had great difficulty in joining the army at all, having several times failed the entrance examinations to both Sandhurst and Woolwich. He finally gained his commission without examination via the Longford Militia.[3] It was perhaps a reflection on the inappropriateness of those early academic hurdles that he was now considered to be one of the cleverest and most astute of British generals. Wilson had no great love of politicians, whom he habitually called 'the frocks'; indeed, a military colleague is said to have observed that 'he got into a state of sexual excitement whenever he saw a politician'.[4] But he was certainly much better than his predecessor as CIGS at dealing with them. Wilson submitted his views on the Russian question two days after the Armistice in his 'Memorandum on our Present and Future Military Policy in Russia'.[5] Like Lockhart, he considered three options. His first was the withdrawal of all British forces from Russia and the building up of a *cordon sanitaire* of states to protect western Europe from the advance of its revolutionary ideas. He dismissed this as politically unacceptable defensiveness that was, in any case, militarily impracticable. Next, he examined a proposal to 'grasp the nettle firmly' and take active military measures to crush Bolshevism at an early date. This too he rejected, despite his instinctive preference for it and the undoubted benefits that might flow from having a strong, united, politically acceptable Russia as a barrier to Germany's eastern ambitions. He believed correctly that the Allies would be quite unable to mobilise the necessary military power at the end of such a long and exhausting war. His third and recommended option was 'to do all we can in the way of material to give our friends a fair start, and then to withdraw'. The 'friends' were the White forces in the three main theatres, north Russia, south Russia and Siberia, to whom he saw Britain having a continuing moral obligation. To give them a 'sporting chance', it seems, was all that the CIGS was proposing. His paper was discussed at a Foreign Office meeting on 13 November which was chaired by the Foreign Secretary himself and attended by his chief advisers, as well as senior officers from the Admiralty and War Office. The discussion extended Wilson's preferred proposals somewhat, and finally resulted in a series of decisions which were endorsed by the War Cabinet at its meeting the following day. They were:

> To remain in occupation of Murmansk and Archangel.
>
> To retain the battalions and military mission in Siberia and encourage Canada to retain her troops there. To try to persuade the Czechoslovak Corps to remain at the front in Siberia rather than seek repatriation. To recognize the Directorate at Omsk as the *de facto* government of Siberia.
>
> To establish contact with General Denikin in South Russia and give him all possible assistance.
>
> To occupy with British troops the railway running from Batum on the Black Sea to Baku on the Caspian.
>
> To supply the Baltic states with military materials should they appear to be able to make effective use of such assistance.[6]

These decisions reflected the Foreign Secretary's opinion that the country would not stand an 'anti-Bolshevik crusade', but also his view that 'If we now withdrew our forces from European and Asiatic Russia we should suffer a serious loss of prestige, and should be letting down our friends'. They also seemed to accept Secretary of State for War Lord Milner's apparent belief that where a friendly anti-Bolshevik government was established on what was previously Russian territory, Britain ought to support it. Beyond that scarcely unanimous opinion, there was no general policy principle established for the conduct of relations with Russia. Most of the dispositions agreed were simply a continuation of those which had first been brought about by the war with Germany. Before the year was out the exasperated CIGS would be forced to return to the War Cabinet to ask for a more definite policy to be given him. He was to get no satisfactory answer on that or subsequent occasions, beyond the promise that Russia would be the first topic for decision at the Paris Peace Conference.[7] It was hardly a comforting response for the commanders and soldiers on the Russian front.

In one area of Russia's borderlands, however, British troops were being deployed in considerable strength even before the Cabinet's less than satisfactory policy decisions had been taken. By 17 November 1918, after travelling along Dunsterville's old route via Enzeli, Major-General W.M. Thomson, with 1200 British and 800 Indian troops, had arrived at Baku on the Caspian Sea. He was soon followed by Major-General G.T. Forestier-Walker with an entire division from Salonica, which deployed at the western end of the Caucasus at Batum. Before long they were fanning out along the railway and oil pipeline, the commanders were suggesting policies that seemed far in excess of what the government had determined, and were calling for reinforcements. General Thomson proposed a plan for British troops not only to occupy all the important towns and communication centres in the region, but also to take on the principal administrative responsibilities of local and regional government. These were matters for the Cabinet's Eastern Committee to determine. Yet at one of the committee's early meetings the Foreign Secretary, Balfour, declared that he did not even know about the troops' deployment. 'I am much alarmed at our having sent a division there', he said, 'It may be necessary, but I was never consulted about it. I was rather shocked when I heard it and am still.' The Eastern Committee proved to be deeply divided on the need for any deployment at all, with Lord Curzon, who headed it, arguing strongly in favour of it on the grounds of protection for India's flank, helping the new states of Georgia, Armenia and Azerbaijan to get to their feet, securing the oilfields, and keeping the French out. But the Foreign Office ministers, Balfour and Lord Robert Cecil, and the Prime Minister himself, all opposed the deployment.[8]

The troops, however, were already there: the withdrawal of the Turks and Germans needed to be supervised, the strategic railway had to be guarded and, once in position, it was rapidly evident to the commanders that the social, economic and political dislocation of the region, still riven by ethnic animosities, forced them to take a larger political role. Thus Thomson imposed martial law on Azerbaijan, became military governor of Baku, and supervised the city's return to ordered public life and active commerce. The military police maintained law and order; the state banks were amalgamated and a note issue was supervised; a system of food rationing was instituted; labour disputes were settled by a labour control office; Bolshevik agitators were arrested and deported; the shipping and oil industries were privatised. All these developments were managed by Thomson and his officers, often calling on those with specialist skills and experience from civilian life. Similar close control was maintained by Forestier-Walker in Batum, whose territory was disputed by Georgia, Azerbaijan and General Denikin. In Tiflis he used a lighter touch (though heavier than the Georgians would have wished) since its government had remained largely unchanged even during German occupation. These British Transcaucasian deployments, though larger than those elsewhere in Russia, were of a different character than the rest. They had limited, defensive purposes and were not, in general, a prelude to campaigns against the Bolsheviks, designed to topple its Moscow regime from power.

The Armistice was soon followed by the Prime Minister's decision to hold a general election. The existing Parliament, extended by the wartime emergency, had already run three years beyond its statutory term. There was, besides, a much expanded electorate with the extension of the vote to all men and many women. The opinion of these new voters had yet to be tested. The government also needed a fresh mandate to negotiate the peace settlement with Germany and its allies. After a turbulent campaign at the hustings the nation went to vote on 14 December. It was a curious affair, for there was no return to traditional party politics. General Wilson put it more strongly, 'The bribery of L.G. [Lloyd George] at this election is simply disgusting. I won't vote tomorrow'.[9] Lloyd George and the Unionist leader Bonar Law decided to continue the wartime coalition and introduced a device which became known as the 'coupon', a letter of approval from the two leaders which as many as 541 candidates received, whereby they were not opposed in the election by a candidate from the other coalition party. The 'Khaki Election' produced an overwhelming victory for the coalition led by Lloyd George, which won 533 seats against the 101 (excluding the Sinn Fein Members, who refused to take their seats), gained by its opponents. It was a great personal triumph for the Prime Minister, for the election had really been fought on his personal standing, his past record, his status as the war leader and his promises for the future; but it was as considerable a party triumph for the Unionists. While the Coalition Liberals, even with the protection of the coupon, returned only 136 members, 339 Coalition Unionists were elected. The Prime Minister was now even more dependent on their support. The independent Liberals were destroyed. Every one of their former ministers lost his seat; only twenty-six of their Members were returned. The Labour Party now became the Official Opposition.

There had been no full parliamentary debate on Russian policy since the Bolsheviks had come to power and none was to take place until the spring of 1919. On 18 November the government was asked in the House of Commons to state the objects of British military operations in Russia. The reply from Ian MacPherson, the Under-Secretary of State for War, was that it was not in the national interest that any such information should be given: an unsatisfactory, lame response with the Armistice now a week old. The matter was then taken up in the Lords, where the government spokesman, Lord Robert Cecil, declared that the government was certainly not disposed 'to entangle this country at the close of a great war in serious military operations', but that he was not free to elaborate any further. It seemed that the veil of secrecy and censorship which been drawn across operations in the war proper was continuing into the peace. The Coalition's policy towards Russia, if it could be called policy, did not feature at all significantly at the hustings; it seemed almost to be a private matter. In none of Lloyd George's major election speeches, nor indeed in the Coalition's election manifesto, was Russia even mentioned. On the other hand, 'Bolshevism' was. Both Lloyd George and his colleagues frequently asserted that a vote for the Coalition would assist in keeping Bolshevism out of Britain. Lloyd George also made sure that the Labour Party, which had declined to continue in the Coalition, was tarred with the Bolshevik brush. But what precisely it was planned to do to keep Britain safe from Bolshevism was not declared.[10]

Despite the Prime Minister's jibes and the Coalition's silence on the matter, the Labour Party did have something to say about Russia. During the war the Labour trade unionists had been predominantly pro-war and remained quiescent about the Russian intervention, even if they did not support it as a necessary part of operations. They were quiet no longer. 'What are our boys doing in Russia?', demanded one election candidate. 'We feel that the time has come to break the self-imposed silence which we have observed with respect to the British Government's attitude towards Russia', the *New Statesman* solemnly declared as the election results were awaited. Lord Milner made one of the few Coalition pronouncements in response when he issued an unusual open letter to the press in which he argued that to leave in the lurch the thousands of Russians who had taken up arms on the side of the intervention powers would be 'an abominal betrayal, contrary to every British instinct of honour and humanity'. This was an admirable sentiment; but hardly a satisfactory basis on which to pursue undeclared hostilities. Even the *Daily Telegraph* was unimpressed. 'We have at present a war on our hands in Russia', it intoned, 'such as would have filled the newspapers at any normal time; and the nation is entitled to know how the war is going, and to what end it is contemplated by the Government.' But it was the left-leaning *Daily Herald*, the Liberal *Manchester Guardian* and the *Express* newspapers which provided the consistent press opposition to the Russian involvement over the ensuing months. The *Express*'s Conservative owner, Lord Beaverbrook, was no lover of the Bolsheviks but held steadfastly to the simple view that 'once peace was declared the only thing to do was to evacuate Russian soil and leave the Russians to order or disorder their own affairs'. The unrelenting demand in the *Express* newspapers for British troops to quit Russia became the first of Beaverbrook's great press campaigns.

'A most amazing state of affairs ... No opposition of any sort', wrote Sir Henry Wilson on 28 December when the election results came in. He dined that night at 10 Downing Street where his fellow guests 'all agreed that it was a bad business having no opposition'. The government's opponents certainly lacked political stature and experience as well as numbers. The fifty-nine Labour Members were all working-class men, almost all with trade union sponsorship, and the majority were trade union officials. Such influence as they had in the House came less from debating skill and political *savoir-faire* as from the support of the unions they represented. Union militancy was developing and many industrial issues were coming to the boil. The most effective parliamentary opposition to the intervention in Russia, though for most of the time it did not discomfit the government unduly, came from three men of upper middle-class, even aristocratic lineage. Though of different parties, they often sat together in the House and were dubbed by the *Daily News* 'The Three Musketeers'. They were Josiah Wedgwood, J.M. Kenworthy and Cecil L'Estrange Malone. All had distinguished war records. Perhaps the most considerable among them was Colonel Wedgwood, the scion of the Staffordshire pottery family. He had served with distinction in the South African War and in several theatres in the Great War, and had gained the DSO amid the dreadful carnage of X Beach at Gallipoli. He then became Assistant Director of Trench Warfare before being despatched on his fruitless venture to Tomsk. Initially an independent Liberal, he soon moved to the Labour Party. His views on Russian affairs carried the more weight because of his parliamentary skill, his political connections and his first-hand knowledge of the Siberian theatre. 'He is an opposition in himself', declared one lobby correspondent. Both Wedgwood and Kenworthy had declined the proffered 'coupon'. Commander Kenworthy, heir to an ancient baronry, was not returned at the post-Armistice election but caused a tremendous sensation a few months later when, as an independent Liberal, he won the safe Tory seat of Hull Central in a by-election, turning a Unionist majority of ten thousand into a Liberal one of almost a thousand. Campaigning on a programme of opposition to conscription, a just peace and an end to intervention in Russia, Kenworthy caught the temper of the times. The third 'musketeer', Mr L'Estrange Malone, chose to discard military rank. He was younger, more passionate and less genial than his colleagues and, though sitting as a Liberal, had pronounced Bolshevik sympathies. Such was the active opposition.

In other circumstances Lloyd George might have found common cause with the Russian policies of the 'Musketeers'. The possibility of forming an alternative left-of-centre administration, by reuniting the Liberals and drawing in Labour, was now, however, denied him by his party's shrunken numbers. Although unassailable in his position as Prime Minister, he had to take account of the very strong Unionist majority in the House of Commons, a chamber which Kenworthy later described as 'horribly intolerant' and 'the most sentimental, the most uncontrolled and the most passion-driven' of the five Parliaments in which he sat. Wedgwood was similarly critical, 'This Parliament of 1918–22 was quite the wickedest I have known', he later wrote. 'Some called them the hard-faced men, I should have said empty-headed. Heaven knows how they made their money, or got there.'[11] Lloyd George's instincts were certainly for conciliation of the new Bolshevik government. He felt that the ferocity that had accompanied their seizure and maintenance of power in Russia was more than explained, if not excused, by the 'exactions and oppressions' of the 'inept, profligate and tyrannical' old order they had overthrown. Like President Wilson and Lord Beaverbrook, he believed that, by removing the causes of their extremism, the Bolsheviks would finally settle down. This analysis was certainly not shared by many of his Unionist colleagues. 'The trouble with the P.M. is that he is a bit of a Bolshevist himself', Curzon confided to Balfour, 'One feels that he sees Trotsky as the only congenial figure on the international scene'. The remark gave some hint of the difficulty Lloyd George would have in constructing an acceptable Russian policy.

The Prime Minister had other difficulties with Russia. He was concerned at the limited reliable information available about the immense kaleidoscope of territories, parties, movements and events which made up the Russian problem. 'We were, in fact, never dealing with the ascertained, or perhaps, even ascertainable facts. Russia was a jungle in which no one could say what was within a few yards of him', he complained. It was also a jungle which Lloyd George's imperfect knowledge of geography rendered the more impenetrable: he thought, for example that Kharkov, an important Ukrainian city, was the name of a Russian general. Over the next six months he also found difficulty in monitoring his Cabinet colleagues because of the demands of the Peace Conference. From 12 January, when he first met the other chief peacemakers, Clemenceau, Wilson and Orlando, at the French Foreign Ministry on the Quai d'Orsai, he was to have more than a hundred meetings with them in Paris. Finally, he had to reckon with the man he chose to manage the country's military affairs, his erstwhile fellow radical, Winston Churchill.

After Churchill's chequered service as First Lord of the Admiralty culminating in the Gallipoli disaster with its huge casualties and bitter recriminations, he had spent some time out of office, much of it commanding the 6th Royal Scots Fusiliers in Flanders. In 1917 Lloyd George risked the wrath of the Unionists in the Coalition by recalling him to government as Minister of Munitions without first consulting his Cabinet coalition colleagues. Churchill did well in the post. Now, after the remarkable election victory which secured his personal position, Lloyd George decided to promote his old colleague to senior Cabinet rank. Churchill would have preferred to return to the Admiralty, but the Prime Minister finally offered him the War Office, with additional responsibility for the Air Force as Secretary of State for War and Air. He knew well Churchill's enormous energy and determination, but was also conscious of the burden of responsibility the combined post would bring. A fresh demobilisation plan was urgently needed, for the existing scheme was already proving hugely unpopular. With enormous numbers of conscripts and Kitchener volunteers now filling the ranks, there was also the task of creating a new Regular Army, the old one having been effectively destroyed at the first battle of Ypres in 1914. Despite the peace, large numbers of uniformed, disciplined men were needed for the substantial Armies of Occupation required to police the defeated powers, while across the Irish Sea there was the worsening republican emergency. Within days of the general election the Irish Volunteers had reconstituted themselves as the Irish Republican Army and the first of its campaigns of civil resistance coupled with physical violence was under way. The pacification of Ireland was beyond the resources of the Royal Irish Constabulary and was making increasing demands on the army. Beyond that there was the traditional role of policing the Empire. Adding to these responsibilities, the Secretary of State would have the new challenge of remodelling and developing the nation's air power in an era of rapid technological change. In sum, it was a substantial task even for a man of Churchill's ability, confidence and stamina. To all these concerns was added the undeclared war with Russia.

Offering the War Office post to Winston Churchill carried significant political risks for Lloyd George. It was not that Churchill lacked the necessary experience. Although still only forty-four, he had already held four important ministerial appointments, whilst on the military side his experience appeared unrivalled. Despite his initial difficulty in passing the Sandhurst entrance examination, Churchill had subsequently served in eight different front-line regiments and had seen active service in Cuba, India, the Sudan, South Africa and most recently, as a lieutenant colonel, in the trenches of the Western Front. All this martial activity had been crammed into less than six years of service. The risk for Lloyd George lay in the widespread unpopularity of Churchill in the Tory Party from which his defection fourteen years earlier had never been forgiven or forgotten. The right-wing press was particularly hostile. It was Churchill's judgement which was most often called into question. Northcliffe's *Daily Mail* declared that the union of War and Air Ministries 'under such a man as Churchill is asking for trouble, and is a sure cause of future mischief', while the ultra-Conservative *Morning Post* believed that he was unsuitable even for the War Office alone. In a leading article, it asserted that 'there is some tragic flaw in Mr Churchill which determines him on every occasion in the wrong course ... It is an appointment which makes us tremble for the future'.[12] Some prominent parliamentarians were distinctly cool. Leopold Amery of the War Cabinet Secretariat felt sufficiently strongly to write directly to Lloyd George, 'Don't put Churchill in the War Office. I hear from all sorts of quarters that the Army are terrrified at the idea'.[13] The army was certainly less than delighted. In mid-December Sir Henry Wilson wrote, 'Winston came to tell me he was going to succeed Milner as War Minister. Whew!' Three days later his surprise had given way to consternation: 'It seems quite clear that Winston is going to succeed Milner and I have grave doubts about the situation'.[14]

From the virulence of the new Secretary of State's opposition to the Bolsheviks it is difficult to believe that he had once advocated an accommodation with Russia's new masters, or that twenty-one years later he would risk Britain's home and imperial defences by rushing to their aid. A year after moving to the War Office Churchill was to claim in the House of Commons that he had taken up his post with 'no strong and vehement convictions ... as to what is right and proper for the country to do' with respect to Russia. Yet he had already made his position clear to both the War Cabinet and his own electorate. The language in which he chose publicly to denounce the Russian regime was eloquent of the depth of his detestation and more than rivalled that which he directed at his adversaries in the Second World War. It was then that Ed Murrow would claim that Churchill 'mobilized the English language and sent it into battle'; but he gave it an equally thorough military workout in 1919. His language was replete with images of pestilence and savagery. Bolsheviks were 'swarms of typhus bearing vermin'; their creed was 'a foul combination of criminality and animalism' or else 'not a creed, it is a pestilence'. Lloyd George's secretary reported him as declaring that 'the Bolsheviks are the enemies of the human race and must be put down at any cost'.[15] This was extreme language even for one habituated to its graphic use. In an election speech to his constituents he declared: 'Russia is being reduced by the Bolsheviks to an animal form of Barbarism ... Civilisation is being extinguished over gigantic areas, while Bolsheviks hop and caper like troops of ferocious baboons amid the ruins of their cities and the corpses of their victims.'[16] There was something almost visceral about Churchill's hatred, but this passion did not make for level-headed policy-making. An understanding of this perhaps lay behind Balfour's cool response to one of Churchill's outbursts in Cabinet, 'I admire the exaggerated way you tell the truth'. Churchill was to argue his case for continued, and indeed much expanded, intervention in Russia's civil war in lengthy minutes to the Prime Minister and his ministerial colleagues, in vigorous debates in Cabinet and by contact with his colleagues among the Allied powers. The problem for Churchill was that Britain's policy towards Russia had to be determined within narrow limits. Making peace with the Bolsheviks – a policy which attracted Lloyd George – would be vetoed by the House of Commons in which the right-wing dominated; but a policy of full-blooded intervention would not be acceptable to a nation and an army overcome with war-weariness and now prostrated by the influenza pandemic.

On Christmas Eve 1918 Sir Henry Wilson was visited by a Canadian officer, Colonel Boyle, just returned from two and a half years working on the Russian railways and in Roumania. He had brought with him the King of Roumania's son for schooling in Britain. Boyle gave Wilson a most lurid account of the excesses of the Bolsheviks. 'He really was very terrifying', wrote Wilson. Two days later he was still recalling the interview: 'I must confess Boyle's account of the Bolshevists frightens me', he wrote. Yet Wilson was only too aware of how difficult it would be for Britain to take any significant direct action against them.

The war-weariness in the ranks showed itself most dramatically in impatience with the slowness of demobilisation and the unfairness of a system that was letting out those soldiers who had trades and jobs to go to first. Since these generally had been the last to volunteer or be conscripted, the policy operated against the interests of the great majority who had served longer and done the most fighting. This, plus an unending round of apparently needless guard duties and time-filling fatigues, brought many units in Britain near to boiling point. A further factor in the growing truculence in the ranks was the fear that, after all they had endured in France and Flanders, they might now be sent to Russia. Active recruiting had already begun for the Military Missions and for reinforcements for those already on Russian soil. As Commander Kenworthy put it, 'The atmosphere was distinctly revolutionary in January and February 1919 and the troops under arms were in no mood to be trifled with'. The view of the CIGS was that 'We are sitting on top of a mine which may go up at any minute'.[17]

The 'soldiers' strikes' – strictly speaking many were actually mutinies though they were seldom treated as such – began in January a few days before Churchill took post, though the censor kept reports of most of them out of the national newspapers. Their outbreak seems to have played some part in Lloyd George's decision to offer Churchill the War Office rather than the Admiralty. In Folkestone ten thousand soldiers assembled at the town hall and refused to go to France. The following day the strike had spread to the harbour and to Dover. A *Daily Herald* reporter noted that everywhere the feeling was the same, 'The war is over, we won't fight in Russia, we mean to go home'. This episode and a similar one in Calais (whose ringleaders General Haig wished to have shot, an action from which he was dissuaded by Churchill himself) are probably the best known and documented; but many more took place the length and breadth of the country while escaping mention in the national press. With the disturbances occurring, as it were, on their doorstep, it was the local newspapers which generally managed to get the details of the mutinies printed before the censor's pen could get to their copy. From airmen at Beaulieu Camp in Lymington and Biggin Hill, where 700 refused to parade, to bluejackets in Liverpool and at Rosyth, where crews of several minesweepers refused to go to sea, to raw and disturbing defiance at scores of army camps throughout the country, a wave of unrest was sweeping through the nation's military forces. The general demobilisation issue was often exacerbated by factors which were purely local and administrative. At Uxbridge 400 strikers from the Armament School complained about the slowness of demobilisation, but also that 'the food has been rotten since the Armistice, one loaf between eight men, five days a week sausage'; at Biggin Hill it was poor food and sanitation, with eight washbasins for 700 men. But Russia also featured among the men's concerns. At Osterley Park in west London, where 150 Army Service Corps men set out in a lorry convoy as a delegation to Whitehall, the demonstration is said to have resulted from rumours of a Russian draft. At Aldershot, where a deputation of a hundred representing various regiments went to see the garrison commander about demobilisation, there were cries of 'Will they send us to Russia?' On Salisbury Plain, where on 4 January Australian troops burnt down the Larkhill theatre, ninety-nine of the hundred men recently transferred to the RE Meteorological Section declared that they would not go to Russia. The local commander at Bedford addressed several hundred protesting Royal Engineers and, according to the local newspaper, explained that the slowness of demobilisation resulted from the fact that 'the war was not yet won, and we still need drafts for overseas, including Russia'. The most substantial and serious demonstration in the London region was at Park Royal camp where a 'soldiers' committee' (a title with worrying Bolshevik overtones) representing four thousand ASC men presented a list of ten demands to the authorities; one was 'No drafts to Russia'. Despite a mollifying response from their commanding officer, a delegation set off for Whitehall to see the Prime Minister. The GOC London District promised the men demobilisation as soon as possible but could give no guarantees as to Russia. The men defied him and marched on to Downing Street where the CIGS found himself having to elbow his way through the throng of soldiers to get to the door of No. 10. General Sir William Robertson, Commander-in-Chief Home Forces, agreed to see a deputation. Finally, it was conceded that no one over forty-one or who had served overseas would be sent on a draft.[18]

Churchill's published account of the episode hardly conveys the seriousness of the disturbances and records that the only serious rioting was in Luton, where the town hall was burnt down by the mob; but this occured six months later and was a protest by ex-servicemen over pensions.[19] A letter he wrote to Lloyd George later in 1919 candidly admitted that 'the army was in a state of general incipient mutiny in January and February of this year'. A memorandum from the Lord Chancellor, a copy of which reposes in Churchill's own files, recalled the situation equally soberly. After noting 'the very grave dissatisfaction' which existed throughout the army, the Lord Chancellor went on to give some details. 'In a single week breaches of discipline of a serious character were reported from fifteen or twenty different places.' He noted that the Calais mutiny was 'the most grave case which occurred. But in these weeks there were many which approached it in seriousness, and there is no doubt that a psychological tremor passed over our splendid army which could not but be a cause of very profound anxiety.'[20] It is against this background of the intense dissatisfaction of troops on home ground that one must imagine the state of mind of those who were already fighting in Russia or journeying north to join them, as the demobilisation began.

The new Secretary of State moved swiftly to remove the principal cause of the grievances: the grossly unfair system for getting the volunteers and conscripts out of uniform. With the aid of Wilson, Haig and others, Churchill quickly devised a scheme to release those who had joined prior to 1916 or were over forty or who had two wound stripes, whilst retaining those who had been conscripted later, so as to furnish the Armies of Occupation. In the category 'Armies of Occupation', the 'Detachment of the Far North and of Siberia' was somewhat incongrously placed. Unlike the genuine Armies of Occupation, these men in Russia were not sent there to impose 'the just terms which the Allies demand' or 'to make sure we are not tricked of what we have rightfully won', as Churchill's explanatory note to the army put it. As he described the plan in a note to the Prime Minister, 'Briefly the scheme consists in releasing two men out of three and paying the third man double to finish the job'. At the same time he introduced plans for a new all-volunteer Regular Army. Demobilisation progressed as quickly as the trains could carry the men, with priority in subsequent phases being given to those who had been wounded. By this rapid reversal of policy, much of the sting was taken out of the government's introduction of the novel decision of compelling a million men to serve abroad in time of peace, albeit mainly in the territory of their former enemy and with much better pay. But it hardly served to explain the detachments in the land of their former ally, Russia. The Prime Minister and the Chancellor of the Exchequer initially opposed the scheme on the grounds of its great cost, and some reductions were negotiated, but Churchill managed to keep ten divisions on the Rhine with three more available in France and Flanders – as well as the men in Russia, who did not feature largely in the discussions. He arranged a special press conference to announce the scheme, which succeeded in gaining the support of the newspapers. By a private and secret appeal to Lord Northcliffe, he had already achieved the immediate backing of the man who controlled the bulk of the London press. The scheme was a considerable personal triumph for the new Secretary of State; but not all aspects of this early example of news management entirely convinced his old friend but now political opponent, Max Aitken, newly ennobled as Lord Beaverbrook, whose newspapers were already leading the way on the issue of troops for Russia.

Beaverbrook's campaign against the Russian entanglement began as early as 3 January 1919 with a Daily Express banner headline 'ARE WE TO BE COMMITTED TO A WAR WITH RUSSIA?' and the first of a series of leaders warning the public of the government's possible plans to commit the country 'without a word said to another gigantic campaign'. A second headline, 'WITHDRAW FROM RUSSIA', appeared the following day. Soon after Churchill had taken up his War Office post, Beaverbrook called at his Whitehall office to warn the new Secretary of State that the offensive against the Bolsheviks on Russia's own territory was beginning to anger the public, who, after four years of war, longed only for peace. The press was starting to be very critical, he told him. What was Churchill's view? At this questioning of Allied policy Churchill exploded with rage, Beaverbrook later recorded. 'As for the Press, he thundered, it must be squared; if he couldn't square it, he must squash it.' This riposte in turn incensed Beaverbrook and a *froideur* descended on the relations between the two men. Though accustomed to dining together frequently, they did not meet again for many months as Churchill's anti-Bolshevik campaign gathered pace and Beaverbrook's opposition to it grew more strident.

To The Workers of the Entente.

A protest against the Russian blockade and support of the Counter-Revolution.

Workers of the Allied countries!

The workers and peasants of Russia, the first to free themselves from the yoke of capitalism, call to you to be on your guard and not to desist from bringing pressure to bear on your government to prevent them from throttling the revolution in Russia.

You are being deceived when you are told that your government has given up the intention of intervening in Russian affairs and crushing the liberty of the Russian workers. On the contrary. they are preparing a new attack, and continue to gather all their strength to enslave us.

More than a year has passed since the Allied troops entered our territory to crush the Russian revolution and turn Russia into a slave colony of the great capitalist countries. Japanese and English troops invaded Vladivostoc at the beginning of April last year, and soon after the English and French troops refused to leave Murmansk. A new expedition was sent to their aid which at once began the march into Russia. Allied troops occupied Archangel and from there attempted to pierce into the very heart of Russia. The Tchekho-Slovak counter-revolutionary rebels were declared to be Allied troops under the protection of the Entente, and Allied hordes hastened to their aid through Siberia. Insurrections, supported by Allied money, Allied officers and white guards broke out, and Allied agents prepared plots against the Soviet Authority.

Your leaders explained to you that all this was necessary for the fight with Germany on the east, who was threatening the existence of France. Nevertheless, your troops never made any attack in Russia against the Germans, for which they were supposed to have been sent here. On the contrary, they became Germany's ally even when the us war was still proceeding between your governments and that of the Central Powers. Although the Allies did not fight together with Germany they, however both fought against their common enemy,— against the revolution of the Russian people. The invasion of Allied troops prevented the Russian revolution from defending itself against the invasion of German troops, and the attack of

Bolshevik propaganda leaflet.

6

General Denikin

As the people of Britain savoured their first peaceful Christmas for five years, the Imperial War Cabinet was trying to develop its policy on Russia ready for the Paris Peace Conference. In particular they had to decide how to respond to the peace feelers being put out by the Bolshevik government in Moscow. Maxim Litvinov, the chubby Anglophile only recently released from a British jail and now Soviet Deputy Commissar for Foreign Affairs, was making proposals in Stockholm through the agency, it was believed, of the British journalist Arthur Ransome. Churchill had been invited to join in the Cabinet deliberations, although this was several weeks before he took over at the War Office. The discussions rapidly exposed the cavernous divide between the views of Lloyd George and those of his fellow Liberal, Churchill, even before the latter was in his new position. At the first meeting which he attended, on 23 December, Churchill made his position very clear. He opposed the current intervention by 'small contingents' and said that the Russians should either be allowed 'to murder each other without let or hindrance', or else, and this was his clear preference, the Allies should intervene 'thoroughly, with large forces, abundantly supplied with mechanical devices'. This was a policy which he was to advocate with vigour and from which he scarcely wavered throughout the discussions of the following weeks in London and Paris. Lloyd George's view, however, was that intervention was opposed by the people at large and that soldiers would not volunteer to serve against the Bolsheviks. Nor were the Russian people themselves any more likely to do so. General Poole at Archangel had hoped to raise an army of a million men, but so far Ironside had managed to recruit only three thousand – and half-hearted ones at that. Lockhart had reported that the workers were loyal to the Bolsheviks and that the peasants could not be relied upon to oppose them. People complained that the Bolsheviks were waging war by propaganda against Britain, he noted, yet it was Britain that had troops on Russian territory, men who, he added with sarcastic understatement, 'not infrequently shot Bolsheviks'. The Dominion Prime Ministers supported Lloyd George, as did Bonar Law, his Unionist Deputy, and Balfour, the Foreign Secretary, who generally followed his master's line. Aligned with Churchill in support of the Whites was his predecessor at the War Office, Lord Milner. The rest of the Cabinet were largely silent in this first debate, which concluded with the decision that unofficial discussions with

Moscow might begin. The proposal, however, was abortive. The attempt by the Foreign Office to clear it with the Allies drew support from President Wilson but flat rejection from the French, whose Foreign Minister Pichon found the idea 'inopportune and dangerous'.[1]

The War Cabinet revisited the Russian problem on 30 and 31 December; but its deliberations were notable less for the emergence of any new arguments than for the clear collision of views between Lloyd George and Churchill. The War Minister again argued for collective action by large contingents from all the Allied powers; or, if the US proved unwilling, by the British Empire, France, Italy and Japan. He was not opposed to negotiation, but this had to be from strength. If the various Russian parties would not agree to hold free elections, the Allies should use force to set up a democratic government in Russia. Churchill made his case with considerable passion, but at no point did he explain how the forces to execute his policy might be provided. The Prime Minister agreed with Churchill solely on the urgency of reaching a decision about Russia: a further few weeks of drift could leave the isolated detachments on Russian soil dangerously exposed. Although bothered by the contradictory information being supplied by Britain's representatives, Lloyd George remained opposed to intervention. Even the vast armies of Austria and Germany had become stuck in the Russian morass, he noted. The Bolsheviks had already raised their forces to 300,000, were increasingly well organised and might have a million in the field by March. Any intervention to unseat them would require huge numbers of troops. The Dominions would not supply them and Britain could not. Even with conscription he doubted if the troops would go. Besides, he argued, an attempt to emancipate Russia from Bolshevism by force of arms would end in disaster. He cited the example of the French Revolution, where equal horrors to those charged to the Bolsheviks had taken place; British intervention had served only to enable Danton to rally the people and reinforce the Terror. 'The one thing to spread Bolshevism was to attempt to suppress it', he declared.

Lloyd George took up a suggestion made earlier by the Canadian Premier, Sir Robert Borden, that all the warring Russian factions should be invited to Paris, not as full participants but 'with a view to composing their differences'. As at the previous meeting, Churchill provided the only real arguments against the Prime Minister's support for this view, though at this final discussion Lord Robert Cecil emphasised Britain's moral obligation to continue supporting the White groups already receiving aid. The War Cabinet supported Lloyd George's position and endorsed his peace proposal, but left in place the contradictory policy of providing the Whites with war *matériel* and leaving in place the British troops supporting them.[2] At the 10 January War Cabinet, General Wilson sat between Lord Milner and Churchill, the old and the new War Ministers, He brought up the need for a decision about Russia, 'whether at Murmansk or in Siberia or in Poland or Ukraine or Caucasus. Absolutely *no* policy'. There was no further advance in deciding on a Russian policy before the discussions moved to Paris.

When the national delegates to the Peace Conference finally assembled on 16 January 1919 in the splendour of the Salle d'Horloge in the Quai d'Orsay, Russia was the most significant absentee. Clemenceau believed it was not entitled to attend, having betrayed the Allies by coming to terms with the enemy, leaving France to the mercy of the Germans. But the truth was that Russia, at enormous cost, had saved France from the full might of the German army on several occasions, and the 1917 Treaty of Brest-Litovsk forced upon Russia by Germany had now been torn up. Nor was there much truth in Pinchon's claim that 'every shade of opinion' in Russia was already represented in the bizarre collection of anti-Bolsheviks now gathered in Paris and which called itself the 'Russian Political Conference'. Lord George retorted that the conference 'represented every opinion except the prevalent opinion in Russia'. He made his case for the proposed all-Russian conference to 'try to find a way to bring some order out of chaos'. President Wilson concurred with Lloyd George's forceful arguments, but the French, followed faithfully by the Italians, flatly refused to invite the contending Russian governments to Paris. If the Allies had to meet the Bolsheviks, it had better be somewhere else, where the wholesale corruption of French society would not be risked by their presence. Ultimately the Allies agreed that the competing Russian governments should be invited to meet the Allied delegation on Prinkipo, the largest of the Princes Islands in the Sea of Marmara, south of Constantinople. President Wilson drafted the invitation in a communication filled with disclaimers about the intentions of the Allies which were typical of the double-talk in many Allied declarations of the time. 'It was not their [the Allies'] wish or purpose to favour or assist any one of those organised groups now contending for the leadership and guidance of Russia as against the others', the President primly declared, quite ignoring what was going on at Archangel and Murmansk, or the aid even then on its way to Kolchak and Denikin. The invitation itself was clear enough. Every regime attempting to exercise authority or control anywhere in the erstwhile Russian Empire was invited to send up to three representatives to Prinkipo. The main condition for the conference was a 'truce of arms' amongst the countries invited. The invitation was issued by wireless, so as not to compromise the senders by direct communication with any particular regime, and required the representatives to be 'at the place appointed by the 15th February 1919'.

The reply broadcast by the Bolshevik Commissar for Foreign Affairs, Chicherin, was long, sarcastic and challenging, but at the same time conciliatory. Since it was only the support of the Allies that was keeping the Whites in the field, it was precisely with them that the Bolsheviks wished to negotiate. Chicherin held out the prospect of financial and commercial concessions to the Allies, as well as an end to the anti-Western propaganda campaign, but also wished to discuss the annexation of its territory. Beyond these issues the Soviet government asked only for details of how it was to get to the proposed meeting. In fact the Prinkipo conference was damned from the start by the White Russians' refusal to countenance it. General Yevgenii Miller (now the White Russian Governor General at Archangel) declared it 'morally unacceptable'; Denikin in the Don lands sent a personal protest to Marshal Foch; the White government in Siberia rejected the invitation as soon as it was received. The British parliamentary majority and the Conservative press were also violently opposed, as were the Allied representatives serving with the White forces. General Knox in Siberia, displaying the anti-Semitism that was never entirely absent from the attitudes of the British armed forces at the time, cabled London in exasperation: 'Suddenly the whole of Russia [the White Russians] is informed by wireless that her Allies regard the brave men who are fighting here as on a par with the blood-stained, Jew-led Bolsheviks'. In the War Office, General Wilson was contemptuous not only of the Prinkipo idea but of the basic idealistic premiss of the Wilson-led Peace Conference. He looked forward to a time when 'we shall work our way back to a balance of the Great Powers'. Secretary of State Churchill simply ignored Prinkipo, telling a Russian confidant that he would continue to send supplies to the forces struggling against Bolshevism 'until I receive categorical instructions to cease'.

On 23 November 1918 an Allied naval squadron headed by HMS *Liverpool* and supported by a French cruiser and two Australian destroyers steamed across the Black Sea towards the Kuban Cossack port of Novorossisk. The squadron carried military missions from the French and British governments to General Denikin whose Volunteer Army was based in the Kuban territory. By the following morning Lieutenant Colonel A. P. Blackwood, the head of the British mission, was already ashore and had met the town's military governor – the first formal British contact with the White Russian forces in South Russia. Blackwood's team had been sent at the initiative of General Sir George Milne, commanding the British forces at Salonika, who had been briefed by the Director of Military Operations (DMO) in London on the government's decisions on the Russia question. There was some urgency about Blackwood's visit since the DMO was concerned about competition from the French, despite the fact that General Denikin was operating largely within the agreed British sphere of influence. Milne was shortly to be made commander of the Army of the Black Sea based at Constantinople and no longer subordinate to the French General Franchet d'Esperey. Blackwood bore a letter from Milne to Denikin. His small party came ashore to an ecstatic welcome from the local population, who were delighted that the Allies were apparently at last coming to their aid and firmly believed that they would transform the fortunes of the Volunteer Army and the various Cossack forces keeping up the

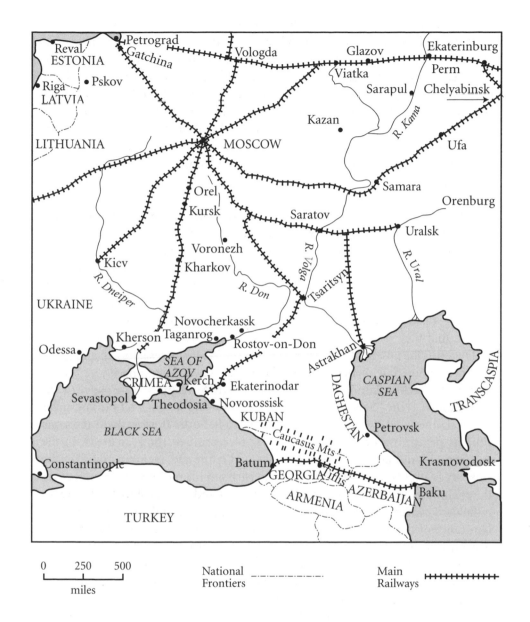

Reval
ESTONIA
Petrograd
Gatchina
Vologda
Glazov
Ekaterinburg
Viatka
Perm
Riga
Pskov
Sarapul
Chelyabinsk
LATVIA
R. Kama
LITHUANIA
Kazan
Ufa
MOSCOW
Orel
Samara
Kursk
Saratov
Orenburg
Voronezh
Uralsk
Kiev
Kharkov
R. Volga
Tsaritsyn
R. Ural
UKRAINE
R. Dneiper
R. Don
Novocherkassk
Kherson
Taganrog
Rostov-on-Don
Astrakhan
Odessa
SEA OF
AZOV
CRIMEA
Kerch
Ekaterinodar
CASPIAN
SEA
TRANSCASPIA
Sevastopol
Theodosia
Novorossisk
DAGHESTAN
Petrovsk
BLACK SEA
KUBAN
Caucasus Mts
Krasnovodosk
Constantinople
Batum
GEORGIA
Tiflis
AZERBAIJAN
Baku
ARMENIA
TURKEY

0   250   500
miles

National
Frontiers
— · — · — · —

Main
Railways
+++++++++++

The Southern Front

struggle against the Bolsheviks. Little time was lost in showing their gratitude to the members of the missions. After a formal civic and military reception at the quayside, a long and wearying lunch of welcome awaited the missions, followed by a military display and then tea with the Kuban Ataman. Apparently they met General Denikin himself only briefly. With admirable forbearance, Blackwood asked to be excused as much official hospitality as possible during his visit. A great deal of it was arranged by the local authorities to exploit the great propaganda value which this earnest of British and French support provided. A few days later the Allied battle-fleet, led by the Commander-in-Chief, Admiral Calthorpe, landed 500 Royal Marines at Sevastopol. The Allies, it appeared, had arrived.[3]

After a joint meeting with Denikin's Chief of Staff, General Romanovsky, the French Mission left on a separate programme and Colonel Blackwood began an intensive round of visits to the heads of all the branches of the Volunteer Army. He also met a representative of General Krasnov, Ataman of the Don Cossacks, and various government figures from the Cossack states, as well as local British residents. The White military leaders were at pains to paint as exaggerated a picture of their military manpower strengths as possible to ensure that they received the maximum aid. Blackwood was given a figure of 1,200,000 as the potential military strengh of the White forces in north and south Russia combined. It seems to have been a particularly beguiling figure for the authorities back in London, where it was shortly to reappear in a paper to the War Cabinet as the likely White strength the following spring.[4] Yet the Volunteer Army claimed that it was not at present able to fight the Bolsheviks at the same time as preserving order and continuing to recruit in the rear areas. In the report on his military needs which Blackwood requested, Denikin asked for the support of twenty-two Allied divisions to garrison his mobilisation areas, cover the main lines of advance to Moscow and Petrograd, and protect the Caucasus oilfields. This outrageously inflated and optimistic request displayed a complete ignorance of the war-weariness in Britain and France, and of the fact that the Allies had no intention of returning the Caucasian 'republics' to the control of the 'Great Russia, One and Indivisible' for which Denikin declared he was fighting. Blackwood made it very clear to his hosts that his mission 'held out no promise of troops'; the use of foreign troops being, in any event, 'highly undesirable'. By 6 December, after a hectic round of visits and hospitality, Blackwood and his party were back in Constantinople, his report was written and accompanied by Denikin's separate, extravagant request for assistance. By 3 January he was back in England at the War Office. In the circumstances it had been a remarkably brisk yet searching visit and its result clearly impressed the CIGS, whose covering note to Blackwood's report hailed it as 'very valuable' and declared that 'the action called for by the situation is admirably summed up in the conclusion to Colonel

Blackwood's report'. 275 copies of it were distributed. Wilson's note, confirming 'the sturdy nature of the efforts of the Volunteer Army and the Cossacks', clearly indicated that their case for assistance which Blackwood reported was to receive very sympathetic treatment.[5]

Blackwood, who declared that the Volunteer Army was the only body capable of coping with the situation in the south, in his report made twelve recommendations, all of which his mission regarded as 'indispensable'. The first, and perhaps the most important, concerned the need for political representation by the Allies in the region. 'The Volunteer Army, the Kuban Cossacks, the Don Cossacks, the Ukraine and the Crimea are all striving towards a common goal, viz., the extermination of Bolshevism', argued Blackwood, but they were 'held apart by minor differences of policy chiefly due to the personal ambitions of certain individuals'. In truth much more than mere ambition held them apart, but Blackwood's recommendation for British political representation at the highest level to bring about their cooperation was, nevertheless, most important, as were his ideas for financial, commercial and industrial advice. Britain was to act on all this much too late in the day. Even the cooperation between the Allies themselves in south Russia, which Blackwood recommended, was never fully achieved. The authorities, however, did accept four of his more practicable military proposals. These called for the vesting of Denikin with the supreme command of all Russian forces in south Russia and the establishment of a permanent Military Mission with his forces, together with a special Railway Mission to look after the technical requirements of the all-important communications in the region. Blackwood also recommended the immediate despatch of war material and other necessities for the armies of south Russia, based on a notional force of 100,000 men. This report thus triggered the massive material support which Britain was to provide over the following months. The pity is that its political, financial and economic recommendations were ignored until too late.

Blackwood's was the first of three British Military Missions of Enquiry which visited the White forces in south Russia in the space of a few weeks shortly after the Armistice. The second was an Allied Naval Mission aboard the French destroyer *Briscon* and the Australian destroyer HMAS *Swan*. Commander Arthur Bond RAN, the *Swan*'s captain, led the British Mission. Bond's principal aim was to report on the state of the harbours at the ports of Mariupol and Taganrog in the sea of Azov north of the Crimea, but his terms of reference included investigation of 'the surrounding countryside' and his chief, Admiral Calthorpe, appears to have agreed to a more extensive programme ashore in the Don heartland, which Blackwood had not visited. The Don authorities seized the opportunity to exploit Bond's visit to the maximum. This was the fiefdom of General Peter Krasnov, the Don Ataman, who had previously looked to Germany for support in his struggle for independence from the Bolsheviks and whose relations with Denikin were competitive to say the least. Bond's visit presented a great opportunity for Krasnov to realign himself with the Allies and assert his independence from Denikin. Bond was accompanied throughout by a Russian, Admiral Kononov, ostensibly as interpreter, but really present 'to attain the result that the importance of the Don country should not be overlooked by the Allies'. Like their predecessors, the two destroyers received a rapturous welcome wherever they went, starting at the small port of Kerch in the Crimea, after which they proceeded to those ports whose harbours were their main concern.

The mission then travelled by train to Novocherkassk, the capital of the Don republic, where they met General Krasnov himself and endured a gruelling programme of banquets and visits which extended as far as the fighting front itself. The tour seemed to have been carefully orchestrated to emphasise the strength, importance and independence of the Don forces. The entire garrison of the Don Cossack regiment lined the streets of Novocherkassk for the mission's arrival, after which Bond's party attended mass in the cathedral with the local hierarchy and in the evening a long official dinner with speeches from the local notables about their epic struggle for the regeneration of Russia. Commander Bond gave as diplomatic a response as he could muster. 'It was clearly stated by us', his report explained, 'that we had come to guarantee nothing, but to gather information only, which it is even hoped, would be of use in deciding what means of help may be given to Russia.' The Cossacks nevertheless regarded the whole visit as an indication of intent and Bond had politely to restate his position the following day at a second banquet given by the Don Krug, the territory's national assembly. This caveat was repeated wherever they went.[6]

There followed a journey by train and motor car to the front itself, where the local commander outrageously claimed that a force of 60,000 Cossacks was holding at bay a force of 720,000 Bolsheviks. A local Red breakthrough forced a hasty retirement by the visitors; but not before Bond had it explained to him that the Cossacks depended for field guns and ammunition entirely on what they could capture in their cavalry charges. Certainly, when Bond returned south via Taganrog, he found that the big armament factory there had only 1200 of its original 10,000 workman, since the Bolsheviks held the main munitions factory at Tul, which had once supplied the explosive for its shells and percussion caps. Bond then journeyed south to Ekaterinodar, the Kuban Cossack capital, to make his report, bearing a letter from Krasnov detailing his requirements.

The third and largest of the missions, and the first to be exclusively British, resulted from the concern of the DMO in London at the growing French influence on Denikin. To counter this a 'big gun' was required. 'I regard it as of importance', the CIGS wrote, 'that a senior officer with knowledge of the Russians, who is personally known to Denikin, should be sent to General Denikin at the earliest opportunity to obtain authentic details of the situation.' The officer chosen, despite his decidedly chequered performance in North Russia and removal from the Archangel command at American insistence, was Major General Frederick Poole. Poole had already written a paper for the CIGS entitled, 'Proposals for Mission to South Russia', suffused with his usual optimism, which recommended the seizure of the Russian Black Sea fleet and all the Black Sea ports. This would result, he believed, in a general outburst of feeling in favour of the Allies, wholesale enlistment in the ranks of the Whites and the ultimate downfall of the 'forces of anarchy', the Bolsheviks. He had earlier forecast something similar for the Archangel command, but it had yet to materialise.[7] Various delays meant that Poole did not reach Constantinople until 2 December. General Milne, under whose overall authority he was operating, was away in Salonika when Poole arrived. He did, however, have discussions with Milne's senior staff. Poole had a brief meeting with Colonel Blackwood, who had just completed his own mission and received a copy of his report. He then moved on to Sevastopol, Novorossisk and Ekaterinodar. It was at the Kuban capital that he met and was briefed by Commander Bond and was handed the letter from Krasnov. Poole was thus in possession of the general conclusions of the earlier missions, particularly concerning Ataman Krasnov's ambitions, as he began to undertake his own.

Poole's terms of reference made very clear the cautious approach he was to adopt: 'to enable the War Cabinet to form an opinion as to the extent of support, if any, which it would be necessary or advisable to extend to General Denikin's or similar movements in the North Caucasus and Don Territories'. He was warned to 'be careful not to extend any promises of assistance of any kind'.[8] On their first evening in Ekaterinodar, Poole and his team were treated to a banquet which lasted, according to Major Clayton, one of his staff, until 6 a.m. In reply to Denikin's speech of welcome, Poole immediately entered treacherous diplomatic waters. 'We share with you', this envoy of the government declared, 'the same desire and have the same aim – to recreate United Russia.' This was on the very day that the War Office was advising Salonika of Britain's policy of seeing in the Caucasus strong, independent states in Georgia, Daghestan and Russian Azerbaijan. 'I am sent by my country', Denikin reported Poole as declaring, 'to see what we can do for you. We shall be only too ready to assist you.'[9] At no stage did Poole make it clear that his mission was simply one of enquiry and therefore of a temporary nature. Among the several false impressions left with General Denikin was that Poole was the permanent military representative attached to the Russian's headquarters to organise the distribution of assistance which Britain was certain to provide. Poole also appears not to have invoked the Paris Convention to prevent French aid from reaching the Whites in the British zone of influence and seems not to have appreciated the importance of this zonal division. Denikin claims not to have been informed of it until May 1919.[10] Some measure of Poole's imperious approach to the command problems of the Whites can be seen in an exchange with him reported by Denikin.

> *Poole:*   'Do you consider it necessary in the interests of the cause that we get rid of Krasnov?'
>
> *Denikin:* 'No, I wish you to use your influence in changing his attitude to the Volunteer Army.'
>
> *Poole:*   'Good, then we shall talk.'[11]

Poole conducted his enquiry less by observing the situation, taking views and then compiling his report than by attempting to have action taken on events in the region as they were occurring. Throughout his tour he directed a fusillade of messages at the War Office and General Milne's headquarters, a practice which appeared to confirm the impression that he intended to remain permanently in the region, giving the War Office authorities his opinions and much fragmentary information, at times in several separate telegrams a day, rather than by conducting his enquiry and then writing up his recommendations.[12] General Milne began to get quite testy at this freewheeling subordinate who was already sending requests for assistance from Milne's local resources. By 10 January he was querying Poole's role with the War Office: 'Please inform me to what extent General Poole's Mission is under my orders and what his position generally is.' The War Office itself was becoming concerned at Poole's poor grasp of the government's policy for the Caucasus and instructed General Milne to make it 'quite clear to General Poole and General Denikin that they are not to interfere with the Trans-Caucasian republics under British protection'.[13]

Poole visited Denikin's front line and on the basis of his inspection quantified the request already made for tanks and aeroplanes (two squadrons and forty-six respectively) and finally visited the Don region. Here he was careful to visit the government first and made it clear that unity of command under Denikin was a precondition for any help to the Don country. The round of welcoming banquets and displays for Poole's benefit continued after his meeting with the Don commander, General Krasnov, who laid on 'a tremendous orgy for him, with plenty of gypsies, which must have impressed Poole, whose weakness for these girls was well known'.[14] The following day he was shown Krasnov's best cavalry regiments and formed an excellent impression of the Don Cossack Army, which he declared to be of a 'very much higher standard than anything else I have seen in Russia'. MI6 agents were also reporting separately on the situation in south Russia and were surprised at this optimistic evaluation by Poole. One wrote, 'I gather that the latter's well-known weakness for female society has much to do with his point of view'.[15] Nevertheless, when Krasnov repeated his request for aid, Poole made it clear that Allied help, from which he did not exclude the despatch of British troops, depended on unity of command under Denikin. Poole kept up his pressure on the Ataman until an agreement was formalised and proclaimed on 26 December. This was Poole's single significant achievement during his extended visit. Denikin confirmed that unity of command was the result of 'pressure brought to bear on Ataman Krasnov by the Allied Missions, particularly by General Poole'.[16]

The War Office, however, was becoming increasingly concerned at the length of Poole's stay, the absence of a report from him and the extravagant promises he seemed to be making of support by British troops. He had already recommended the despatch of two brigades and two battalions. He had to be specifically warned off to 'discourage any hopes for assistance in despatching troops'. By 9 January even Poole's keenest supporter, the DMO, was becoming concerned at his extended sojourn. 'We are anxious that you should return as soon as possible to give your personal report unless you have much further information to collect, in which case you should telegraph your intentions', he wrote.[17] It was, however, to be a further thirteen days before Poole began his journey back to London. It seems that he was involved in something other than official military business in south Russia. On the day the DMO despatched his signal some local Russian noblemen and senior officers in Ekaterinodar, the Kuban capital, drew up the legal documents establishing a joint stock company for the purposes of exploiting 'the natural resources of the north-eastern shores of the Caspian Sea'. They gave the right to a free issue of the company's shares to the value of £150,000 to 'Major General Feodor Albertovich Poole of the English Service'.[18] Quite what part the negotiation of this gift may have played in the length of Poole's stay, or in his recommendations for the despatch of British troops to the region, must remain a matter of speculation.

Poole's report, which was not formally issued until 14 February, was long and descriptive and did not include a separate section of recommendations which he had earlier sent piecemeal. It ran to some fifty pages, mostly describing the Volunteer Army and Cossack organisations and their requirements. He still insisted on recommending the despatch of troops, which he declared to be 'essential to restore the morale of the Cossacks and peasantry', who believed that 'material assistance in guns, tanks, armoured cars and aeroplanes alone is not sufficient'. He recommended the despatch of an infantry brigade and an artillery brigade to the Kuban, and two battalions and two batteries to the Don. With this aid, he declared, the Bolshevik organisation, 'based as it is on compulsion, must speedily crumple up'.[19] Aside from the important agreement which subordinated Krasnov to Denikin, Poole's mission achieved very little that was positive. Blackwood's recommendations were already being implemented by the time the general reported. The appointment of a permanent Military Mission to Denikin (Denmis) had already been announced on 31 January and its head, Lieutenant

General Sir Charles Briggs, arrived at Ekaterinodar on the day Poole's report was finally published.

In London the War Cabinet again discussed Russia, with Churchill arguing for a decision: either to get the troops out altogether or else, always his preferred alternative, to send much larger forces against the Bolsheviks. The CIGS was ordered to produce a paper on the choices available: evacuation, full intervention, or the recognition of all the anti-Bolshevik forces and full support for them. Churchill recommended the third course. Again Lloyd George demurred, demanding to know the costs of the options. Churchill pressed for a decision, since it was known that President Wilson was due to return from Paris to the United States the following day. Prinkipo remained the Prime Minister's favoured solution, though it seemed to be dead in the water if the Whites would not attend. The clarity of Cabinet thinking was not helped by the presence of General Poole, newly returned after his lengthy stay with the White forces in south Russia, whom the CIGS had brought to the meeting. Poole's advice to the Cabinet contradicted all that he had recommended so far. Contrary to what his report was to advise, he now declared that there was nothing the Russians would like better than to sit down and watch the British fight for them. It would be sufficient for Britain to send tanks and aeroplanes and the crews to man them.[20] Poole's report, arguing for the despatch of troops to south Russia, was published the following day. Perhaps unsurprisingly, the Cabinet meeting again ended in a fudge. Lloyd George would not accept the larger commitment to intervention which Churchill wanted, but could not bring himself to agree the complete evacuation of all imperial troops which the Dominion premiers preferred. He still had hopes of the Prinkipo option. Whatever was to happen about Prinkipo, or whatever process might succeed it, needed President Wilson's endorsement. In the end the Prime Minister took the surprising decision to send Churchill post-haste to Paris to settle the Prinkipo matter for good with the US President and his Allied colleagues at the Peace Conference.

It is not easy to account for this extraordinary move. It was clearly difficult for Lloyd George to leave London when industrial troubles were coming to a head and a general strike was threatened. Yet he was well aware that Churchill's views were diametrically opposite to his own, and he knew him well enough to appreciate that he would never be satisfied with the role of simply taking to Paris views which he found distasteful. Perhaps he believed that to leave the decisions in Paris to the indecisive Balfour, now *de facto* head of the British Mission, would have been a worse alternative. Churchill's War Office was certainly the department likely to be most immediately affected by any decisions on Russia. Perhaps he believed that Churchill would accept the rejection of his intervention schemes more readily from the US President than from his own political chief.

Whatever the reason, the Prime Minister handed a very loose rein to his old colleague. The absence of clear instructions enabled the Secretary for War to leave for Paris, accompanied by the CIGS, with clear ideas of his own for the settlement of the Russian problem.

Churchill arrived in Paris in the nick of time: President Wilson was preparing to leave the specially convened Russian session of the conference to take his train to Cherbourg for the voyage back to the United States. Answering Churchill's enquiry about the prospects for Prinkipo, the President declared that he believed Allied troops were doing no good whatsoever in Russia and should all be withdrawn. If Prinkipo could not be held, he favoured informal contacts with Moscow to get a true picture of conditions there. Churchill disagreed. Allied withdrawal would mean the destruction of all anti-Bolshevik armies in Russia. He proposed instead that the Allies should send 'volunteers, technical experts, arms, munitions, tanks, aeroplanes'. The President remained unconvinced: volunteers would be hard to find and sending supplies 'would certainly be assisting reactionaries' in some areas. The President was tired and eager to catch his train. He left, remarking only that the others knew where he stood, but stating (and this was quite uncharacteristic) he would abide by any decision they might reach. Churchill took the remark to mean support for any joint measures which he might persuade the Allies to take.[21]

The following day the French outlined an extravagant, optimistic and quite unrealistic proposal for the encirclement and destruction of Bolshevism – a multinational operation in which the French would have the starring role. After this Churchill presented his plan, a two-pronged scheme that it would not be too dangerous to summarise as being designed to scotch Prinkipo once and for all and replace it with preparations for the massing of all available resources for a combined military effort for the destruction of Bolshevism. As to Prinkipo, his proposal, which Balfour had approved, was to address a demand not to all the Russian factions, as had the original plan, but merely to the Bolsheviks. It called for a cease-fire and a five-mile withdrawal on all fronts within ten days. If the Bosheviks complied, the White forces would subsequently be required to do the same, whereupon the Prinkipo discussions could go ahead. If the Bolsheviks refused, Prinkipo would be deemed to have failed. It is plain that Moscow would never have agreed to such a one-sided arrangement and equally surprising that Lloyd George, once the terms were telegraphed to him, should have agreed the proposal. The plan's only merit was its clear abandonment of Britain's spurious role of 'honest broker' in a conflict in which it was an active participant. The second prong of Churchill's scheme was for the setting up of suitable machinery 'to consider the possibilities of joint military action by the Associated Powers acting in conjunction with the independent border States and pro-Ally Governments in Russia'.[22] This plan, on which the British Military

Delegation had already undertaken some preliminary work, was nothing less than the first step in the creation of a staff to coordinate Poland, the Baltic States, Finland and the Allies in a combined effort to destroy the Bolshevik regime.

Churchill reported his plans to the Prime Minister in England. So also did Philip Kerr, Lloyd George's assistant at the Peace Conference. He warned the Prime Minister that the following day the Conference was likely to decide that the Prinkipo proposal had lapsed, which would leave the delegates confronting Churchill's plan for war against the Bolsheviks with 'allied volunteers, tanks, gas, Czech, Polish and Finnish conscripts and the pro-Ally Russian armies', which he felt would be a 'fundamental and collossal mistake'.[23] Lloyd George wrote back to Churchill in some alarm at his 'planning war against the Bolsheviks'. 'The Cabinet', he emphasised, 'have never authorised such a proposal.' He warned him against committing the country to a 'purely mad enterprise out of hatred of Bolshevik principles' and urged him to consider the domestic consequences. 'Were it known that you had gone over to Paris to prepare a plan of war against the Bolsheviks, it would do more to incense organised labour than anything I can think of.' Churchill was asked to show the telegram to the Foreign Secretary, Balfour; Philip Kerr, who also received a copy, was asked to show his to the US representative, Colonel House – a sure sign of declining trust between the Prime Minister and his Secretary of State. The CIGS called it 'a low down trick' about which 'Winston was very angry'.[24]

The crucial meeting of the Peace Conference took place the following afternoon. Some of its deliberations were so acrimonious that it was decided not to produce minutes. Churchill's ultimatum to the Bolsheviks was never sent and Prinkipo met its expected death. His proposal for the military commisssion to plan joint action against Russia drew bad-tempered exchanges between the delegates. House opposed Churchill's proposal and Balfour, now stiffened by the sight of Lloyd George's views, backed the American. 'Although Churchill had received his instructions from Lloyd George', House's diary noted, 'he was persistent in pursuing his plan for a military committee to examine the question as to how Russia could best be invaded in the event it was necessary to do so.' This opposition to Churchill's plan provoked an outburst from Clemenceau for which he was forced to apologise. Finally it was agreed that the individual nations would consult separately with their military advisers about possible action. But such routine action did not require the imprimatur of the Peace Conference. Churchill's plan was dead. 'I think this is the greatest depth of impotence I have ever seen the Frocks fall to', wrote Wilson in his diary. British policy towards Russia was no further forward than the early decisions taken before the end of the previous year.

These exchanges did not give the CIGS the answer to the other urgent question he had long been asking: what to do about the British troops already on Russian soil. If these were to stay on in North Russia, they needed reinforcing. If no reinforcements were to be sent they would have to consolidate their positions by reducing the area under their control. General Ironside at Archangel was already endeavouring to increase his force by recruiting more local Russians, but he needed reinforcements from home, technical and support troops as well as infantry. At Murmansk, General Maynard needed railway specialists to maintain the line running south on which his advanced detachments depended for all their supplies, whilst engineers were urgently required to build proper wooden housing for the troops. The one concession Churchill did manage to wring from the Prime Minister was his agreement to the despatch of these support and specialist troops. His visit to the Peace Conference had not, however, strengthened the relations between the two men. Churchill regarded Lloyd George's actions in having his letter of criticism shown to House as a serious betrayal of trust; Lloyd George considered that Churchill had failed to follow his instructions. A gulf between them was developing.

General Poole's legacy in south Russia was one of disappointed expectations among the Whites and the creation of a 'relationship of insincerity' with Denikin who had been led to expect speedy assistance and British troops.[25] 'Time went on', the Russian leader wrote, 'All the fine speeches had been made, and still help was not forthcoming.' He recalled that there was a 'loss of faith in the Allies, of whose speedy arrival Krasnov had so often and incautiously spoken to the wavering front'.[26] Months later Sir Henry Wilson was writing to General Briggs, 'That Denikin has been led to expect assistance in the shape of Allied troops is greatly to be regretted, as public opinion is absolutely opposed to such a measure in this country. There are, too, other grave objections to this course.'

After Poole's indiscretions, General Wilson had written to General Milne at Costantinople: 'It seems very important that we should now have a Senior Officer of experience and force of character with General Denikin as permanent liaison officer.' He suggested General Briggs. Milne demurred, arguing that 'to supervise the distribution of stores is not in his line'. On the other hand, 'if you wish to send a fighting soldier to infuse spirit into Denikin's Army and run his campaign, by all means send Briggs'. Milne suggested other candidates, but Briggs was chosen.[27] Churchill later wrote of Briggs as being 'a competent cavalryman'; in fact he was a distinguished one, having commanded the 1st Cavalry Brigade at the start of the war and, most recently, the 16th Army Corps at Salonika, whence he was summoned, at fairly short notice, to take up his new appointment. He may have known nothing about stores, but he quickly offered the post of ADOS, effectively chief stores officer, in the mission headquarters, to one of his staff, Lieutenant Colonel (substantive lieutenant, temporary captain, local lieutenant colonel) De Wolff, telling him that he could keep his rank. De Wolff was soon sent down from Ekaterinodar to be Base Commandant at Novorossisk where the move of the supplies could best be supervised and controlled.[28] Other early members for Briggs's Mission were drawn from troops already in the general theatre.

The difficulty was that Briggs had not wanted the job with Denikin, spoke no Russian and knew little of the complications of the Russian political scene. He was to find Denikin similarly, if perhaps more understandably, ignorant of the military diplomacy of Britain and France. When Briggs arrived at the Kuban capital he was received in an atmosphere of resentment and disappointment which it took him some time to lighten. Since the visits of the early British missions the Whites had suffered a succession of reverses at the hands of the Bolsheviks, and both the Volunteer Army and the Don Cossacks had been hit by a severe outbreak of typhus. Their line had been pushed back to the Donets basin and part of the Don territory. Moreover, Denikin was now being hampered by an obstructionist Rada in the Kuban, a critical financial situation, and manifold problems with the intractable local railway authorities on whom his operational flexibility depended. There was much for General Briggs to do.

At their first meeting Denikin listened with some impatience as Briggs urged the Russian general to stop fighting the Georgians and turn his attention to the Bolsheviks, for which struggle Britain was to provide him with arms and equipment for 250,000 men, if only the Russians would sink their political differences and face the main enemy. If there was any meeting of minds between the two generals at this stage, it was simply the mutual acknowledgement of direct soldiers talking bluntly to each other. The exchange gave Denikin the opportunity to express some of the bile which had built up within him during the three months since the Armistice when no Allied help had arrived, but only a succession of missions bearing, in his view, false promises. 'You may implicitly rely on the aid of Great Britain and free France', one of the French representatives had assured him, 'We are with you! We are for you!'[29] Yet at Tiflis, Denikin declared, there had been enough war material for a whole army, which the British had handed over to the Georgians, while a similar amount at Odessa had been seized by the French. In Roumania there had been enough Russian material for three armies, but the Roumanians had seized it. Meanwhile Denikin had to beg assistance from England. He was also baffled by the notion of French and British 'spheres of influence' in his country and wanted to know what the British were doing in the Caucasus. Who had invited them there? Denikin believed firmly in 'one united Russia' and could not understand Britain's policy of supporting the independence of some of the putative border state regimes. He needed to recruit in those areas. He would rather fight on for his ideals with his own resources than obey British orders merely to get their supplies. 'I felt more like a prisoner at the bar than head of a Mission', Briggs confessed at the end of this recitation. He left his first meeting with the Russian commander with a developing respect for him. 'I came to the conclusion that Denikin was a strong, clear-headed and determined man who would stand no nonsense from anybody.' It was a respect which Denikin came in time to reciprocate.[30]

Several accounts of General Briggs's first arrival at Novorossisk follow Denikin's written recollections in stating that he was accompanied by eleven British transports bearing supplies.[31] Alas this is not so; Denikin's memory was at fault. There were ultimately sixteen shipments of supplies during the four months Briggs spent as head of the British Military Mission, delivering a total of 34,000 tons of supplies; but the first, aboard SS *Twickenham*, did not begin to discharge its cargo at the Kuban port until 10 March, almost a month after Briggs's arrival, and did not complete it until 15 April. It brought almost 5500 tons of guns, ammunition and much needed supplies.[32] Not that Briggs was in the least tardy in recording the plight of the Volunteer Army and its desperate need for speedy aid. He reported the appalling medical situation with typhus rampant, and the makeshift hospitals at Ekaterinodar lacking drugs, linen, medical supplies or even disinfectant to arrest the spread of the disease. He wrote of the critical financial state of the Volunteer Army, without roubles to buy its supplies,* but confronted by a peasantry which would accept nothing else; and of the refusal of the Don and Kuban regional governments to cede control of the railways to the army, despite its critical dependence on them in a region of very poor roads. He reported that the 20,000 railway workers were 'truculent, lazy and inefficient. They demand boots, clothing and food for themselves and their families'. The provision of such material assistance might serve to bring the railways under Denikin's control, Briggs believed. He also estimated that the total forces under Denikin's command were about 110,000 – 80,000 Volunteers and 30,000 Don Cossacks; supplies for 250,00 would therefore be excessive. The 100,000 sets of kit originally promised would suffice. Denikin's men were presently managing with a consignment of old Russian kit acquired by the French in Roumania and passed on to them the previous November – the rest they had captured themselves. With these the soldiers at the front were fighting gallantly under regimental officers of a high order; but they were opposed by double their numbers and their supply organisation and medical system were poor. 'General Denikin is worthy of every sympathy', Briggs believed, 'He is a great patriot and an honest man who has never wavered in his allegiance to the Allied cause.' Nevertheless, writing his report in mid-March, Briggs took a pessimistic view of the situation, doubting

---

* De Wolff claimed that Denikin's main source of revenue was the sale of wine and champagne from the imperial vaults, which the Russian guarded with his most reliable troops. Of a visit to the vaults De Wolff wrote that they walked for miles through lines of bottles of which the German manager said he had six million champagne, ten million white wine and eleven million red wine. By the distance they walked, De Wolff noted that he could well believe it.[33]

if Denikin could stem the numerically larger Bolshevik armies. He might be able to hold the Don region, he reckoned, but even with the extra equipment now on its way an advance would not be possible.[34]

The shipments of supplies which began to arrive regularly from early March onwards came from London and the two nearer military bases at Salonika and Alexandria. But much that was delivered was of poor quality or inappropriate for the Russians. The guns supplied were not new; many had only 40 per cent of useful life left. This, coupled with the Russian practice of using them at extreme ranges and without proper servicing, meant that their life was shorter still and breakdowns frequent. Seventy-five per cent of the vehicles supplied were also faulty and had to go into workshops before they were fit for the road. The Studebaker ambulance wagons proved too heavy for the poor Russian roads. The War Office supplied over 116,000 horseshoes, but they were too large for the small Russian ponies, as were the harnesses, which required much modification, whilst the modern British breast collars 'were a complete mystery' to their handlers. The Russian ponies seem to have had a particularly hard time, for many of the guns supplied were heavier than the Russian ones to which they were accustomed. They had great difficulty drawing them, especially over wet ground. The 102,000 steel helmets sent out were entirely out of place; the Russians had never used them, even in the trenches of the early campaigns. Seventy thousand bayonets were provided but the Cossacks had no use for them, nor did they find the 13,000 cavalry swords to their liking, preferring the Indian lance or the old pattern cavalry sword. Briggs appealed for a committee of officers to be set up in England to ensure that no useless equipment was shipped. This ought to have been a routine procedure but appears to have been entirely overlooked. Briggs's entreaty seems to have been a vain one: long after he had left the southern front his successor was complaining that 'Twenty-five per cent of the mortars arrived rusty and fit only for instructional purposes. Fifty per cent were deficient of spare parts'.[35]

None of these shortcomings should obscure the great boost to White Russian morale which came from the arrival of the items of which they stood in such great need. Clothing, which came as complete sets with personal equipment, was very welcome, as were the desperately-needed medical and veterinary supplies. The horses and mules supplied were ideal for the artillery units, though mules had apparently not previously been seen in south Russia. The Russians were particularly impressed by the tanks which the British supplied, and also wanted aircraft. Sadly, the former came only in small quantities and the latter very late. Both were a great boost to morale, but the tanks were potential battle winners. Only twelve tanks, six Whippets and six Mark Vs, were delivered during Briggs's time, but he was able to report their great success. As to aircraft, the Russians were actually offered a hundred RE 8s as early as 30 December 1918, but the first did not arrive until 14 June – the day Briggs left. By April Briggs was appealing for thirty-six more tanks as a matter of priority, and in June increased the demand to fifty Mark Vs, but the War Office, affecting an omniscience which its previous failings in supply matters ought to have banished, questioned their suitability for the region and the Russians' ability to operate them. The exasperated Briggs was driven to fire back: 'All tanks with exception of six retained for training purposes now in action with excellent results. Expert opinion therefore at fault in both instances. Much delay in the provision of such essentials would have been avoided had my demands, which were formulated on the spot with expert advice, been considered'. Delay in the timely supply of sufficient tanks and aircraft was a not insignificant factor in the ultimate outcome of Denikin's campaign.[36]

Aside from the unwisdom of the War Office in not accepting the advice of the general on the spot, much of the difficulty with the equipment supplied lay in the fact that many military units were withdrawing from the Middle East at the time and the military *matériel* earmarked for despatch to Novorossisk was at risk of being pilfered by departing units to bring their stocks up to scale. When one artillery officer in the officers' club in Salonika complained to another of his unit being deficient of spare parts, the advice he received was 'Why don't you go to Denikin's dump?' At this park of stores destined for the Russians, 'apparently there was no guard of any kind, and breech blocks, sights, wheels, anything the heart of the battery commander might desire, could be acquired there for the asking'. Nor did Denikin's needs seem to have any sort of local priority. Even at Constantinople, to whose British commander, General Sir George Milne, Briggs was technically responsible, there was, in the view of one major *en route* to the Mission, 'a profound indifference, even opposition, to any action that might be taken by the British Mission in South Russia. Nobody knew anything, nobody seemed to want to find out anything, and nobody cared'. As Milne's biographer noted, 'He showed little enthusiasm for the Volunteer Army'.[37]

Similar hazards lay in wait for the supplies once they had made their journey across the Black Sea. 'We are pouring supplies into Novorossisk for General Denikin', wrote Commander Goldsmith of HMS *Montrose*, 'but his people are so apathetic and lazy that the ships are being unloaded by our Turkish prisoners'. The initial arrangement was for the supplies to be turned over to the Russians as soon as they were landed. At Novorossisk they were dumped unceremoniously at the docks where, as one officer noted, 'great piles of the stuff were rotting on the quaysides, untended, uncared for and the target of every pilferer in the town'. Some even found its way onto market stalls in the town where British soldiers, searching for souvenirs, came upon familiar items of military equipment. The problem was exacerbated by the turmoil of the war-torn region and the many shortages. It became common to see Russians in the headquarters and the rear areas wearing the kit that was desperately needed by those fighting at the front.

According to one British observer, nearly every petty official and bureaucrat in south Russia wore a British uniform. Supplies were equally vulnerable as they made their laborious train journeys to the fighting lines. On one occasion three trainloads of badly needed ammunition failed to appear at the front. After a search, the trains were discovered in a siding where the Russian guards were entertaining some local ladies in the wagons. The heavy ammunition boxes had been loaded over the wheels leaving a space in the middle of each wagon. It was there, surrounded by ammunition, that the guards and their guests were sitting, warmed by open braziers! The practice was later instituted of British Mission detachments accompanying all stores on their journeys to the front. One young subaltern wrote of collecting a consignment of supplies at the quayside and his party 'riding shotgun' on the trucks until they reached their destination.[38]

In ensuring that the Russians units took delivery and then made best use of the weapons and equipment supplied to them, much depended upon the members of Denmis itself. The initial establishment of the mission was roughly three hundred: ninety-nine officers and 132 other ranks, with the remainder being support staff, including many batmen. Of this total twenty-eight officers and fifty-six sergeants were to form the training section charged with familiarising the Russians with the use of the British pattern arms and equipment. But it was one thing to write a desired establishment of men, quite another to fill it with volunteers as the Cabinet had stipulated. More difficult still was getting men, and particularly officers, of the right quality for the testing circumstances of south Russia. The officers came forward for a variety of reasons, some better than others. Churchill made a broadcast appeal for volunteers on the wireless, making it clear that he wanted men to help south Russia, not fight there. Mr Lever, a civilian, but once a Royal Engineer, wrote that he 'felt compelled to answer this appeal (Churchill had been an idol of mine for many years) and so I found myself back in the forces with the rank of captain'. Major Williamson, a regular gunner, offered himself 'in a spirit of adventure and of preservation of the caste to which I belonged ... I saw myself committed to a crusade to preserve something which I thought was good'. Lieutenant Ashton Wade, a signals officer, volunteered 'to gain further experience and to escape the boredom of the demobilisation period'. Another young regular, Lieutenant George Wood, came forward because 'as a professional I wanted far more active service experience, and the shocking news of the Czar's five lovely young children pointed to that [Bolshevik] regime as one very proper to fight against'. Lieutenant John Kennedy (later the very capable Director of Military Operations in the Second World War) volunteered from a similar spirit of professional zeal and even took the trouble to take Russian lessons on the boat out. The enthusiastic young regular officers quoted here all subsequently rose to general officer rank and left accounts of their experiences.[39]

Not all were of this kind. Many were 'temporary' officers who had served for the duration of the main war and now, for various reasons, wished to prolong their time in uniform. In the view of General Holman, the final head of the mission, they were 'neither keen nor capable'. Some, he declared were 'prospecting for an opening in Russia' and for 'opportunities of which they took full advantage, and their mischievous activities only came to light when it was too late to prevent the harm done'. One regular officer wrote, 'Some were pure adventurers, and others for various reasons were in no hurry to return to the bosom of their families'. An example was a fraudulent paymaster who disappeared, ultimately to South America, with several months' worth of overseas allowance due to his brother officers. Others were drawn by the additional pay which Russian service attracted and by the promotion which service on the mission generally gave. All the training appointments had a minimum rank of captain for the officers and sergeant for the other ranks; many were promoted to fill them. A further category of volunteers were ex-prisoners of war of the Germans who had missed out on the earlier action and a chance of distinction. Holman found them 'of little use'. Towards the end, the non-regular officers came to represent almost half of the mission's strength. The other ranks, in Holman's view, were a mixed bag, but better than the less desirable officers. One of his unexpected conclusions was that 'the men made better progress than the officers in learning the elements of the Russian language'. Lieutenant Wood found his group of sergeant machine gun instructors 'splendid men who were to set a fine example'. On the other hand, a sergeant who formed up with his contingent at a London station ready for the journey to Russia declared his fellows to be 'a bright lot! If Scotland Yard burns down before we return, 90 per cent of them will breathe more freely'.[40]

Recruitment for the Mission remained slow, despite Churchill's plea for recruits and the despatch around the commands, at his behest, of 'good officers eager for service' to act as recruiters. At the start, a major disincentive to service in south Russia was pay, as the cost of living there was high and rose dramatically as the campaign of the Whites developed. Pay had to be made attractive if volunteers were to come forward, or if those already serving were to extend their engagements; but the Treasury opposed the early proposals for a flat rate addition of pay. Churchill took a hand in arguing the case himself, but to no avail. It was not until late May that a special addition, unfortunately called a 'colonial allowance', was finally negotiated. The Cabinet did not approve the arrangement until July, and the terms of service which advertised the new rates were not published until the following month. The result was that, from the start, the mission lacked sufficient staff to carry out its responsibilities and many of those who did volunteer were quite unsuitable for their appointments. Since the mission's tasks demanded men of dedication, loyalty, discipline and ability, these shortcomings did not bode well.

The British Military Mission was established initially in the industrial sector of the port of Novorossisk. Its training section was split in two. One part was despatched to establish a school at Armavir in the Kuban for training the Volunteer Army and the Caucasian Cossacks. The other was sent to set one up at Novocherkassk, the Don capital, for training the Don Army. Even when they had volunteered for Russia, the mission members from England came out slowly. The journey took three weeks and the shortage of transport and general disorganisation at a time of great military upheaval meant that there were many delays and changes of plan. Key officers, like the head of the training section of the mission and the officer in charge of supplies and transport, did not arrive until Briggs was himself about to be replaced. Writing of his journey out from England, one officer recorded: 'At this distance of time it is impossible to remember the number of similar orders and counter-orders I received. I believe it was close on a dozen. On one occasion I got as far as Le Havre before being recalled.' Others who volunteered were determined to take their full entitlement of home leave before they went abroad again. Once in Russia there was an inevitable period of acclimatisation and familiarisation with the local scene and the workings of Denikin's command before they became effective. Some never did.[41]

Then, as at Archangel and elsewhere, there was the language problem. A few officers could speak a little Russian, others took lessons while they were with the mission; for some, communication with Denikin's officers was in the halting schoolboy French which they shared. Many local interpreters were employed. Some proved loyal and valuable, others were working to their own agenda; some simply disappeared from their posts. Efforts were made in London to recruit interpreters and some officers were selected purely because they spoke the language, although quite lacking in military training and experience. Interpreters should be carefully selected, General Holman was later to emphasise, and the 'employment, as British soldiers, for example, of East End of London Jews, simply because they have a knowledge of Russian, is fraught with danger'. Very true, no doubt, but an undertow of anti-Semitism was also evident, perhaps reflecting the extreme and barbaric prejudice against Jews amongst members of Denikin's army. Language difficulties were yet another brake on the effectiveness of the mission.[42]

Nevertheless, some able and enthusiastic young officers were now arriving. Lieutenant George Wood, not yet twenty-one but quickly promoted to captain, was one of the few infantrymen in the first batch. Consequently, he was immediately designated a machine gun specialist, which he was not, but remained so regarded throughout his time in south Russia. He was sent to the Don Cossack capital, Novocherkassk, with the warning that 'all Cossacks are ruffians whom no genuine Russian would trust an inch. They would probably cut our throats'. From there he and a fellow infantry captain visited the fighting front on the Donets river where the Cossacks were skirmishing with their opponents.

'We were watching', Woods wrote, 'a genuine military antique, an army raised on the feudal system; every man holding his land with the obligation of serving with his own horse, first in an active regiment and then the reserve.' Then it was down to Novocherkassk, to the Don Army School to set up the machine gun instruction section, as the British warrant officers and sergeants began to arrive to man it. The complicated British technical terms for machine gun parts proved too difficult for their Russian interpreters and were substituted with Russian ones 'as crude and ribald as possible'. The 'extractor', for example, became '*preomnik*', Russian for the hated tax inspector. Similar improvisations were resorted to by the artillery instructors, who were additionally hampered by the incomplete and often faulty equipment which was being sent out.. The Russian commanders, however, seemed less interested in their men being trained on the weapons than on both being sent immediately to the front.

The difficulties with Denikin over the trans-Caucasian republics was the cause of considerable annoyance. In Baku, General Thomson commented: 'It is always incomprehensible why Denikin, with the local forces in the hands of old and not unsympathetic colleagues and the British in occupation as well, does not more resolutely make his objective Moscow, instead of bickering with the republics behind him.' The issue was also the subject of much animated discussion between Curzon and Churchill. Curzon wished to keep British troops in the Caucasus as protection for the new states as well as for the route to India. Churchill considered the new states 'little weak pawns'; his priority was the toppling of the Bolsheviks and therefore the support of Denikin. He hoped that, in return for more supplies, greater support and a larger mission, Denikin would agree not to interfere in the republics and that the British troops there might be withdrawn. It was ultimately decided that the British Caucasus mandate there would be taken over by Italy, but, with a change of government in Italy, this did not happen. These problems with Denikin, and the opposition of Briggs to some of the War Office proposals, led Churchill to write in strong terms to General Milne. 'I attach the greatest importance to helping Denikin', he emphasised, urging Milne 'to travel swiftly yourself to [Denikin's] headquarters … to reach a thoroughly good working arrangement for our common interests'. Milne had taken little interest in the White cause hitherto, but duly paid Denikin a visit, travelling on the same ship as 'a smart lots of officers' whom he thought 'a bit young to train Denikin's Army'. The conference between Denikin, Milne and Briggs no doubt helped to clear the air; but it hardly solved the central problem. 'Conference does good', wrote General Milne, 'and though we skim over the dangerous points, I think a good impression is made and improvement in the situation affected.' In fact, the basic problem remained, as Briggs had often pointed out: it was impossible at one and the same time to give maximum assistance to Denikin and yet deny him access to the physical and manpower resources of the trans-Caucasian republics.[43] After much wrangling the War Office finally agreed that Daghestan, in the northern foothills of the Caucasus, should be in the sphere of the Volunteer Army.

General Milne supported Briggs on other issues, particularly in opposing Churchill's idea of having an extra 800 British volunteers as 'stiffening' for Denikin's front line units, for a variety of very good reasons. He also endorsed Briggs's favourable opinion of Denikin, whom he believed worthy of support. He found the Russian leader 'a calm and determined man standing out amongst the mediocre and rather reactionary crowd of followers whose administrative capacity does not seem great'. Churchill agreed with this judgement, but he was not happy with Briggs: too many of his early reports had been pessimistic and depressing, something Churchill never liked in telegrams from his commanders. Briggs had actually been commendably realistic, but Churchill decided to replace him nonetheless. Once again Denikin was to see a man for whom he had come to develop some regard replaced by another.

Meanwhile, the Russian commander was beginning to get some positive help from the British in the Caspian Sea. During the winter freeze-up there was great activity in the dockyards of Baku, rearming and refitting ships brought from the Black Sea by rail and ones captured from the Bolsheviks. By May 1919 the flotilla comprised eighteen ships in all, including supply ships and tugs, with a CMB depot at Baku, a smaller one further north at Petrovsk and a refuelling point for seaplanes at Chechen Island, 'a lonely sandbank' one young pilot called it, for the RAF was soon supporting the navy's effort against the Bolsheviks along the Caspian littoral.

Across the sea in Transcaspia, however, Britain was now withdrawing. There had been extended discussions in the Cabinet's Eastern Committee as to whether, after the Armistice, there was any reason at all for General Malleson's mission and his small force opposing the Tashkent Bolsheviks. The case for their retention was much weakened by the corrupt nature of the Ashkhabad regime. Malleson called them 'an insignificant collection of adventurers, who maintained 'a precarious, partial and purely temporary control over the armed mob'. Such had proved to be the case, for another, equally corrupt, anti-Bolshevik regime soon replaced them. Though Lord Curzon argued for the force's retention, the Treasury could not justify the costs involved and the Indian government itself could see no reason for keeping it. Finally, in February 1919, after further heavy losses had been inflicted on the Bolshevik forces, the order to withdraw was finally sent to Malleson. He managed to postpone the pull-out until reinforcements from General Denikin were sent to support the shaky successor Ashkhabad regime. By early April these had begun to arrive. The last of Malleson's troops were withdrawn on 5 April 1919. The protection of India's flank was thenceforth to be secured by British formations available in Persia.[44]

7

The Winter War

As the first mission to General Denikin was beginning its voyage to Novorissisk in south Russia, the British generals and their forces at the northern extremity of Russia's land mass were having their initial experience of the problems of surviving and fighting in the rigours of a winter on the fringes of the Arctic Circle. Furthest north were the troops of General Maynard. The first phase of his campaign from Murmansk was an undoubted success. With very small forces he had repulsed the attack on Pechenga and driven the White Finns back across the frontier from his new bases at Kem and Kandalaksha, besides dealing, temporarily at least, with his erstwhile allies, the Bolshevik Red Guards. Finally, he had prepared 'last-ditch' defences on the coastal tip at Alexandrovsk, in case he should be forced back to this extremity. A stand there would still have left Murmansk unusable by the enemy; but nothing so dire had been required. Indeed, the aggressive tactics of his small force had been so successful that his German opponents seemed to be crediting him with commanding a much more substantial army. In the early autumn of 1918, when his numbers were scarcely six thousand, Maynard tells us that 'papers were found on a German agent instructing him to ascertain the number of divisions on the Murmansk side, together with the names of their respective commanders'.[1] Von der Goltz, it seemed, was being deterred.

Years later, when reflecting on his Russian campaign, Maynard declared that his little army was 'one of the most motley forces ever created for the purpose of military operations', and that it campaigned 'under climatic conditions never previously experienced by British troops'. It is difficult to dispute either of these judgements. In fact, these circumstances determined virtually all that Maynard managed to achieve in north Russia and do much to explain the unfortunate reality that his army spent most of its time and energy not fighting any opponents but merely administering itself, and Maynard much of his simply ensuring that his soldiers remained a cohesive and disciplined fighting force. A great part of the difficulty, for him as for Ironside at Archangel, stemmed directly from the climate. In November, the month in which the Armistice came into effect, the sun disappeared from Murmansk. It did not reappear until January. For much of the intervening period there were at most about three hours of daylight each day into which all significant military activity had to be crammed. Andrew Soutar, the war correspondent of *The Times* who arrived during this time, explained that between 12 noon and 2 p.m. 'it was possible to write a letter with the aid of candlelight if one didn't want to strain the eyesight unduly; for the rest – darkness, save for the glare of the snow'.[2] The condition 'seasonal affective disorder' may not have been diagnosed in Maynard's time, but the consequences for a soldier's mood and morale of a life lived in half-light, at a temperature varying from zero to minus 40, and with snow always thick on the ground, were very clear to the commander.

Since the town of Murmansk was a recent creation with a civilian population already swollen far beyond its capacity, additional accommodation was a desperate need, made the more urgent by the rapid expansion of the garrison in the weeks before the Armistice. For months Maynard and his staff lived and worked in railway carriages in one of the sidings of the port before being able to move into a decent building in the township. Many departments, messes and a proportion of the civilian population continued to be based in trains throughout the campaign. This was not only cramped and unhygienic but reduced the amount of rolling stock available for the railway itself, which was the only lifeline across the vast and empty tundra to the troops spread out to the south. The building of extra housing was therefore a priority and never-ending task. Great quantities of timber were delivered from the forests, and the dragging and sawing of logs for hut building filled the waking hours of many troops besides the engineers, one of whose major preoccupations it became. The sawing of wood for fuel in the harsh winter was another continual chore. Masses of stores, delivered to the port since the crisis of the previous spring, still lay at the quayside: barbed wire, sandbags, prefabricated Nissen huts and so on, all of which had to be transferred by hand to the railway wagons for delivery to the garrisons further south as well as to the ever-expanding local settlements. Although some of the civilian labour force was employed on these chores, many of Maynard's troops were fully engaged on them for months.

In early November Maynard's command was declared independent of Archangel. A few days later the coming of the Armistice finally sundered what little amity, born of shared fears, still remained between the general's garrison and many of the local residents. Moscow's repeated demands that the local soviet end its cooperation with the Allies were not obeyed; indeed the local soviet issued orders for conscription into the White Russian forces which Maynard was endeavouring to build up and train in accordance with his War Office instructions. But there was little active cooperation from the general population, which contained nothing in the way of an indigenous bourgeoisie that might have been expected to support the intervention. Understandably, few of the Tsarist officers or members of the St Petersburg and Moscow nobility had chosen to flee to the hutted town, preferring the more developed and sophisticated Archangel. Although the locals were now almost wholly dependent upon the

Allies for their food and other essentials, they were essentially a working-class group, sympathetic to the Bolsheviks. Many were openly hostile and anti-Allied incidents were frequent. The notion that there was a substantial indigenous White movement in Murmansk which the Allies were merely supporting was a fallacy. *The Times*'s correspondent's first evening at the headquarters ended with Maynard showing him to a small bedroom adjoining his own and handing him a loaded rifle with the advice to keep it handy 'just in case'.[3]

With money and goods of all kinds in short supply, thieving was widespread and full-time guard duties occupied 300 men of the garrison. 'Until I have cleared the place of the gangs of robbers and hooligans who have been giving much trouble', Maynard told the War Office, 'their number cannot be reduced.'[4] Military guards had to be put on all the stores, vehicle compounds, pay offices, messes, canteens and billets, as well as on the port itself. Similar security measures had to be taken with the 'pack trains' which supplied the garrisons down the railway. There was generally three of these each week. So often did a guarded, fully-loaded train arrive at its destination deficient of some of its cargo that train guards had to be increased to an officer and eleven men for each journey. With every return trip taking about a week, the drain on manpower was considerable. Yet even with these precautions losses were frequent, aided by the slow progress and frequent stops necessitated by the state of the permanent way and the fuelling arrangements, but also by the wiles of thieves and saboteurs. All these factors ensured that, although the garrisons based at Murmansk and in the healthier and more welcoming village of Kola were considerable, not many men were available for active military operations or even training. Indeed with Kola a cold, half-hour's train ride from Murmansk, where all the labouring duties was undertaken, more time was taken from the working day.[5]

Another consequence of the Armistice was the steadily declining relations between Maynard's force and their other local allies. Recruiting for the Finnish Legion, the 'Red Finns', had been brisk in the early days when they were thirsting for revenge on the Whites who had driven them from their homes in the turmoil of the Finnish civil war. The Legion had played a valuable role in frontier defence in the first months of the campaign, but it was now becoming something of a liability. When originally expelled from their homeland, many of the Finns had made their way first to Petrograd, before some 1400 of them journeyed up the railway to join the Allies. There they were armed and equipped and operated under British and Canadian officers and NCOs. Some, however, had remained in the south with the Bolsheviks when the Russians began organising their 8th Red Army, whose original front had been in the Soroka area until Maynard cleared them out. Now that the threat from Finland itself had disappeared, the Legion did not look kindly at the idea of fighting their Russian Bolshevik comrades, still less their fellow-countrymen who had joined the Reds. Indeed, with their civil war now over, most simply wanted to go home. Maynard had a justifiable fear that the Finns might try to join their brethren on the Bolshevik side and become part of the 'enemy'.

Closely related to the Finnish Legion was the Karelian Regiment. Karelia consisted of the corridor of land between the White Sea and the Finnish frontier. It covered an important stretch of Maynard's line of communications between Kandalaksha and Kem. Recruiting for the regiment had also gone well in the early months, with several thousand volunteers forming the large regiment which operated, like the Finns, under a handful of Allied officers. They had done good work at the start of the campaign, clearing the White Finns from their district, whose main defence force they then became. As time went on, the regiment's numbers in the Kem district swelled until they were between 3700 and 4000 strong. It had been guaranteed that the men would not be called upon to fight outside Karelia; but after the Armistice that region no longer faced German threats. Furthermore, like the Finnish Legion, most of the Karelians had left-wing sympathies and friends on the other side. Their language was Finnish and they shared with the Finnish government a keen desire for independence nurtured by President Wilson's peace principles. But the idea of Finnish, let alone Karelian, independence was anathema to the White Russians whom both Ironside and Maynard were doing their best to support and strengthen. The two groups made uncomfortable comrades in arms. The problems posed by both the Finnish Legion and the Karelian regiment grew greater for Maynard as the days went by.

If the coming of the truce with Germany produced these political and nationality problems, at least it limited the Murman campaign to a single fighting front, that against the Bolsheviks in the south, and one which was only as wide as the railway corridor and its immediate environs. Even so Maynard had few men to man it. In the north, besides the considerable numbers at Murmansk and Kola, there was still the reinforced garrison at Pechenga. Though the tiny port was now considered relatively safe from German attack, it was more vulnerable to attack from Finland, since its land approaches were frozen over and usable. Given Finland's well-known desire to incorporate the port into its territory, Maynard could only maintain a 'worst case' view of its defence. Aside from the Pechenga garrison, there were also small bodies of men at a series of tiny outposts nearer the Finnish frontier, such as the detachment of one officer and eight men who occupied the diminutive and remote post of Restikent, which guarded a river approach to Murmansk from Finland. Restikent was thirty miles from the railway, from which all its supplies had to be hauled over a track of compressed snow. Its unfortunate defenders had been there since the previous June, finding what amusement they could amongst themselves and a similar number of inhabitants of the tiny hamlet. To the south, the front line had now advanced beyond Soroka on the White Sea to the railway village of Olimpi, about twenty miles further on. From the front line northwards the railway line was dotted at each significant town with a small garrison. These men were largely occupied with looking after their own needs, building huts and blockhouses, drawing water, sawing wood, unloading trains or collecting their supplies from the railway if they were distant from it, in addition to keeping an eye on the local population. Maynard had organised his men into two 'brigades', though they hardly fitted the conventional understanding of the term. The northern, 236 Brigade, area ran from the Arctic coast down to Polyarni Krug, a small railway village near the White Sea, a distance of some 200 miles. The southern, 237 brigade, covered the White Sea coastal area from Polyarni Krug down to Olimpi, a similar distance further on. Immense tracts, small forces.

Despite the great drain on manpower caused by the bitter winter and comfortless conditions, Maynard did manage to strengthen the position of his force and organise some winter training ready for an offensive planned for February. As further troops arrived to strengthen the garrison at Pechenga, including a field battery and some French ski troops, the numbers outgrew the accommodation available in the pilgrims' log huts. The infantry platoons moved into an outer perimeter of blockhouses which they built on the hills ringing the fjord. They also sited an observation post for the guns of HMS *Cochrane* on an imposing, isolated crag with excellent visibility. It was a measure against the rapidly receding possibility of a major attack. The Pechenga garrison was well prepared for most eventualities and relatively cosy in its fastness, for wood fuel was in plentiful supply. As the winter advanced, *Cochrane* withdrew for fear of being iced in and was replaced by a couple of trawler-minesweepers, aided in the worst conditions by an icebreaker. These did the weekly ration runs for the garrison throughout the winter. With no enemy to bother them, for there were no attacks from Finland despite the intelligence reports, the garrison platoons were able to form one of the mobile ski columns which Maynard had ordered to be formed for winter warfare.. The Pechenga column was trained by Canadian instructors and supported by reindeer-drawn transport. The animals were plentiful in the area after the locals brought them down from the hills, where they were put to graze during the brief summer to avoid the tundra mosquitoes of the lower ground. The Pechenga ski troops became so proficient and well organised that their mobile company, 170-strong and maintained by 200 sleighs and 600 reindeer, once made the journey to Kola, across a hundred miles of trackless desolation, in just three days.[6]

Shackleton had been designated 'staff officer in charge of Arctic equipment', a post which made him little more than a glorified storekeeper. In fact he seems to have played a more important role in the organisation of the mobile ski columns. Some measure of the extent to which general fatigues were taking up the time of the fighting troops may be gained from the fact that only five of these mobile forces were ever formed and trained in the northern sector where, for a time, five battalions of Maynard's troops were based. One ski column each was formed by the 6th Yorkshires at Murmansk, the Royal Sussex battalion at Kandalaksha, the Italian battalion at Kola, the French *skieurs* and the Pechenga garrison. The company-strong mobile columns were supported by light artillery, medical and wireless sections. The idea was that they should be able to operate unsupported for a period of fifteen days. They were a relatively new fighting unit for the British Army and their equipment was organised in minute detail by Shackleton and his polar experts. Since the companies were composed of men who knew nothing at all of skis or this kind of winter warfare, the training was lengthy and the companies were kept unchanged throughout the winter. Many emerged from the experience well trained and fighting fit, just as the spring thaw put an end to all hope of operations by ski and sleigh. But at least their morale was generally high; more than could be said of the remainder who had spent the winter in an unending round of guard duties and fatigues amidst an increasingly resentful civil population. The comforts were few, the mail was irregular, the diet monotonous, recreations limited and the cold relentless. One young officer wrote home to his mother, telling her little about the war beyond the news that the main activity was building huts. He asked her to send him 'big felt boots, pickles, Clara Butt singing "Abide with Me" and a record of "Destiny" or some good valse'.[7]

Shackleton had worked enthusiastically and under pressure at his new task in the War Office before he sailed north, and in general the equipment he chose appears to have stood the test. 'We had fur coats, fur hats, fur gloves, fur-lined sleeping bags', wrote one of the early arrivals. The exception was the canvas 'Shackleton boots', which were on general issue although intended only for use with skis. Without skis their smooth soles provided no grip on packed snow and many men lost their footing wearing them. During a visit to Archangel, Shackleton asked one man on guard duty why he was not wearing his Shackleton boots, only to receive the reply, 'Lor Lumme, Gov'nor, I must give my backside a chance'.[8] An issue of football boot studs put the matter right while the snow was still hard; but the boots were not waterproof and became useless once the spring thaw began. Always short of funds and ever searching for his eldorado, Shackleton harboured dreams of making his fortune by exploiting the natural resources of Russia and cultivated various of his Russian contacts in the hope of furthering his schemes. When Maynard sailed back to London in late December he took Shackleton with him as a sort of unofficial military assistant. On the return voyage they travelled with the new Russian commander for Archangel, General Miller. 'I cultivated him assiduously and he repays keeping in with', Shackleton wrote to his wife. On his return Shackleton was openly in contact with various Russian officials in furtherance of his plans, particularly Yermoloff, the deputy governor of Murmansk. It seems that he alienated some of his fellow officers by the way he exploited his military position. Nothing, however, came of these schemes and by March the explorer was back in London, a civilian again after five months in uniform but still sufficiently a celebrity to justify an interview in *The Times* on his Russian experience. Unfortunately, his enthusiasm for his commercial projects was not shared by the City's venture capitalists, who clearly did not rate the chances of the North Russian Government very highly. Shackleton's dream quickly evaporated and, ever penurious, he was soon reduced to supporting himself by twice-daily lectures on the story of the *Endurance* at the Philharmonic Hall in Great Portland Street.[9]

Having pushed the Red Guards beyond Soroka and as far south as Olimpi, Maynard was in possession of a valuable 'winter only' overland route to Archangel around the southern coast of the White Sea. Soroka lay midway between Murmansk and Archangel, about 300 miles distant from each. Its link with Archangel was a 200-year-old snow trail which was refirmed by sleigh each winter. Midway along the trail lay the important small town of Onega, a collection of wooden houses and huts standing on a tiny islet on the fringes of the White Sea, with a monastery on an island nearby. Small hamlets dotted the rest of the trail and served as overnight stops on the journey which, when well supplied with ponies, could be accomplished in ten days. To the chagrin of the Murmansk commander, the reinforcements which Ironside was demanding could now readily be detached from his garrison and sent overland by the snow route, as well as via the White Sea along a channel slowly carved out by ice-breaker, until the Archangel estuary became too deeply iced-up even for these powerful craft.

Despite his larger garrison, Ironside seemed in a much more difficult situation than the Murmansk commander. At his back the ice-bound port prevented a rapid withdrawal until the early summer; to his front was an increasingly well-organised enemy with troops available in quantity and backed by strong artillery. At Murmansk, General Maynard had ambitious plans for a southern offensive to gain a larger area from which to draw more recruits to build up his White Army. But the War Office was well aware that, with the Finnish threat diminishing, his position was not nearly so critical as his colleague's and that he always had an open port behind him. The inevitable result was that the Murmansk command was repeatedly bled of its best troops to relieve the plight of Archangel. 'Out of the 5000 Britishers shipped to me originally, 1000 only would remain in my theatre', the bruised Maynard was later to write, 'half of whom were claimed at the time by Pechenga.'[10]

First to go had been the King's Liverpools, another battalion that had begun its journey to Russia from the barracks in Mychett. 'They locked us up in a train and sent us up north. I can remember stopping at Preston – but not getting out – the doors were locked', wrote one of them. The 'Liverpool Pals', as this service battalion was known, and a battery of artillery, spent only a few days in Murmansk before sailing on to Archangel. Next, and the first substantial reinforcement to use the snow route via Soroka and Onega, were the 13th Yorkshires. They had passed their time since landing at Murmansk on grinding guard duties, fatigues and train protection, while based, for the most part, on the small Popov Island in the White Sea. Neither this experience nor their earlier troubled voyage to Murmansk did much for their morale, but at least a commanding officer was appointed to them in time for the transfer to Archangel. About a company's worth made the journey by ice-breaker across the White Sea, the last contingent to do so before the thickness of the ice around Archangel made the link unusable, but the remainder took the snow route around the White Sea coast. It was an epic journey which the battalion made in three columns, leaving Soroka on successive days, travelling in two-man sleighs drawn by sturdy Russian ponies in a remarkable logistical operation which the RASC arranged. It required a huge number of ponies and drivers. Although Maynard had plenty of reindeer at his disposal, these animals could subsist only on moss and none was available on the Onega trail. There were stops at villages about two hours apart where supplies were renewed and the ponies rested or changed. It was intensely cold and at one stage a blizzard blew up and for about ten hours the temperature dropped to 70 degrees below zero, halting all progress. Remarkably, there was not a single case of frostbite on the journey and only four men were admitted to hospital after it. General Ironside met each company column as it came into his command area and told them that they would be going to the front to relieve American companies which had been in the line all winter. 'I asked them', he said, 'to put up a good show for the credit of the British Army.'[11]

The Archangel winter was more severe than that at Murmansk, which had the good fortune to lie in the path of the Gulf Stream. In the posts along the Dvina the cold was intense, dropping frequently to minus 40 degrees centigrade. One battle took place in 85 degrees of frost. Coffee froze in mugs, eyelids stuck together, touching bare metal with uncovered hands brought instant frost burns; and the *droshky* drivers stopped regularly to massage the noses of their ponies lest they became frost-bitten. In these conditions the evening rum ration was a boon to the forward troops; even the Americans, though technically 'dry', took it with enthusiasm. The raw red wine *pinard*, which was the equivalent French issue, often froze in the forward blockhouses. During the intense cold of the night there was a curious cracking of the tree branches in the forest, which often gave the unnerving impression of an enemy stalking up. Even soldiers with experience of the worst of the Western Front found the conditions difficult and dispiriting. 'Doing night sentry outside a blockhouse gave me a lonely and uncanny feeling', wrote one of the Liverpool Pals, 'ever alert for the Bolsheviks whom we could not hear as they moved about in the perpetual snow of the silent forest. Compared to duty on the Flanders front this was another world ... You weren't in the company of anybody in Russia. When you were doing a duty you were alone unless you were in a party going scrapping. Even going up there with your rifle cocked it was a bit tense, because you didn't know which side they would come from, you didn't know where they were'.[12] Common to both theatres was the general puzzlement as to what the campaign was all about, now that the Great War itself was ended. Few things are more corrosive of discipline and morale than doubts about the reason for fighting. 'The Armistice caused a flutter here', wrote an articulate and indignant young signaller in the GHQ Signals office at Archangel, 'and much regret that we are unaffected, for everybody is fed up ... The men are all "category", most having been wounded in France and it is simply scandalous that they should have to be fighting now and under such conditions, when there is peace on all other fronts.' There was further resentment over the censorship of mail: the troops were not allowed, as they had been in other theatres, the 'green envelopes' which held them on their honour not to divulge military secrets. All mail was read by the censor. 'We are muzzled and cannot get the truth out of the country', complained the signalman.[13]

The Bosheviks' Armistice Day offensive took place when the climatic conditions gave them a brief but crucial advantage. After a severe frost, accompanied by a bitter north wind from the Arctic which had frozen the river at Archangel and the seas around it, there was a brief thaw. This did not affect the northern end of the river but further south the water flowed freely and enabled the Bolshevik gunboats with their heavy artillery to return to the front and begin a sustained shelling of the Allied positions along the Dvina. Supported only by the short-range Canadian field guns, the Allied forces could make no effective reply. Under cover of their bombardment, the Bolshevik infantry advanced unseen through the forest fringes to make their attack. Their main thrust was on the left bank of the river where Brigadier Finlayson had his headquarters and so was able to attempt some coordination of the defence. The attack on the Dvina lasted for four days and was defeated by small arms fire and the Canadian gunners firing shrapnel at short range. This took heavy toll of the Bolsheviks. The defences held, but only just. For a brief period the attackers got so far behind the main position at Toulgas that the artillery pieces were in danger of capture. Heroic action by the gunners saved the day. It was not until 14 November, after a sharp drop in temperature and a heavy snowfall, that the offensive slackened and then ended in full retreat. The Bolsheviks lost some hundreds of men killed, the Allies only twenty-eight killed and seventy wounded, but this was a severe loss for the small force, which also had five of its blockhouses demolished by direct hits.

The railway town of Plesetskaya, held by the Bolsheviks and controlling the road which led from that front to the Emptsa river and across it to the Dvina, had been assailed unsuccessfully once already during Poole's time in command. It was tactically so important that Ironside determined to make a fresh attempt to take it, using troops from the railway and from the Seletskoe column on the Emptsa river as the two arms of a pincer movement. Once again the operation ended in failure. The left arm of the pincer, two companies of Americans supported by Canadian gunners, succeeded in driving the enemy out of Kodish but could get no further, since a British machine gun company failed completely in its task of coordinating with them for a further advance. According to Ironside, its commander had 'succumbed to the festivities of the season'. The Archangel Regiment, which was to have pursued the retiring Reds from Kodish, also failed to appear. As for the right arm of the pincer moving down the railway, the French commander Colonel Lucas failed to coordinate the two parts of his force and, when Bolshevik artillery began to shell the line, he called off the main frontal attack. The failure denied Ironside the nodal town and the benefit of its good accommodation for a winter defended post. The railway column, supplied daily from Archangel with most of its necessities, settled to a relatively comfortable winter developing its existing defence line. Kodish, too, with its line of strong blockhouses, became the forward defensive position on the Emptsa, so that the road, at least from railway to river, was secured. The Bolsheviks, however, continued to probe further east of it. In this vast territory there could be no continuous front; with enough determination and sufficient men any position could be turned.

The most serious threat to Ironside's front developed later against his positions on the River Vaga, the southernmost of the two major tributaries of the mighty Dvina. Here his troops were in occupation of the town of Shenkursk and the group of villages which lay scattered along the river for thirty miles to the south of it. Shenkursk was unlike any other of the general's forward positions in that it was a major town, second in size and importance to Archangel itself. Built largely of brick and stone, Shenkursk was a popular summer resort with fine churches, schools and the inevitable monastery, as well as some elegant houses and an army barracks. It had a substantial bourgeoisie, some of whom had taken up permanent residence in their country properties to escape the Bolshevik convulsions further south. In mid-September the town had been occupied with great ease by a column of 200 Americans, who arrived by barge and took the place without a shot being fired, the Bolshevik garrison having fled in panic and disorder. But the ease of Shenkurk's capture and its attractions as a town of some distinction where 'pony sleighs, bearing bearded men and fur-clad women, cantered briskly through the hard white streets towards brightly lit engagements behind steamy panes of glass',[14] carried no implications for the ease of its defence. The place was 240 miles from Archangel on a narrow, fast-flowing river.

When it was first occupied it already represented an isolated salient about forty miles further south than the most advanced of Poole's positions on the Dvina and about a hundred beyond those on the railway. Since then there had been some retrenchment after the Bolshevik offensive, leaving Shenkursk even more exposed. Aside from Poole's disdain for the Bolshevik opposition, Shenkursk had been taken because the Archangel government recognised the recruiting opportunities its substantial population represented. Finally, since the Vaga's junction with the Dvina lay behind the Allied forward positions on the latter river, some positions on the Vaga had to be held lest the main front be turned. Already consisting of 400 men, the 'Shenkursk battalion' had been recruited in the town and had begun their training there, since no suitable buildings were available further back. Ironside had visited Colonel Graham, the commander at Shenkursk, seen its well-organised defences and even visited the US company and its outpost platoon holding the forward position. The local commanders seemed calm and confident, but Ironside realised how exposed the town was and that he had no means of reinforcing it. He left to Graham the decision of when to withdraw if a siege seemed likely.[15]

The Bolsheviks began their assault on the Shenkursk positions on the morning of 19 January when the temperature stood at 45 degrees below. They attacked in considerable strength, directing their initial efforts against the forward hamlet of Nijni Gora, which was held by a platoon of US infantry. The rest of the company, together with some Russians and a couple of Russian guns, was deployed in hamlets close behind, all near to the Vaga. The Americans fought resolutely against overwhelming odds but, after taking casualties, were forced to withdraw from the two forward hamlets to the main company post at Visorka Gora about 1100 yards to the rear. They had lost seventeen men, a great blow for a single platoon. The Bolsheviks took huge losses both from small arms fire and, once Canadians had replaced the panicky Russians in manning the guns, from artillery fire as well. Shrapnel at short ranges was again lethal to the Soviet foot soldiers. Despite heavy attacks supported by their own artillery, the Reds made no headway against Visorka Gora, the Canadian gunners again operating very effectively. There was, however, already intelligence that a large enemy envelopment was nearing Shenkursk itself, so the US company was ordered back. The withdrawal came none too soon: the Bolsheviks had begun firing incendiary shells at Visorka Gora and the village was soon alight. Supplies and the wounded were sent back on pony sleds and the company column followed on foot, heavily loaded with equipment. They spent long enough in a delaying action in another small village to be able to assess the strength of the growing Bolshevik envelopment. A mounted Cossack patrol which was operating with them reported thousands of Soviet troops converging on Shenkursk; long columns of artillery and infantry were observed moving along the roads towards the town. Having lost the Canadian artillery commander and his sole gun to opposing artillery fire, and with their own company commander evacuated wounded, the American lieutenants decided to abandon their delaying action and head directly for Shenkursk. The company arrived utterly exhausted: they had fought for five days against overwhelming odds and taken heavy casualties for so small a force. With very professional Canadian support, they had made their enemy pay a heavy price for their gains.[16]

Colonel Graham's own intelligence confirmed the strength of the Soviet envelopment and the fact that they were bringing up their heaviest artillery for the assault on the town. His other outposts were already under fire and taking casualties. Even more worrying was the realisation that the intensifying bombardment of Shenkursk was coming from all points of the compass. In the choice between staying in the beleaguered town to be pulverised by the heavy artillery of the Red Army – for it seems it was indeed the bulk of Trotsky's 6th Red Army which was concentrating against him – and attempting to break through the encirclement to the safety of the river junction and the Beresnik base, Graham had no hesitation in choosing the latter. After some hasty planning, and hurried and at times chaotic reorganisation, a night withdrawal was decided upon. Avoiding the main road which the enemy had no doubt blocked, he chose to follow a little used loggers' trail which a Cossack patrol found but the enveloping forces had apparently not discovered. This led across the frozen river, directly north through the forests, before regaining the main road about twelve miles further on. It was along this track that the garrison column made its escape from destruction at Shenkursk. The Canadian guns took the lead, with ninety sleighs bearing the wounded from the hospital following behind them. Then came the marching foot soldiers loaded down with stores and equipment: American, British and Russian (half the garrison at Shenkursk was Russian), stumbling and sliding in their Shackleton boots, and finally the laden sleighs carrying the 500 citizens of Shenkursk who had decided to throw in their lot with the Allies. The column of 2000 stretched for more than a mile along the trail. The night withdrawal was hazardous, but it was successful. By daylight Shenkursk was left far behind with the heavy Red artillery beginning a relentless pounding of the defenceless town, clearly believing that Graham's garrison was still in occupation.

Four days later, after intervening halts, the column reached the river town of Kitsa. Guns had been lost en route and equipment discarded; but the journey was largely unmolested by the Bolsheviks, though the Canadian guns had to deal with patrols which, after some time, approached the tail of the column. The 'Shenkursk battalion' of recruits were sent along another little-known track, perhaps as a kind of decoy for the main withdrawal, perhaps because their loyalty was doubted. While the hospital sleighs travelled on from Kitsa to Archangel, the fighting troops halted at the former and began to construct defences in the riverside town. It lay roughly parallel with Toulgas, the forward position on the Dvina, and was only twenty miles from Bereznik, the main base near the junction of the two rivers, from which it could be easily reinforced. Kitsa, with Vistafka behind it, became the new front line on the Emptsa. Territory had been surrendered, but at least the garrison was now safe and the front line straightened and rendered more defensible. It may be that the Red Army leadership was only too pleased to have eliminated the Shenkursk salient without needing to take the casualties which the destruction of its garrison would have demanded. They had learnt to respect the effectiveness of Allied artillery at short ranges. Their primary aim seems to have been to keep the Archangel forces as far as possible from the forces advancing from Siberia, elements of which were now reported to have crossed the Urals and reached Perm. A junction between the two would have been a severe setback to the Red cause.[17]

The withdrawal from Shenkursk marked something of a lull in the fighting on the Archangel front, but it was a major psychological reverse and caused considerable consternation in Britain where Churchill, spurred by a memorandum from the CIGS, wrote to the Prime Minister to draw his attention to 'the safety of our troops in North Russia'. He noted that the Cabinet had decided against sending any reinforcements there, but warned that 'a disaster might easily occur on this front during the four months which must inevitably elapse before these men can be withdrawn if that is what the Government decide'. He asked for a modification of the policy to allow the specialist reinforcements – railway units, medical staff, electricians and so on – which the CIGS had requested, to be speedily despatched. Lloyd George readily agreed; but this did not effect the fighting strength on the battlefield or relieve the exhausted and demoralised front-line troops.[18] If Ironside was to have front-line reinforcements they could come from only one source – Murmansk. Over the following weeks General Maynard was to lose not only the 13th, but also the 6th Yorkshires and the 280th Machine Gun Company to the Archangel Command. Despite his need for reinforcements, Ironside was rather more sanguine about the military situation in his command than were either Churchill or the CIGS. The reverse at Shenkursk notwithstanding, he realised the great power of the defensive in the Russian winter. Now that the Bolsheviks' artillery superiority was being countered by the arrival of 60-pounders from England, his well-built blockhouses, fully wired-in beneath the snow, were immensely powerful. Their Bolshevik attackers, still inexpert and with brittle discipline, would need overwhelming superiority and complete disdain of casualties to overcome them. In fact, in some respects the strength of the enemy was of less concern to Ironside than the morale and cohesion of his own troops.

It was now clear that the Bolshevik forces, dismissed as derisory by General Poole, were beginning to improve. Brigadier General Finlayson, worn out by his time in sole charge of the Dvina force, returned to UK in the course of the winter. He wrote an appreciation for Churchill of the state of the campaign in north Russia which included this evaluation of the enemy:

> There appears to be an impression in Great Britain that the Bolshevik Forces are represented by a great rabble of men armed with sticks, stones and revolvers, who rush about foaming at the mouth in search of blood and who are easily turned and broken by a few well directed rifle shots. On the contrary, the Bolshevik Army on the Archangel Front is a well-equipped, organised and fairly well trained one.

He emphasised that their staff was composed of officers who had war experience, with a sprinkling of staff-trained people among them, and that their infantry leaders were brave and bold in attack.[19]

The attack to eliminate the Shenkursk salient was the major part of a powerful offensive largely directed at the vast expanse of territory between the railway and the main river positions. Whilst the salient was being attacked, strong forces were also attacking positions much further north around Shred Mehengra. which guarded the easterly approaches to the Emptsa river. On 27 January Major Gilmore, the forward commander there, reported that 'the enemy used a certain percentage of gas shells with no effect'. Ironside realised that this was a significant development, if only small in scale, and immediately notified the War Office: 'Report that 3 gas shells fired by enemy; my 1 gas officer has gone up to investigate. This is first suggestion of enemy using gas in any form but if it is verified I shall ask for some gas officers and means of repair for masks. There is a plentiful supply of latter here'. Three gas shells were hardly a major event and Ironside's reaction, it will be noted, was entirely defensive. Not so the response from Churchill. The same day, without waiting for confirmation, he made this 'first use' clear to the nation at large in a formal press statement and at the same time notified Ironside that a ship would be sailing in the middle of the month loaded with gas shells for his various artillery pieces. Ironside still demurred, asking for instructions, since he had not yet verified the report that the Bolsheviks had indeed used the weapon. Plainly the general had residual inhibitions. The clearest of directives from the War Office, however, soon followed. On 7 February the GOCs at Archangel, Murmansk and Constantinople received a message in cipher from the Director of Military Operations: 'Fullest use is now to be made of gas shell with your forces, or supplied by us to Russian forces, as Bolsheviks have been using gas shells against Allied troops at Archangel.' The Secretary of State had wasted no time.[20]

Since his days as Minister of Munitions, Churchill had been an enthusiastic proponent of gas. He had wished to see its use increased fivefold on the Western Front, regarding it, like the tank, as a technological development whose benefits should be rapidly exploited. When the French Munitions Minister, Louis

Loucheur, had appeared to be succumbing to pressure from the International Red Cross for a multilateral abstention from its use, Churchill wrote to him in protest, declaring, 'I am on the contrary in favour of the greatest possible development of gas-warfare, and on the fullest utilisation of the winds, which favour us so much more than the enemy'.[21] His enthusiasm for what he called 'this hellish poison' carried over into the intervention in Russia despite conditions, particularly in the north, being entirely different. Some critics have claimed that Churchill, in his keenness to use gas, falsely charged the Bolsheviks with using it first.[22] This is plainly not so: further reports came in of gas being used by the enemy on two occasions on the Vaga front, though once again its use was limited and ineffective. The press carried the reports, no doubt prompted by the War Office: 'It is reported that the Bolsheviks have commenced to use gas shells against the Allied troops: all of the latter are, however, completely equipped with anti-gas apparatus', *The Times* noted. However, even a couple of months later Brigadier General Turner, the new commander on the railway front, was writing to Ironside, 'Personally, I don't want to use the beastly stuff, for in case of retaliation we are not properly prepared'.[23] Ironside took advice from one of his staff who had some experience of gas warfare and requested one or two Livens projector companies and half a company with 4-inch Stokes mortars. He did not want cylinder gas, as the close conditions of north Russia with limited clearings shut in by forest made it unsuitable. It was some days before Churchill replied, saying that he could not supply the equipment requested, but instead offered Ironside twenty-four officers and 'a new gas, which can be easily manipulated and used with the infantry'. It was a new and very secret weapon, required a special respirator as protection and should only be used 'if specially necessary'. It was plain that, if the Cabinet would not let him have fresh soldiers for his Russian campaign, Churchill was determined to use the latest version of an effective weapon. In the context of the Bolsheviks' very limited use of gas, it did rather smack of massive retaliation.[24]

Spirits were now low in all the Allied detachments in north Russia, not least among the Americans in the Archangel Command, who had taken something of a battering in their front-line positions. They had been ill-prepared for the conditions they found there and for being under direct British command. The American soldier, one of their number wrote, 'does not like the idea of serving under English officers, carrying out English plans for English purposes on English rations dealt out by English ASC. Because of this implied inferiority to Britons there has grown up a live enmity between English and Americans'.[25] He might have added that the US policy for its troops' employment in the theatre was muddled in the extreme. Ironside found the American infantry at first very inexperienced and trained only for trench warfare, but they improved quickly under active service conditions. He was particularly critical of their officers, of whom only two were regulars. 'I should say', he confessed, 'there are only four officers in the whole Regiment capable of commanding a detachment above a company.' But he praised 'two exceptionally fine company commanders who distinguished themselves in the heaviest fighting. He thought their engineers were 'excellent, commanded by capable officers ... I could not ask for better'. But among the US rank and file he was disturbed to find 'a large proportion of self-inflicted wounds almost invariably amongst men of Polish and Russian extraction', of whom there were many in the Michigan-recruited force.[26] Others were even less complimentary. After the loss of Kodish one British officer wrote, 'The whole thing despicable. I put the Yanks below the Bolsheviks even ... they're a hopeless mob and windy as hell'.[27] The quality of the junior commanders in the US companies seems often to have been the determining factor. Yet in the early days it was on the Americans that the defence of the Allied positions predominantly depended.

The Canadians artillerymen Ironside knew well from France. They were very professional and he valued them highly; but even they were deeply troubled by their anomalous position in this unexplained war. He visited them in the front line at Shredmehengra: 'They asked me two questions', he noted, '1st whether there is any chance of relief and 2nd what was the actual position between ourselves and the Bolsheviks. I gave as good an answer as I could ... There appear to be questions troubling all men here of whatever nationality.'[28] There were indeed; it was a factor of which the government was taking far too little account. As to the French, although their ministers in Paris and their diplomatic staff in north Russia displayed the most violent opposition to the Bolsheviks, the troops on the ground in both commands did not share these sentiments. The 21st Colonial Infantry, Ironside's main French unit, had been involved in a mutiny at Lyon in 1917 and had been sent to Russia, it was said, to keep them out of trouble. In early November 1918, when there were rumours of an armistice, the men had refused to return to their front line in the railway corridor. By February 1919 Finlayson was calling them a sullen band of 'strikers and shirkers'. The unit and its commander proved valueless to Ironside as the failed attempt to take Plesetskaya exemplified. But from the commander's viewpoint, the most worrying case of indiscipline came not from the soldiers of his allies but from British reinforcements of whom so much was expected.

The 13th Yorkshires, who had been reported by Ironside as being 'in very good order' when he saw them arrive at Onega after their journey across the snow trail, mutinied shortly after their arrival. It was not the action of the whole regiment, only of the mobile ski company which had trained for winter warfare under Maynard, and a few men from another company. They refused to go forward from Seletskoe to relieve the Americans in the front line at Shredmehengra. The men of this same company had at first resisted the order to make the overland transfer to the Archangel command. Only after their new commanding officer,

Colonel Lavie, had talked to the men for an hour were 'his orders … quietly carried out'. So read Ironside's telegram to the War Office on 23 February notifying the mutiny. He later recorded that when the adjutant first reported that the battalion had refused to fall in for front-line duty, the astonished CO personally ordered them to parade without arms, which they did, whereupon two sergeants stepped forward and declared that the battalion would do no more fighting. Lavie had the men arrested by armed soldiers. When Ironside received news of the mutiny he travelled quickly to Seletskoe, which he reached about 6 p.m. on the 27th, being 'much relieved by the news that the battalion had marched that morning'. He later wrote that the two sergeant ringleaders of the mutiny were recent transferees to the regiment who had done no fighting before coming to north Russia, having 'served all the war in the Army Pay Corps in England'. He promptly sent them for trial by court martial. They were found guilty of mutiny and sentenced to be shot. Since Ironside had received secret instructions from the King that no death sentences were to be carried out after the Armistice, he commuted their sentences to life imprisonment. Such was the general's account of the first British mutiny in north Russia, of which, he declared, 'very garbled and much exaggerated' accounts' had reached the railway and Archangel before his return.[29]

In fact the mutiny was both more significant and more understandable than Ironside's published words suggest. His telegram to the War Office after visiting the battalion on 27th described it as a 'quite serious situation' and noted that although 'the men were orderly they were very obstinate and persistent'. The mutiny occurred on 22nd, but it was apparently not until the morning of 27th that the men moved off to the front, though the following companies of the battalion had concentrated with them at Seletskoe by 24th. One Russian account suggests that along the road to the front the Yorkshires were covered by Russian machine guns at the request of the British commander.[30] Furthermore, Ironside's second telegram confirms that he remanded for court martial not just two NCOs, but three NCOs and thirty men.[31] There were dire consequences for the men found guilty – inevitable given the operational context of their offence. It appears that the night before their mutiny the Yorkshires company had held a soldiers' meeting with two platoons of the Liverpools and two sections of the MGC, who no doubt told them about the conditions at the front and may have played a role in fomenting the unrest.[32] The meeting apparently passed resolutions 'that they must be withdrawn from Russia immediately … that censorship be removed from letters in order that the people in England get to know the true state of affairs out here … and that a cable be sent to Lloyd George demanding immediate withdrawal of all troops in Russia'. So affirmed the diary of a RAMC stretcher bearer whose record added, 'They all positively decline to go up the line or obey any orders but are conducting themselves in an orderly manner'.[33]

Similar meetings and refusals of duty had been widespread in England only weeks before and comparable resolutions had been passed without any disciplinary consequences. The differences in north Russia were the active service conditions, the closeness to the front line and the fact that the action kept other soldiers, who deserved relief, facing the enemy for longer. It also encouraged similar action in other operational units. Ironside admitted that 'the ill-discipline communicated itself quickly to the French infantry'. He already had 160 wretched French mutineers in custody waiting to be returned to Africa, and declared the rest of their colonial battalion to be 'completely demoralized and … useless for military operations'. It has to be remembered, since mutinies are a blot on any regiment's escutcheon, that the cap-badged Yorkshires, who themselves represented only a modest proportion of the composite regiment, had suffered rather more than four leaderless months and slack discipline before a commanding officer was appointed – a serious failing by the appointing authorities. The regiment went on to serve with distinction in the campaign. In April its soldiers earned one Distinguished Conduct Medal and seven Military Medals after an operation which reflected great credit on them. In the same month a platoon under a second lieutenant was involved in heavy fighting in harsh conditions and managed to survive in the forests for about ten days. A considerable achievement.[34]

The discontent of the British troops was not restricted to the front-line infantry. Resentment at serving in Russia was just as intense at the Archangel base. In February the troops were given a lecture by a civilian at the Archangel YMCA on the 'Aims of the Allies in North Russia'. 'I have very strong opinions on this subject', wrote Lance Corporal Thompson of the GHQ Signals Office, 'and after the lecture I made a short speech. Judging by the applause, I voiced the opinions of the majority of the "Boys" present, and the lecturer was not a little disconcerted.' Yet Thompson was no trouble-maker. He was a conscientious signalman who was promoted to sergeant during his time in Russia and even received a Russian decoration. By March he was declaring, 'Everyone is fed up with the whole show and there is much unrest'.[35]

It was the unreliability of the Russians themselves, however, that had the most serious implications. The only element of British policy which was at all clear to the local commanders was that they were to help develop and train the White Russians. Whilst Ironside did not have the nationalities problem which afflicted Maynard, this did not mean that his Russian forces were as yet a reliable adjunct to his own. One British sergeant who was training Russians at a machine gun school located in a monastery outside Archangel recorded that 'the rank and file of the Russians were not a bad lot and I couldn't blame them for wishing to join their folk on the other side, but occasionally they got panicky, and God help you if you find yourself in their way when they madly rush for safety'.[36] Two companies of the troublesome Archangel Regiment refused to go to the front in December and the following month a Russian company refused to attack at Shenkursk. Desertions were frequent. On the other hand, some spoke highly of the Russians fighting alongside them. Major Gilmore, commanding the left wing of the front on the Vaga river commended some officers and NCOs of the Archangel Regiment and Archangel Dragoons, a small body of whom held a position against an attack by a Bolshevik force many times their strength. 'During the many weeks they were under my command', he wrote, 'there were only three cases of desertion to the Bolsheviks. Not only did they fight steadily and well, but there was never a lack of volunteers for dangerous work. They were well officered.'[37] Perhaps that was the key. Some Russians also fought well on other fronts, but as a whole they were far from reliable. Ironside was particularly critical of the Russian officers who, in the Tsarist manner, seemed to despise their men and took little interest in their welfare. 'Many of them did not believe in their hearts that they could beat the Bolsheviks, though they still firmly believed that they ought to be suppressed … As they were, they could not expect their men to follow them in the exacting conditions of civil war.' The general saw 'a terrible hopelessness in their eyes'.[38] It would not have been surprising if a little was reflected in his own.

Ironside took considerable personal interest in the expansion and training of the Slavo-British Legion. Begun initially as a means of employing ex-Tsarist officers and others whom, for one reason or another, the Archangel government found unacceptable, the SBL was considerably expanded by Ironside. It became the embodiment of one of the great contradictions in the intervention policy. Ironside was charged with helping the Russian government to develop its army to oppose the Bolsheviks, yet at the same time he was building his own force of Russians. This included numerous Tsarists who declined to fight for the Chaikovsky regime and whom Chaikovsky, in his turn, found unacceptable. The Slavo-British Legion was also a silent witness to the British lack of faith in the Russian officer system. The general took the risk of recruiting to the SBL's ranks some of the doubtful characters in the refugee population and many of the peasants who had been conscripted into the Bolshevik forces in other parts of Russia and subsequently captured and brought to Archangel. These were not ideological Bolsheviks, Ironside believed, and keeping them idle and under guard in the perpetual twilight of the northern winter was a severe drain on manpower. This was an act of faith on his part: faith in the efficacy of the British training system. His belief was that decent food and regular pay, and the enlightened and professional training and disciplinary practices of the British Army, would work wonders even on such unpromising material. The aim was to turn the SBL into the backbone of the developing Russian forces. In the same improving spirit, Ironside also established a junior unit of the SBL into which were drafted the many homeless, orphaned and delinquent youths among the Archangel population. The unit clothed them in British uniforms, fed them well, gave them discipline and taught them trades. A similar enthusiasm lay behind his support for the establishment of the first groups of Girl Guides and Boy Scouts in Russia started in Archangel by an English lady. Ironside inspected their first jamboree; 'a tall, imposing if slightly arrogant figure' was how one girl remembered him as he passed along the ranks, stopping 'to say a word or two to some of them in his broken Russian'.[39]

The new SBL infantry recruits were first drafted into companies and mixed with the original volunteers, who then formed the NCO and some of the junior officer element. Several small detachments fought at the front for short periods, as did one platoon with the King's Liverpool at Kodish and another under Major Gilmore at Shredmehengra, both with some credit, though there was also indiscipline and a few defections. Finally, they were formed into battalions under British officers and given intensive training on Bakaritsa Island in the Dvina estuary, where Ironside frequently visited them. They, too, wore British uniforms and were officered down to company level by the British, who also provided a proportion of the NCOs.[40] They were even given their own regimental band formed from the musicians of the once-mutinous crew of the cruiser *Askold*. The first SBL battalion was known as Dyer's Battalion, in memory of the young Canadian officer who died of overwork and Arctic cold while commanding it. In all it seemed a promising start.

8

The Baltic Knot

If nationalism and the nationalities issue was a lasting problem for General Maynard at Murmansk, it was an even greater bedevilment for British policy in the other northern theatre of the intervention in which Britain became progressively embroiled: that of the Baltic States. The question of British intervention against the Bolsheviks in the Baltic region did not arise until Germany had been defeated and the Armistice was in place. Had Germany triumphed, it is likely that the Baltic States would have become German provinces – a Prussian-dominated grand duchy perhaps – with the more robust Finland also closely associated with Germany. As it was, the German defeat resulted in all the states concerned, Estonia, Finland, Latvia and Lithuania, declaring, or reaffirming, their independence from the defeated imperial Russia and wishing to shake off German influence as well. The Allies accorded them *de facto* recognition. This did not count for a great deal at the time, since most of them had already been invaded by the Bolsheviks as, after the German downfall, Lenin sought to regain control of the provinces under the guise of creating a federation of Soviet Republics. At times he expressed his aspirations rather more bluntly: 'Soviet troops must occupy Lithuania, Latvia and Estonia. The Baltic must become a Soviet sea.' Despite having significant groups of Bolshevik sympathisers among their populations, the new Baltic States had no wish for such liberation.

The Allies had been excluded from the Baltic Sea by the German High Seas Fleet for more than five years and consequently had no troops in the area. In wishing to come quickly to the aid of the new states, they had, therefore, little choice but to use the German occupying forces which had rapidly taken over parts the Baltic coast after the Russian Revolution. For this reason the Armistice terms did not require the German troops there to return home immediately, but 'as soon as the Allies shall think the moment suitable, having regard to the internal situation of these territories'. Using the Germans to try to keep the Bolsheviks out was very much the lesser of the two evils, but it was replete with danger nonetheless. The key to understanding the difficulties it presented lies in the recognition that, although Latvia, Lithuania and Estonia had spent two centuries as part of the Russian Empire, the preponderant economic, political, and cultural influence in all three was German. Both Estonia and Latvia were keen to assert their national freedom from both Russia and Germany. Only in

Lithuania, which had suffered German occupation for more than three years and was also flanked by a resurgent Poland, was this desire muted and circumspect.

When the German army first occupied the territories, after the enforced peace with Bolshevik Russia, they had been welcomed by the German element of the population, the 'Balts', the Baltic barons who formed the powerful local landed aristocracy which the historian H.A.L. Fisher, Churchill's Cabinet colleague, described as 'the proudest and hardest aristocracy in Europe'. They and the subsequent German settlers in the region were known by this collective name. But with the breakdown of German military power at the end of 1918, the occupying German troops were demoralised, mutinous and often frankly Bolshevik themselves; hardly a suitable instrument for the Allied policy makers. On the other hand, when General von der Goltz arrived from Finland in February 1919, having assured Mannerheim's victory over the Red Finns and created such temporary alarm in the mind of General Maynard, he began to reassert discipline and stiffen his war-weary troops with fresh, nationalistic volunteers from Germany. He had considerable local sway around Libau in Latvia and showed little inclination to leave the Baltic lands. His reasoning appeared to run along the lines of hoping that, although Germany had been beaten in the west, he could perhaps ensure a compensating victory in the east with a reassertion of control over the Baltic lands. The Bolsheviks, on the other hand, held power in nearby Petrograd and over the substantial Russian fleet lying in its well-defended naval base of Kronstadt. From this bastion they were moving to re-establish control of their Baltic empire. Soon they had occupied half of Latvia and were moving into Estonia. It was against this background of the manoeuvring of the defeated powers that the new, weak national governments of the Baltic States were struggling to establish their own authority free from the control of either, yet with large groups of White Russians beginning to collect on their territories and with numerous Bolsheviks among their own nationals. It was a complex and confusing mix.

The White Russian troops in the area, later to be dignified as the 'North-Western Army', at British insistence, in order to distinguish them from the White forces of Maynard and Ironside, had their origins in an anti-Bolshevik underground of very reactionary Russian officers established at Petrograd in the final months of the war. Initially they hoped to operate from German-occupied territory, and with German support, to challenge Lenin's regime. Recruits were required to take an oath of loyalty to the Tsar. Their objective was the capture of Petrograd, where their commander was to declare himself military dictator. By October 1918 the movement had become the 'Northern Corps' and was established at Pskov, in the strip of territory known as Ingermanland, within Russia but very close to the Estonian border. It numbered little more than 3500 men. With the signing of the Armistice, all hope of German support ended and the Bolsheviks began to advance against Pskov. The result of this threat was a marriage of convenience between the new Estonian government, already hard pressed by the Bolsheviks, and the Northern Corps, according to which the latter came under Estonian command and was paid and victualled by Estonia, and based on its soil for joint operations against the Reds. It was an uneasy alliance born simply of shared danger, for the White Russians were as opposed to an independent Estonia as were the Bolsheviks. The Estonians knew this well and had little trust in their temporary allies. By April 1919, Supreme Commander Admiral Kolchak, as he then had become, appointed General Yudenitch, an experienced commander from the Russian campaign against the Turks, as Commander-in-Chief of the Northern Corps and any other anti-Bolshevik Russian troops in the Baltic area. Yudenitch held court with a substantial staff in the Hotel Societenhusen, the largest in Helsingfors (Helsinki), surrounded by a motley collection of speculators and hangers-on, all optimistic about the fall of Petrograd that was to be effected by Yudenitch's modest force in Ingermanland.[1]

The outline of Britain's policy had been established very soon after the Armistice, when a Foreign Office conference decided 'to supply the Baltic states with military material if and when they have governments ready to receive and utilise such material'. Within a week an Estonian delegation had arrived in London asking for help in the shape of troops, ships and arms. The War Cabinet quickly took the key decision to send a substantial naval force to the Baltic but on no account to provide troops. The naval force was a light cruiser squadron and a destroyer flotilla supported by minesweepers, with auxiliary cargo vessels loaded with weaponry for the embryonic Baltic governments, all sailing under the flag of the young Rear Admiral Alexander-Sinclair whose nebulous orders were to 'show the flag and support British policy as circumstances may dictate'. The force was sent in some haste: the cruisers had put into port only the day before, their crews expecting some Armistice leave after their extended period away from home. This they were not to enjoy for many weeks. The many 'hostilities only' crew members in the flotilla were particularly disgruntled.

Significant support for the new Baltic regimes was not easy for the navy to provide, since the main threat to their existence was plainly on land rather than at sea and the politics of the area were in a state of confusion. It was fortunate that the admiral was given a Foreign Officer official as an adviser. Moreover, if the commander's assignment was imprecise, carrying it out was beset by practical hazards. The shallow, stormy and often mist-shrouded waters of the Baltic had been liberally sown with mines by both Russia and Germany during the late war and these were now a constant danger. Only days into his mission the admiral lost the cruiser *Cassandra* to a mine as it travelled between the Baltic capitals, though the great majority of the crew were rescued. Aside from such dangers, there was the constant threat of a sortie by the Bolshevik fleet at Kronstadt, aimed at negating any assistance the Allies might try to give the new states, or indeed to Yudenitch's Whites.

At the Estonian capital, Reval (Tallinn), Alistair-Sinclair found the new government short of virtually everything needed to protect and sustain its independence and facing a Red army less than forty miles distant. The Estonian Prime Minister was desperate: he asked for a British training mission, a garrison for his capital, and ships for his non-existent navy. He even requested that his state be declared a British protectorate. All these were pleas which Alexander-Sinclair was quite unable to meet. He did, however, give the Estonians 5000 rifles and other equipment. Turning a blind eye to what his orders had said about 'coastal reconnaissance only', he also sailed along the coast close to the Russian border and used the combined guns of two light cruisers and five destroyers to lay down a devastating barrage on the advancing Bolsheviks' supply lines. This severed their contact with Petrograd by destroying a bridge on the river frontier and forced their retirement. Risking leaving only part of his flotilla in support, the admiral took the remainder down to Riga to encourage the Latvians. The Bolshevik high command then responded to Britain's inteference in its affairs by ordering the assembly of a naval force under the command of the Soviet Naval Commissar K.K. Raskolnikov for a sortie from Kronstadt to destroy the squadron which had so effectively disrupted the land advance. The venture ended in disaster. Only two Bolshevik destroyers got as far as Reval and one of these ran aground when the British opened fire. It quickly hoisted the white flag. The other was surrounded as it attempted to get back to Kronstadt and was captured as well. The captors found both destroyers new and up-to-date in every respect, but there was little fight and not much discipline in their crews. Their naval commissar was discovered on one of the vessels, hiding behind some sacks of potatoes! The destroyers were handed over to the Estonians and became the nucleus of their navy. A combined force of Estonians, Finns and White Russians, supported by another naval bombardment, subsequently removed the immediate Red land threat to the new state. It was not a bad start for the Baltic squadron.

At Riga the Latvian situation was even more desperate. The admiral was begged to put his ships' crews ashore to support the government. The Bolsheviks already held large tracts of the country and Riga itself was threatened. Although the Armistice terms were invoked by the British, the indisciplined German garrison declined to help. The German High Commissioner had his own plans to extend German control over the territory and tried to induce the desperate Latvian Prime Minister to grant citizenship rights to members of a local German volunteer corps he was forming to oppose the Bolsheviks. All that Alistair-Sinclair was able to do was use his ships' guns to help put down a mutiny among the Latvian troops and to embark some of Riga's prominent citizens and transport them to the relative security of western Latvia. Riga fell to the Bolsheviks in

Petrograd and the Baltic States

early January. This rescue mission completed, Alexander-Sinclair withdrew his squadron to Copenhagen to escape the winter ice of the northern Baltic.[2]

The Admiralty was continuing to press the government for clearer direction and arguing for more appropriate action. The naval view was that, if the government really wished to assure the independence of the Baltic States, it should 'put in hand the immediate preparation of a land expedition of considerable strength'. This the Cabinet refused to consider. Instead it chose to end the Baltic squadron's extended tour of duty and send out a new force of cruisers and destroyers under Rear-Admiral Sir Walter Cowan with a similarly vague remit. Cowan was a small, pugnacious officer, highly-strung and with a short fuse. A fine horseman, and devoted to hunting when he was not at sea, he had no liking for parties and female society He lived for combat. 'He was, I think', a fellow admiral recalled, 'the only officer in the Grand Fleet who was sorry that the war was over.'[3] His task, Cowan was told, was to prevent the destruction of Estonia and Latvia which the Bolsheviks were threatening. Where this was possible by attacking from the sea, he 'should unhesitatingly do so'. Any Bolshevik men-of-war operating off the Baltic coasts were also to be treated as hostile. Only in 'very exceptional circumstances' was he authorised to land men from his ships. Cowan was also told that he was only to supply further arms if the local government was stable and in full control of its forces. In truth, British and Allied policy for the region was becoming progressively less effective as the Baltic situation grew in complexity. With the arrival of General von der Goltz and fresh troops from Germany, the Germans were proving more of a menace than a support to the embryonic governments of Estonia and Latvia. And despite the antipathy of the other putative opponents of the Bolsheviks, the Whites of the Northern Corps, to any notion of independence from Mother Russia for these new states, Britain was apparently intent on supporting these Russians as well as the new governments. To cap it all the German reinforcements for von der Goltz, together with their supplies, were coming by sea through the blockade of Germany which Britain and the Allies had imposed. Admiral Cowan was plainly to have no easier a time in the Baltic than his predecessor. 'It seemed to me', he declared, 'that there was never such a tangle, and my brain reeled with it. An unbeaten German army, two kinds of belligerent Russians, Letts, Finns, Esthonians, Lithuanians, ice, mines – 60,000 of them! Russian submarines, German small craft, Russian battleships, cruisers, and destroyers all only waiting for the ice to melt to ravage the Baltic.' In his first few weeks there, however, he supplied the Letts with rifles, machine guns and ammunition and managed to shell the advancing Bolsheviks out of Windau in support of the Germans who were at last playing some part in the defence.

The Naval Staff were quite exasperated by the situation in which their forces were placed. A very strongly worded memorandum pressing for 'a definite and coherent policy' was sent to the First Lord, who passed it untouched and without comment direct to the War Cabinet. In response Lloyd George pressed the Supreme War Council in Paris to send military missions to the Baltic States, but it was two months before a satisfactory agreement was reached on even this relatively toothless measure. By the time the decision was taken, Britain had decided to withdraw its troops altogether from north Russia and Lloyd George was refusing to consider a fresh entanglement, despite Churchill's arguments for a more active intervention. Thus, as the Baltic ice began to melt and the political situation in the infant coastal republics to worsen, Cowan was left to execute a policy without any appropriate means to do so. In mid-April the Latvian Balts, with the knowledge of von der Goltz, took control of Libau and arrested the provisional Lettish government. When Cowan returned from a visit to England, he demanded that the Balts' ringleader leave Libau, that the ministers be released and the government restored. Von der Goltz, aware of the admiral's inability to enforce his orders on land, agreed only to the first demand, protesting that the Latvian ministers were Bolshevik sympathisers. Cowan was powerless to do other than report back the German's refusal; the truculent behaviour of the Balts and the German troops in Libau continued. One group even trained their machine guns on the British destroyers drawn up at the port and later attempted to put to sea themselves in two armed trawlers. On another occasion, when Cowan himself was returning to ship from visiting the British Mission at Libau, he was held up by a German sentry and asked for his pass. Few Allied demands, unsupported by the necessary force, ever drew a complaisant response from the determined Prussian. Within weeks, confident that he was firmly established in Latvia, von der Goltz sent his troops north to attempt an occupation of Estonia.

Stung by von der Goltz's actions and his force's clashes with the Estonians, as well as by Cowan's vigorous protests at the possible extinction of two small countries which had been encouraged to rely on British support, the Allies at last took some action. The Foreign Ministers agreed that the German troops should be replaced by locally raised levies and the Allied Military Mission, on which they had agreed, finally arrived in the Baltic. Britain was to staff and run the mission, which was to be the main executor of Allied policy in the region. This was not exactly the display of force the Admiralty wanted, but it did suggest that the ministers deliberating in Paris were at last taking the Baltic situation more seriously. In May 1919 Churchill telegraphed Sir Henry Wilson, 'I have offered the mission to Gough, who I think will accept'. Lieutenant General Sir Hubert Gough had commanded the Fifth Army in France until removed from command when his understrength army's defences broke under the German onslaught of March 1918. He had been without an appointment since. Churchill considered that Gough had been hard done by over the March disasters. Cowan was of the same opinion and might also have had something to do with his selection for the Baltic post. He had written to his old friend General Wilson, suggesting Gough as one of two generals who had 'been through the furnace of undeserved defeat' and who merited another chance as head of the mission. Churchill was already considering what part Britain might play in supporting an attack by Marshal Mannerheim or General Yudenitch, or both, on Petrograd. 'When Gough has got out there and reported fully', he wrote, 'we shall be in a position to make up our minds.'[4]

The affairs of the Baltic region were complicated enough without the contradictory briefings Gough received before he left to take up his new post. Although he was appointed by, and operated under, War Minister Churchill, he was called first to a private briefing at the Foreign Office by Lord Curzon, the acting Foreign Secretary, at which Curzon explained, according to Gough's recollection, that Britain's policy was one of 'non-interference' in the Baltic. Curzon 'was anxious that Mr Churchill's hostility to the Bolsheviks should not lead me into committing Britain to any action which was contrary to the Government's view, which might happen if Mr Churchill's views were my sole guide'. He was also at pains to caution Gough against giving General Mannerheim, the Regent of Finland, any encouragement or support for a march on Petrograd. Subsequently, Gough had an interview of an altogether different character with Churchill himself. Pacing about his room and constantly referring to the large map of Russia on the wall, Churchill optimistically explained to Gough how the various invasions then under way against the Bolsheviks – Kolchak from the east, Denikin from the south and the British from the north, together with the one proposed by General Yudenich from the Baltic – would encircle and crush the Reds. 'He seemed to overlook the scale of the map', Gough noted, 'and that these four movements, separated by immense distances, were handicapped by very inferior numbers and equipment.' He put these points to Churchill, who swept them aside with the comment that Bolshevik morale was low and the resolute advance of even small armies would cause their organisation to disintegrate. It was a typically over-sanguine judgement of the kind Churchill was to make throughout the intervention. As to advice from the War Office itself, Gough claimed that he received none – not even a clear statement of what the object of his mission was. 'A most surprising ignorance existed there as to the actual situation in the Baltic Provinces', he declared. This was not entirely true and perhaps reflected Gough's subsequent difficulties with his Whitehall masters.[5]

In fact Gough received very clear instructions for his mission, whose British element was sixty-six strong (including two brigadier generals and thirty-one other officers of various ranks) and was to be spread across the four capitals of Finland, Esthonia, Latvia and Lithuania. The control of German activities was stated to be 'the most important, as well as the most difficult', of the mission's duties. Gough was also instructed to advise the War Office on the best means of assisting the Baltic States in providing for their own defence and reducing

German domination of their affairs. In addition, he was to examine the practicability of the Russian Northern Corps continuing its operations against Petrograd from Estonia and the measures needed to assist it in doing so. But if the mission's objects were plain enough, carrying them out was a different matter. Gough had no troops with which to support his orders and decisions, only the authority the Allied Powers in Paris whose agent he was, and the power of the British fleet which, even under the fiery Cowan, was severely limited in what it could do to bring sea power to bear. But the appointment of Gough and also of a Chief Commissioner for the Baltic States, Lieutenant Colonel Tallents, a senior Foreign Office official, with a subordinate in each of the state capitals, did seem to herald clearer policy and firmer action. More than that, it relieved Cowan of an onerous and inappropriate responsibility ashore and freed him to concentrate on bottling up the powerful Russian fleet in Kronstadt and supporting the new states, where he could, with the guns of his ships.

Expecting a general without troops, rather than an admiral without any, to control the activities of von der Goltz forces was not really very much of an improvement. Von der Goltz declined to obey Gough's orders, or even to shake his proffered hand when they first met, and employed all manner of prevarication to avoid doing what the Allies required of him. His early efforts to enlarge and discipline his force, and then to drive the Bolsheviks from Latvia, were generally in accordance with Allied wishes. But his actions were taken to establish German authority rather than to allow the Letts to govern themselves. They were too weak to oppose him and von der Goltz regarded them as Bolsheviks or at least Red sympathisers. His 'Iron Division' took Mitau in early March and Riga in late May. The expulsion of the Soviets from both places, however, merely replaced their terrorisation of the population with that of the German troops and their assistants, the Baltic *Landeswehr*, who behaved with great harshness and cruelty: 'a veritable reign of terror' was how the Foreign Office described the occupation of Riga, where 3000 inhabitants lost their lives. Intervention by British representatives did something to moderate these excesses; but ultimately it was countervailing force which put an end to von der Goltz's larger ambitions, if not to the high level nuisance he continued to represent. In June, aiming to extend German control, the Iron Division started an advance towards Estonia, but was met in northern Latvia by a joint force of Latvian and Estonian troops which decisively defeated the Germans. Von der Goltz suffered a double blow, for later in the month the Treaty of Versailles was signed. Within four days his troops had fallen back forty miles. Colonel Tallents arranged an armistice which required the *Landeswehr* and all German troops to be out of Riga within forty-eight hours and all German troops out of Latvia as soon as possible. The agreement also gave General Gough the right to nominate a new commander for the *Landeswehr*. This appointment went to a young Irish Guards lieutenant colonel on Tallents's staff, Harold Alexander, later a distinguished field marshal. Alexander, still in his twenties, took command of the 2000 Balts of the *Landeswehr* and led them out of Riga to the front against the Bolsheviks. There, dressed in his Irish Guards uniform, but wearing Russian high boots and a grey astrakhan Cossack-type hat, he 'succeeded brilliantly', according to Tallents, in keeping his men uninvolved in the further machinations of von der Goltz. With German power at last on the wane, the Latvian premier, Ulmanis, was finally able to leave the security of a British ship and attempt to govern his impoverished country.[6]

In 1919 Kronstadt was probably the best protected fleet base in the world. It lay on the southern side of Kotlin Island at the narrow, eastern extremity of the Gulf of Finland. East of the island was the Gulf of Petrograd, the wide estuary of the River Neva which flowed down from Petrograd itself, ten miles distant. Built initially by Peter the Great, and even then immensely strong, the defences of the Kronstadt had been developed over the centuries and were formidable. Westward of the base were minefields stretching from coast to coast with a single swept channel. Closer in, the northern and southern routes around Kotlin Island had further protection: the northern channel was spanned by a chain of forts linking the island to the northern mainland; the southern, main approach to the base itself and the River Neva also had several sea-based fortresses watching over the swept channel. The forts of the northern chain were known to be linked by submerged breakwaters. On the higher coastline around the narrow neck of the bay were large fortresses armed with powerful artillery, 12-inch guns in the case of the major fortress of Krasnaya Gorka on the southern coast. With a view commanding all approaches to the island base was the Tolbukhin lighthouse. Behind this formidable protection, sequestered in the Kronstadt basin itself, lay the Bolshevik Baltic Fleet. It was known to include one dreadnought-type battleship, one older model, a large cruiser and numerous heavy and light destroyers, besides a flotilla of submarines and numerous patrol craft. A seaplane base lay close by. The Baltic fleet was of a size and strength which could brush aside Cowan's force should it choose to emerge from the security of its base and the comfort of its minefield, and if it was handled with skill and resolution.

As the ice began to clear from the Gulf of Finland in the late northern spring, Cowan gave warning of a more aggressive posture towards his opponents by moving his base from Helsingfors first to Reval and then, after several warnings from the Admiralty not to take any risks, into Biorko Sound, off the island of Selskar, only thirty miles from Kronstadt. He regarded Reval as too distant for a swift reaction to any sorties by the Bolshevik fleet, whereas from Selskar all activity from the base could be closely monitored. This important advantage was gained at some risk to the hard-worked destroyers of the squadron on constant watch for any attempted foray, and at the expense of harder living for the ships' crews alongside the remote island. On 17 May the Bolsheviks tried a reconnaissance in strength in which a heavy destroyer led four other vessels out of the base. The cruiser *Oleg* and the dreadnought-type battleship *Petropavlovsk* also slipped out of harbour past the defences. The destroyer opened fire on the British squadron, which immediately went forward to the edge of the minefield. Returning fire, the squadron scored a hit on the Bolshevik destroyer and the Red force slowed to a few knots before returning to base. Cowan finally had to turn his force away when it came under fire from the big guns of the shore batteries. Brushes of this kind became common throughout Cowan's difficult watch. They served to emphasise the strength of Kronstadt (if not the skill of the Bolshevik sailors) and the difficulty of getting to grips with the fleet sheltered there.

A means of breaching the apparently impregnable defences of the base had, however, already been devised. Lieutenant Augustus Agar and some seamen volunteers, working in plain clothes directly for the Secret Intelligence Service (SIS), had been sent to the Baltic in charge of a pair of recently developed weapons, 40-foot coastal motor-boats (CMBs), with orders to make contact with a British agent operating in Petrograd who was having difficulty in getting messages in and out of the city in view of the increasing activity of the Bolshevik counter-intelligence service. Agar was given the job of landing and collecting couriers and, ultimately, of rescuing the agent himself. Based at Helsingfors whilst awaiting the secret arrival of his CMBs, Agar studied the charts of the coastline, including Russian ones of the Kronstadt base provided by an agent, and considered how best to insert and retrieve the couriers. The Russo-Finnish border was too well policed to offer a realistic entry route for them, whilst landing them at suitable locations on the southern, Estonian coast would not only involve making a dangerous sea trip across the Russian section of the Gulf of Finland, but would also give the couriers an equally hazardous 100-mile trek north to Petrograd. Ultimately Agar decided upon a plan of spectacular audacity which exploited perfectly the characteristics of the new naval weapon, the CMB. He planned to take the couriers right to the outskirts of Petrograd itself by the most direct route possible – through Kronstadt's seaward defences and up the River Neva. Relying on the cover of darkness and the skill of a local smuggler (bribed for the occasion) as pilot, his idea was to take one of his small boats through the north channel's chain of forts, relying on the small size and shallow draft (the CMB drew only two feet nine inches) of his craft to evade the defenders and surmount the mine and breakwater defences and its great speed to keep him out of trouble subsequently. It was a matter of nice calculation and great risk: whilst the mines he might encounter were set at a harmless depth of six feet, the breakwaters were believed to be at only three; he would have perhaps three inches to spare. With the agreement of the Finnish authorities, who at first had no inkling of his true role, Agar based himself secretly at a tiny Finnish harbour less than fifteen miles from the critical line of forts (indeed it was actually inside the main Russian minefield) from which good observation of Kronstadt was possible via the local church tower.

The plan worked perfectly, assisted by a single element of good fortune – the garrison of the important fortress of Krasnaya Gorka, which commanded the approaches to Kronstadt's southern channel, was in revolt when Agar made his attempt and was distracting the defenders of the naval base from their primary task. The mutinous garrison apparently believed that a counter-revolutionary coup was already under way in Petrograd and they wished to join it. The following day, safely back at his secret base with his mission completed, Agar watched helplessly as the Bolshevik battleships, which had come out of the basin for the purpose, shelled the fortress which was now flying the white flag of opposition to the Soviets. A day later he repeated the trip through the defences, bringing the agent out again onto Finnish soil. Once again the small size, great speed and shallow draught of the CMB, matched by Agar's courage, saw the tiny craft safely through. On the return jouney Agar could see the battleships of the base, protected by a screen of destroyers, continuing their bombardment of the mutineers in Krasnaya Gorka. It would plainly be only a matter of time before the place capitulated, unless the battleships could be forced to retire. He resolved to try to do something about it.[7]

Agar already had SIS agreement for the arming of each of his CMBs with the single torpedo they were designed to carry, but this was for defensive purposes only. He now contacted London for permission to use them for a torpedo attack on the exposed battleships. The reply, of uncompromising clarity and directness, was: BOATS TO BE USED FOR INTELLIGENCE PURPOSES ONLY – STOP – TAKE NO ACTION UNLESS SPECIALLY DIRECTED BY SNO BALTIC. Speed, however, was vital if the fortress was not to fall and also because the shroud of darkness on which Agar's operations depended would soon disappear in the 'white nights' of the northern summer. With the assurance that Admiral Cowan would 'support', though could not 'direct' him, Agar decide to attack on his own initiative that very night, 15/16 June, using both boats. The short period of darkness meant that the boats could not leave until after midnight. All went well for the first half hour, but then the second boat struck an obstruction which shattered its propeller shaft. The venture had to be aborted as Agar's boat towed its crippled partner back to base. Crestfallen but undeterred, he determined to try again the following night with the remaining boat, hoping that a single torpedo could do sufficient damage. By this time the battleships had returned to the base and the 6600-ton heavy cruiser *Oleg* had taken over the bombardment. Despite a succession of mishaps, Agar managed to slip undetected through the cruiser's screen of destroyers, close to 500 yards at high speed, despatch his sole torpedo and then race away under heavy fire from the escort destroyers as a large flash followed by a huge column of black smoke confirmed that the torpedo had found its mark. It was a brilliant operation for which Agar was later awarded the Victoria Cross: three men in a 40-foot boat had sunk a 12-gun heavy cruiser with a single torpedo without loss to themselves.

The only shadow to fall across the achievement was that the action failed to save the rebellious garrison of Krasnaya Gorka. Unsupported by a coup in Petrograd or any advance by Yudenitch's Northern Corps, whose attack had now come to a halt, the rebels finally succumbed to the sustained shelling. Flying over the base the following day in a Finnish plane, Agar had the satisfaction of seeing the *Oleg* lying on the bottom of the shallow gulf but the mortification of observing red flags again flying over the fortress. His action had, of course, been technically without authority, but he received Cowan's strong endorsement when he finally reported his exploit to the pyjama-clad admiral in his cabin at 2 a.m. a couple of nights later. The fact remains, however, that despite Cowan's determined brush with the force from Kronstadt on 17 May, and Agar's spectacular sinking of the *Oleg* a month later, the Admiralty was still unclear as to the rules of engagement for their ships in the Baltic and the legality of their actions.

The First Sea Lord, Admiral Wemyss, and Admiral Fergusson of the Naval Staff used the occasion of these successes to argue for more freedom of action for Cowan and his captains. Attending the meeting of the War Cabinet with his chief on 4 July, Fergusson demanded to know, 'whether, in the event of the Bolshevik Fleet coming out, our ships were authorised to engage them ... Both the Admiralty and the Naval Officers on the spot were really in ignorance as to the exact position: were we or were we not, at war with the Bolsheviks?' Prime Minister Lloyd George replied in a form of words which became among the most memorable of the intervention: 'Actually we were at war with the Bolsheviks, but had decided not to make war. In other words, we did not intend to put great armies into Russia to fight the Bolshevik forces.' This was hardly a satisfactory answer. The First Sea Lord then asked the War Cabinet to 'give the Admiralty authority to take any action they might think necessary to meet a change in the situation in North Russia'. The meeting finally concluded (and this over a year after the first land engagements between the two sides) that a state of war did exist between Britain and the Bolsheviks and, in consequence, 'our Naval forces in Russian waters should be authorised to engage enemy forces by land and sea, when necessary'. These formal decisions never reached the public, where the consequence would surely have been uproar; nor, presumably, did they reach the Bolsheviks. Cowan, however, now had the freedom and authority, if hardly yet the strength, for more decisive naval action.[8]

9

Plan of Attack

Churchill's efforts in Paris to substitute a massive, coordinated, international offensive against the Bolsheviks for the Prinkipo peace proposal was the most extreme of the interventionist schemes to come before the Peace Conference's Supreme Council. It suggested an operation which would combine the armed forces of the Allied Powers with those of the states bordering Russia. When President Wilson, sailing back to the United States, heard of Churchill's scheme he was 'greatly surprised' and quickly repudiated the throwaway line he had made to the council as he hurried to catch his train. He had not meant that the United States would fall in with any Russian policy the conference decided upon, but only that he would not take any hasty, separate action. 'It would be fateful to be led further into the Russian chaos', was his verdict on Churchill's plan.[1] Subsequent interventionist proposals were made by Marshal Foch in his position as chief military adviser to the council. His ideas were a little more modest in that they suggested employing only the armed forces of the east European states, while supporting them with military *matériel* supplied by America and the west Europeans. But even within these parameters they were impractically ambitious and politically unacceptable. His first proposal involved mobilising the Finns, Poles, Czechs, Roumanians and Greeks, as well as the White Russians, against the Bolsheviks – with massive support from the Western Powers. Lord Balfour, speaking for Great Britain at the Supreme Council, argued that, since both President Wilson and Lloyd George were absent from Paris, the council could not possibly consider such a gigantic scheme. When the principals returned, and Foch submitted an apparently more limited proposal, he met with the firmest of objections from the President and Lloyd George. 'To attempt to arrest a revolutionary movement by means of deployed armies is like trying to use a broom to sweep back a high tide', was the President's view. 'If this Bolshevism remains within its own frontiers, then it should be no concern of ours.' Lloyd George entirely agreed. One might have imagined from this agreement of high principle that neither of them had a single soldier on Russian soil. Thus the proponents of a concerted, international drive on Moscow lost their case.

It remained for the other extreme of Supreme Council opinion, the one which desired some sort of deal with the Bolsheviks and a resumption of relations with Russia, to make its last effort. On the initiative of President Wilson's representative, Colonel House, it had already been arranged for a young State Department Russian specialist, William Bullitt, to travel to Soviet Russia with a radical journalist colleague, Lincoln Steffens, unofficially and secretly, to gather first-hand information about the Bolshevik regime and to discover its conditions for a peaceful settlement. Bullitt had discussed the visit with Philip Kerr, a colleague of his on the British delegation, and received from Kerr his personal views on the terms which the British government might find acceptable. Kerr produced a list of suggested terms which included a general ceasefire, *de facto* recognition of the territory held by the various Russian governments, withdrawal of Allied troops, and the restoration of trade relations. Whether these had actually been discussed with Lloyd George or any of the Cabinet remains a matter of debate. Nevertheless there seems little doubt that the American delegation went to Moscow with British approval and assistance. It was some time before Bullitt and his colleague reported back.[2]

Despite the conference's efforts to agree and coordinate a miltary policy towards Russia, unilateral national decisions continued to rule the day. By this time Britain's policy had at last been determined, and without any reference to Paris. Sir Henry Wilson had accompanied Churchill back to London after the latter's brief interventionist foray at the Quai d'Orsay. The bitter divisions which the CIGS had witnessed at the Supreme Council's session on 17 February convinced him that there would never be an agreed Allied policy for dealing with the Russian problem. 'I think this is the greatest depth of impotence I have ever seen the Frocks fall to', he commented in his diary. He therefore prepared a paper for the Cabinet recommending a Russian policy for Britain alone. It proposed the complete withdrawal of British troops from Archangel, Murmansk, the Caucasus and Siberia as soon as conditions allowed, the continuation of the policy of supplying Denikin and Kolchak, and the protection of the states whose integrity had already been guaranteed, namely, Poland, Roumania, Finland and the Baltic states. When Churchill received Wilson's paper, he declared that its proposals were 'most cold-blooded'; but they were, in fact, less radical than might appear. The north Russian theatre, from which, under Wilson's plan, two major generals' commands would disappear, had never presented a significant challenge to the Bolsheviks, certainly not once Lenin and Trotsky had been properly apprised of the diminutive size of the Allied forces deployed there. The substantial Caucasus deployment had also never been more than a temporary arrangement, concerned with the security of oil and India rather than the toppling of the Bolshevik government. The important challenges were coming from Kolchak and Denikin, whose advisory and training missions and material support from Britain the CIGS proposed to strengthen and increase.

Churchill perhaps appreciated the inevitability of the troop withdrawal from the north, although he bitterly resented it and did all he could to limit or evade it. He continued also to propose other challenges to the Bolsheviks, even within the context of what he regarded as Sir Henry Wilson's dispiriting proposals. In commenting on the CIGS's paper, he declared that, in defending the new border states against Russia, there was no need for the Allies to 'stop their pursuit of the Bolsheviks when they reach the frontier'. Nor did support for the border states suggest that Britain would have to abandon the White Russians, for, in Churchill's view (from which logic was entirely absent), the stronger the latter became, the easier would be the task of protecting the new states. 'He talked much wild nonsense about sending 6000 men each to Denikin and Kolchak', recorded the CIGS. In fact Churchill proposed a great deal more. He suggested not only an expanded Military Mission to Denikin but also much advanced weaponry and the specialist volunteers to man it: forty tanks (400 men), two RAF squadrons (500 men), fifty armoured cars (300 men) and a machine gun battalion (1000 men), all supported by a General Staff of 800. To these he added 2000 volunteer Chinese coolies as a tank maintenance force.[3] This last proposal seemed neatly to balance the bands of 'Chinese executioners' whom British propaganda claimed the Bolsheviks were employing to do their dirty work. General Wilson's more temperate and realistic proposals, however, set out in subsequent papers, finally won over his chief. The problem was getting Lloyd George to agree to a unilateral British policy for Russia, and in particular one which involved a substantial degree of indirect intervention and considerable cost to a Britain already finding difficulty in making ends meet in the post-war world.

The Prime Minister was in his customary delicate position, leading a Conservative-dominated Parliament keen to unseat the Bolsheviks, but responsible to an enlarged electorate and restive working class which wanted no part of the Russian war. His own view was closer to theirs. Besides, he already had something of a vested interest in the fresh peace approach to the Bolsheviks which Colonel House had put in motion with the Bullitt Mission. He also wished to see the response to Marshal Foch's proposals before finally determining his own position. His reply to Churchill's repeated demands for a definite policy on Russia, and for a more strongly interventionist one at that, was to insist that policy must be decided in Paris, since it was an Allied decision. In addition, and here was a genuine concern given Britain's parlous post-war economic position, he had no infomation on the costs of the proposals which Churchill was making. The War Office hastened to provide these. As the Secretary of State and his General Staff pressed for a decision, so the Prime Minister continued to stall.

The weather, which in north Russia determined much of what was possible and what was not, now took something of a hand in the proceedings. Churchill was to make the most of the apparently serious position of the forces 'icebound in the far north'. If Ironside and Maynard were to be withdrawn from north Russia they needed to know soon. Once the spring thaw began the military situation would be transformed; land movement would become a problem, but the rivers would enter into their own, with a return of the dangers from the powerful Soviet gunboats which had been so effective the previous autumn. For Ironside would come the risky few weeks when the river to the south of him would be open to the Bolsheviks, while the port channel and the sea behind him were still icebound and closed to shipping, and the Soroka trail support route to the Murmansk command rapidly changed to impassable mud. These were indeed important factors in the situation; but Ironside had now been reinforced with heavy artillery, and the railways on his and Maynard's front were soon to be maintained by a substantial reinforcement of professional US railway engineers. His English troops were now operating with courage and effectiveness, and he had the promise of support from a much more sustantial river flotilla come the spring. His Russian troops were growing in number and commitment. There had been, Ironside noted, 'surprisingly few desertions and no further acts of ill-discipline'. Although the Russians were not highly trained, he believed 'they were better than anything the Bolsheviks could produce'.[4]

When Churchill presented the Army Estimates on 3 March he explained to the House of Commons that the country was 'half way between war and peace'; that was why he was presenting a budget for an army of two and a half million men to carry out the immense peace-building responsibilities which still fell to Britain's lot. On the matter of the troops still in Russia, he took care to explain how the main deployment had first taken place as part of the struggle against the Central Powers. He went on, 'That reason has passed away, but the troops sent in obedience to it are still on those wild northern coasts, locked in the depth of winter, and we must neglect nothing for their safety and well-being. We must look to the House of Commons, to the public generally, and to the newspapers', he added significantly, 'especially to those whose influence upon the opinion of the troops is so marked – we must look to them to support us in everything the military authorities think it requisite and necessary to do to support those men.' These were sentiments with which no one in the Chamber was likely to disagree: none did. This was not, however, Churchill's last word on Russia. He went on to explain that Britain had 'incurred heavy commitments towards the people of these districts who have espoused our cause, and to the Russian armies, which were encouraged and called into being largely by the Allies'. One Opposition Member, Sir Donald Maclean then asked, 'What Russian people and what Russian Army?', making the point that there were two sides to the civil war in which Britain was getting involved. He called the appropriation for which Churchill was calling 'a vast sum – a staggering sum', and explained that, 'right throughout the country, and in the Army itself, there is nothing which is causing graver unrest and anxiety than the commitments of the country with regard to Russia'. Another Member, Mr J.M. Hogge, expressed the general view of the Opposition when he declared that, 'I am perfectly willing, if we have troops on the Murman coast, or in the Caucasus or in Siberia, to stand by any expedition to fetch them away. But I am radically opposed to do anything which would involve us as a result in a conflict with Russia. The people of this country do not want such a conflict. The soldiers do not want it.' He, too, was astonished by the continuing military costs. 'It is not every Minister', he noted, 'who can spend £500,000,000 inside an hour as my Right Honourable Friend did this afternoon!'

Churchill's plan to continue supporting the Whites was backed by a phalanx of supporters on the government benches, whose preference seemed to be not only for the troops to remain in Russia, but for much more positive action to be taken against the Bosheviks. They had little patience with the international statesmen attempting to determine the Russian policy; 'the lotus eaters of Paris' one called them. The language of many of those who spoke in support of the policy of backing the White Russians echoed some of the more colourful expressions displayed in Churchill's speeches on the subject. Sir Samuel Scott backed 'the determination of the government to protect those who have helped us from murder by the Bolsheviks. If we leave them unprotected we hand them over to be killed by Chinese executioners.' Major Archer-Shee called for a volunteer army to destroy the Bolsheviks, warning that, 'Unless the Allies make up their minds to intervene in Russia and upset this Government of bloodthirsty barbarians, the whole of Europe is likely to be infected and the fall of civilisation will be almost complete'. Major Henderson considered that Bolshevism was 'really a contagious disease' not merely 'some internal question with which we have no concern'. Another believed that Britain was 'entitled to put some sort of ring fence about the evil'.[5]

It was with sentiments such as these still vivid in their recollection that the Cabinet met the following day. Churchill once again asked to be given a definite Russian policy. The Prime Minister replied, for the umpteenth time, that the matter would be discussed in Paris as soon as he returned there. The general British policy, as Churchill knew, was to withdraw its troops from Russia and then supply the White Russians. Churchill argued that it was impossible to evacuate north Russia before June and that the British troops had to be properly reinforced before then to ensure a safe withdrawal. The Second Sea Lord supported him and declared that the navy was already planning to send additional vessels and 2400 ratings to support the land forces, whether an advance or withdrawal was decided upon. This plan for substantial reinforcements for north Russia, against which the Cabinet had previously set its face, was a new factor in the situation. Both major services were now pressing for an early decision, with Churchill 'deeply apprehensive that without it the consequences might be absolutely disastrous'. Foreign Secretary Lord Curzon finally stepped in, supporting a decision for withdrawal. The War Cabinet now appeared agreed on this and on allowing the

War Office and the Admiralty to take the necessary steps to cover the evacuation. At a separate meeting two days later, at which Lloyd George was not present, ministers similarly determined to withdraw the troops deployed in the Caucasus. Curzon, who had earlier argued the case for defending the new states there, now agreed with Churchill. In return for the withdrawal of these 30,000 troops, which in essence had always been acting defensively, Churchill proposed to make it up to Denikin with a British Military Mission of 1800 and also to send a similar training mission to Kolchak in Siberia, whence the two British battalions, the Hampshires and the Middlesex, would also be withdrawn.

Even these substantial additions to Britain's commitment to the cause of the White Russians did not appease the Secretary of State. 'Winston says he will seriously consider resignation before submitting to ignominious withdrawal from Russia', noted H.A.L. Fisher, the Education Secretary, 'After conquering all the Huns – tigers of the world – I will not submit to be beaten by the baboons', Churchill declared.[6] There was soon evidence that he intended to use the freedom he had now been given to reinforce north Russia, to assist in the withdrawal, actually to undertake a major offensive there. In addition, he planned to support Denikin and Kolchak substantially and help train their armies for further ventures against the detested Bolsheviks.

No sooner had the Cabinet taken the Russian decisions than Sir Henry Wilson telegraphed Ironside at Archangel asking what forces he would need to cover a withdrawal, should the decisions be confirmed by the Allies, and the latest date for him to receive the withdrawal order. Churchill also fired off a lengthy minute to the General Staff asking for plans for a June withdrawal to be drawn up by, it is important to note, 'the Generals on the spot ... I wish the Generals on the spot to know that they are free to claim reinforcements, etc., for the purpose of covering the withdrawal ...' But despite this emphasis on local decision-making, he went on in his minute to make his own proposals. 'It seems to me', he wrote, 'that we ought to be preparing without delay a force of 5000 or 6000 men who could be sent if necessary to extricate these North Russian expeditions ... It is not necessary even to wait for the reports of General Ironside and Maynard.'[7] Ironside, however, was quick to reply, on 5 March, that no Allied troops would be needed to cover his withdrawal, though the navy would have to be reinforced along the River Dvina and at Archangel itself. Furthermore, he believed the Russians (meaning the White Russians; the Bolsheviks were generally denied their nationality in Allied references to them) would melt away once the British withdrew.[8] A couple of days later Churchill travelled to see the Prime Minister in Paris where Lloyd George was again attending the Peace Conference, informing the Supreme Council of Britain's decision to withdraw. The two old Liberal colleagues, now a gulf apart on the issue of Russia, breakfasted together, discussing the Cabinet's recent decisions for which Churchill wanted the Prime Minister's formal approval. Once Churchill had returned to the War Office, aware of Lloyd George's true preference for a negotiated settlement and no doubt mindful also that the Bullitt Mission was yet to report, he wrote the Prime Minister a long and careful letter summarising the War Cabinet's decisions to which Lloyd George had just agreed.* 'If I have wrongly interpreted your decisions in any respect', he concluded his circumspect words, 'I hope you will let me know what you really wish, in order that I may see whether it can be done.' In the course of the letter Churchill took care repeatedly to reiterate that the decisions he was confirming were Lloyd George's and the War Cabinet's rather than simply his own. The Prime Minister did not reply to the sober recital, but Churchill promptly circulated it to his Cabinet colleagues and it became the basis of Britain's Russian policy for the next five months. Churchill now had the freedom 'to make whatever military arrangements are necessary' for the safe evacuation of the Archangel troops. It was a freedom of which he was to make the fullest use.

Despite the confirmation of these long-awaited decisions, Churchill, as Secretary of State for War and Air, continued to press for more action against the Bolsheviks. On 14 March he wrote bitterly to Lloyd George complaining that 'You and President Wilson have, I fear, definitely closed your minds on this subject and appear resolved to let Russian affairs take their course'. He repeated his warnings to the War Cabinet on 17 March, declaring that 'It was idle to think we should escape by sitting still and doing nothing. Bolshevism was not sitting still'. This warning became all the more effective when, a few days later, the Communists under Bela Kun seized power in Budapest and set about trying to establish a Bolshevik Hungarian regime. The War Cabinet, however, baulked at the idea of trying to equip counter-revolutionary forces to topple Bela Kun, whereupon, according to Thomas Jones of the Cabinet Secretariat, 'Churchill grew very hot and prophesied vast and immediate disaster …'[9] In fact, Bela Kun's Bolsheviks were in power for only eight months. On 26 March Churchill spoke in the House of Commons, again warning of the iniquities of Bolshevism in typically colourful and sensational language. The Bolsheviks, he explained, 'destroy wherever they exist', and, 'by rolling forward into fertile areas, like the vampire which sucks the blood from his victims, they gain the means of prolonging their own baleful existence'.

When the Cabinet met again, on 31 March, Churchill was not present at the meeting's start. In a discussion on Russia, Lord Curzon argued against an early evacuation from Archangel, because of the disastrous effect this was likely to have on the various states fighting alongside Britain against the Bolsheviks. The Chancellor of the Exchequer, Austin Chamberlain, ever mindful of costs and suspicious of the interventionist arguments, put forward the opposite case

---

* The letter is reproduced as Appendix 2.

– that the troops should be withdrawn without delay and that there should be some arrangement with the Bolshevik government to allow this to happen. A negotiated withdrawal of this kind had, of course, been a realistic and practicable proposition ever since the Armistice, when the rationale for the intervention disappeared; but it was never seriously considered. At the time General Ironside had hoped that, even at that late hour, 'something might happen to save us from our winter campaign', and had taken the view that 'had we been ordered to withdraw I had no doubt that we could have done it as a military operation'. The fact was, however, that he 'was never asked to consider the question of evacuation after the Armistice'.[10] The issue of a negotiated withdrawal had been raised in January during discussions in Stockholm between the US diplomat William Buckler and Maxim Litvinov. Litvinov had agreed to a negotiated withdrawal, and indeed for the evacuation of any Russians committed to the Allies' cause who wished to go with them.[11] Nevertheless, Chamberlain's proposal was dismissed on the grounds of the prestige such a withdrawal would give to the Bolsheviks. Prestige was still looming large. Churchill finally arrived at the meeting to bemoan the disastrous French withdrawal from Odessa on the Black Sea which had just occurred, which he believed completely compromised the position of the troops in North Russia, whose lives might be 'gravely endangered' thereby. He seemed, at every opportunity, to be emphasising the dire straits of the British troops in the far north.

Churchill subsequently wrote privately and in secret to the French Prime Minister Clemenceau, appealing against the French intention to withdraw from north Russia and complaining that the French Foreign Minister Pichon had publicly announced the precise Allied strength there, letting the Bolsheviks know how weak the forces were. He protested at the declaration of another French Minister, Abrami, 'that not another single man would be sent to the aid of this small force'. He went on to explain the authority he had been given to send reinforcements to Ironside and his plans to send 'a strong brigade of volunteers' to Archangel, as soon as conditions allowed, to help extricate the British element. He suggested that Clemenceau might do the same. 'I should have thought you would meet with similar support', he wrote, 'as long as the operation was clearly defined as one of succour and extrication.' He wrote again to Lloyd George complaining of these public exposures, declaring 'It was shameful of the French to disclose our weakness and intention to withdraw to the enemy'. It was a disclosure which 'might easily lead to the destruction of our whole force while it is still cut off by ice'. In the wake of the French disaster at Odessa, and perhaps fearful that a similar one might befall his troops in the far north, Lloyd George replied by telephone the following day, regretting the French disclosures and confirming the freedom that Churchill sought. 'I do not wish any interference with any arrangements you may have made for making evacuation of troops and those associated with them in Northern Russia, perfectly safe.' Churchill immediately circulated the message to his Cabinet colleagues.[12] With this reassurance he no doubt considered he now had *carte blanche* for the substantial reinforcement he had in mind.

He promptly wrote to General Harington in the War Office, who was holding the fort during Sir Henry Wilson's absence in Paris advising Lloyd George: 'I am ready, therefore to receive proposals for strong action. I consider the force we are forming should be known as "The Rescue Force", which will in every way shield it from criticism and gain it support. I do not see why we should not call for volunteers in addition to those we have already selected. It would be interesting to see what response we got.'[13] This suggested that Churchill was considering a further force for north Russia, in addition to the brigade from the new Regular Army which had already been decided upon.

Churchill's repeated statements about the perilous position of the Archangel force, and his very clear intentions to send reinforcements to extricate them, seemed to stand in sharp contrast to the judgements which Ironside was sending back from north Russia to the effect that he did not need any reinforcements in order to get his troops out. His opinion of 5 March was repeated on 10th, when he said that he could not yet give his withdrawal plans since these needed to be concerted with the Murmansk command, and again on 17 March when he welcomed the War Office proposal to ask the French government to send to Archangel the Russians troops whom they were training in France. The real need at Archangel, emphasised Ironside, only too conscious of where the potential weaknesses lay, was for good Russian officers; but he needed no British reinforcements. The situation of his own troops was indeed hardly threatened by the destruction which Churchill claimed to fear. It had been critical in late January when Shenkursk and other positions had been lost, and the Yorkshires had momentarily wavered, but that crisis had developed largely because the forward positions to which Poole had allowed his troops to penetrate had been perilously isolated and the forces there were completely outgunned by the Bolsheviks. Since then much had changed. Ironside, an experienced gunner himself, had ensured that his artillery was reinforced with 60-pounders which, by a huge logistical effort, had now arrived at the front. Every ice-breaker in the region had been used to get the guns and ammunition through: 'after three weeks' strenuous battle the ammunition ship *Wardown* staggered into port almost in a sinking condition' to discharge its vital cargo, wrote the artillery commander. Then 118 sturdy Russian ponies took over and, under the direction of the Canadian gunners, hauled the guns to the front where they outranged anything the Bolsheviks had available.[14] It was an important and timely achievement, given the improving weather that would free the upper river for the Bolshevik gunboats. British morale had been restored and capable senior commanders and further troops were filtering through to Ironside along the Soroka trail. More

Russian units were replacing the tired men in the line. It was at this juncture that some good news from the front and two important messages from London served to change the Archangel commander's mind about reinforcements.

The first message, on 18 March, was a wire from the CIGS asking Ironside whether, if 5000 fresh British troops were sent to him, he would be able to strike a hard enough blow to prevent a Bolshevik offensive this year, so as to give the Archangel regime 'a fair chance of holding out' after the British had gone. This message reached Ironside at about the same time as he received news that a small Anglo-French volunteer detachment from his force, accompanied by a representative of the Archangel government, had managed to penetrate inland as far as the Pechora river, just west of the Urals and some 400 miles from Archangel, though much further by the circuitous overland routes. There it had made contact with advanced contingents of Kolchak's northern army. The significance was obvious: if a summer campaign could firmly link the two fronts, the strategic situation would be transformed. Kolchak would have a nearer and more reliable base at Archangel and a secure line of communications to it; all the White forces would be heartened and the Archangel administration immeasurably strengthened; the British would be able to make their withdrawal without disaster overtaking the Russian administration they left behind. Ironside replied on 22 March. Provided he was given 5000 fresh British troops, that the Dvina flotilla was brought up to strength, that Kolchak's troops cooperated in the move and that Bolshevik forces elsewhere were held down, he *guaranteed* to drive the Bolsheviks from the main Dvina port of Kotlas. This was the Bolshevik base for their Dvina flotilla and their 6th Army, besides being a terminus of the main central railway line connecting with the rest of Russia, including its White heartlands. But Kotlas was also 400 miles from Archangel and over a hundred beyond Ironside's most advanced positions. The guarantee was bold, but not foolhardy over-optimism on the commander's part, for his caveats were substantial. He was planning to use his Russian troops as well in the offensive. These were as yet largely untried, but by the end of March there would be almost 14,000 under arms, with more in prospect.

The second communication from London was a 'personal and secret' letter, drafted by Churchill himself and sent on 2 April. It read as follows:

> In your E.1191 of 17th March you express opinion that no extra troops will be needed to carry out evacuation. Nevertheless on the advice of the General Staff we are preparing a Mixed Brigade and proposing to send it through as soon as the ice allows. This is a measure of precaution to guard against unforeseen dangers like a Bolshevist rising in your midst, the discouragement of the troops, or an unexpectedly heavy attack by the enemy. Of course we do not want to send the troops if they are not needed. Pray consider the whole position in the light of recent events and wire me whether your present opinion is still unchanged.[15]

The message reads somewhat oddly in the light of the exchange between the CIGS and the local commander: 'recent events' had served to strengthen Ironside's position rather than weaken it. Was this 'Mixed Brigade' the 5000 troops to which Sir Henry Wilson had referred? Was the Secretary of State merely attempting to temper the optimistic judgement of an able but overconfident young general? Was it an effort by Churchill, mindful of his brief from Lloyd George and the Cabinet which his developing plans were already in danger of exceeding, to ensure that the reinforcements, intended for an offensive to put the Bolsheviks out of action for a whole season, would be justified by Ironside as wholly necessary simply to extricate the British force? Encouraged no doubt by the CIGS's message, Ironside's response provided the reply to which Churchill's letter guided him. 'It is very desirable', he wrote on 1 April, 'that a compact force should be despatched which could bear the brunt of any fighting during evacuation and which will enable me to relieve exhausted troops tried by service under conditions which have existed.'[16] The War Office could now concentrate on recruiting the volunteers which the so-called 'Rescue Force' and the expanded missions for Kolchak and Denikin required. Henceforth Churchill was to refer to the Kotlas operation as 'Ironside's Plan', as though the young commander had been the originator of the whole scheme.

Over a year previously Churchill had written to Beaverbrook, when the latter was his colleague as Minister of Information, declaring that he was 'increasingly convinced that there can be no more valuable propaganda in England at the present time than graphic accounts of the Bolshevik outrages and futility, of the treacheries they have committed, and what ruin they have brought upon their county and the harm they have done to us and our fighting men'.[17] Beaverbrook agreed, but did not like Churchill interfering in a matter which was the concern of his ministry. By the end of the main conflict the War Cabinet had taken up the 'Bolshevist horrors' idea, intending 'full and speedy publication' of whatever it uncovered. Material was collected, much of it second- if not third-hand and a great deal of it spurious; but by the end of March 1919 nothing had appeared in public. Churchill nagged Curzon for the Foreign Office to hasten publication of the 'Bolshevik atrocity blue-book', explaining that, 'I find it a difficulty in supplying the necessary reinforcements for Archangel and Murmansk; public opinion is not sufficiently instructed'. Curzon replied that he was pushing the matter on as hard as he could. A few weeks later the eighty-eight-page White Paper appeared. It was entitled *A Collection of Reports on Bolshevism in Russia* and painted a graphic and frightening picture of the excesses and barbarity of Lenin's regime.* The

---

* The circumstances of the publication of this report bear some comparison with those of Prime Minister Blair's 'dossier' produced eighty-four years later, written in justification of a similar number of British troops being sent to invade Iraq.[18]

Foreign Office ensured that it was widely available on the news-stands at the lower than cost price of twopence. The booklet has been described as a 'wildly hysterical piece of propaganda' and 'one of the most absurd documents ever to appear in the United Kingdom as an official government paper'.[19] It was, nevertheless, taken at its face value by many at the time and certainly by the right-wing MPs who dominated the government benches in the House of Commons. It was laid before Parliament on 3 April 1919.

The press had featured Bolshevik horror stories for some time. One member of the Foreign Office Political Intelligence Department remarked that he found it 'easy to get "horrors" into the press', adding that such stories were 'doubly useful if properly authenticated', thereby implying that they did not need to be.[20] Typical was *The Times*'s article on 3 April which presaged the White Paper. Its headlines give the flavour: HORRORS OF BOLSHEVISM. A CRY TO HUMANITY. MONSTROUS TREATMENT OF WOMEN. Countless similar stories of Bolshevik excesses had been featured for some months. There is little doubt that some of them were true; though how many were attributable to Lenin's regime is another matter. The social dislocation caused by the civil war, particularly outside the metropolitan centres, the freedom accorded to the secret police, the notorious Cheka, and the poor quality of many of its operatives did much to account for them. The situation was also seriously exacerbated by the food shortages for which the Allied blockade was partly responsible. But just as many of the gruesome stories originated in the areas of Russia under control of anarchist groups and robber bands who bore no allegiance to the Bolsheviks. Such was the case with the notorious Saratov Manifesto,* which snowballed from a brief item in a Moscow newspaper into a major story taken up uncritically by many of the British papers, as in *The Times*'s headline above. That the Bolshevik authorities repudiated the story, and the practices it authorised, escaped the attention of most. Two themes, sex and race, guaranteed to arouse uncritical indignation, seemed regularly to feature in the propaganda.[21] Hence the emphasis on the alleged debauchery of the Bolsheviks (who actually did much to liberate women) and the activities of the notorious 'Chinese executioners' whom they were said to have employed.

The press was similarly involved in painting the picture of the critical situation of the forces in North Russia and the need for reinforcements to relieve them. The fact that these extravagant accounts were engineered by the War Office is clear from Ironside's admission: 'At first I was annoyed at this exaggeration,

---

* According to a decree issued by the Anarchist Club of Saratov, all women between the ages of seventeen and thirty-two became the property of the state; the rights of husbands being abolished, though as former owners they retained the right of using their wives without waiting their turn.

until I woke up to the fact that the War Office was pressing for a relief force to be sent out to us in the spring and that their task in getting authority to sanction this move was being considerably lightened by reports of heavy fighting.'[22] As the spring thaw approached, the worrying reports reached a crescendo. A selection of the headlines on 4 April makes the point. NORTH RUSSIAN ALLIED ARMIES ENDANGERED BETWEEN BOLSHEVIKS AND THE SEA – URGENT CALL FOR REINFORCEMENTS declared the *Manchester Guardian*; while for *The Times* it was ARCHANGEL DANGER – TIRED AND ISOLATED FORCES that headed the main news story featuring the following imaginative news: 'On the Archangel front the enemy continues his menacing preparations, and all the signs are that he proposes to make an attempt to drive us into the sea.' There followed a leading article which explained the need for an offensive at Archangel with a homely analogy. 'You nearly always have to attack before you can withdraw – if your fingers are trapped you have to push the door open before you can get them out.' All true, but to push the door open as far as Viatka seemed a little excessive. 'There are no politics in this new appeal', declared the editorial soberly. *The Times* that day also included an interview with Sir Ernest Shackleton, whom it introduced as the 'Director of Equipment and Transport to the Northern Russia Expeditionary Force'. The famour explorer had just returned from Russia, his mission completed. Shackleton pressed all the right buttons, underscoring the critical situation of the forces in the north, but also emphasising the larger purposes which a volunteer relief force might serve. 'The situation in northern Russia is undoubtedly an anxious one', he explained. 'The Bolshevists … are not ignorant of the possibility of unlimited rapine and loot if Archangel falls.' He went on to declare, 'I am certain that if volunteers were called for, sufficient fit men would respond, and that within three months the Bolshevist power would be broken … A three months' campaign by a volunteer Army would break the Bolshevist monster'. The justification of simply ensuring a safe withdrawal seemed to have disappeared.

The *Daily Herald* was understandably more circumspect. Beneath a headline declaring BOLSHEVISM: WHITE PAPER TO JUSTIFY NEW WAR, it proceeded to intone gravely, 'Yesterday it was announced that more troops were to be sent to Russia. This morning the Government produced a White Paper of eighty-eight pages on Bolshevik atrocities. The connection is not difficult to see.' The *Daily Express* delivered the 'acute danger' message under the banner headline, ARCHANGEL FORCE IN GRAVE PERIL, but its leader turned to larger issues. 'We want to know clearly and at once who has been responsible for the hare-brained policy which has put this force in peril.' Beaverbrook's mouthpiece accepted the need for reinforcements to bring the Archangel force away safely, but it was clearly suspicious of Churchill's intentions and issued a blunt warning to the government. 'Against any idea of a large punitive expedition the whole country sets its face like flint ... Russia must be left to stew in the juice of Bolshevism ... One step beyond the rescue of our helpless men, and the Government is dead.' The newly-ennobled Lord Beaverbrook was no longer a political insider, but his suspicions were well-founded. He would later do his best to make good his threat.

Then came the White Paper, which was debated and much quoted, in an angry session of the House of Commons on 9 April, against a background of rumours and leaks from the Paris Peace Conference about the Bullitt Mission's contacts with the Bolsheviks and the proposals for the recognition of their regime. The idea of recognising the 'murderers and villains' who now held power in Moscow was anathema to the Tory majority and was widely condemned in the Northcliffe press. When Colonel Josiah Wedgwood called the White Paper 'anonymous tittle tattle' (which much of it was), he was howled down with cries of 'Shame!' At the end of the debate over two hundred Members of the House took the unusual step of signing a resolution in the form of a telegram to Lloyd George, again absent in Paris, opposing any recognition of the Bolshevik government by the Peace Conference. There seemed to be an incipient mutiny within the parliamentary coalition. The telegram was forwarded to the Prime Minister the following morning.[23] The day of the 'Bolshevik horrors' debate was, very appropriately, the day when the press carried the details of the War Office's appeal for volunteers for the 'North Russian Relief Force', as it had now come to be called. Churchill had chosen the new and more ambiguous title to leave it unclear whether the force was merely to rescue the existing troops or to relieve them in the line. Two brigades, rather than the one about which Churchill had initially written to Ironside, were now to be raised, a total of 8000 men.

Meantime the Bullitt Mission had been going about its business. The two young men had travelled by boat to Norway, and then across Sweden and Finland, before meeting Chicherin and Litvinov for initial discussions in Petrograd, journeying on with them to Moscow where their consultations continued. The emissaries were given the red carpet treatment by the Russians during the week they spent with them and were suitably impressed. 'The Soviet Government is firmly established', Bullitt later reported. 'Perhaps the most striking fact in Russia today is the general support which is given the government by the people in spite of their starvation.' It was his conclusion that 'No government save a socialist government can be set up in Russia to-day except by foreign bayonets, and any government so set up will fall the moment such support is withdrawn'. This may have seemed a starry-eyed judgement to those who read Bullitt's reports. Bruce Lockhart, however, had intimated something similar when he had first returned from Moscow. Following a long conference with Lenin, Bullitt was given a statement of the peace terms acceptable to the Bolsheviks. These were similar to, though certainly stiffer than, those which Kerr had judged the minimum his government would accept. For example, whilst Kerr had proposed that *de facto* governments should remain in full control of the 'territories which they at present occupy', Lenin's proposals substituted 'territories they occupied at the moment of the Armistice'. This was a significant difference. Lenin's was perhaps the better legal position, but it was one which Lloyd George would have found impossible to sell, not only to Clemenceau, but also to an increasingly hostile Cabinet and House of Commons. It is uncertain whether Lenin was negotiating in good faith or was merely, as at Brest-Litovsk, playing for time. Nevertheless, the Soviet proposals suggested that they were prepared to surrender, at least temporarily, parts of the Archangel and Murmansk areas, as well as Finland, the Baltic states, much of Siberia, the Caucasus and the Ukraine. They required an acceptance of their proposals by 10 April. Bullitt was very sanguine about the prospects and in mid-March, as soon as he had quit Soviet territory, he cabled Lenin's terms to Paris, where he arrived himself on 25th.

Although Lloyd George breakfasted with Bullitt a few days after the return of his mission and discussed its outcome with the young official, he was clearly not prepared to take the negotiations any further, certainly not without a lead from the American administration. He was only too aware of the strength of Churchill's position, which had been confirmed by the unusual telegram from the MPs, and the widespread opposition to any recognition whipped up by White Paper and the press campaign. He was also distracted by a serious dispute with the French over the German treaty, whilst Bela Kun's seizure of power in Hungary, only a few days before, had reminded everyone of Bolshevism's international, indeed global, aspirations. At home he had the growing problem of the Sinn Fein rebellion and the increasingly militant trade unions with which to grapple. According to Bullitt's testimony, Lloyd George showed him a copy of that day's Paris edition of Lord Northcliffe's *Daily Mail*. Pointing to a leader entitled 'Peace with Honour', which forewarned of the possibility that the Allies were considering making a dishonourable peace with the evil Bolsheviks, Lloyd George declared, 'As long as the British Press is doing this kind of thing, how can you expect me to be sensible about Russia?' Bullitt, nevertheless, believed that Lloyd George was giving his negotiations serious consideration. The Prime Minister had apparently discussed with his colleagues, in Bullitt's presence, whom he might send to take up the negotiations. Bullitt quoted General Smuts, who was also at the breakfast meeting, as averring that the Soviet offer should not be allowed to lapse.[24] All this was a false dawn for Bullitt; Lloyd George did nothing further. His political position was too weak for him to press for negotiations until the Russian civil war, extended as it was likely to be by Britain's involvement, had fully run its course. As for President Wilson, dogged by recurrent illness, he seems to have been too absorbed by the problems of the German treaty even to read Bullitt's report, let alone see the young diplomat.

On 11 April Churchill made an impassioned speech at the Connaught Rooms denouncing the Bolsheviks in the most violent language. 'Of all the tyrannies in history, the Bolshevik tyranny is the worst, the most destructive, the most degrading', he declared. He described Russia's decision to desert her allies in the Great War as a betrayal of honour and an act of murder, even claiming that 'Every British and French soldier killed last year was really done to death by Lenin and Trotsky, not in fair war; but by the treacherous desertion of an ally without parallel in the history of the world'. In the passion of his diatribe he seemed to have forgotten that, after its series of massive defeats and appalling casualties, the Imperial Russian Army had crumbled to pieces, as had much of the empire's social order, by the time Lenin's peace overtures began. The speech was reported to Lloyd George and clearly made an impression on him. One of his dinner guests recorded his comments on Churchill's performance: 'In certain moods he is dangerous', declared the Prime Minister, 'He has Bolshevism on the brain … he is mad for operations in Russia'.[25]

The comment illustrated, if nothing more, the difficulty of the task which confronted the Prime Minister when he faced the suspicious and hostile House of Commons on 16 April, the last sitting before the Easter recess, to move the adjournment. It was his first address to the House since he had received the rebel MPs' telegram and was inevitably largely concerned with explaining the policy towards Russia. His speech was an astonishing mix of political contradictions and intellectual gymnastics as he tried to preserve his position and retain a vestige of principle and moderation in the nation's policy. Without mentioning the Bullitt Mission or the Bolsheviks' stated terms for peace, he emphasised that there was no question of recognising a Russian regime, for there was no *de facto* government of the whole of Russia that might be recognised or with which Britain might negotiate. He attempted to explain his policy with an analogy of contemporary Russia as a volcano. 'Boundaries advance and boundaries recede', he declared. 'It is just like a volcano; it is still in fierce eruption, and the best you can do is to provide security for those who are dwelling on its remotest and most accessible slopes, and arrest the devastating flow of lava, so that it shall not scorch other lands.' It seemed an apt comparison. He went on, however, to declare against military intervention, which was counter to 'the fundamental principle of all foreign policy' of never interfering in the internal affairs of another country, no matter how badly it was governed. He seemed to see no contradiction between this principle and the huge quantities of military aid now flowing to the Whites from British dumps and on British ships, nor with the force being readied by Churchill for despatch to Archangel. Besides, he explained, military intervention in Russia would be a gigantic undertaking which would be ruinously costly and 'the surest road to Bolshevism in Britain'. Britain, nevertheless, was 'standing by her friends, General Denikin, Admiral Kolchak and General Kharkov [sic].

Without the support of the White forces which Britain had improvised after the Treaty of Brest-Litovsk', Lloyd George declared, 'the Germans would have broken the Allied blockade.' This claim had a tenuous connection with the historical facts – even as they were then imperfectly known by the Prime Minister. The time for negotiation with Russia, he declared, would be when Bolshevism, already rapidly on the wane, finally disappeared.

Lloyd George managed to complete the Russin section of his speech without any mention of the Bullitt episode, but was then directly questioned by one Member about the suggestion that he had been involved in receiving approaches from the Bolsheviks. In his reply the Prime Minister was studiously dismissive: 'No, we have had no approaches at all. Of course there are constantly men of all nationalities coming from and going to Russia always coming back with their own tales ... But we have had nothing authentic ... I think I know to what the Right Honourable Gentleman refers. There was a suggestion that there was some young American who had come back. All I can say about that is that it is not for me to judge the value of these communications.'[26] Bullitt was furious with Lloyd George's Pilate-like repudiation of him. 'It was the most egregious case of misleading the public, perhaps the boldest thing that I have ever known in my life', he declared. He was little mollified by various members of the Premier's delegation who visited his hotel to apologise. But Lloyd George's misleading reply was not entirely indefensible: the Bullitt Mission had initially been secret and therefore 'deniable'. However reprehensible Bullitt found the performance, the Prime Minister had managed to preserve the unity of his Coalition Government by effectively capitulating to Churchill and the right wing; but it was only to a limited further intervention that he had surrendered; not what the Secretary for War had hoped to achieve in Paris, nor indeed what he was planning. Besides, the Bolshevik deadline had already passed, and with it had gone the last real chance of a negotiated peace. The Peace Conference's efforts at devising a Russian policy, of whatever kind, were effectively at an end.

The Commons adjournment debate did not conclude without a long and rousing intervention from Josiah Wedgwood, Churchill's personal friend but avowed political opponent on the intervention question. Wedgwood welcomed the return of the Prime Minister to the country where his liberal principles were much needed. 'The reactionary Foreign Office under that eighteenth-century Tory, Lord Curzon, was going from bad to worse', he declared. He went on to attempt a summing-up of the process by which the Russian policy had recently been determined.

> The papers one day are suddenly filled with news of the critical situation of our force at Archangel, where we are told we may expect another Kut unless something is done at once ... the public gets into a panic. The result is that the War Office gets *carte blanche* to

send troops to Archangel and we are committed, without the consultation of the Prime Minister, by the Foreign Office and the War Office combined to an enlarged expedition to Archangel.

He admitted that there might be real danger at Archangel, but his information was that the chief danger was 'the fatal habit' of the Russian troops with whom we were cooperating of 'deserting to the other side whenever they get a chance'. He wanted an assurance that the demand for relief troops 'was not merely a mask for getting there a force which will make a further advance and, indeed, make a dash upon Petrograd'.[27] Wedgwood was awry with his Petrograd suspicions; but in light of the secrecy surrounding both the political planning and military arrangements for the projected Archangel offensive, it was an inspired suspicion.

10

Maynard's Offensive

The Murmansk Command was not favoured with anything like the important role given to Archangel in Churchill's developing plans. There was nothing General Maynard would have liked more than sufficient reinforcements to make a dash for Petrograd: that had been his strategic ambition all along, and the developing support for General Yudenitch in Estonia seemed to harmonise with his ideas. But for Churchill and the CIGS Murmansk had none of the significance of Archangel, with its large population, developed port facilities and allure of becoming the supply base for the White Army from Siberia. Nor, it seemed, did the smaller Bolshevik army opposing Maynard have much intention of moving northwards against him. Maynard's troop strength had been steadily reduced during the winter to help deal with the apparently critical situation of Ironside's force, and thereafter his theatre was put largely in the shadow as the plans for Ironside's command began to take shape in Churchill's mind. The latest unit to go was the 6th Yorkshires, which made the move to Archangel in early March. Maynard was nevertheless keen to continue his offensive down the railway and was already making substantial progress as the hidden agenda for the Relief Force was being developed. By March the worst trials of winter were over; the temperature occasionally rose above freezing. At the end of the month the Murmansk commander began a series of minor but cleverly planned operations which were to take his troops to within striking distance of the vast Lake Onega.

First, in mid-February, came the capture of Segeja, a railway village which controlled an important bridge forty miles beyond the Allied front line. It was taken largely by surprise tactics, for the first stretches of forested land now created the opportunity for an unobserved approach by an attacking force. A column of two hundred men, travelling by horse sleigh, made a wide detour and reached the outskirts of the village before the garrison was aware of their presence. After a brief stand by the Bolsheviks, the village was taken with the bridge intact, much of the garrison managing to withdraw southwards, blowing a minor bridge behind them as they went. Meanwhile other columns converged on the villages bypassed by the main assault and dealt with their isolated detachments. The operation was carried out whilst the cold was still intense, but it was a complete success. A further forty miles of railway corridor had been gained and over two hundred Bolsheviks killed or captured at the cost of one killed and ten wounded on the Allied side. Most importantly, much needed engines and rolling stock were captured.

The Bolsheviks in reply hurried men forward to Urosozero, now their forward position on the railway, and began preparations for a counter-attack. They made a half-hearted attempt the following week but were easily driven off. The Canadian commander at Segeja, Major Anderson, now aware that the Bolsheviks were receiving further reinforcements and planning a stronger attack, boldly decided to pre-empt them. Without consulting his superiors, he had the partially destroyed bridge quickly and secretly repaired, although it was within sight of the enemy, and then launched an attack straight down the railway in an armoured train, with a troop train following. His total force was less than a hundred men and included some untried Russians. The defenders of Urosozero were taken completely by surprise. Two lines of trenches north of the railway station were taken in enfilade by the armoured train and then 'mopped up' by the troop train following. Fifty of the enemy were killed and forty captured, together with two field guns and much booty. Instead of reproaching the major for his unapproved enterprise, Maynard promoted him to lieutenant colonel and awarded him the DSO. The newly battle-tested Russians went on to clear the small hamlets which protected approaches to the railway town. It was a very successfully climax to the winter campaign and set things up nicely for the spring. The tactics for these railway engagements were developing as cover became available for flanking columns to advance unobserved. The plan was often for a subsidiary force to capture and dismantle part of the line behind the defenders to prevent their escape and to forestall the move forward of enemy reinforcements. Then there would be a speedy, direct advance down the railway by the main body, in an armoured train when one was available.[1]

The Murmansk Command had not, however, lost all of the *opéra bouffe* quality which the First Lord of the Admiralty had discerned when he had visited it the previous spring. The Finnish Legion were one factor in the increasingly bizarre situation. These 'Red Finns' had grown steadily more disaffected since the civil war in their homeland had ended and the German threat had disappeared with the conclusion of the Armistice. Unwilling to be used against the Bolsheviks, they were also too numerous to disarm, yet they remained on the army payroll. Then there were the Karelians. The Karelian Regiment was not formally part of the Allied force and had an agreement that it would not serve outside its own region; but, after the regiment's very successful autumn campaign, much of Karelia was now free of incursions from the White Finns, leaving the men with very little to do but draw their pay and become increasingly restive at the growing White Russian influence in Maynard's headquarters. Since these were essentially political problems, Maynard had always to refer them to the local Foreign Office representative, or even direct to London for advice. Both issues might have been resolved had it not been for the ever-changing international situation and the developing moods of the local national leaders, together with the intransigence and hostility of the White Russians, who were chronically mistrustful of both Finns and Karelians and determined, as ever, to hold onto every element of the old Russian Empire. It was these very Russians whose authority General Maynard was attempting to bolster and whose tiny army he was trying to enlarge. The unfortunate and at times tragicomical reality was that the sympathies of the Finnish Legion and the Karelian Regiment, both formally substantial elements of Maynard's multinational force, lay almost entirely with the Bolsheviks. These problems peristed throughout the spring and summer of 1919 and provided a constant anxiety for the general as he attempted to continue his advance with a very mixed Allied force whose own morale was at times far from unshakeable.

In early March, Maynard reported to the War Office that the men of the Finnish Legion were refusing to be deployed in penny packets. A couple of weeks later they were opposing any action at all against the Bolsheviks, becoming, the general wrote, 'a very serious menace to our safety'. At the end of the month he telegraphed the War Office that the Finns intended to join the Bolsheviks and fight against the British, with large numbers of Karelians expected to join them. 'My British troops have been so reduced by reinforcements to Archangel that I am left with an exceedingly small force on which I can rely', he wrote in exasperation. He asked for a warship to be sent to Murmansk with landing parties of four hundred men: an expensive precaution against a force which still remained in British pay. A mutiny which the Finns were planning (which involved an invitation to the British officers to join their Easter celebrations, to be followed by their speedy assassination) was forestalled when Maynard got wind of it and mustered a British force of infantry and marines to arrest the ringleaders. To considerable surprise, instead of punishing these putative mutineers, Maynard granted them safe passage to join the Bolsheviks in the south. The problem might have been solved if the Finnish government had been prepared to grant an amnesty to the Red Finns and had allowed them to return to their homes; but this was proving very difficult to negotiate with the eternally mistrustful Finnish government of General Mannerheim. The Red Finns themselves feared extermination if they went home. Maynard's lenient treatment of the mutineers, together with a promise to send a delegation to Helsinki to help speed repatriation, sufficed, however, to keep the lid on the Finnish problem until, after lengthy negotiations, repatriation finally took place at the start of September. Upon their return to Finland, the legionnaires had to attend a form of court martial at which their Canadian commander from Murmansk acted as 'prisoner's friend'. A few were given a spell in jail, but most returned free to their homes. Their own leaders, however, including General Lehtimaki, a hot-headed and troublesome Bolshevik, were refused repatriation and chose to join the Reds. Lehtimaki even asked Maynard's Chief Administrative Officer, Lieutenant Colonel Schuster, for a recommendation. Schuster provided it. Using a standard British Army form, he recommended Lehtimaki for command of a division in the Bolshevik forces![2]

The late winter advances had brought a much extended area under Maynard's control, but the region freshly acquired was very sparsely populated, being for the most part bleak tundra that would yield few fresh recruits for the White Army. As yet his Russians had little prospect of standing alone after the British departure. But the topography to the south of Maynard's new front line was changing Beyond it the railway passed through country which was largely flat, densely forested and broken by innumerable lakes, some tiny, others extensive. The land was arable and sustained a much larger peasant population. Village settlements were frequent, and around them were stretches of open land where the trees had been cleared and summer crops were grown. Communications were also better; the single-track railway was supplemented by minor roads linking some of the larger villages. Despite being bedevilled by the nationalities problems on his line of communications, Maynard calculated that an advance of another fifty miles would at last bring him to this recruiting eldorado: a region which might produce several thousand volunteers who would welcome the opportunity to turn their backs on the Bolsheviks. If this judgement was quite untested, the idea of a further advance was supported by other valid strategic arguments. Some fifteen miles ahead of him was the railway town of Maselga and a similar distance further south were the two large towns of Medvyeja Gora and Povynets which guarded the northern approaches to the enormous Lake Onega, the second largest lake in Europe. The Finnish frontier lay close to the west of the lake. These features therefore narrowed the front line; the two towns lay across the only avenues leading north from Bolshevik Russia. A further advance to capture them would not only create a defensible front for the White Russian forces to take over, it might pose a sufficient threat to the Bolsheviks to take some of the pressure off the Archangel sector.

Maynard's troop resources were also improving: two British companies (one of the King's Royal Rifle Corps and one of the Middlesex Regiment) had reached Murmansk on 17 April in response to his entreaties, and two companies of American railway engineers arrived a week later to maintain the vital but ramshackle single-track line behind him. These skilled and willing volunteers were particularly welcome, being able to maintain the line and defend it as well. Maynard was never entirely free from worries about his ever-lengthening line of communications. In January two British officers had been murdered in Murmansk. The same month a fire at Kandalaksha station destroyed five locomotives and much stock. A few days later the largest barracks at Murmansk was burnt to the ground with the loss of two NCOs' lives. In late March Maynard was warning the War Office that 'Bolshevik tendencies throughout district are far from being eradicated'. A RAF officer who joined the force a little later expressed surprise at 'the state of utter uncertainty as to the real loyalty of the White Russians we were helping. Immediately on arrival I was told to wear a loaded revolver at all times and to sleep with it under my pillow or it would be stolen during the night.'[3] Despite these concerns and buoyed by his new, if still modest, accretions of manpower Maynard now felt secure enough to mount a more considerable offensive operation – if only the War Office, which now actually wanted him to turn to the defensive, would permit it.

The serious difficulties with the Karelian Regiment, which had similar comical undertones to the problem with the Finns, had simmered on throughout the winter months. The regiment's British commander, Colonel Woods, spent the winter in Kem, where the influenza pandemic had taken hold and brought two or three deaths daily for many weeks. Woods was very loyal to his Karelian charges and believed that the rumours of the regiment's disaffection were much overplayed at Murmansk, where the malign influence of the White Russian officers was all too evident. At the end of March intelligence reports apparently warned that in early April the Karelians planned to rise in revolt, demanding separation from Russia and incorporation into Finland. It seemed that Finland would support them. In fact the option of joining Finland was very much a second choice for the Karelians, who would much have preferred complete independence but realised that this was a political impossibility. Woods's diary explains that a new commander for Maynard's southern, 237 Brigade, Brigadier General Turner, arrived in Kem with instructions that 'Woods must be sat on'. A fresh crop of British officers, appointed to the Kem garrison, at the very time when the Karelian Regiment was under suspicion, confirmed Woods's fears that he and his regiment were not trusted. His diary even records the serious but not incredible charge that the Russian Governor-General at Murmansk had 'arranged the poisoning' of the Karelian officer in charge of the regiment's depot at Kem. By this stage another new commander, Brigadier General Price, had been appointed in the south with similar orders to reduce the influence of Colonel Woods. Woods protested that the Karelians were loyal and honest, and that some of the Russian officers at Murmansk were treacherous. GHQ, he believed, had a misplaced confidence in the latter.[4]

A Karelian deputation to the British high command requested that the province be put under the protection of the British flag, but the Foreign Office refused. Subsequent requests to be represented at the Prinkipo Conference and for their Finnish language to be recognised for electoral porposes met a similar rebuff. The Karelians accepted these rejections sullenly and refused to serve under Russian officers. This presented a considerable difficulty for Maynard, who was busy trying to extend the force under Russian command as part of the withdrawal plan. The promise to introduce Russian commanders gradually, with the regiment remaining under overall British control and with a Briton commanding each of its battalions, proved little more than a palliative. Eventually doubts about the loyalty of the regiment, and the increasing desertions from it, decided Maynard to disband it, despite Woods's protestations, The regiment was paraded and addressed by Maynard and then, with considerable passion, by the Russian Commander-in-Chief from Archangel, General Maroushevsky. The Karelians were offered alternative employment in the Russian Army, or as an unarmed labour battalion supporting it. Only eleven of the Karelians' 250 pioneers chose the labour battalion and only 300 of the 700 in the fighting unit volunteered for the Russian Army: only 311 of the 3700 in the whole regiment who were drawing pay. But the men's decision was unsurprising: many of the Karelians, like the Finns, were 'Red', with friends and relatives on the Bolshevik side.[5]

Finland's intentions to free Karelia from its Russian overlords later became clear when a force of 5000 Finnish 'volunteers', supported by local Karelians from the Bolshevik-occupied section of the province, crossed the border about a hundred miles south of Maynard's front line and began an advance on Petrozavodsk, the Karelian capital, which the Bolsheviks still held. In some ways this was a not unwelcome development for General Maynard. The Finnish leader said that he would cooperate with Maynard in any way against the Bolsheviks, providing, however, all Maynard's White Russians were withdrawn. The Finns, pressing for their own independence, were now against all Russians, of whatever hue. But much as he welcomed the military cooperation of the Finns, Maynard could not, of course, accept their condition; cooperation with the White Russians remained his first concern. The Finns were later to demand that the Finnish Legion be similarly withdrawn. Maynard's reply emphasised what a useless force this had become: 'The Finnish Legion has not been employed for any military operations for seven months, and no portion of it has ever operated within 300 miles of my present force.'[6]

Meanwhile, the general was planning his advance on Lake Onega. He had cabled the War Office explaining its advantages and requesting sanction for an immediate advance. The War Office response to his plan came quickly at the end of April. It approved the offensive but enjoined caution. London could not afford to allow any more troops to be sucked into the Murmansk theatre by the ambitions of its commander: 'As no further reinforcements of railway or other troops can be sent it must be clearly understood that this advance must be undertaken with the resources now at your disposal'. Nothing daunted, Maynard pressed on. His advance began on 1 May. It was planned to take his force in two bounds to the shores of the lake and the capture of its gateway towns of Medvyejya Gora and Povynets. To assist his control of operations, he set up a small operational heaquarters at Kem, leaving one of his brigadiers to run the

12. Churchill inspecting British troops, 1919.
(*IWM, Q 34659*)

13. General Knox (seated left) and members of the Military Mission to Admiral Kolchak. (*IWM, GSA 042/Q 81130*)

14. White Russian Supreme Commander Admiral Aleksandr Kolchak with members of the Allied Missions and part of his large *Stavka*. (*IWM, GSA 042/Q 81115*)

15. General Poole (centre) and his mission in south Russia. On Poole's left is General Krasnov, the Ataman (leader) of the Don Cossacks. (*Lucy Sheppard*)

16. An armoured train leaves for the front in Murmansk Command. (*IWM, Q 16826*)

17. British armoured wagon with naval gun mounted. Part of Captain Wolfe-Murray's Royal Marine detachment from HMS *Suffolk* at Vladivostok. (*IWM, GSA 046/Q 70448*)

18. The Baltic Theatre. British tanks in the harbour at Reval. (*IWM, GSA 045/Q 69731*)

19. Ice-laden CMBs in Biorko Sound: three of the force which attacked the Bolshevik fleet in Kronstadt. (*IWM, Q 107940*)

20. Six Victoria Cross holders on their way to north Russia as part of the Relief Force aboard SS *Stephen*. Standing are Brigadier General Grogan (second left) and Lieutenant Colonel Sherwood Kelly (third left). (*Royal Hampshire Regiment Archives*)

21. Lieutenant Colonel Sherwood Kelly. (*Royal Hampshire Regiment Archives*)

22. General Holman (seated left), on a tour of the front, pictured with Cossack children. On the right is Harold Williams of *The Times*, according to Philip Knightley 'by far the worst war correspondent in Russia'. (*IWM, GSA 043/Q 75872*)

23. British guns, British uniforms, British artillery officers: Russian trainees. Novocherkassk, June 1919. (*IWM, GSA 75897*)

base and line of communications from Murmansk. The attacking force, though tiny, was nevertheless a remarkable patchwork of nationalities. Its right column was a mixture of Karelians and Russians; the centre, commanded by a Canadian, consisted of a hundred Royal Marines, a hundred Russians, thirty Americans, thirty Canadians and sections of French and British artillery; the left column was another small force of Russians. Despite growing enemy resistance and greatly increased, though wildly inaccurate, artillery fire, the force pressed on to take its series of railway objectives, culminating in the capture of Povynets on 18 May and Medvyejya Gora on the 21st. It was a considerable triumph, since it took place during the spring thaw when progress was difficult and turning movements practically impossible. Yet a speedy advance had been all-important lest the thaw enabled the enemy to deploy its considerable armada on the hitherto ice-bound lake.

The capture of Medvyeja Gora was of particular importance. It was a substantial town with considerable accommodation, and ample open space for the erection of tents, extensive railway sidings and a long lakeside quay protected from the worst of the weather in a sheltered neck of the lake. The town was connected, but for a broken bridge, to the main railway line to Murmansk. Its occupation opened up new fields of operations by water and air. No longer would Maynard's troops function in 'blind' columns unsupported by the other services. After a major bridging effort was completed, Medvyeja Gora was reconnected with the main line and became a centre of great activity. Motor boats for a lake flotilla which had been parked in a siding further north were now hurried down to the lake, quickly followed by RAF material for a seaplane base. A large landing strip was laboriously constructed at Lumbushi nearby. So much did confidence develop after this important advance that the initial rather over-optimistic withdrawal plan for the British force involved the Russians themselves taking over the advance south of Medvyeja Gora, supported by British gunners and aircraft operating from the new advanced base. The Bolsheviks were well aware of the town's significance: captured documents indicated that Trotsky, the Bolshevik War Commissar, had forbidden any retirement by his men defending it. Certainly the resistance of the Bolsheviks was strengthening in this southern region.

The effort required for this important advance and its successful conclusion brought difficulties as well as advantages for both Maynard and the War Office. Whilst the fight for the lake towns was still in progress the War Office telegraphed Maynard to stop recruitment of Russians, since there were no further British troops available to administer them. 'Limit yourself to what you have raised and trained already', decreed the message, and 'to operations which you can execute with present forces and occupy such territory as you can administer'. This was wise advice; but it confounded the main purposes of the whole advance: the creation of a viable Russian army which could hold the narrower front line.

Maynard had already commandeered deserted buildings at Medveyja Gora as training schools for the Russians and arranged instructors for them. He replied that recruits were now coming in 'with enthusiasm' because of his advance to the lake. Russian mobilisation, he declared, 'was a farce' until he had made this move. He asked for details of future policy so that he could put a safe limit on his advance. It seems, however, that the safe limit had already been reached.[7]

The following month was a time of great activity on the Murmansk front as the commander did his best to consolidate his advance, take control of Lake Onega and enlarge and strengthen the Russian forces. His advance had now brought him to the northern end of the Shunga peninsula, a long limb of land which stretched far out into the lake. It was a populous area, generally anti-Bolshevik in its sentiments but resolutely defended by the Bolsheviks with a strong stiffening of Red Finns – perhaps including those very men to whom safe passage south had been granted. Encouraged by the proximity of Maynard's force, the population of the northern section of the peninsula rose in revolt against the Bolsheviks and appealed for arms and assistance. Maynard's Allied troops were already fully occupied, so he risked using the more reliable and experienced of his Russians to pass rifles and ammunition to the insurgents. That was the first risk; the second was sending the consignment across twenty miles of lake from the nearest available point at Povynets to Shunga village, despite the lake not yet being under his control. The venture was a success and the rising spread. Fighting continued on the peninsula for some weeks before Maynard's force fully controlled it. The effort seemed to be worthwhile since the peninsula produced 2000 volunteers for the growing Russian Army under the command of General Skobeltsin. The concern was that this was all happening very late in the day. Was it realistic to suppose that an army so recently recruited could be trained in time to hold off the Bolsheviks as the British withdrew?

Great efforts were made to take control of some the lake as well. Maynard's RAF resources had previously been limited to six unreliable RE8s, but he had requested seaplanes in anticipation of using them on the lakes, and two flights had been railed south and were now waiting in sidings for the capture of Medveyja Gora. Once they were in use, their bombing and gunfire sank four Bolshevik vessels and three other substantial ones were captured: a 300-ton steamer, a small armoured destroyer and an armed tug. Other vessels were captured as the lake thawed. These were all substantial achievements for the small Murmansk force, but the effort had been considerable and signs were beginning to appear that the tiny army had had enough.

In early May, when Meselskaya on the approach route to the lake had been captured, General Maynard had singled out his Royal Marine Field Force for particular praise, saying that it had 'displayed splendid fighting qualities' and remarking that all troops were in the 'best of spirits'. But by late June the tone of

Maynard's telegrams had completely changed. He reported 'great enemy activity' at the front and noted that they were mostly Finns who 'fought with great determination'. In a counter-attack pressed with some vigour, they managed to cut off the troops on the peninsula from those defending Medvyejya Gora on the lake's north-western littoral. In his report Maynard was bitterly critical of some of his British troops, the Marines in particular. His words, which were a souce of considerable embarrassment to their corps and to the Royal Navy and became the subject of an acrimonious exchange between the War Office and the Admiralty, are worth quoting verbatim:

> Regret to inform you that Royal Marine detachment has shown such exceedingly bad spirit that I am sending them from Medvyejya to Murmansk at once to await first opportunity for embarkation to England. I am very disappointed in behaviour of both officers and men.
>
> Grave signs of bad discipline are also being displayed by the 253rd Machine Gun Company and the half company in reserve refused to go to the front to relieve the other half company. Matters have been settled for the present by threats of the strongest disciplinary action. Needless to say above two incidents have affected Russians adversely but I think removal of Marines will have good result.[8]

It seems that discontent among some of the troops in the Murmansk Command was of long standing. Puzzlement at why they were fighting the Bolsheviks at all, while home demobilisation was proceeding apace, was certainly a factor in their ill-discipline; the conditions in the Murmansk Command were another. It will be recalled that the trouble among 13th Yorkshires after their transfer from Murmansk to Archangel had something to do with the 'grinding fatigues' which the troops had endured during their winter in Maynard's command. Now there was evident discontent, even technical mutiny, afflicting other units as well. Most is known about the trouble among the Royal Marines because Maynard singled them out for criticism. Formal, and revealing, enquiries by both Royal Navy and Army were held as a consequence. Disgruntlement among the Marines seems to have been simmering for many months. As early as February 1919, fifty-five men of the Royal Marine Detachment at Kandalaksha had addressed a very threatening letter to their Officer Commanding. The letter complained that an earlier letter submitted by the men for consideration of their complaints by General Maynard had not been acted upon. 'The delay', wrote the men, 'has kept us in suspense. If after tomorrow's parade we have no satisfaction as to going home, we will down "tools" for forty-eight hours. If nothing happens then, we will commandeer the first train travelling in the direction of Murmansk.' They claimed that the other detachments of Marines were of the same mind. 'We think we have been out here long enough and what is more have been messed about like a flock of "sheep" without a Shepard [sic]. They complained about the cold, the conditions, the absence of medical attention and the lack of leave which army units were apparently getting. In short, they said, 'we have been nothing but a dung heap for the Army'. The letter caused a flurry of action, but apparently no serious disciplinary measures were taken; nor did the men carry out their threats, but continued at duty.[9]

There was a further and much more serious incident in May 1919 when the detachment went forward from Maselga to take part in operations for the capture of Medvejya Gora. The brigade commander gave orders for a strong reconnaissance patrol to go out on the night of 18/19 May to locate the exact enemy positions. The patrol was to be a joint one of marines and infantry. The detachment commander said that his men were very tired and footsore. When the infantry commander said that he had to have a hundred marines for the operation, the marine officer produced a doctor to say that the men were unfit for any strong exertion. The infantry company, equally exhausted, had to undertake the patrol alone. They were ambushed by the enemy and the worn out men panicked and took to their heels. Officers were unable to restrain them. The failure of the marines to undertake the duty was blamed for this humiliating reverse. There were further incidents in June culminating in the the detachment commander admitting, in a telephone call to the brigade major, that unless his men were relieved he could not be responsible for them holding their position. Apparently two platoons had refused to go on duty. The detachment commander was himself deeply disenchanted with the way his unit was being treated. He claimed that the men, having volunteered to go on outpost duty for four days, were kept there for fourteen without a chance to change their verminous clothing. He had already asked to be relieved of his command, having lost faith in General Maynard, who had promised him that the men would not be used south of Maselga except in 'case of unforeseen emergency'. These and other incidents, which seem to have passed without serious disciplinary action, formed the background to Maynard's telegram which aroused such indignation in both the War Office the Admiralty, if for different reasons.

The court of inquiry set up by Admiral Green, on which sat two RN captains and a RMA captain, concluded that there was no excuse for the officers and men to have refused duty as they had done. They criticised Maynard, however, for keeping the men at the front until the last possible moment, although they were well overdue for repatriation and had rendered service which had been recognised and valued by their local commander. They also made the telling point that the Royal Marine detachment 'had been on continuous active service in North Russia without leave for fourteen months and longer than any other military unit'. They declared that 'General Maynard is to blame for sending this report which they do not consider is just to the officers and men of the

Royal Marine Detachment known as Glory 3'. Subsequent comment within the Admiralty noted that the force had contained only four regular officers, the rest being temporaries, while among the men there were only two hundred Active Service ranks, the rest being 'Hostilities Only'. The naval authorities had expected the men to remain in Russia for a maximum of three or four months before being relieved by army troops. Repeated applications for their return had been met with the GOC's reply that he could not spare them. They also noted that the platoon which had given most trouble had been 'left to face an Arctic winter under the command of a temporarily promoted warrant officer with a temporary young subaltern under him'. They might have added that the overall commander of the Royal Marines in Murmansk, Colonel Paterson, had been transferred from his detachment to be Base Commandant at Murmansk while another of the experienced officers, Captain Drake-Brockman, had been moved to the staff of one of the brigades. The Lords of the Admiralty concurred with these serious findings and asked the Army Council to consider withdrawing the Maynard telegram. The matter dragged on between the corridors of Whitehall and the Admiralty for several months.

These were the days, it must be remembered, when the War Office and the Admiralty were separate, sovereign departments of state, each headed by a Cabinet Minister. When the nation went to war it depended crucially on cooperation between them. Besides threatening to put this cooperation at risk, the developing row was also beginning to expose the true responsibility for the problems of General Maynard and his Royal Marines. This was the policy of military intervention itself which the government had espoused, and particularly the decision to continue it once the main war with Germany was at an end. Secretary of State Churchill and his War Office were unaware of, or unwilling to face, the reality of its unpopularity among the troops in the north. They also continued to labour under the illusion, an illusion which their two local commanders were attempting, without too much success, to turn into a reality, that a substantial, loyal and reliable White Russian Army could be created in north Russia. Bearing the burden of the consequences of these misappreciations, Maynard was reaching the end of his tether. The affair of the Royal Marine detachment was only one of a series of setbacks for the Murmansk commander which made the months of June and July 1919 the low points of his time in command.

Things had begun to unscramble in early June when a signal from the War Office informed Maynard that all the men who had overwintered in the north were to be out of Russia by 1 September, that there was no prospect of fresh British troops for his command, and that the Russians had to be made self-supporting. A few days later a newly-trained, 500-strong Russian regiment, supported by seaplanes and artillery, refused to advance under fire and made no attempt to move on to occupy the western flank of the lake. 'This affects military situation very materially', wrote Maynard in some desperation, 'as my allied troops are gradually becoming a negligible quantity … It looks that the best we can hope for is that the new Russian Regiment will not turn against us.' So lamentable was the general's manpower situation becoming that he was reduced to asking for at least 'one reliable Russian Battalion from Ironside'.

He had a further shock the following week when he reported, 'nearly 2000 Russian troops on whom I had every reason to rely are untrustworthy'. He complained that the Murmansk Government had no money and that the railway workers had not been paid since March and were planning to strike. 'I am at low ebb for time being', he concluded. But worse was to follow. On 21 June he heard that the US railway troops were to be withdrawn, an 'extraordinarily selfish action' with the strike threatening. Furthermore the Serbian troops (perhaps his best infantry fighters) were now becoming unreliable as a result of the withdrawal of the others. The situation continued to deteriorate. A month later, on 21 July, Maynard had to pull the Italians out of the line as 'unreliable': this was his euphemism for their outright refusal to fight. Apparently one of them had addressed Russian civilian and troops, saying that the Italians were in sympathy with the Bolsheviks and had no intention of fighting them. By this stage news of serious mutinies in the Archangel force had percolated through to the Murmansk units. Maynard also learnt that some of the mutineers were moving along the road to Soroka, threatening his link with Ironside's command. His hopes now rested on the battalion of French marines he had been promised. Their early despatch was 'imperative', he told the War Office.[10]

11

The North Russian Relief Force

The public announcement of the recruiting of the North Russian Relief Force was made on the morning of 8 April and by 3 p.m. over sixty men had already presented themselves for enrolment.[1] 'Recruits are still pouring in dressed in civilian clothes, with medal-ribbons on their waistcoats and red handkerchiefs round their necks. They have all seen previous service, and look the most ideal material from which to form a battalion.' Thus wrote Major E.M. Allfrey of the volunteers coming forward.[2] The London *Evening News* commented that it is 'the soldier without a bit of [medal] ribbon who is conspicuous'. By 11 April Churchill was able to write to Sir Henry Wilson with some satisfaction: 'The volunteers are coming in well for Murmansk and Archangel. We had on the Horse Guards Parade today a scene which recalled the early days of the war, when a compact body of about a hundred magnificent men marched from the recruiting office to the depot. The Adjutant-General seems quite confident that he will get all he is asking for and more.'[3]

The economic incentives for enlistment were certainly very powerful: in drab and depressed post-war Britain employment was hard to find and there would soon be two million men out of work. That most of the volunteers were drawn from the ranks of the workless was clear from their appearance: 'Worn clothes, jackets in which the pockets drooped pitiably, collars devoid of all ties, ties to which no collars give effect, baggy trousers, boots thin and cracked.'[4] They were all seasoned soldiers nonetheless. The same economic imperatives seem to have applied to the ex-officer volunteers, for many were quite prepared to take places in the ranks as ordinary soldiers. The *Evening News* correspondent noted, 'The corporal of whom one enquires the way to the orderly room is no ordinary corporal. He has the DSO, and till lately was a major. Another NCO has twice been second in command of the battalion in France. The men who form a trench mortar battery are nearly all ex-officers'. Allfrey noted a man in the ranks who was a wartime captain with a MC and the Mons Star; and another until recently a pilot in the Royal Flying Corps. One officer in the naval flotilla was later to write of the Relief Force battalion which arrived near his position, 'They are all volunteers, and any quantity of ex-officers in the ranks, colonels etc galore; fellows wearing DSOs and MCs in private's uniform. I have never seen a finer crowd of men anywhere.'[5]

These were the civilian volunteers who would fill the ranks of one of the brigades of the Relief Force. The other brigade was to be composed of volunteers drawn from the regiments of the new Regular Army, steadily forming from the ashes of the old. Persuading the regulars to volunteer for Russia seems to have been a more difficult challenge, though many officers, who would, of course, take charge in both brigades, seem to have come forward quite readily. Some were no doubt motivated by the stories of the perilous situation of their comrades in the frozen north; others felt they had been hoodwinked by them. A few weeks into the preparatory training, Major Allfrey was confiding to his diary that the papers had recently been saying that 'if forces were not sent to Russia at once, Grousik [Ironside] and his forces would be driven into the sea', to which he added tartly, 'there was never a word of truth in this statement and I hope the men will never find out'.[6] No doubt others considered they had a moral responsibility to deal with the Bolshevik threat to civilised society which Churchill was regularly articulating so forcefully. Yet more complained that they had not volunteered at all. Such was the case of Major Wimberley, of 8th Machine Gun Battalion, who was to take part in the force's first operation in north Russia. One battalion adjutant wrote that they were given to understand that the expedition would be a picnic. 'The officers were told that North Russia abounded in game, and were advised to take fishing rods and guns, the better to enjoy a summer holiday.' The regular soldiers, many newly enlisted, some hardened veterans, proved more difficult to recruit to the venture. Although the two infantry battalions of the brigade of regulars were embodied as the 2nd Hampshires and 1st Oxford and Bucks Light Infantry, it is clear that the authorities had to scour all the regiments of the line in an attempt to find sufficient volunteers to fill their ranks. In the 2nd Hampshires men were drawn from twenty-seven other regiments, ranging from the Grenadier Guards to the Connaught Rangers; fewer than 20 per cent were Hampshires. Half their officer complement similarly wore other cap badges, while their commanding officer was not even a regular.[7] The same was true of the Oxford and Bucks, which was ultimately composed of men from twenty different regiments. There were also many 'pressed men' in the force. 'Relief was to be effected entirely by volunteers – that was emphatically stated', recorded the regiment's official historian. 'Actually, of course it was nothing of the kind'. One pressed man was Sergeant Pond, who had the misfortune to be on leave when the call for volunteers went out to units. On his return he was greeted by the company sergeant major: 'Pond, since you went on leave an urgent letter was received asking for volunteers for the North Russian Relief Force, you have the qualifications required so I have sent in your name.' Pond was astounded and protested, 'Sir, I have no wish to go to North Russia, I had enough in France'. The only consolation the CSM could offer was that Pond might not in the end be accepted. Needless to say he was.[8]

The Director of Military Operations had already determined that only 'officers of the highest stamp' would serve in the force. The call for volunteer soldiers aimed similarly for the best: it asked for fully trained troops in excellent physical condition who would be given service in the rank at which they were demobilised. The pay, allowances and bonus were to be on the enhanced scales which Churchill had negotiated for the Armies of Occupation. Besides this, they were to be given two months' leave with full pay and allowances at the end of their period of service in Russia. It was an attractive package. In addition to the infantry battalions of the two brigades, there were to be support units of the Royal Field Artillery, Royal Engineers, Machine Gun Corps and the ancillary services. All were to wear a distinctive white polar star on a dark blue background on their tunics. The day after the civilian recruitment began, an advance party of the regular element of the force was already beginning its journey to Murmansk.

The enlistment into the Relief Force was to be for one year, or such shorter period as was needed to complete the operation. The advertisement emphasised that the troops were to be used for the defence of existing positions, not for offensive operations.[9] This explanation, although vital for the public acceptability of the recruiting campaign, hardly accorded with the plans which Churchill was developing with his senior War Office advisers. The misstatement was to have unfortunate consequences. Sir Henry Wilson noted in his diary, after he returned to London on 23 April from a further advisory stint with the Prime Minister in Paris, 'Winston and I discussed a good punch towards Viatka to join with Kolchak before we cleared out'.[10] Viatka was over 600 miles from Archangel, in the heart of Russia, 200 miles beyond Kotlas, which had been the last provisional target given to Ironside. The extent of the misinformation was growing perceptibly. The General Staff Policy Paper which embodied these plans recognised that they 'may lay us open to the accusation of breaking faith, on the ground that these troops were provided and despatched to rescue our beleagured [sic] garrison, and not to undertake offensive operations against the Bolsheviks'. The General Staff believed that the offensive could be justified on the grounds that 'it is impossible to tie down General Ironside as regards the details of his operations or to forbid him to advance beyond a certain line'.[11] In other words the responsibility for the breach of faith was to be transferred from the Secretary of State to the commander at Archangel. By the time of Wilson's return to London the recruiting was still going reasonably well; 3500 men had already volunteered. This was fewer than the General Staff had hoped for but sufficient to make their developing plans practicable.

Unlike the brigades of the Great War, the two of the Relief Force were known throughout by the surnames of their commanders. Brigadier General Grogan VC, small, chubby-faced and young-looking, was an experienced and well-liked

Western Front commander. His brigade included five other holders of the Victoria Cross, including two who were members of his small brigade staff. The other brigade commander, Brigadier General Sadleir Jackson DSO, was a flamboyant and energetic cavalryman who had achieved some notoriety on the Western Front by motoring around the battlefield's rear areas in a blue Rolls Royce gathering up stragglers. He had later commanded 54th Brigade, one of the most successful of Kitchener's 'New Army' formations. Major Allfrey cast an experienced and sceptical military eye over Sadleir Jackson and concluded condescendingly: 'He is a pushing sort of man who enjoys a splash … he is a thruster, young and ought to command well. His hair wants cutting badly, otherwise he is a set-piece and a promising soldier.'[12]

One key characteristic of the early part of the previous year's campaign on the Archangel front had been the close cooperation between Royal Navy and Army, both in the descent upon the port itself and in the subsequent thrust southwards along the Dvina. Until the rivers finally froze, supplies and reinforcements for the troops on all three main river fronts had been delivered along the rivers themselves by the improvised and soon overtaxed Dvina flotilla, which had also provided the Army's sole substantial artillery support. Once the rivers iced up – and in these northern waters the ice could form to a foot deep in a single night – all naval support ceased and Captain Altham sailed his light cruiser *Attentive* back to Portsmouth where it paid off, appropriately enough, on Trafalgar Day. Altham had learned much in the brief campaign, during which his flotilla was generally outnumbered and outgunned. It was evident that the Bolsheviks had facilities for improving and strengthening their flotilla during the winter. If the Allied force was to remain in Archangel for any part of the coming summer, a much strengthened flotilla would be vital if Ironside were to hold his position and have his withdrawal adequately covered. At the War Cabinet meeting on 4 March, the Second Sea Lord had made clear his intentions to send substantial reinforcements to the White Sea station for the summer campaign. What he did not make clear, however, was that Admiralty approval for the fitting out of a fresh flotilla was based on the assumption that it would be designed only to cover a withdrawal and that it was 'not to advance beyond the immediate vicinity of our existing front up the river'.[13] Captain Altham was selected to command the enlarged force and given the roomier old cruiser HMS *Fox* as his mother ship. Admiral Kemp was also replaced by Admiral Green as commander of the White Sea station. Kemp had endured a lengthy and taxing stint at this cold and gloomy naval outpost, but a fresh commander at this stage in the unusual circumstances of this isolated posting was not, perhaps, the best arrangement.

The nucleus of the flotilla was already at Archangel: four river gunboats, built for the China rivers, which had managed to get into the port just before the winter freeze ended all movement. There they joined the monitors *M23* and

M25, already laid up in winter quarters. The plan was to send out a substantial reinforcement of four more small monitors, two more China gunboats, four shallow-draft minesweepers (also fitted to lay mines), six coastal motor-boats and a great number of auxiliary craft, as soon as conditions permitted. There were to be fast, shallow-draft steamers for the use of the Commander-in-Chief and the flotilla commander, as well as a roomy depot ship which could act as military hospital, bakery, refrigerator and general supply ship for the front-line units. 'Refrigerator' may read rather oddly in the catalogue of the ship's appurtenances; but in the short northern summer the temperature at Archangel could rise to almost tropical levels. In addition there would be a need for many small utility vessels for transporting the wounded, prisoners of war and the like, as well as lighters equipped as small workshops to modify ships for their river roles and keep them all in service. With two additional brigades set to join Ironside's army, a fleet of river transport craft was also required to carry the troops about the rivers. Finally, barges were needed for the personnel servicing the eighteen seaplanes which Altham was to have with his substantial flotilla. Seaplanes were much more useful than the land-based version with their immobile bases and hangars fifty miles behind the front. Altogether the proposed flotilla seemed a large and more than adequate force.[14]

Whilst the brigades of the Relief Force were beginning their training, the question of the use of the 'new gas' reappeared on Churchill's desk. In mid-April Sir Keith Price, a head of production at the Ministry of Munitions, wrote to his old chief's new department urging the use of the new weapon in the north Russian campaign. The gas was now available in two variants, DA and DM. 'Do not let the powers that be ignore the new Gas Generators', he wrote, 'I really believe they are the most deadly weapon which has yet been produced ... The DM generator knocks people out for say twenty-four hours but does not kill them, the DA kills alright; which is the right medicine for the Bolshevist, I don't know.' His letter also noted that 'gas would drift along very nicely and certainly put the wind up someone. I believe if you got home only once with the Gas you would find no more Bolshies this side of Vologda.'[15] This advice contained a remarkable pair of misunderstandings for an official so highly placed in the munitions specialism: neither DA nor DM was lethal, though both were effective incapacitants; and in the conditions of north Russia gas would certainly not 'drift along very nicely'. Despite Churchill's enthusiasm for using the new gas in his earlier note to Ironside, he was now hesitant about doing so. He wrote to Sir Henry Wilson's deputy, 'Are you sure that it is wise to give away the secret of our new gas for the sake of such a small application as would be possible in North Russia?' When the General Staff were able to reassure him on this point, Churchill concluded, 'of course I should very much like the Bolsheviks to have it, if we can afford the disclosure as proposed'.[16] A considerable time was to elapse before a satisfactory method of delivering the new gas was developed to meet the difficult circumstances of North Russia.

On 9 May General Lord Rawlinson, the respected ex-commander of the 4th Army on the Western Front, arrived at Crowborough Camp in Sussex, to which Grogan's brigade of young, untried regulars and veteran NCOs and officers had moved to complete their training and preparations for the move to Russia. Rawlinson was accompanied by General de Radcliffe, the DMO, who had played an important part in arguing for the formation of the Relief Force and its use in an offensive. Rawlinson inspected the brigade and liked what he saw. 'Very pleased with them', he noted in his diary, 'I made them a speech and saw them march past. Very fine lot.' Within a few days the brigade was moving to its embarkation ports for the voyage to Murmansk. By 26 May its vessels were approaching the mouth of the Dvina. General Ironside took a tug out to meet them as they steamed slowly up the narrow channel to Archangel. His tug ran alongside the brigadier's ship and the Commander-in-Chief transferred to it via a rope ladder and met the new commander and his staff. The brigade's vessels tied up at the dockside, but the battalions remained aboard ship until their formal welcome to Archangel the following day, when they marched ceremonially along streets lined with Russian troops under training. Grogan inspected a guard of honour provided by Dyer's battalion of the Slavo-British Legion, Ironside's particular creation. A crowd of some 20,000 assembled to witness the welcome ceremony of the city fathers. As Ironside surveyed the crowd, he estimated that it must have contained at least three thousand able-bodied men, of whom no more than 150 had chosen to come forward for the defence of their country. Unsurprisingly, he was heartily glad to see Grogan and his men. He addressed the battalions separately about the forthcoming operations, to the disconcerting accompaniment, in the case of one of them, of 'a sort of running commentary' from the Commanding Officer of the 2nd Hampshires standing behind him. 'I said no more, but told Grogan of the incident', Ironside recalled, 'telling him to watch this CO carefully'.

As Ironside's messages to London had repeatedly emphasised, the new Russian units which Generals Maroushevsky and Miller had formed, half of which had now taken their place in the line, still lacked good officers. The commitment and discipline of many of the battalions remained shaky. Sporadic fighting had already resumed with the Bolsheviks on the river fronts when a fresh crop of mutinies among the White Russians began. The 2nd Battalion 3rd North Russian Rifles had taken its place in the front line on the Dvina with a complete Russian field battery and a subsection of a heavier battery in direct support. The Russian regiment's commander had been arguing for some time for an independent command, and was finally given the position of Toulgas on the left bank. The Canadian gunners who had been there with them crossed the river and occupied the village of Kurgomen. In the early hours of 25 April the Russian battalion mutinied. After murdering seven of their officers, 300 mutineers made off into the woods where Bolshevik troops awaited them. Then the whole force turned to attack the remnants of the force holding Tulgas, where the Russian machine gunners and artillery together with some riflemen, had stood firm. Heavy fire from the artillery, supported by that of the Canadians at Kurgomen, when they found out what was going on, sufficed to halt the attack on the battalion's remnants, who became practically surrounded. Under cover of the supporting fire they were able to withdraw six miles to the next village, which was also attacked, but the assaults were beaten off with heavy casualties. Then, on 30 April, the enemy flotilla appeared – twenty-nine river craft armed with guns of various calibres – supporting a combined attack by 2500 troops on the Tulgas bank, with 3000 massing aginst the Kurgomen positions across the river. The Allied garrison numbered 550 all-ranks, British, Canadian and Russian. Only superior discipline and very professional artillery work saved the day, with the Bolshevik flotilla first wavering and then retiring under the fire of the 60-pounders. By 6 May the first of Altham's monitors was nosing its way gingerly upstream, through a channel specially dynamited for it in the still icebound Archangel waters. Days later two 6-inch gunboats followed. The situation stabilised and Toulgas was later recaptured.[17]

The mutiny had precipitated a brief tactical crisis on the river front, but Ironside remained optimistic. He blamed the situation on the unsatisfactory Russian commanding officer, who had subjected two of his men to 'severe corporal punishment' shortly before the mutiny occurred, arousing the enmity of the battalion. This did little to explain how well coordinated the incident seemed to have been with the Bolsheviks. Although the indiscipline did not spread to any of the other local units, and the Russian artillerymen and machine gunners had behaved courageously, to the considerable satisfaction of the Canadians who had trained them, this was not the end of the general's troubles. Whilst the Tulgas affair was still raging, a second mutiny took place in the Shenkursk battalion, whose machine gun company mutinied, killing two of their officers before scattering into the forest, some to the enemy. Ironside reported that, in this case, much of the trouble was caused by panic and indiscriminate firing, in the control of which 'the British officers did not do so well'. He needed in 'almost every company of Russian troops good liaison officers'. He also admitted with some candour, 'I have made in my appointments one or two bad shots'. Then in mid-May came another rising, hundreds of miles to the east of Archangel on the Pinega river front. In this area there appeared to be little Bolshevik influence and the garrison was composed entirely of Russian troops. 'I have just returned from Pinega', Ironside wired the War Office, 'where there arose trouble with two companies and two officers were killed. I regret to report I had to shoot fifteen but the companies are back on duty, the weather is now settled.' A bland announcement of a Draconian punishment. The reason for the trouble appeared to be 'non payment of men's pay and dependence allowance owing to incompetence of financial authorities and no fault of military', Ironside confirmed. 'I do not think it will occur again as I have thoroughly frightened the former.' Three significant mutinies in widely separated areas in little more than three weeks seem not to have dented Ironside's optimistic assessment of the development of the White Russian forces. The same day as he reported the Pinega executions, he was telling the War Office in a separate telegram of the proposed organisation of the Russian National Army in his command. It was to consist of eight regiments of infantry, each 3000 strong, four brigades of artillery and one of cavalry with supporting engineers and labour battalions.[18]

On 9 May Captain Altham, Senior Naval Officer of the Dvina flotilla, arrived from England at Murmansk for his second stint in charge of the river war. 'It was a surprise', he wrote later, 'to be told on arrival that it had been decided to advance on Kotlas at once, and my river "armada" (as it was called) would probably be too late for the fray.' This startling information came to him in a telegram from the Admiralty awaiting him at the port. But it was not simply a question of his armada being too late for the fray, it might also be quite unsuitable for the shallower conditions further up the Dvina where the projected offensive would require it to operate. This would be a severe handicap. 'Obtain opinion of experienced local people', demanded the Admiralty, 'and telegraph what will be probable minimum depth in navigable channel of River Dvina during each month May to October inclusive.' Perhaps in his concern to orchestrate political acceptance for his ambitious plan, Churchill had forgotten to consult his naval colleagues about it. If so, it was an egregious error by a man who was not entirely ignorant of river wars.[19] The naval preparations for the campaign were now a race against time.[20]

It was over two weeks before Altham had sufficient reliable information to be able to reply. Based on figures from 1915 to 1918, he wrote, the minimum depths would occur from July to early September (the precise months of the projected operations) when much of the lower Dvina in Allied hands would have an average depth of four feet one inch; but in the upper section from Nikolski to Kotlas the depth would be as little as three feet 9½ inches. In years of particularly low water, depths as low as two feet had been recorded. Already there were local predictions that the river would be unusually low in the coming summer. The implications for the navy's ability to support Ironside's projected operations were obvious: even the lighter of the two monitors in dock at Archangel drew five feet nine inches. They would both risk grounding if they operated any distance from the port itself, while the four gunboats, drawing four feet, would be similarly at hazard if they tried to get as far upriver as the present advanced base at Bereznik. Only the four minesweepers (drawing three feet six inches) would be safe until they neared Kotlas, when they too would risk grounding. The only hope lay in the various shallow-draught barges and lighters, if suitable guns could be found and mounted on them in time. At Altham's urgent request, the Admiralty promptly sent out spare guns and mountings to turn them into makeshift gunships. The flotilla commander was later to record, with evident exasperation, 'between the claims of the water-transport service and the inability of the base repair ship to undertake the work, not one of these gun barges ever materialised, with the result that ships of heavy draught had to be taken up-river to provide the necessary artillery afloat'. This involved frantic efforts to lighten some of the vessels. 'Floating cranes enabled us to remove big guns, mountings and even main engines, and to strip the two biggest monitors to mere shells. *Humber* took off all her side armour.' But these desperate efforts also rendered the stripped-down craft less effective and particularly vulnerable. Altham's actions were loyal efforts to support the land offensive, but they were far from successful in a summer in which the Dvina levels fell remarkably, with predictable results.[21]

On 12 June monitor *M27* went aground within six hours of starting to go up-river; minutes later *M33* was aground as well. Once afloat again *M33* picked its way cautiously through the shallow waters to Beresnik, where it grounded again. It was finally refloated, but two days later went aground again several times. These groundings left the vessels helpless and occupied the time and efforts of lighter craft which had to be diverted to refloat them. But the navigational hazards of the shallow river were not the only threats which the makeshift flotilla had to face. Others came from the increasingly accurate fire from the 'Bolo' gun barges and shore batteries, from mines floated downstream by the enemy, and from the occasional air raid. Crews had to put up with excessive heat, inadequate food and vessels which were often inappropriate to their task. Also in June, the crew of HMS *Cicala*, dissatisfied with their conditions, refused to sail up the Dvina to engage the Russian shore batteries. The men did not budge until they were in the gun sights of other ships on the river and threatened by Admiral Green: 'Do your duty or you will be shelled by other ships of the British squadron.'[22] By late July, as the river shrank still further in the brief but intense summer heat, the first officer of the monitor *Humber*, now unarmoured, was writing of the extremities to which the Senior Service was reduced, making plans 'for landing the whole ship's company ready to walk back to Archangel in case the expedition had to be abandoned'. But the comical side of their predicament did not escape him: 'We are absolutely isolated up here', he wrote, 'and have got into quite a hole, and there is a sense of humour about it, as we were originally the relief force.' Others were destined never to get near the action. HMS *Moth*, a large, flat-bottomed river gunboat, had been brought home especially from Mesopotamia, given a hurried refit at Chatham and then sent to Archangel in a great panic without its guns. It never went up-river to the front line or even received its guns, being fitted instead

with one cannibalised from the crippled *Cockchafer*. The commission diary of
the boat's first officer records more about duck shooting expeditions than any
warlike actions, though he does note, of the up-river naval activity, 'they said the
[sand]bar was like a flypaper on a hot day – vessels of every kind were stuck fast
all over the length and breadth of the river'. The Dvina was recording its lowest
levels for twenty years.[23]

As Grogan's Brigade was receiving its welcome and then moving off to
newly-built wooden billets in Archangel, its sister brigade, Sadleir Jackson's, was
beginning its journey north. This force, the civilian volunteer brigade, was much
the more experienced. The 45th Fusiliers was commanded by an Australian and
the 46th by a South African, both in the British service. The 45th Fusiliers and the
brigade's machine gun battalion contained significant numbers of Australians,
about 150 in all. Some had enlisted too late to join the fighting in France and were
determined to see some action before they returned home. Others were veterans
of Gallipoli and the Western Front. All had to be formally discharged from the
Australian Imperial Force and enlisted in the British Army before they could
participate. They served together in Australian sub-units and were allowed to wear
their AIF uniforms. Some were to distinguish themselves in the short campaign
in Russia. Lord Rawlinson inspected the brigade in camp at Sandling before its
departure and presented it with colours. 'A very fine lot under Sadleir Jackson'
was his judgement. The 45th Fusiliers displayed some other characteristics of a
war-hardened unit: there were problems with absentees who disappeared days
before they were due to move to Newcastle and then miraculously turned up
at the last minute. There was more trouble aboard ship at South Shields: forty
men of Allfrey's battalion tried to rush the gangway and get ashore again when
they discovered they were to be in dock overnight. Allfrey managed to quieten
them down, not without thinking his usual forthright thoughts: 'How the War
Office have the audacity to put 1400 men alongside an amusing town and order
them not to go ashore I'm blowed if I know.' Some indeed did manage to rush
the sentries on the gangways and wander off into town, not unlike the Yorkshires
before them. One sergeant in the battalion was later to write, 'I feel heartily sorry
that I ever joined such a mob as this. The lack of organisation and control is
dreadful. The NCOs are snubbed while the men are pandered to.' The battalion
sailed the next day with a great public display, as did its sister battalion from
Tilbury. By 3 June their ship had arrived at Murmansk, taken on some additional
naval personnel and was making her way to Archangel in a fourteen-ship convoy
headed by ice-breakers across the still icy White Sea.[24] They received a warm
welcome at the port and were briefed on the tactical situation and plans before,
some days later, making their journey up-river. One young platoon commander,
a South African not long out of Sandhurst, explained his understanding of the
adventure on which he was about to embark:

We were now given the object of the campaign for the first time. We were to move south down the Dwina river to Moscow, which was quite a long way. To protect the lines of communication would take most of our Brigade. General Denikin was said to be holding out with a few White Russians in Moscow and if any of our Brigade was to reach there we would then, with Denikin's help, take on the rest of Russia.[25]

This seemed a tall order for a single brigade; but the young officer, who had found his platoon of veterans 'a tough lot, very tough indeed', and was on a steep learning curve on most aspects of his duties, appeared undaunted. By the middle of the month the two battalions were beginning their slow progress up the River Dvina to the front. The 46th Fusiliers found themselves, the entire battalion, crammed into a single, huge, shallow barge drawn by a wood-burning paddle steamer. They camped under canvas at Ossinova, near the men of Grogan's Brigade.

Events in Archangel were now getting ahead of those in London. Ironside was already starting to plan an attack to secure a new advanced base for the Kotlas operation, though this larger venture had yet to be broached politically. On 1 June the King's Birthday Parade was held in Archangel at which Ironside presented colours to Dyer's Battalion of the Slavo-British Legion, which was now a well-drilled unit. 'In their khaki they presented a strikingly smart appearance on parade', recalled one onlooker. After the parade, in expansive mood perhaps, and doing all he could to build the morale of the Russian Army, Ironside gave an interview to a representative of the Information Bureau of the Northern Russia Provisional Government. The details of the interview were later reproduced in the first issue of G.A.F., the Gazette of the Archangel Expeditionary Force, a British Forces newspaper which, somewhat belatedly in view of the acute sense of isolation long felt by many of the forward troops, had just been started at Archangel by the correspondent of The Times, Andrew Soutar. The two-column front-page spread was headed GENERAL IRONSIDE'S PLANS. In it Ironside explained that his forces would soon advance up the Dvina, take Kotlas, link up with the Siberian Army and enable it to transfer its base from Vladivostok to Archangel, where the supply lines would be shorter and more reliable and the warehouses would be filled with war materials and stores for it sent from England aboard ships released from duty in Mesopotamia, the Balkans and Africa. His intention, the general declared, was to support the Russian Army until a firm footing was obtained at Kotlas, Vologda and Petrograd. In case of need, Ironside explained, the British expeditionary forces could 'remain as reserve for the Russian Army'. He followed with a paean to the developing Russian forces which were being 'not only recreated but re-educated' along English lines. 'Look for example at the results obtained by our system in Dyer's regiment', he declared. This remarkably indiscreet interview outlined a policy quite different from that which the War Cabinet had authorised, or for which the volunteers in the Relief Force had come forward. Parts of it, indeed, the Cabinet was never to sanction. The cat, it seems, was out of the bag.[26]

When Churchill learnt of Ironside's disclosures a few days later he wrote to General Harington, again deputising for the CIGS, 'This is very disquieting. I have lately been dwelling on the process of evacuation in public in order to conceal any impending movement. I cannot understand how General Ironside could have allowed himself to use language of this kind in an untrustworthy quarter. Apart altogether from the military disadvantages, political difficulties will be caused here if it is thought that an offensive operation is impending.'[27] Copies of the *G.A.F.* (a gaffe indeed) were quickly withdrawn from circulation – the process of preparing the Cabinet for the idea of the offensive had not even been started. It was only on the day of Churchill's letter of complaint to Harington that the CIGS, in Paris with Lloyd George, sent a brief telegram to his chief confirming that he had, as requested, put 'Ironside's proposals' (they were of course essentially Churchill's) to Lloyd George and had 'explained the whole situation to Prime Minister who raises no objections'. It had not been quite as straightforward as the telegram suggests. In his diary Wilson confessed that it was only 'after great struggles' that Lloyd George agreed to the proposition that Ironside should advance to join the Siberian Army at Kotlas. At the time the Prime Minister was consumed by acrimonious disputes with his colleagues over the final drafts of the German Peace Treaty. Lloyd George's 'mind was full of Fiume & terms for the Boches & against the Roumanians, & anger against Winston for giving Gough a GCMG!', wrote Wilson.[28]

Finally, two weeks after the arrrival in Russia of Grogan's Brigade and a week after Sadleir Jackson's, the War Cabinet finally met, at Churchill's request, to consider the north Russian venture since, as he put it to his colleagues, 'for the first time we proposed to depart from our previous defensive policy and embark upon definite aggressive action against the Bolsheviks'. The meeting was chaired by Lord Curzon, who was actually the only formal member of the War Cabinet present. Sir Henry Wilson outlined Ironside's plan for the Kotlas operation. He explained that one Russian and one British brigade would make the main attack down the Dvina, with a second Russian brigade advancing, in a subsidiary operation, down the Vologda railway. The First Sea Lord confirmed the Royal Navy's cooperation; his statement that the monitors would not form part of the flotilla supporting the offensive was the only reference he made to the hectic and partly futile arrangements which the Admiralty was having to make in order to play its vital part in the venture. He did, however, mention the threat from mines and the need for the force to proceed with caution. There were mild queries from other Cabinet members as to whether the offensive was indeed part of the announced withdrawal operation, and whether it was 'in no sense inconsistent with any pledges that we had given in either House'. The

THE
G.A.F.
The Gazette of the Archangel Exped. Force.

No 1.   Archangel, Russia.   June 7, 1919.

THE G.A.F.

ARCHANGEL JUNE 1, 1919.

Published Weekly by the British Archangel Expeditionary Force for the British troops. Address all communications to the Editor, 78, Troitsky, Archangel.

ABOUT OURSELVES.

In offering to you the first number of "The G.A.F." we do not make the usual apologies, nor do we ask for any bouquets. If it is our privilege to entertain you during the time you are in Russia, we shall be more than rewarded.

In the first place, we wish to tender our thanks—and yours—to the American Red Cross who have handed over to us the "copyright" of the "American Sentinel" which has been run so successfully by Captain Roger Lewis. Secondly, we, the editors, offer thanks to those members of the Force who have kindly contributed to the pages of the paper. So far the Navy, the Gunners and the Air Force have been silent, but we understand that they are thinking hard. Anyone who has any thing of interest to say, either about himself or the particular department in which he serves—any item of news that is calculated to interest the Force—is heartily invited to send it to the Editor, "G.A.F.," 78, Troitski.

Anything of a political nature is not wanted—we have enough troubles of our own. And we do not hanker after "moanings." We want cheeriness. We want to feel the happiness of a nigger with a "skolkered" melon; not the misery of the clam that has been left up by the tide. All kinds of news will be acceptable because we haven't a large staff of reporters to run around North Russia collecting information. We want the news early in the week; don't hoard up your paragraphs until you have a pile. We are anxious that the "G.A.F." shall be a success, and success depends as much on you, the readers, as on those who are responsible for the production. As no one wants a halo, or his leg pulled, we shall not sign articles save with a pseudonym; so select one. And we cannot return unsuitable M.S.—fuel is too scarce.

The paper is to be delivered free of charge, to the troops, but those other than the troops must pay one rouble per copy.

THE NEW TROOPS.
How Archangel received the Relief Forces.

The new troops which have been sent out from England to relieve the Archangel Forces arrived on May 26. A further contingent is on its way, even if it does'nt beat us in our race to press with the first number of the newspaper.

The men who arrived last week belong to the Ox. and Bucks. and the Hampshires, and Brig.-General Grogan is in command.

The official reception took place on the 26th and was an impressive ceremony. The civil population of the town searched its wardrobe for the best it contained, and with glorious sunshine flooding the city of wood, the scene was kaleidoscopic. The barishna came into her own that day; she was as a multi-coloured butterfly emerging after a rain-storm.

General Grogan arrived in a launch from Smolny where the ship on which he came out was anchored. On the quay he was met by Governor-General Miller who welcomed him in the name of the Russians of the Region. General Ironside, attended by a few staff officers, shook hands with General Grogan and invited him to inspect the guard of honour drawn up on the quay. These men belonged to Dyer,s battalion, and, in themselves formed a tribute to the perseverance of the G.O.C. in C., for out of Bolshevik prisoners he has trained a battalion of first class fighting men.

The new troops lined the road up to the town, under the floral arch of triumph erected by the civilians in honour of the forces, General Grogan was presented with bread and salt and three massive cakes, this being a time honoured custom.

During the remainder of the week, the new troops filled the town, picked up that little of the language which always serves the British soldier wherever he may be, learned the difference between a new and an old rouble, grappled with and conquered the subtleties of "pajuluster", and (who shall reproach ?) cast an appraising eye on the barishna. These new troops not brought out a cargo of arrogance with them. They have not come out to teach the tired ones how to fight. They know that in North Russia, since the beginning of this expedition, the Royal Scots, the D L.I.'s, the K.L.R.'s, the Yorks, the Canadian Artillery and the other troops have been fighting with the verve and courage that has made the British Empire what it is to-day.

The new troops went up to the Front on Monday last.

DERBY RESULT.
ODDS-ON FAVOURITE BADLY BEATEN.

The "Victory" Derby was run at Epsom on Wednesday last, with the following result :

Grand Parade.	1
Buchan.	2
Paper Money.	3

Prices: Grand Parade, 33-1; Buchan, 7-1, Paper Money, 7-1. Panther, a hot favourite, delayed at the start and got away badly. The King and Queen and other members of the Royal family were present. The Avro Company took many passengers to the famous downs by aeroplane.

GENERAL IRONSIDE'S PLANS.
CREATING A RUSSIAN ARMY.
KOTLAS — VOLOGDA — PETROGRAD.

On Sunday last, after the Parade, the G.O.C.-in-C. discussed his plans with a representative from the Information Bureau of the Provisional Government of Northern Russia. General Ironside said :—" I have now all I require to fulfil my plans." He then outlined his plans, which are briefly:—

Advance up the SVINA River and take Kotlas.

Link up with the SIBERIAN Army and thus transfer the base of the Russian National Army from SIBERIA to ARCHANGEL.

Fill the ARCHANGEL Warehouses with War Materials and Stores sent from ENGLAND.

Support the RUSSIAN Army until, in conjunction with the MURMAN Forces, a firm footing is obtained at three points : KOTLAS, VOLOGDA, PETROGAD. Afterwards deal with Central and Southern RUSSIA.

Create a purely RUSSIAN Force which will permit RUSSIA to free herself.

Finally, when those objects have achived, go Home.

The full text of the interview is given below :—

The Commander-in-Chief of the Northern Forces said :—

"I am very satisfied with to-days parade ; the new Russian unit has taught and trained by us, quite came up to our expectations. I need not say anything about the newly arrived British troops, their appearance speaks for itself.

Now with the British and local Russian troops I have all I require to fulfil my plans. My plan is very simple—to utilise the summer months for transferring the base of the Russian National Army from Siberia to Archangel. Only eight days are required for the transport of men and materials from E.g.,and to Archangel. You will easily appreciate what material and strategic advantages are involved in the transfer of the Base from Siberia to Archangel ; also the saving of time, energy and labour. It means that no consideration of an International, Allied or National character can any longer affect the timely supply of Ko nchak's front.

When the second contingent of volunteers arrives, which I am expecting shortly, I shall move up the river to Kotlas which I am perfectly certain will be taken. At the Archangel Base everything is in readiness to receive all the stores sent from England, barracks, warehouses and vessels.

The Russian National Army requires only the necessary equipment and supplies, and, lust at first, the support of our Expeditionary forces, which in case of need can remain as reserve for the RUSSIAN Army. This reserve, remember, consists of picked men who have fought for years on the Western front and of Officers from the Regular Army. The training they have received you can judge from today parade. Their fighting capacity, morale and discipline half been proved on all fronts during this World War.

These are the elements which make me sure of fulfilling successfully my plan here in the North. The ARCHANGEL Basetogether with the MURMANSK and PETROGRAD regions, will enable a firm footing to be secured at three points: KOTLAS, VOLOGDA, PETROGRAD. This is not everything, but it is a good deal, and as we shall have the whole Northern Base in our hands, we can then take serious measures against the Centre and the South. Sufficient unto the day is the evil thereof'.

Our shipping facilities are now reinforced by ships which before were required for AFRICA, MESOPOTAMIA etc., and during this summer everything we require will be brought to ARCHANGEL.

Already a lot of work has been done but there is more still waiting for us. The most important task has been accomplished the creation of a purely RUSSIAN Force. This is after all our chief, not to say, our only, object, and this will enable RUSSIA to free herself.

Having attained our object of creating a RUSSIAN Military Force we shall go away, and this should be borne in mind. We have no other aims, either of a political, commercial or otherwise egotistical charactercted. The RUSSIAN Army at the present time is being not only recreated but re-educated on new principles. Our ENGLISH discipline will be a splendid lesson for the new RUSSIAN Army, It is strict, sensible and instructive. Thanks to it and to our Regular Officers, we, who started the war with a small army of 350,000 men. created a mighty force of 5,000,000. Thanks to our discipline, our training and officers, our Army is energetic and healthy.

In every village in ENGLAND we have introduced games, healthy occupations and amusements, in my opinion you must do the same thing here and not confine it to the army, but this again is a question of education which is not within my province.

Look for example at the result attained by our system in 'DYER'S' regiment. You saw them on parade today, two companies of them have already fought at the front and have done excellent work. Our officers worked with them all the time and, in not a single instance, was it necessary under our strict discipline, to meet out punishment, either disciplinary or otherwise Now, I have given them several Russian Officers whom I am gradually introducing at all points of the front Thus by degrees, giving over the Command to the RUSSIANS. This is how I am endeavouring to solve the problem of the creation of a RUSSIAN Army.

When my Mission is fulfilled and the formation of the RUSSIAN Army with the help of the RUSSIANS, themselves, is an accomplished fact, we will go Home!

Commenting on the interview the RUSSIAN Government's Representative said:-

General IRONSIDE has obviously complete faith in RUSSIA's resurrection and future greatness. He spoke with assurance and with evident sympathy and referred in terms of great praise to several of his colleagues in the organisation of the RUSSIAN Army. He expressed the pleasure it gave him to work with men like General MILLER and General MARUSHEVSKY.

With his usual modesty, the G. O. C. forgot only one—himself. But RUSSIA will not forget him, nor the great task he has performed in reconstructing our Army. He has proved himself a true Ally and devoted friend to RUSSIA".

CIGS assured the Cabinet that 'the men taking part in these operations were not "driven conscripts", but were, on the contrary, tremendously keen about the whole expedition'. Churchill foresaw no difficulty in justifying to Parliament the present plans, 'which were simply designed to secure our withdrawal from north Russia'. He then voiced some sanguine expectations about events on the other Russian fronts, after which the Cabinet approved the proposed operations. London, it seemed, was now squared with Archangel.[29]

The details of the latest Russian mutinies at Archangel were not the only bad news which the Secretary of State and his CIGS were soon confronting. Information, always delayed by the uncertain communications with the Siberian Front, had been coming in for some time suggesting that Kolchak's forces were meeting serious setbacks. They might not, therefore, be in a position to join up with Ironside's Kotlas offensive. With the Prime Minister still detained in Paris by the peace negotiations, Lord Curzon decided that the Cabinet should re-examine the advisability of Ironside's offensive. It met for this purpose on 18 June. Queries were raised about the need for mounting the operation at all if a junction with the Siberian forces could not be effected. Austen Chamberlain said that he would not object if it were necessary for a safe withdrawal, but if it was simply a question of prestige he saw no point in advancing into central Russia and then at once withdrawing. The DMO (deputising for the CIGS, again away in Paris) retorted that the British troops would not be advancing on their own. Ironside now had a substantial force of Russian troops who would do their share of the fighting and then hold the territory gained when the British troops withdrew. When Curzon suggested that the news from Siberia seemed blacker even than the military reports indicated, Churchill, ever optimistic, noted that the Siberian reserves were now entering the battle and there was still the possibility of Kolchak making the junction with Ironside. The Cabinet finally decided to discuss the matter again on 27 June, when the situation might be clearer and Sir Henry Wilson would be free to attend the meeting. Meanwhile Ironside was to continue with his plans but make no 'definite advance' until the Cabinet gave the word. These decisions were telegraphed to Ironside, who was also asked his view on the chances of a junction with Kolchak (he knew even less about Kolchak's movements than did the Cabinet) and whether the Kotlas operation should go ahead as 'an indispensable part of the process of evacuation' independent of any hope of the junction.[30]

By this time, with the strong and reliable brigades of the Relief Force available, Ironside decided that it was time to give the Russians a leading role in an attack along the Dvina to secure the new forward base. It was important for them to gain combat experience at unit level as soon as possible. The main objectives for the attack, to be undertaken by a composite force under Brigadier General Graham, were the two groups of villages around Topsa and Troitsa, situated on the right bank of the river. There was to be a corresponding advance on the opposite bank. Topsa stood on a bluff overlooking the Dvina and south of it the land fell away gently to Troitsa, which had a deep channel and was a valuable landing place for river traffic. The two villages were joined by a rough road that ran along the river bank. Once Troitsa was captured, Ironside would use it as his forward river base for the main attack on the Bolshevik 6th Army's Kotlas base. The attack on the Topsa villages was to be made by two battalions of 3rd North Russian Rifles, with a simultaneous outflanking attack on the more distant Troitsa villages by a much smaller force of two companies of 2nd Hampshires under their redoubtable commanding officer Lieutenant Colonel J. Sherwood Kelly VC, CMG, DSO. The four-times-wounded Kelly, a thirty-nine-year-old South African, was not a regular officer but a formidable and experienced commander with a combat record stretching back to the 1896 Matabele Revolt. In the late war he had been hailed as 'one of the Twenty-Ninth Division's most reputed fighting men'.

Both columns were to advance under the cloak of the forest flank and then turn westwards to pin their assailants against the river. Kelly's objective, on which the new forward line would subsequently be established, was Troitsa church. The attack, especially its Russian element, was to have artillery support from the land batteries and also from the gunboats, as well as some supporting bombing by the RAF. The Russian regimental commander, Colonel Voulichevitch, Sherwood Kelly and the brigade commander himself carried out a reconnaissance on 16 June: an exhausting operation which saw the men cover thirty-five miles in seventeen hours. Although the enemy positions were entrenched, with, it was believed, roughly 700 men in the Topsa village complex and about 500 at Troitsa, and were supported by machine guns and some light artillery, their morale was reported to be low and there was every expectation of complete success. Nevertheless, as we examine the plan today, there was a worrying disparity in the strength of the two attacking forces and the tasks which confronted them. Kelly's men had been awake since about 2 a.m. on 19 June. It was 4 a.m. when their commander led his two companies out of the Kurgomen defences; the Russian battalions, which had a much shorter approach march, set out about an hour later. Throughout the day the two columns struggled in the intense heat along the marshy forest tracks and across the muddy Topsa river to their start lines. The attacks were scheduled to begin the following morning at 4 a.m. after a short artillery bombardment.[31]

The operation by the White Russians, supported by the gunboat *Cockchafer* after some difficult navigation up the narrow river channel, was a complete success: the entire Topsa group of villages was in their hands by 8.20 a.m. The Bolsheviks left roughly 150 dead in the positions and the North Russian Rifles took 350 unwounded and a hundred wounded prisoners. Their victory was later hailed by *The Times* under the headline, GENERAL IRONSIDE'S CONFIDENCE JUSTIFIED – RUSSIANS' BRILLIANT OPERATION. But it was a victory gained at considerable cost. A hundred White Russians were killed or wounded, as were seven of their accompanying British liaison staff. Whilst such losses would have been routine the previous year in Flanders, they would have been quite unacceptable to any of the British battalions in the very different circumstances of north Russia. There is no sign that the expensive victory did much to hearten the Russians. As for the Hampshires' attack, as Ironside later explained the situation in his published version of events, 'they failed to take any part in the fight'. When he interviewed Sherwood Kelly the following day, he said the CO 'could not explain why he had acted as he had'. Had Kelly been a Regular officer, Ironside explained, he would 'certainly have had him court martialled', but, in view of his outstanding war record, he merely withdrew the battalion from the line and sent Kelly 'down to the Base with orders that he should be sent home for demobilisation'. This account seems to have been taken at face value and accepted in subsequent accounts, though it is very much at variance with the primary evidence. Perhaps Ironside's recollections were influenced by his subsequent troubles with the hot-blooded Colonel Kelly, for the Troitsa operation proved to be the opening round in a notorious and politically embarrassing episode in the British intervention.[32]

There is no doubt that the Hampshires did not take their objective, which was occupied some time later, and that their attempt to do so, particularly in the light of their CO's fearsome fighting reputation, was a disappointment. There is much evidence, however, which belies Ironside's account, not least his own contemporary reports to the War Office, one of which reads, 'Successful operation carried out by 2nd Battalion Hampshire Regiment and 3rd North Russian Rifle Regiment on right flank of Dvina. Enemy put up strong resistance. Enemy was prepared for attack and stood to all night. 2 Companies of 2nd Hampshires repulsed 3 counter-attacks on night of 20–21 June.' This is supported by the Archangel HQ War Diary for 20 June which records: 'Enemy morale by no means low and were forewarned of attack by deserter from 4th North Russian Rifles. Stood to all night – communists with MGs posted behind his infantry.' The Brigade Operation Report recorded that Kelly's column was successful at first and got to a position within close range of its objective, but after holding it 'from 0800 to 1030hrs the troops were withdrawn into the woods to the east of it, owing to the position being considered insecure by the Column Commander, and to the difficulty experienced in getting up ammunition supplies'. An additional concern was the difficulty they would have in getting any wounded back through the forest marshes. When Kelly got back to his bivouac position, a couple of miles away, and in touch with his brigade commander, he is said to have spoken as follows: 'Is this General Graham? This is Colonel Sherwood Kelly. I have retired from Troitsa. I consider I have been shamefully let down.' Perhaps it was the failure of the flotilla to provide adequate artillery support, or the intelligence failure, which drew this charge from him. He is reported to have been ordered to resume his attack, which he declined to do. Kelly offered a very detailed explanation, if not to Ironside at least to his brigadier, to whom he penned a three-page report the following day. He blamed a series of factors for his decision to withdraw: the difficult approach march through the marshy forests which prevented the tail of his column reaching its bivouac position until midnight; a failure of communications which deprived him of information about the progress at Topsa; the stiff resistance of the enemy, which belied the 'low morale' about which the troops had been specifically briefed; his force's critical tactical situation with enemy troops threatening to encircle him; and a growing shortage of ammunition. He might also have added 'utter exhaustion': he and his officers had only a couple of hours' rest from the time they left the base at Kurgomen until he called off the operation thirty-two hours later. This account was corroborated by a separate report submitted by the major commanding the supporting Machine Gun Corps section who finally returned to base, 'tired beyond all description'.[33]

Further evidence is found in a letter home sent by one of Kelly's subalterns who had won the VC as a second lieutenant on the Western Front. Clearly no shirker, he wrote of the action:

> they gave us a very warm time but our own better shooting told heavily. However we were nearly surrounded and cut off so, fagged out as we all were – we had to retreat at 9.30 a.m. in the blazing heat, no rest, little food. My platoon was the last to leave, the enemy had worked up to within seventy yards, covering us with very heavy fire the whole time. We just got out and had to trek right back over our old trail, and we got back to TOPSA at 12 midnight.[34]

This does not read like the account of two companies which 'failed to take any part in the fight'. Their concern over the likely fate of the wounded, of which the column sustained only a handful, was borne out by one subaltern's fate: 'poor old Gorman ... got one in the stomach and died sixteen hours later after having been brought back through that awful forest'. Lieutenant Gorman had been wounded twice previously in France. 'We learnt afterwards', wrote another of Kelly's officers, 'that the Bolos had discovered our plan some days before the attack started. They had hurriedly brought up strong reinforcements and laid a trap for us at Troitsa.' It was known that the Bolsheviks had 1500 men eight miles to the south at Gorodok, which Brigadier General Graham had been unwise to ignore.

The improvement in the enemy's defences and in their determination was borne out by the fate of the companion attack by the Hampshire detachment on the left bank of the river, over which Kelly had no direct control. This too was not pressed to a conclusion; 'the task was impossible without involving heavy casualties', wrote its commander. The enemy were strongly posted on an embanked road with nearly 300 yards of bog between it and the attacking column. Brigadier General Graham had ruled out a proposed frontal demonstration to divert attention from the flank attack and had allocated no artillery support to the operation. Perhaps, because of the flotilla's problems, he had been unable to do so. Here again it was 'only owing to bad shooting on the enemy's part that the casualties were so few'. In north Russia the Hampshires were, understandably, not prepared to take heavy casualties. One Hampshires sergeant reported of Colonel Kelly, 'He said he is not going to get any more of his men or officers killed for the sake of this ***** country'. Major Allfrey, of the companion brigade, commented on the Hampshires' operation: 'In my opinion, and also in Colonel Davies's, the show is tactically wrong ... After five years of war good troops ought never to be placed in such a rotten predicament by some damn fool of a muddle-headed broken-down old regular soldier.' This was a reference to Brigadier General Graham, who had planned the attack on Troitsa and Topsa. Kelly's views of the brigadier were similar.[35]

Kelly was not relieved of his command and sent home. Ironside wrote elsewhere that he had 'decided to give him a second chance', which is what happened. With Kelly still in command, the battalion was moved to other parts of the front where emergencies were occuring: two companies to Pinega and the remainder, under Kelly himself, to the Onega area whence 400 Russians had defected to the enemy. Kelly was not finally replaced in command of the Hampshires until 17 August, almost two months after the Troitsa affair, and for quite a different reason than the Troitsa operation. The battalion continued to serve satisfactorily in north Russia; one MC, one DCM and nine MMs were among the decorations which its members were subsequently awarded. Apart from the disappointment which the Hampshires' failure gave General Ironside, the improved performance of the Bolsheviks at the start of the new campaigning season must have given him pause for thought.

The day before the attack on Topsa and Troitsa took place, Ironside sent Churchill a long telegram replying to the Cabinet's message of the previous day. 'Preparations for advance on Kotlas are nearing completion', his message began, before going on to examine the operation's viability and value if no junction with Kolchak's army were possible. In such an eventuality Ironside saw the Kotlas venture as a 'peace operation', designed to allow his own forces to disengage and embark safely and to place General Miller's Russian troops in a position to maintain themselves without him. He had three objectives. The first was to capture the Bolshevik base and communications hub at Plesetskaya on the Vologda railway, thus preventing an enemy winter campaign in that sector; secondly, to clear the Pinega area so that the whole northern region was free of the Bolsheviks. Thirdly came the advance on Kotlas itself, with the object of destroying all the workshops, depots and wharfs there, capturing all the enemy boats and rendering the place useless as a base for an enemy advance during the summer or winter. He conjectured that the advance might also 'bring in' the right wing of the Siberians. Having achieved these objectives, the evacuation could begin before the winter freeze, leaving behind a British mission of a size to be determined later. He envisaged the Russians themselves being largely responsible for the first and second objectives with some help from Grogan's Brigade. The main attack on Kotlas would be in the hands of Sadleir-Jackson's Brigade together with Russian troops, including those of the Slavo-British Legion. 'In no case', Ironside emphasised, 'do I think that any advance less than to Kotlas will have any effect of disengaging our forces and it does offer possible chance of bringing on Kolchak.' He did not believe he would be endangering the Relief Force at all by undertaking the operation.[36]

This important telegram was dangerously misleading in two respects. First, Ironside knew that a withdrawal was quite possible without an advance to Kotlas, though he was equally well aware of Churchill's wish for him to take the place and make the junction with the Siberian army if at all possible. He was, let us remember, a recently promoted major general, not yet forty, with no experience of military politics, heading an unusual and isolated command in very unconventional circumstances. More significantly, Ironside already knew that the Kotlas operation was no longer a practical proposition. The water level in the Dvina, he had noted in his diary a week earlier, had dropped to the lowest point in fifty years. It was more 'a series of pools and sandbanks than a river'. A glance at Captain Altham's river chart confirms this judgement. On the day of this apparently confident telegram to the Secretary of State, Ironside was confessing to his diary, 'I do not think for a minute that I can get to Kotlas but I do not want to be left wiring for permission to do things just when I want to be doing them'. The day before the Cabinet was to meet to reconsider the venture, Altham was wiring the Admiralty, 'River is falling rapidly' and Ironside was confirming in his diary, 'all hope of any operations to Kotlas is over'. If the message to Churchill was a calculated deception of his political master, this hardly gave Churchill the moral high ground, for he and the CIGS were preparing similarly to mislead the Cabinet.[37]

When the War Cabinet met on 27 June to make its final decision on the Kotlas operation, it looked principally to the CIGS, now back from Paris, for guidance. Sir Henry Wilson explained that Kolchak's armies had fallen back successively in the south, the centre and the north. The chance of a junction with Ironside was now remote. But in his view this made it all the more important for British troops to reach Kotlas and destroy the Bolshevik steamers and stores there, so they could withdraw in safety. He strongly advised the Cabinet to allow the operation to proceed. Churchill concentrated on what he called the 'remarkable' growth of the Russian Army in the Archangel region where there was the most democratic Russian government of the three Britain was supporting. The Russian Army there now numbered 22,000 men. It bore no comparison with the best European troops but 'the material was quite good' and included the Slavo-British Legion with its considerable proportion of British officers. In supporting the judgement of Sir Henry Wilson, he noted that the CIGS had 'complete faith' in General Ironside, who was confident about the projected operation. The most incisive critical questioning of the plan came from H.A.L. Fisher, who ran the Board of Education, and the Chancellor of the Exchequer, Austen Chamberlain. Fisher asked whether, since the River Dvina was the only means of advance and retreat, it could not simply be mined before a withdrawal. The CIGS honestly admitted that 'there was a good deal to be said for that point of view', but (an unfortunate lapse in his argument) that course ruled out all possibility of a junction with Kolchak. Churchill interposed to emphasise the need to deal with the Bolshevik steamers at Kotlas and declared that they 'had to give the Archangel Government every chance' and could not 'slink out of the country, and leave nothing between them and the Bolsheviks but a few mines in the river'. The Chancellor of the Exchequer did not share Churchill's optimistic views of the 'soldierly qualities of the Russian troops' or the 'capacity of the Archangel Government'. He was, however, 'greatly impressed' by Sir Henry Wilson's statement that the operation was necessary to secure a safe withdrawal of the troops. This professional advice of the CIGS ultimately carried the day. The War Office telegraphed Ironside: 'After consideration of all provisions and arguments contained in your telegram of 19 June ... you are authorised to carry out advance as proposed.' Ironside had misled the CIGS and the CIGS has misled the Cabinet.[38]

On 2 July, when the implications of the flotilla's difficulties were clear to him and the advance down to Kotlas was plainly ruled out, Ironside decided that all he would be able to do was break the Bolshevik line above his present positions and then settle the Russian troops in at the front before starting his evacuation. Whilst still keeping the War Office in the dark, he flew down to Archangel to break the news confidentially to General Miller. He had a two-hour meeting with the Russian and they continued their discussions the following day. He told Miller of the bad news from Kolchak and that the British forces would have to withdraw from the upper Dvina by 1 October at the latest. 'When I told him the news hardly a muscle of his face moved. I could only see in his pale blue eyes how desperately tired he was.' The Russian's urgent plea that Ironside call for volunteers from among the British to remain over the winter was rejected by the British commander. To Miller's flurry of questions as to whether he would be given sufficient currency, guns, ammunition, winter clothing and river transport to carry on the struggle, Ironside assured him 'that all he needed would certainly be supplied'.[39] Meanwhile, Russian units continued to move to the front in preparation for the major role they were to play in the coming offensive. Dyer's battalion of the Slavo-British Legion was the next to take its place in the line. By this stage, after more than two months of intensive training, it had become, in the Ironside's words, 'a very fine unit'. The general's plan was to 'blood' it behind one of the battalions of Sadleir-Jackson's Brigade in the main attack. It reached the Dvina front on 4 July and was inspected on arrival. 'The men were reported upon as being in particularly good heart', Ironside noted, and that they had been 'very jolly and had amused themselves playing games' on the journey up-river. Staff officers also visited the battalion and reported favourably on it. The battalion's headquarters was established at Kucherika with its 'B' and 'C' companies forward and 'A' and 'D' in reserve. Not far away men of the Relief Force were still moving into position at the front.[40]

In the early hours of 7 July, Dyer's Battalion mutinied. A nucleus of determined men in C company killed, in cold blood, three of their British officers and four of their Russian ones, together with several of their British and Russian orderlies. Others were wounded, including two further British officers who subsequently died of their wounds. One of the latter, Captain Barr, made a brave bid to raise the alarm by swimming out to the monitor *Humber* in the river nearby. The ship's captain reported that Barr had about ten bullet wounds in his body and had taken one in a lung. Unsurprisingly he soon died, but not before Ironside had visited the ship and personally awarded him a Military Cross for his gallantry. The bodies of the dead were 'mutilated beyond recognition', the battalion commander later reported. The mutineers ordered the company to follow them over to the Bolshevik lines, which many did together with some men from the neighbouring B company. Altogether about 150 men defected to the Bolsheviks. When the firing had first started the remainder of the battalion remained under discipline and stood to, imagining it was under attack itself; but 'the Russian officers did practically nothing to quell the mutiny', Ironside reported, 'Many simply ran away and deserted their posts'. Units nearby were alerted at once: one of the flotilla vessels immediately put six Lewis gun teams ashore and the commanding officer of 46th Fusiliers took up two companies aboard the commander's launch, accompanying his pyjama-clad brigadier who then addressed the remainder of the Russian battalion which had stood firm. Discipline was rapidly restored.[41]

The loss of five young officers was a tragedy for the British force and, in view of the close personal interest Ironside had taken in the training of the battalion, the mutiny itself was a great blow to him and to British prestige. It was a defining moment in the whole campaign. The general confessed that it had caused him 'a greater shock than I liked to admit even in my innermost thoughts. I now felt a distinct urge to extricate myself and my troops as quickly as I could.' Echoing the post-mutiny report of the battalion's commanding officer, Lieutenant Colonel Barrington Wells, Ironside attributed the trouble to 'a carefully arranged plot in one company only, made by eight determined men', all deserters from the Bolsheviks, including two ex-officers who came or were sent across deliberately. He declared that it was 'due to active propaganda and came without any warning'. In fact, it seems that the disaffection was more widespread than he supposed and that there had been a clear warning of trouble, though neither he nor Barrington Wells was aware of it.[42]

The Times reported the mutiny some days later in a gloomy and critical despatch in which its correspondent, Andrew Soutar, supported the view that the men of the battalion had given 'not the slightest sign that any conspiracy was being organised'. But Soutar knew that this was untrue. Years later he explained that he had made particular friends with Captains Barr and Finch, two of the company commanders of Dyer's Battalion, whom he had first met in Archangel during the unit's training. He encountered them again when the battalion moved to the front, when he found the young officers 'quiet and reserved' with a sense of foreboding. They explained that they had had trouble in the battalion on the way up the river, trouble which they claimed to have nipped in the bud by getting rid of ten of the men, the ringleaders, who were making mischief with the others. They had not told their commanding officer of the incident, believing that he had worries enough. This was a serious misjudgement which cost the young officers their lives and seriously compromised Ironside's plans. Colonel Barrington Wells remained in ignorance of this earlier trouble when he came to write his report, in which he noted that 'There has been no discontent at any time among the men'. Yet after order had been restored, and the supposed ringleaders separated from the main battalion, he apparently came to believe that further mutinies in the unit were being planned, though how reliable his judgement was at this point it is difficult to say. As one close observer noted, 'He is very overdone, poor fellow, and is also a good deal gone in the nerves'. In fact Major Allfrey's searches did find that one man had hidden a bomb in a sock in his kitbag. 'I put him in the condemned cage, and he will be shot with the others', his diary noted. Forty-eight hours later the *Humber* intercepted a Bolshevik wireless message urging the sailors to mutiny, 'Look at the uprising amongst the White Russian troops', it read, 'it is significant for you. Let us shake hands and do away with Tsars, Kaisers, Kings, Terrible Capitalists and Bankers.' The Bolsheviks opposing the Dvina force were aware of the mutiny and were probably complicit in it. The following day they opened an offensive along the Dvina which required the intervention of the 46th Fusiliers and the supporting artillery before it was driven back with heavy casualties.[43]

Ironside's published account make no mention at all of an incident which had occurred five day's earlier in the 4th North Russian Rifles at Troitsa when two officers and a newspaperman had been locked in a local bathhouse in the course of another mutiny. The officers subsequently escaped and the mutineers scattered when shelled by artillery from Topsa. They were later rounded up by men from 46th Royal Fusiliers and some sailors and marines from the flotilla. The flotilla commander concluded that these mutinies 'had been carefully timed by enemy agents to coincide with a short period when two British brigades were changing over'. Most of Grogan's men were already away dealing with other emergencies and Sadleir Jackson's force was still arriving at the front.[44]

A disconsolate Ironside, whose bold experiment in training methods had so publicly failed, disarmed the men of Dyer's Battalion and used them once again as a labour force. He also planned exemplary punishment: 'Eight men who engineered the mutiny have escaped', he wired to the War Office, 'but I am having about twenty executed.' The War Office replied quickly, 'The execution of so large a number of men as twenty cannot be approved'. It entered various caveats about circumstances in which he might execute more and then suggested, 'the number executed should not exceed the number who lost their lives as a direct result of the mutiny. Please telegraph action taken.' This was a fiat quite without legal support. Ironside replied the following day (action having been taken very quickly in the emergency circumstances of north Russia): 'Eleven men, against whom [there was] direct evidence of complicity, have been shot. Varying terms of imprisonment have been given to remainder. The number of deaths of British and Russian officers is greater by one than the number of executions.' According to Major Allfrey, who was closely involved in the proceedings, fifty Russians were initially placed in the mutineers' cage, but since it would be possible to get a sentence for only about twenty-five of them under the British system, 'the remainder will be transferred to the Russian Army, where they will be tried under the Russian method, in which it is much easier to secure a conviction'. Twenty-five were indeed charged with mutiny and court martialled by the British. Eighteen death sentences were handed down in all, though some were commuted. The court martial records show that eleven men were ultimately shot. This, like the fifteen whom Ironside had had shot at Pinega, was still an unusually large number to be executed under British arrangements. By comparison, only fifty-six British soldiers were sentenced to death for mutiny in the entire Great War and the sentence was carried out in only four cases. The facts of the executions were for a time omitted from the published records. In North Russia Ironside had been particularly requested by the King not to carry out any executions of British troops. Whatever the position in law, the execution of Russian soldiers by the order of a foreign general in an undeclared war caused resentment among the Russian civilians, whether Bolshevik or not.[45]

The British garrison reacted angrily to the killing of the British officers. 'We all had some excellent friends amongst the officers of Dyer's Battalion', wrote Major Allfrey whose company had the task of guarding the disarmed battalion. 'If there is the slightest trouble I shall pump lead into them harder than they have ever seen bullets fly before.' Five hundred newly-conscripted Russians were sent up by GHQ to witness the execution of the guilty men, which was to be by machine gun. The disarmed Russian battalion and the other spectators were drawn up on three sides of a square, with the condemned men tied to posts along the fourth. Then there arrived 'an enormous influx of naval people and some sightseers who suddenly came along' to join the now silent parade. 'I felt a little ashamed of them', wrote Major Allfrey, with an appropriate concern for the proprieties of the occasion, 'the arrival of a British contingent of sightseers seemed in awfully bad taste'. The executions, intended no doubt as an object lesson for the Russian trainees, did not go according to plan. Since the shooting was to be carried out by the loyal machine gunners of the mutineers' own battalion, Allfrey had trusted them with only five rounds each and kept them covered by British machine gunners. Whether the firing party was overawed by the occasion, nervous at being in other gunners' sights, or simply 'aimed off' deliberately is not clear, but when the fusillade was over they had 'only killed about four of the twelve, and the remainder were left kicking tied onto big posts'. The spectators were then treated to the grisly spectacle of Allfrey and his officers having 'to go with our revolvers and polish the prisoners off'. One sergeant, still very much alive, even 'took the bandages off his eyes and shouted out: 'Long Live the Bolsheviks!', before being despatched. As a ceremony designed *pour encourager les autres* it was hardly a great success.[46]

When Churchill received Ironside's report of the mutiny, which included the names of the suspected ringleaders who had escaped, he wrote in anger to the CIGS and the Adjutant-General, 'The names of these Russians should be carefully recorded and never lost sight of. They are guilty of the blackest treachery conceivable ... When it is possible for us to demand their exemplary punishment, we must not fail to do so.' A flurry of correspondence followed between Whitehall and the various far-flung missions on Russian soil, with Churchill calling for a system to ensure that the ringleaders' names were brought up each year on the anniversary of their crime. Needless to say, the culprits were never caught; some of their names were misrecorded in any event. It was a futile and time-wasting gesture.[47] The larger damage was done: Ironside had lost faith in the Russian units of the Slavo-British Legion, which his officers had largely trained and officered and which he had hitherto regarded as the backbone of the Russian Army. The British soldiers in north Russia had never had much time for their Russian colleagues in the White forces; now they were beginning to lose faith in them altogether. Some of the Russians had fought reasonably well alongside the hard-pressed winter garrison at Archangel, but the men of the Relief Force had little time for any of the Whites; they even pitied them, while their Russian officers were widely despised. Ironside had considerable trouble with Sadleir Jackson, who wanted to disarm the entire Russian force and rely on his own men for any offensive action. 'It took me some hours reasoning with him, to convince him that I could not accept his ideas', wrote Ironside years later. By contrast, his contemporary diary recorded, 'I am contemplating doing away with the Army that I practically forced them to mobilise. It is a wretched situation if ever there was one.'[48]

It was not until 4 July that Ironside finally informed the War Office of the situation that he had been aware of for almost three weeks. 'Latest news of loss of Perm [and] Kungur, coupled with the Dvina at very low ebb, makes even a raid on Kotlas at the moment impossible', he wrote. The mutiny of Dyer's Battalion confirmed the decision; but even that depressing affair was not the end of the general's troubles. On 20 July Ironside received news that the Russians on the Onega front had mutinied. Only a few days previously General Marushevsky, the Russian battlefield commander, had inspected the regiment there and reported it in excellent condition. (Marushevsy and Ironside did not get on too well. Their disparity in size cannot have helped: the one five feet and one inch tall, the other six feet four.) Now the regimental commander at Onega and most of his officers were murdered and the mutineers handed over their positions to the Bolsheviks. 'This was the last straw indeed', wrote Ironside. 'The whole of our right flank was open.' This was no exaggeration: the entire district was now in Bolshevik hands and the overland link with the Murmansk front was broken. It seems that few of the mutineers chose to join the Bolshevik forces: 'the majority made straight for their homes, where they burned all traces of their having been in our service and started their civilian life again as if nothing had happened to interrupt it'. There could hardly have been a more eloquent testimony to the failure of the appeal of the White cause. Ironside immediately telegraphed the War Office asking for two warships to be sent and saying that he must clear out altogether. 'This is a bad business', confessed the CIGS when he read the message.

Worse was to come. When Ironside travelled over to the railway sector of which Onega was a part, taking 150 recently-arrived Australians from 45th Fusiliers with him, he found that the disaffection had spread. Two of the Russian battalions were planning to mutiny, arrest their officers and hand over their positions to the Bolsheviks with whom their action was being concerted. There would then be an attack on the main position, including the headquarters itself. According to Brigadier-General Turner's brigade major, Charles Hudson, by sheer good fortune the orders fell into the hands of a loyal Russian and the plot was foiled; the two battalions were disarmed and the potential mutineers were arrested. Disciplinary measures were in the hands of the senior White Russian colonel. It seems that, after heavy interrogation, including some torture, 'a large number of NCOs and men were executed'. A similar plot was exposed, and foiled, in a company at Seletskoe, nearer the river. Following these defections, a half-hearted attack by the Bolshevik forces on the railway was easily repulsed.

'For the moment the trouble was over', Ironside later recalled, 'but I felt that we had come very near to a general mutiny.' The need now was to get out of North Russia as quickly as possible.[49]

The situation of the flotilla was also going from bad to worse. An Admiralty study was later to conclude that there had been 'no prospect of providing sufficient vessels for successful operations above Kurgomen'; but this did not stop Altham trying. By taking Troitsa when it did, the army was already outpacing its river support. During June the river level fell by over five feet. Although Troitsa had a fine, deep channel alongside it, the approaches were dangerously shallow and the flotilla was having trouble with a heavy enemy minefield, to which floating mines added a particular menace. 'They have all sorts of mines', wrote one of Altham's officers, 'small ones with horns, large sea mines with horns, and small ones with whiskers (these are awful because they will go off if you look at the blighters almost.' Altham later explained, 'From now onwards our movements were beset with difficulties and dangers from these river mines'. The majority of the craft specially sent out from England were useless, though some of them had been called home from as far afield as Mesopotamia to join the flotilla. The exploratory mine-sweeping in small steamboats had to be done under frequent shelling from the enemy's ships and shore batteries and sniping from the banks. The shallow river boat HMS *Sword Dance* was mined and sunk, and not long after *Fandango* shared the same fate. HM *Monitor 33* was hit by a large shell and its wardroom was shattered. Morale in the flotilla was under strain. Seaman Jowett noted, 'The Bolos send notes over, and drop them on our lines – asking us why we are fighting them, when we ought to be home celebrating Peace etc, after five years of war. Strange to say that is what we all want to know.' The futility of the conflict became an accelerating corrosion. 'Today we are doing a fine thing!', mused Jowett, 'fighting the battles of a people who do not want us, and who turn on us at every opportunity. Probably the Ruskie troops at Archangel will mutiny next, and then there will be some fun … What a wise Government is ours!' Even the naval officers were beginning to lose faith in their equipment and a successful outcome to the river war. 'I wonder what the finish of this outfit will be', First Lieutenant Tyler of the *Humber* ruminated, 'It seems a great waste of life and material and really the sooner it is over the better. Either the expedition should be a very much stronger force – properly equipped with gun barges of light draught – and many more transport barges – light draught tugs – and the proper gear – more aeroplanes – kit balloons etc. or it should be abandoned. We seem to have underrated the enemy's strength and rather overrated our own.'[50]

On 27 July 1919 a memorial service was held in the grounds of the church at Troitsa, the church which had been the objective of the Hampshires' abortive attack. The service was for the seamen lost in the river war: the crews of the *Sword Dance*, *Fandango* and a picket boat. Among those remembered was Altham's young mine-sweeping officer, Lieutenant Brockholes, who had lost his life lying in a small skiff, with a couple of seamen as crew, in a desperate attempt to catch a mine with his hands and render it safe. The mine had been spotted drifting slowly towards the hospital barge. The skiff overran the mine which exploded. All three crewmen were lost. A second mine-sweeping officer was lost later when a mine struck another vessel. Altham proposed Brockholes for a posthumous Victoria Cross which, unfortunately, 'the Admiralty could not see their way to recommend His Majesty to award'.

The same day, General Ironside and Mr R.H. Hoare, the new senior British diplomat in north Russia, met formally with the General Miller and the members of the Archangel Government to inform them officially of the coming evacuation. Until then Miller had still hoped that some element of the British force would remain in Archangel over the winter. Also that day, the two British Commanders-in-Chief in North Russia, Generals Ironside and Maynard, sent separate signals to the War Office. The telegrams originated from distinct but linked circumstances, were different in their wording, but identical in their startling recommendations. They suggested nothing less than a negotiation with the Bolsheviks for the Allied withdrawal. The proposal was that the Allied forces would depart from North Russia in return for the Bolsheviks agreeing not to interfere with the evacuation and not to exact reprisals on Russians who had collaborated with them. The following day Hoare telegraphed a similar proposal to the Foreign Secretary. It was a remarkable change from the strategic optimism displayed in Ironside's interview on 1 June, and a final admission of what had long been obvious to many soldiers on the ground: the White movement in North Russia was entirely a creature of the British; without them it would collapse like a house of cards.[51]

12

The White Advance

Vladivostok was already in the grip of winter when 1/9th Battalion of the Hampshire Regiment arrived there at the end of November 1918, after a not too pleasant voyage from India during which the influenza pandemic had struck the ship and claimed a number of lives; sick men were also dropped off at Colombo, Singapore and Hong Kong. The battalion, now forty-six men fewer than when it had left Bombay, was despatched at General Knox's particular request since it was a first-class Territorial battalion, better able to act as an example to the Russian troops he was attempting to train than Colonel John Ward's garrison men. The Hampshires were to become part of the Canadian-led brigade that was now assembling. The men had trained hard in the heat of India and even taken part in a minor campaign in Waziristan. Their commander, Lieutenant Colonel Robert Johnson, was also of a man of quite a different kidney: an Oxford-educated civil servant, he had been commanding his Territorials since 1911. Like some of his men, he was a little concerned to be embarking on a fresh campaign when the main war was over and many of his fellows were returning to good jobs at home. The Hampshires were issued with Arctic clothing by the Canadian authorities, spent some time at Vladivostok training and getting acclimatised, for the temperature was already twenty degrees below zero, and in mid-December set out on the Trans-Siberian Railway, twenty men to a truck, for their 4000 mile journey to Omsk. By comparison with the chaos and disorganisation around them, the journey went reasonably well, helped no doubt by a revolver-armed NCO being posted on the footplate, keeping the driver and fireman up to the mark. Each truck was heated by a barely-adequate stove, the men had an ample if humdrum diet of black bread, bully beef, cheese and stew, with some variety being provided by the Canadian YMCA truck, where canteen stores were available, other items coming from the various stops along the route at which the battalion detrained to show the flag. At Chita, for example, where they stopped to celebrate Christmas and pay respects to Ataman Semenov, they dined on rum and black pheasants which their colonel had acquired at Harbin. Johnson visited Semenov, who was in bed recovering from an assassination attempt. He knew of Semenov's disagreements with Kolchak and also that he ruled Chita and district with a rod of iron, but this did not deter Johnson, an ex-President of the Oxford Union, from giving the Siberian warlord, lying on his sick-bed and universally feared for his barbarities, a pompous lecture on the need for all to pull together in the war against the Bolshevik. It was one of many bizarre scenes in this extraordinary theatre of war.

After twenty-three days the battalion finally arrived at Omsk to a warm welcome from Colonel Ward and the men of the Middlesex Battalion. There was, however, declared one of the men, 'little to do except to keep fit and kill time'. 'What purpose their presence here was serving', concluded their regimental historian, 'it is hard to say: they made a great impression on the Russians by their fitness', but 'a tiny handful of troops could do nothing to influence the always obscure and rapidly changing political situation'. One man in the ranks, Sergeant Jupe, had no such doubts: 'It was understood that the Colonel's instructions were to proceed to Vladivostok, make our way across Siberia, turn the German Army out of the country, put a stop to the Russian Revolution and await further orders.' If only it had been that simple. Later on, however, they moved further west to Ekaterinburg, somewhat nearer the front line.[1]

Allied policy in Siberia was in complete disarray, which the Armistice served to increase rather than lessen.. The bulk of the American forces remained in the Vladivostok area for the winter, guarding the stock of stores which the Allies had supplied to the Russian Imperial Government and which they wished to prevent being transferred to the Germans. Although this motive disappeared with the Armistice, General Graves was determined that the stores, about 750,000 tons of them, including barbed wire, field guns, many thousands of railway truck wheels and millions of rounds of ammunition, should be inventoried and sealed and not issued to anyone until peace was restored. This immediately provoked trouble with the British and French, who knew how desperate the Omsk authorities were for supplies. General Knox insisted that the stores be released, as they had been provided largely by Britain and paid for by British loans, but endless difficulties accompanied every release. Not until June did Graves get firm orders to release all stores and did President Wilson agree to supply even more. By then, of course, it was too late. Meanwhile, the Japanese continued with their policy of establishing as much economic control as they could, whilst doing their best to keep Kolchak's regime weak and unpopular by subsidising Semenov and Kalmikov, who plundered and terrorised their domains along the railway besides, in the case of Semenov, doing his best to disrupt the flow of supplies and reinforcements upon which Kolchak's armies depended.

The Czech Legion was now a changed force. The Czechs had been delighted when the independence of their distant homeland had been proclaimed on 28 October; with the signing of the Armistice they wished for nothing more than to return to their country as free citizens. They had done the lion's share of the fighting; none of the promised Allied support had arrived; Japanese interference with the railway had left them short of clothing and ammunition; and the

Siberian Directorate, which they had supported, had now been overthrown. On 21 November the Czech National Council formally stated that the Omsk *coup d'état* was contrary to the principles for which they were fighting, and that, 'as representatives of the army that is bearing the brunt of the struggle with the Bolsheviks', they did not sympathise with and would not help the new Omsk regime. In mid-January, tired, disillusioned and increasingly ill-disciplined, the Czech forces withdrew from the front and took over their share of guarding the railway, which was apparently all that the big battalions among the Allies, the Japanese and Americans, were doing in support of the White cause. The exception to this disaffection was the young Czech commander, Gaida, who had fought with such distinction in the Baikal region. Favouring the move to a stronger regime in Siberia, he resigned in disgust and offered his services to Admiral Kolchak. He was promoted to lieutenant general and given command of the Northern Army, on whose advance in the direction of Archangel Churchill and his Chief of the Imperial General Staff were to place such store.

Then there were the Canadians. Major-General Emsley was keen to get his force into battle, realising that genuine battlefield support from the Allies was the only way of keeping the Czechs in the line. He was correct, of course, and despatched a lieutenant colonel and over forty all ranks to Omsk to administer the Hampshire and Middlesex battalions and arrange accommodation there for the rest of the substantial Anglo-Canadian force; but that was as near to action against the Bolsheviks as the British and Canadian battalions were ever to get. With considerable popular opposition in Canada to its army's involvement in the Siberian campaign, and little sign of the imagined economic benefits of participation or even of the prestige of Canadian command, since Emsley was still subject to the direction of the London War Office, the edict finally came from Ottawa that the Canadians were not to engage in military operations, nor was Emsley himself to move west to take command of the British battalions. The main body of Canadians had arrived in mid-January; but there were no further sailings thereafter. Early in February, Prime Minister Borden, who was now forced to change his earlier views, informed Lloyd George that Canada intended to withdraw its troops from Siberia in April. There was no protest from the British Premier. 'Perhaps the Armistice threw a spanner into the entire expedition', Seargeant Jupe correctly surmised.[2]

The decision that the Canadians were not to fight, and subsequently that they were to be withdrawn altogether, led to some heated exchanges between the leaders in Siberia and the government in Ottowa. Sir Charles Eliot, General Knox and General Emsley all protested against the decision. There was also some exasperated corespondence locally between Kox and Emsley, with Knox rather lamely asserting that Emsley should have gone forward to Omsk himself to take command of the British and Canadian forces there before the movement restrictions were applied to him. Knox still hoped for a change of heart in Ottawa, writing, 'I still hope that they [Ottawa] will send troops to go the whole hog. If they only think of playing the American-Japanese sitting game in the Far East, I honestly don't see much use in their coming at all'. The Canadian troops were left in a wholly unsatisfactory position. By the finish there were over 4000 of them in Siberia with no role to play, save for the few who were providing administrative backing for the British. 'Home or Fight' became their cry as boredom and indiscipline developed, which Ward claimed was even spreading to the Hampshires. The first party of Canadians returning home embarked at Vladivostok on 21 April. Even at this late stage, Churchill made one last despairing appeal to Borden as Kolchak's spring offensive gained its successes: 'I cannot help being sorry that Canada has not been able a little to help us in bringing about these good results. I of course agreed to your wish to withdraw the Canadians from Vladivostok ... But is it not possible for us to have a few volunteers from the Canadian Forces to cooperate with the volunteer detachments which compose our various missions to the loyal Russian armies?' A few Canadians did vounteer, but the last main Canadian contingent left Siberia on 5 June 1919.[3]

Protracted negotiation between Britain and France, followed by a series of discussions at Omsk in mid-January involving Kolchak, Knox and Janin, confirmed the relationship and powers of the three men. Kolchak refused to accept Janin as Commander-in-Chief of the Russian forces. Instead, the French general retained his grandiloquent title but was given charge simply of all non-Russian Allied forces west of Lake Baikal. It was a virtually non-existent command, involving a battalion from each of Britain, France and Italy garrisoning towns in the rear areas, together with the now-defunct Czech Legion. Colonel Johnson, the CO of the Hampshires, wrote of General Janin: 'He sits in his railway carriage here, a solitary though dignified figure ... nominally C-in-C of the Allies including the Czechs who refuse to fight under any circumstances, and ourselves. But he gives no orders and takes no responsibility ... A ridiculous and pathetic figure, with his personal escort of twenty men.' General Knox, on the other hand, was confirmed as *Chef de l'Arrière*, responsible for Allied help with the training of fresh Russian formations and for directing the distribution of all military *matériel* from abroad, the great bulk of which, of course, was British. Knox became the most influential foreigner in Siberia; Kolchak much preferred him to Janin and the two men had established something of a relationship long before Kolchak's accession to supreme power. General Knox derived some leverage from his control of the foreign supplies; but it has to be said that all this did not amount to a great deal in the circumstances of Siberia and particularly those of Kolchak's headquarters. Most of the time Knox was in Vladivostok, with Kolchak 4000 miles away at Omsk, where a new man, General Lebedev, was soon appointed as his Chief of Staff. Young, inexperienced but cocksure, Lebedev had originally arrived as a liaison officer from General Denikin. Kolchak had selected him, he told Knox, 'because I can be sure he will not stab me in the back'. This drew the comment from Knox, 'Kolchak forgets that the post requires more positive qualities'.[4]

Despite the defection of the Czechs and the ill-prepared state of his own forces, Admiral Kolchak decided on a winter offensive against the Bolsheviks. Perhaps he considered that an attack was needed to justify his position, an admiral who knew nothing of land warfare but now commanded generals and armies. He determined on an attack to capture Perm in the north west, which would take him in the direction of Kotlas and Viatka and a possible link-up with the Ironside at Archangel. He could not have known, at this stage, that Ironside's command was in no position to link up with him. Wiser counsels in the *Stavka*, Kolchak's military headquarters, advocated a thrust towards the south in an attempt to effect a junction with Denikin, but not until the spring. But Kolchak was impatient for action; besides, Gaida had told him that a plan for the capture of Perm had already been prepared by the Czechs. His sole concession to the *Stavka* advice was to sanction a force to attempt to link up with Dutov's Orenburg Cossacks. General Knox's view, that the immediate task should be 'the raising of a small disciplined army, and that half-equipped levies should not be hustled to the front in the hope of gaining territory that could be conquered later on', was ignored. According to Knox, Lebedev 'thought it was a matter of weeks to beat the Bolsheviks'. Lebedev believed in 'what he called "elemental measures" – that is, calling up thousands of men for whom there were prepared neither instructional cadres, clothing, equipment nor accommodation and of hurling them in their "elemental" state, without training, on the enemy.' In view of Kolchak's determination to attack right away, Knox did what he could to help: the Hampshire Battalion provided guards for troop and supply trains between Omsk and the front, whilst Colonel Ward asked if his men might participate in the coming offensive. A few picked men were allowed to.

There was, however, one British unit, the Royal Marine gunnery detachment, which had fought with Ward's battalion on the Ussuri river and continued to fight with considerable distinction as a small unit integrated with the Russian forces. It had gone forward with the advancing Czechs and Russians and continued to provide artillery support along the railway from Omsk to Ufa, well beyond the Ural Mountains, until the intense cold of late November froze the guns' recoil cylinders and put an end to all artillery support. The detachment returned first to Omsk and then to Vladivostok. Its officers subsequently formed a small Naval Mission to assist Admiral Kolchak in creating a Russian Naval Flotilla to operate on the River Kama, which flows down from Perm, in the foothills of the Urals, to join the mighty and strategically important Volga. The chief of this tiny mission, Captain Wolfe-Murray, proposed that the guns used by the marines on the railway shoud be transferred to vessels on the Kama and become an integral part of the Russian flotilla when this formed at Perm. The Admiralty agreed, providing sufficient volunteers were forthcoming from the Royal Marine Light Infantry detachment aboard HMS *Kent*, an old cruiser then on its way to replace the *Suffolk*, for its fifth period of duty on the China station. Whilst the *Kent* had a two-month delay at Hong Kong for the refitting of its badly-worn engines, its marines were ashore training for the possibility of civil disturbances which the *Suffolk* had warned them to expect at Vladivostok. When the *Kent* finally made its way into Vladivostok harbour, preceded by an ice-breaker, in the intense cold of the Siberian winter, its band and marine guard paraded smartly on the quarterdeck to salute the American cruiser, *Brooklyn*, anchored in the bay. 'The arms drill was faultless', noted the detachment commander, 'but the only effect by the band was by the drums – all wind instruments froze up after the first few notes'.

The Royal Marines were fully briefed about the Kama flotilla proposal and then given some days to think over the matter of volunteering. Of the detachment of sixty-four NCOs and men, sixty-three volunteered for action; the odd man out being then in the cells and without a vote. This was a remarkable result since the Admiralty was already making emergency arrangements to relieve the *Kent* at an early date to enable the 450 'hostilities only' members of its crew to be released, the war having ended four months previously. It might have been expected that some of the similarly-placed marines would be keen to get away. The commander, Captain Wolfe-Murray RMLI, attributed the unanimous vote to the spirit of adventure among his men for this unusual assignment in the heart of Russia. His preparations for the operation were thorough. The detachment was issued with excellent winter clothing by the efficient Canadians; it took two months' supply of iron rations as well as a store of luxuries from the *Kent* canteen, and, very wisely, twice the weight of foodstuffs in disinfectant. He also found three Russian volunteers to add to the crew, as well as an unusual Englishman, Lieutenant Ewing, to act as Russian interpreter; by an odd combination of circumstances, Ewing was actually a lieutenant in the Russian service then serving at the Vladivostok Russian Naval College. Thus staffed and victualled, the Royal Marine force put its one 6-inch and four 12-pounder guns aboard a express train for the 5000 mile journey to Perm, where it would get its next sight of armed vessels on flowing water when the warmth of early spring dramatically broke up and dispersed the three-foot depth of ice which had immobilised all river traffic on the Kama for almost five months.[5]

Gaida began his drive on Perm on 18 December and captured it on 24th. This rapid and striking success was due to the surprise caused by attacking in the depths of winter and the unprepared state of the Bolshevik forces. Only days before the attack Lenin had wired urgently to Trotsky, 'Perm is in danger. I fear that we have forgotten about the Urals'. Gaida captured intact the bridge over the Kama at Perm, as well as 30,000 prisoners and huge quantities of booty: 4000 wagons, 260 locomotives, fifty guns and ten armoured cars. According to the British Consul at Ekaterinburg, the captured wagons were loaded with goods looted from shops and homes by the Bolsheviks, but left behind by their hasty evacuation. Trotsky believed that the loss of Perm would 'bring traffic to a standstill', since the region's mines supplied the factories and all the railways with coal. Scarcely balancing this serious reverse, the Bolsheviks took Ufa, on the southern route to the Volga. Ufa lay astride the communications to Dutov's corps and threatened the possible junction with Denikin. General Kappel's efficient White corps had been withdrawn from the Ufa front, on General Knox's advice, for re-equipment, so the Bolshevik advance was effectively an unopposed occupation. General Knox remained optimistic, however: 'Bolshevism has no lasting force behind it', he wired the War Office after the fall of Perm, 'and requires only one or two knocks to finish it.' Bruce Lockhart's views, quoted earlier, provided a more soundly-based judgement.[6]

By the end of November 1918, the War Office had ordered the despatch to Siberia of 200 field guns and complete sets of equipment for 100,000 men. The following month, it arranged to supply a further 100,000. General Knox consequently agreed to equip Kappel's Corps, which was to be expanded to three divisions, and also three of the five new divisions which Kolchak was raising in the rear areas. He was also doing his best, with limited but steadily growing Mission manpower, to assist with the the training of the new divisions being raised. The transport of supplies from Britain over such huge distances was not a speedy affair; the great bulk of it arrived in the four months March to June. Until then there was only the little which been sent earlier and the equipment which the Canadians had available. In the interval, Knox believed, the front should be held with existing forces while the newly-raised divisions were being trained and equipped. Knox appointed Brigadier General Blair, who had come out initially as his Chief of Staff, to run the base at Vladivostok, whilst Knox himself arranged the training operation with Kolchak and his Omsk Stavka. He was still based at his train headquarters at Vladivostok, from which he clocked up 37,419 miles in his travels between the port and Omsk during his time heading the mission. The first training unit was set up as early as October 1918, on Russian Island in Vladivostok Bay, to train Russian young officers and NCOs. Over the following six months other schools were established at Irkutsk, Tomsk and finally at Ekaterinburg. Unlike the training schools established by the mission in south Russia, in Siberia the Russians were in overall charge, with the British doing such training as they could negotiate and had the manpower to provide. It was a very unsatisfactory situation; but Knox was at least able to use his staff at the schools to ensure that British-supplied weapons and equipment actually got to the men being trained. He naturally kept a closer eye on the Russian Island school, commanded by a reactionary monarchist, General Sakharov, where the training staff included a few British instructors and a demonstration platoon drawn from the Hampshires. All the equipment was supplied by Britain and the cadets wore British uniforms.[7]

Getting supplies and equipment to the fighting troops depended not only on transporting them across the high seas, but also along the Trans-Siberian Railway. As time went on this became an increasingly frustrating task, partly as a result of the machinations of the Japanese and Semenov, but increasingly because of disorganisation, thieving, general brigandage and anarchy. As early as December, a rising of supposed pro-Bolshevik railwaymen was brutally suppressed; many orders to railway workers had to be given at the point of the gun. In February, General Knox asked Colonel Ward to undertake an unusual assignment: a propaganda tour of the railway to persuade the railwaymen to stay at work and support the Kolchak regime. Whether this was a means of getting the busybody Ward away from Omsk or a serious attempt to exploit his position as a union leader is not clear. Lieutenant Colonel Ward, in uniform rather than boiler suit, hardly appeared a representative of the British workers, and his need to speak always through an interpreter cannot have reinforced the credibility of his appeals. Ward's letter to Kolchak asking for authority for his tour made crystal clear where the real trouble lay. He explained to Kolchak that the railway workers needed regular pay. Some had not been paid for 'many weeks, and in other cases, months', and there needed to be regulations for the protection of Russian workmen, once order had been restored. 'If I could get something definite from Your Excellency upon these points, I believe it would do much to help.' That he should have been reduced to writing in these terms betrays the total ineptitude of the regime on a matter vital to its existence. Nevertheless, the doughty Ward, accompanied by a liaison officer, an interpreter, the regimental sergeant-major and an escort of twenty-two men and a machine gun, duly made his tour down the line and back to Omsk, holding workers' meetings at the major stations. He was thanked for his efforts, but what positive impact they had on the attitude of the railway workers remains unclear. At Irkutsk, Ward found that 14,000 rifles had been deposited by a British supply train six weeks earlier with no instructions for their disposal, although they were desperately needed at the fighting front. 'Allied help to Russia is like a jigsaw puzzle', wrote Ward, 'a mystery even to the man who devised it.'[8]

An example of the routine hazards which confronted even the most important rail journeys is provided by the experience of Captain H.K. Peacock, who, in the early days of the intervention, was charged with taking a vitally important train of small arms ammunition from Vladivostok to Omsk where it was desperately needed by the Czech, Cossack and Russian forces who provided the thin front line forces then resisting the Bolsheviks. Peacock was no tyro in Russian affairs:

he had been born in Russia, spoke the language well and had eight years' experience of Siberia. He was given a special express train, recently serviced for the purpose, which was to have priority of travel throughout its journey. It had a ten-man military train guard and was to have a greaser travelling with it to deal with any problems *en route*. The journey began on 28 November 1918, but, after proceeding with difficulty for only 500 yards, the train stopped – the engine was not sufficiently powerful and had to be substituted. The appointed greaser did not appear. These were but the first of a multitude of delays, breakdowns and surprises which plagued the journey. By 4 December the tenth and last of the wagon changes was made, all the originals having broken down when the poorly-serviced axle boxes overheated and ruined the axles; some even caught fire: this on an ammunition train! Peacock also discovered that a wagon-load of caviare and another of tea, one destined for Manchuria and the other for Chelyabinsk, had been secretly added to his train. Attempts to hook on extra wagons were subsequently made at various stations along the route. The train finally reached Omsk on 18 December and delivered a million rounds of ammunition to the Russian forces there before proceeding to Chelyabinsk and providing several million more to the Ural and Orenburg Cossacks and the remainder to the Czechs. It was at Chelyabinsk that Peacock discovered that one ammunition wagon was missing; it had been unhitched earlier for repair but not reattached to the train. Throughout the journey Russian railway officials refused to give the train any priority; there was recurring trouble with engines and always a shortage of materials for repairs. By journey's end several of the train guards were suffering from frostbite in the severity of the Siberian winter.[9]

At the beginning of February, Sir George Eliot told the Foreign Office that forty-eight goods trains, including several of munitions, were backed up on the Trans-Baikal section awaiting locomotives, whilst Ataman Semenov kept five, always under steam, attached to armoured trains from which he and his men ravaged the countryside. Semenov took first call on all repaired locomotives in the area, diverted scarce railway materials to suit his own purposes, and levied taxes on all civilian passengers, who were arrested on the slightest suspicion. Travelling with his Royal Marine Detachment from Vladivostok to Omsk in early April in a well-appointed train complete with restaurant car, Captain Jameson declared that 'evidences of Bolshevik activities were seen almost daily. Twice the railway had been cut by raiding Red bands wrecking trains and shortly after passing Harbin we saw a train which had been derailed and lay at the bottom of the valley.' As the signs of brigandage increased, the civilian passengers appealed to Jameson for his protection. He declared himself OC Train, posted military pickets along it and, in a much resented move from which he granted no exemptions, impressed all able-bodied civilian males on the train to patrol each side of it during the hours of darkness when it was at halt.[10]

Despite these manifold setbacks and difficulties with supplies, Kolchak determined to resume his offensive in the early spring, again attacking on a broad front. Gaida's Northern Army was to strike from Perm in the direction of Viatka to link hands with Ironside; the Western Army would press towards Samara to gain the line of the Volga as a preliminary to a junction with Denikin; in the centre there would be a thrust towards Kazan. The three armies, totalling about 100,000 men, were disposed over a front of 700 miles, quite incapable of mutual support even had the commanders wished to cooperate. In fact, there was rivalry between the principal generals for the limited supplies available. Yet, despite these obstacles, the offensive, which began in early March, quickly met with surprising success. Gaida swept through the Bolsheviks' lines, drove them from the Kama river basin and captured Glazov, midway between Perm and Viatka, an advance of about 140 miles. By this time, however, he had outrun his weak supply lines and could make no further progress. In the centre, the Soviet line was broken and two complete battalions defected to the Whites. Ufa fell to General Khanzhin's army on 13 March; Sterlitamak, sixty miles on, was taken in early April; by the end of the month Khanzhin was only 100 miles from the key objective of Kazan, a total advance of some 250 miles. In the south, the gains of the Western Army were even more spectacular, several important towns falling rapidly, until finally Yertsov, only 35 miles from the Volga, was taken. From there the important Volga towns of Samara and Saratov could both be threatened. These startling successes, however, formed the high watermark of Kolchak's advance. As might have been imagined, given the indifferent state of his armies and their precarious supply situation, the successes were as much the result of Bolshevik weaknesses and their being taken by surprise by the early offensive. The Fifth Red Army, opposing the most successful southern thrust, was well below strength and menaced by risings in its rear areas in reaction to the seizure of the last reserves of grain in the peasant villages of the middle Volga. The White forces, having now expended all their offensive power, were little better placed. Kolchak had very few trained reserves with which to exploit his successes and, significantly, the first serious defections from his own armies were beginning. Shortages of food and clothing were apparent and the competence of Kolchak as Commander-in-Chief was already being questioned.

General Knox was well aware of the precarious state of the victorious armies and concerned that the offensive, however successful, had disrupted training and impeded preparations to sustain the armies in the field. In March he had written, in some ill temper, to the Minister of War complaining about the latter's peremptory decision to send cadets, whom Knox had trained at Russian Island, to quite different formations from those agreed earlier with Knox, and to delay the despatch to Russian Island of the general who was to have charge there. In desperation Knox threatened, 'If matters are not arranged at once I consider it will be my duty to take all British equipment to formed units at the front'. The same month he wrote with similar directness to Kolchak himself, insisting that there could be no spring offensive 'because we will have nothing ready' and complaining that 'the first mobilisation of the Intelligentsia has produced only 2300, largely because of the number of men hiding in the various ministries ...', and the fact that in the attempted Irkutsk mobilisation, 'from 50 per cent to 70 per cent of the conscription of last August deserted simply because they had no clothing, properly prepared barracks or real instructional cadres ...' Knox's frustration was infinitely compounded by the news that Kolchak's spring offensive had begun some days before his letters had been composed, and with a complete lack of consultation with the British.[11]

Little of the truth of the momentous events in Siberia percolated to the British public at large. The Times's man in the region was Robert Wilton who, prior to the Revolution, had worked in Petrograd. He had left the capital a little while before the momentous events there in the belief that nothing newsworthy was happening. He returned to Russia via Vladivostok as a war correspondent when the intervention was in full swing. An ardent anti-Bolshevik and firm supporter of the intervention, his reports were largely propaganda, completely compromised when, for a time, he joined the staff of one of the prominent White generals. He was well aware of the true state of affairs, as a private letter to his editor makes clear: 'It is a truly appalling situation here, far worse than anything we can conceive – almost all due to the divided counsels that prevail among the Allies ...' Nothing so depressing ever appeared in the pages of The Times from its man in Siberia. Wilton achieved the unusual feat for a zealous anti-Bolshevik of arousing the hostility of General Knox by his intrigue and tale-telling. Knox finally wrote brusquely to him: 'I would be obliged if you would mind your own business as Correspondent of The Times and avoid interference in my work, for which I alone am responsible ... It is impertinence on your part to criticise my orders to people working under me. It is a matter of indifference to me what you write in your paper, but if I hear of another instance of your agitating against me in my Mission I will report all details home.' The War Office later supported Knox's request for Wilton to be recalled.[12]

Churchill, however, was delighted with Kolchak's progress. In a letter to the Prime Minister he noted that, 'The advance of Kolchak's armies is all the more remarkable in view of the fact that it is being conducted with Russian troops'. It held out the possibility, he believed, of Kolchak gaining the line of the Volga in the next few weeks, and even of advancing further towards Moscow. He reminded Lloyd George of the important role Britain had played in the Siberian successes: 'We can, I think, claim to have given more effective support to Kolchak than any of the other great Powers, as we have supplied him with nearly 12 million pounds' worth of our surplus munitions, and by the labour of our officers and agents this great mass of stuff has been filtered along the Siberian railway.' He also pointed out how Kolchak's advance 'enables him to stretch out his right hand in the direction of the Archangel forces'. Finally, he recommended the Prime Minister to recognise Kolchak's government, providing he could get the Russian leader to 'carry through a democratic programme about Russian land'. One can only comment that the possibility of such a programme ever being put into effect in Siberia by the reactionary regime which Kolchak headed was so remote as to be quite out of sight, though in his personal views Kolchak was probably the least reactionary of the White Russian leaders. He was, quite simply, incapable of controlling his subordinates or of managing a military campaign.[13]

By this stage, Captain Jameson's marine gunners had reached Perm with their naval guns and had begun hectic preparations to become a sub-unit of the Kama Flotilla, a makeshift force of river craft rapidly being converted to military use, which was to support the White forces fighting near the banks of the river and attempt to destroy any Red vessels opposing them. The open plains west of the Urals over which the Whites were now disposed were crossed by several mighty rivers which were vital for communications away from the railways, for the ground was now boggy from the spring thaw. The Kama itself, two miles wide in places and rising rapidly, was navigable by large river craft. The Kama Flotilla was one of the most professional of Kolchak's forces and the main concern of Admiral Smirnov, the Omsk Minister of Marine, who had been Kolchak's Chief of Staff when he commanded the Black Sea Fleet. Smirnov spoke excellent English and had served for some time with the Royal Navy. Jameson was allocated a large paddle-driven river boat for conversion to a gunboat on which his smaller guns and a machine gun were to be mounted. His other weapon platform was a huge tug-drawn barge which was to take the detachment's main armament, the 6-inch gun. By early May both boats had been converted by the artisans of the railway works at Perm, their guns had been tested and they had sailed about 400 miles downstream towards the front line where their gun-barge promptly suffered the indignity of an ineffective attack from two Bolshevik seaplanes. The *Kent* and *Suffolk*, as the detachment had dubbed its new vessels, were to find their gunnery skills in some demand; but in support of a withdrawal, rather than an advance, of the White land forces.

If Kolchak's front line forces were incapable of further efforts, the British in Siberia were doing their best to devise fresh means of strengthening them. The results of their supply efforts were already being seen, but they had not prevented troops at the front from being sent into battle with bark fibre shoes or even sacking wrapped around their feet and with bags sewn together in lieu of uniforms. General Knox's frustration at his inability to have more control of both the training and supply effort, and his concern at the Russians' hopeless inefficiency and their almost feudal approach to officer–soldier relations, led him to suggest a plan, not unlike that developed by Ironside at Archangel, to create a force of Russians trained and equipped exclusively by the British and led, initially at least, by British officers and NCOs: an Anglo-Russian brigade. Russian junior officers would be called in later for the development of this *corps d'élite* on which the government would be able to rely absolutely. His growing mission staff would provide some of the officers, with volunteers from the Hampshires furnishing the remainder and the NCO element. The scheme was welcomed by Kolchak and his Czech commander Gaida and authorised by the War Office in London. Knox called forward Brigadier General Blair from Vladivostok 'to undertake the delicate task of organising' the brigade. Colonel Johnson, the commanding officer of the Hampshires, who was to do much of the training, also welcomed the scheme. 'The Hampshire Russian Brigade', as he called it, 'will be dressed in British uniform, armed with British weapons and drilled in British style with British words of command ... We hope to march into Moscow as conquerors. Hants and Russian Hants together.' The creation of the Anglo-Russian Brigade, like that of the SBL, was a metaphor for the dilemma facing many British officers involved in the intervenion: they hated the Bolsheviks, but they despaired of the Whites; indeed, many now despised them.[14]

On 12 May 1919 Churchill wrote an enthusiastic letter to General Denikin in South Russia: 'We are sending you from the British War Office General Holman to be the Head of the Mission which His Majesty's Government have authorised me to maintain at your Headquarters.' The letter emphasised Holman's suitability for the post, his 'qualification of speaking Russian well and of being a great admirer and friend of the Russian people'. Holman was being sent, Churchill stressed, 'to aid you in every way in your task of warring down the Bolshevik tyranny'. He was also bearing, the letter explained, the insignia of the KCB which the King had conferred upon General Denikin, and a number of other decorations for award to Russians senior officers. No doubt General Denikin appreciated these honours; he was, nonetheless, resentful at the departure of General Briggs who had fought Denikin's corner well with the British authorities over a range of matters. He did not appreciate him being replaced by an officer of lower rank, which, as a major general, Holman was. But he would have been more heartened had he known that Churchill did not regard the supplies recently authorised for despatch to South Russia as being all Denikin would get. Churchill had recently written to General Harington at the War Office, 'If more can be used, every effort must be made to provide them and to secure the necessary authority. I hope General Holman is asking for everything he requires and will go out with the feeling that his mission is being well provided for'. Lloyd George was much less keen on Denikin than the award of the KCB might have indicated. He wrote to Churchill that other European leaders he had spoken to in Paris regarded Denikin as a reactionary. If British efforts 'simply ended in establishing a reactionary regime in Russia, British democracy would never forgive us', he told him. A couple of weeks later Josiah Wedgwood added to the attacks on Denikin in a stinging House of Commons speech which reported in detail some of the atrocities being committed by Denikin's troops in south Russia. Churchill did not answer Wedgwood's charges but instead spoke enthusiastically of the Russian commander's recent successes.[15]

After many months of hard fighting and at times precarious existence, Denikin's Volunteer Army and its Cossack allies were at last breaking out from their base in the Kuban. They had survived a series of setbacks, the latest of which was the French-led débâcle in the Ukraine and Crimea. On instructions from the Allies, Germany had started to pull its troops out of the Ukraine in the days following the Armistice. The French led the struggle to fill the void, but without any very clear aim, since a Ukrainian nationalist regime had already been established. France landed its first troops in mid-December 1918, the advance guard of a motley force, mainly French colonial troops and two divisions of Greeks, which finally numbered over 80,000. It joined a substantial detachment of the Volunteer Army and it was backed by a naval force, strong numerically but weak in morale. The French quickly managed to alienate the local nationalists, to whom Denikin was, in any case, opposed, and while negotiations continued, a Bolshevik army under the experienced and independent-minded commander Antonov began a steady advance southward. He combined with a powerful Cossack partisan commander, Grigoriev, to sideline the notional Ukrainian Commander-in-Chief, Petlyura, and then to force back the French-commanded Allied force. Grigoriev was greatly strengthened by huge quantities of weapons taken from the Germans. The French troops were indisciplined and proved almost useless; the Greeks were somewhat better but cruel and much disliked. The French even managed to alienate the Volunteer detachment with which they were supposed to be cooperating. Ultimately, every shade of political opinion protested against them. They finally withdrew from Odessa amid scenes of desperation, indiscipline, horror and panic. Most of the Allied force got away, together with some 30,000 civilians and 10,000 men of the Volunteer Army. Commander Goldsmith aboard HMS *Montrose* wrote that the French had 'disgracefully abandoned Odessa to her fate and are taking no steps to defend Sevastopol ... Every English ship is full of refugees whom the French refuse to have anything to do with'.[16] Denikin, however, was not even aware of the evacuation until it was already under way.

The Crimea, from which the British marines had supervised the early German evacuations, was abandoned as well, without much resistance. Engineer Commander Shrubsole, serving with the Allied naval force aboard HMS *Calypso*, witnessed the collapse of the resistance: 'The French had about 4000 troops ashore and the Greeks 2000 but they were never sent to the firing line. We could not understand the apathy of the French Admiral who was in command of the Allied forces. The Greeks wanted to assist more actively but they were never allowed to.' Captain H.W. Wyld, on board the destroyer *Nereide* in the Black Sea, found himself virtually the governor of Kherson, just above the Crimea, during the Red advance, keeping the town quiet and preserving law and order as disaster spread, until he was able to hand over to some French troops. Finally, the Bolsheviks forced the lines and the Volunteer Army contingent 'melted away'. By this time, the unrest in the French navy in the Black Sea was turning to mutiny. Some of the French ships' crews who had refused duty demanded to go ashore, where they fraternised with the Bolsheviks, eventually being fired on by French and Greek troops. Once back on board, Shrubsole records, they 'hoisted the red flag on *all* French ships at the jackstaff' and demanded to go back to France. 'The French', he declared, 'stink in the nostrils of decent Russians and even we dislike them fairly heartily which is a pity.' Commander Goldsmith shared his view, 'The French are awful. We loathe and despise them now almost as much as the Russians do'. The disastrous French adventure in south Russia, against which its local Commander-in-Chief in Constantinople had long advised, was at an end. If Denikin's efforts were to be supported and south Russia wrested from the Bolsheviks, it would be by Britain's assistance alone. It would be incorrect to suppose, however, that direct action against the Bolsheviks had universal support in the British ships which were bombarding the advancing Red formations as they approached the Crimean coast. One seaman's diary recorded a bit of unrest aboard ship 'owing to us firing on the Bolsheviks'.[17]

The last Bolshevik offensive designed to drive Denikin from his south Russian base was beaten off in March 1919; thereafter the White commander, 'a powerful-looking, handsome man with a grizzled beard and moustache', as one British Mission member described him, was reorganising his troops in preparation for his own offensive, though the advance did not begin until late May, just as General Holman was preparing to leave London for his new appointment. On the far right of Denikin's line, securing his right flank, was the British Caspian Flotilla which was now virtually unchallenged on its inland sea. The Reds had brought several light destroyers down from the Baltic by canal and river to the mouth of the Volga, but, as Lieutenant Bilney noted, 'These showed little inclination to leave the Volga estuary', despite being armed with 4-inch guns, since they were now menaced not only by the Caspian Flotilla, but also by British aircraft. Based at Petrovsk, halfway up the western coast, was 221 Squadron RAF, flying DH9 single-engined bombers from an airfield just outside the town. It undertook reconnaissance sorties for the flotilla and bombed the Bolshevik fleet, Astrakhan and the naval bases in the Volga delta. In April it was joined by the seaplanes of 226 squadron (to which Bilney transferred on promotion to captain), which based itself in the Anglo-Asiatic Bank building and developed a seaplane base on the coast. The less buoyant fresh waters of the Caspian made take-off hazardous for the seaplanes until they had been modified. Both squadrons were then able to fly missions in support of Denikin.[18]

By May, the armed forces of south Russia were deployed in three small armies. On the right flank, working from Caspian Sea bases, was the small Caucasian Army, mainly cavalry, about 10,000 strong and composed of Terek and Kuban Cossacks commanded by Baron Wrangel; next were the 20,000 men of the Army of Don Cossacks, drawn entirely from the Don District and part mounted and part on foot until the 'Plastoune' regiments, as these very temporary infantrymen were called, could capture fresh horses. A Siberian Cossack, General Sidorin, was their commander. The small, 10,000-strong Volunteer Army itself was next in line, one small corps holding a front which extended to the Sea of Azov near Taganrog while its fellow, the remnant of the force which had cooperated with the French until their withdrawal, was preparing to begin its advance northwards through the Crimea. Both had officers and cadets fighting in the ranks. This, then, was the combined force which, over the next six weeks, was to advance across the Don and Donets rivers, capture first the major industrial centre of Kharkov and then, a few days later, the key city of Tsaritsyn, of great historical as well as strategic importance. Soon after, Denikin was to order a general advance on Moscow.

Not everyone in the mission had such a high regard for General Denikin as did Churchill and the successive mission commanders. All respected him for the way he had risen from humble origins to high rank, and all acknowledged that he was a great patriot; but most also admitted that he was a poor administrator. Colonel de Wolff also judged that Denikin often could not make up his mind and was largely dependent on his Chief of Staff, General Romanovsky. Romanovsky had a German wife and was never notably sympathetic to the British. 'The Head of the British Military Mission constantly urged Denkin to get rid of Romanovsky, but he refused to do so', another mission officer records. De Wolff also noted disapprovingly that at the height of the campaign Denikin married a comparatively young girl and spent his honeymoon at Sochi on the Black Sea. This indulgence provoked lots of comment and was not, De Wolff considered, likely to boost the morale of those who were fighting for their lives and the Motherland. As to the generality of Denikin's officers, they were widely criticised by the mission members. Captain Williamson found them 'kind-hearted and generous to the point of absurdity', but also 'lazy, arrogant, ignorant and often cowardly, chiefly because they knew their men had no heart for fighting their fellow countrymen ... no one at Mission Headquarters had a very high opinion of them'. Many mission officers were to comment on the preference shown by many White officers, most of whom were unreconstructed Tsarists, for comfortable billets in the rear and at the headquarters, rather than at the fighting front. Other wrote of the situation at the front where the troops 'were largely despised by their officers and treated abominably'. It was all very similar to the officer–soldier relations encountered in the other theatres of the intervention, and as little amenable to alteration.[19]

General Holman, an Indian Army cavalry officer, had served with the Russians as an attaché during the Russo-Japanese War and had spent most of the recent war on the Western Front, finally as one of the principal staff officers of the 4th Army. As commander of the mission, he had two advantages denied to Briggs: he was not subordinated to General Milne (who was angered by this change, about which Holman himself was left to inform him), and he had the full confidence and support of Churchill. Indeed, it was partly the difficulties with General Milne which had led Churchill to give Holman some independence. The young Captain Kennedy drew a very unflattering sketch of the new Mission Commander: 'a fat old man, not at all awe-inspiring or dignified, but rather like a business man which, of course, he is, more than a soldier. He has an extraordinary habit of turning up the whites of his eyes and blinking at you while he talks'. As it happened, Holman soon showed himself to be anything but a 'base wallah'. On the contrary, he was very keen on front-line service. It was less Holman's appearance than his utmost contempt for Regulations which impressed Colonel De Wolff. When Denikin began to advance, Holman was quick to claim the early successes to be a direct result of the assistance given by Britain. This was actually not the case. When the tide of operations turned in the Whites' favour, very little of the British weaponry or supplies had filtered through to the front. The advance had more to do with the success of Kolchak's offensive on the Siberian front, the weakening of the Soviet southern front by the defection of Grigoriev and the partisan leader Nakhno, and the rebellion of the northern Don Cossacks which broke the Bolshevik hold on the Don. However, as the advance neared the two key objectives of the first main offensive, Tsaritsyn and Kharkov, British weaponry began to play an important role in the progress of the campaign.[20]

Holman made several useful changes during the early period of his time in charge of British support. Having reviewed how the mission was operating, one of his first ideas was to stop all attempts at training the Russians. He subsequently relented somewhat, deciding merely that the artillery instruction being given was too theoretical and that tactical training was inappropriate. He also developed a plan to attach liaison officers to each of the White armies, so that the effectiveness of the British training could be evaluated and the liaison officers could assess whether the equipment and supplies were getting through to where they were most needed. It was a sensible idea, but meant that the small supply of high-quality officers was spread even more thinly between the base, mission headquarters and the liaison groups (which they soon became) with the armies. Holman had already emphasised that 'the officers we employ must, therefore, be men of great tact and of real administrative ability'. This was seldom the case and the mission was already seriously understrength. Because of staff shortages, Russian apathy and rapid battlefield movements, some aspects of training never really got under way. Two attempts to start engineer training were overtaken by reverses at the front and the need to move location. Signals training was largely a failure: the Russians had little interest in technical communications and the British specialist staff were always way below strength. As late in the campaign as December 1919 there were still only six signals officers and thirty-one other ranks against an establishment of twenty-seven and 177. Captain Lever was a Senior Wireless Officer with the mission. He had spent over six weeks in Britain waiting to go out and then a further six on the journey to south Russia, only to meet, once there, an 'evasive and befogged attitude' from the Russian officers with whom he had to deal. He subsequently discovered the precious wireless sets, supplied by Britain, frozen solid to the floor of a railway truck. After only four days in post he was reduced to total exasperation. 'Actually I am nothing but a ruddy greaser and mechanic sent to amuse and interest numbers of Russian blokes whose sole mission in life is to stand around and gape – boggle-eyed idiots.' The progress of artillery training was hampered by the delivery to the schools of much defective equipment, an almost universal complaint. The Railway Section had its difficulties too, not so much with its civilian counterparts as with the Military Communications Directorate, whose attitude was positively hostile in the early months of the mission's operations. Like all his predecessors in south Russia, from the small missions of enquiry onwards, Holman emphasised the need for economic assistance and political advice for Denikin, but the Foreign Office reaction was slow and ineffective.

Perhaps the most succesful element of the mission's training was that of its tank section. Despite the earlier failure of the War Office to accept General Briggs's sound judgement on the important role which tanks could play, the relatively small armoured force which was sent had an influence out of all proportion to its size and managed to operate quickly and effectively. A Royal Tank Corps detachment of ten officers and fifty-five other ranks reached south Russia in mid-April, closely followed by a force of six Whippet and six Mark V tanks. The detachment commander, Major McMicking, had the tank school established at Ekaterinburg just nine days after his arrival. But it soon suffered from the traditional and virtually universal determination of the Russian commanders to send men and weapon systems directly to the fighting front, whether trained and ready or not. By early May, with the first hundred officers of the new Russian Tank Corps only partially trained, Denikin ordered six tanks and crews up to the Donets front. They went into action on May 8 and 10 and 'the mere sight of the tanks threw the enemy's ranks into confusion and he fled, panic-stricken, abandoning rifles, ammunition and clothing', as the corps history recorded. By 24 June GHQ at Constantinople was telling the War Office that the tanks were 'successful beyond all expectations' and that the Bolsheviks 'openly state they will not fight against tanks'. The tanks managed to capture six armoured trains, five surrendering untouched, and when some Whippets, loaded aboard a train, approached Siavyarsk, the Bolsheviks evacuated the place hurriedly before the tanks had even detrained. 'All fronts clamouring for tanks', the message emphasised. They went on to distinguish themselves in the capture of Tsaritsyn, which had already resisted two assaults by Wrangel's army. Six tanks went forward with a reinforcing infantry division, the tanks in the lead. They cleared the defenders' trench lines without difficulty and then ran out of fuel. Two days later, with only sufficient fuel collected to refill the one British-manned tank, Major Bruce took command of it and drove into Tsarytsin, with the terrified defenders surrendering or fleeing northwards; 40,000 prisoners were taken. It was a remarkable achievement. Three further consignments of tanks reached Denikin from England, a grand total of eighteen Whippet (Medium) and fifty-six Mark V tanks. By September 1919 all four sections of 1st Russian Tank Division had been trained and assigned to the front and the crews of two more divisions were trained as tanks arrived. This considerable feat, however, came at a price of some discontent among the other ranks in the hard-worked tank training sections.[21]

From the very start of Britain's support for Denikin there had been requests and recommendations for aircraft and flying training for the Russians. The Air Ministry quickly agreed to provide 50 RE8s together with instructors and mechanics, with the possibility of fifty more. A long delay then followed while the Paris Peace Conference got under way. By the time Churchill was alerted to the supply problem the aircraft had lost their place in the queue for shipping and a further hold-up followed. Lieutenant Colonel Maund, an experienced airman who had returned from working with the Russians at Archangel at the end of 1918, arrived at Ekaterinodar in March the following year to head the Air Section of the mission. He could do little to help the Russians, who had only a few worn-out machines, until fresh ones arrived from England; so bad was the situation that Russian Air Service units were being disbanded around him for lack of aircraft. In some desperation Maund appealed for 47 Squadron RAF, based in Salonika, to be shipped over to south Russia. London agreed, with the proviso that the squadron was 'to be filled with volunteers and then move by flights if necessary'. The British-manned volunteer squadron was to support the White Russians' struggle, not fly in combat itself, but this policy decision was cheerfully ignored. Furthermore, the squadron members were not even given the option of volunteering, but were shipped across as a complete unit. The squadron leader, Major Collishaw, wrote later, 'Perhaps, not unnaturally, a good many of the squadron's members, particularly the other ranks, were not too happy with the situation and wanted to go home'. Many were later replaced with volunteers, but not before one of the flights had already been in action for some time, supporting Baron Wrangel's assault on Tsaritsyn. It began its raids on 23 June, attacking river barges, troop concentrations and the Bolshevik cavalry groups which Budenny had just arrived to command. From then until the end of the month, when the city fell to the Whites, the flight was in the air daily. In one raid over Tsaritsyn, a squadron historian records, a 112-pound bomb was landed 'squarely on a building in which the local Soviet was holding a full session. All but two of the 41 Red officials were killed.' Red naval forces on the Volga were also attacked. Baron Wrangel later sent a letter of thanks for the flight's assistance in taking the town. It seems certain that the strategically important city would have held out for much longer without the British in their tanks and aircraft.[22]

One of the most remarkable air exploits of the intervention occurred at about the time Tsaritsyn fell, when two DH9 aircraft, one a photo-reconnaissance plane, the other its escort, took off for an intelligence mission behind the Bolshevik lines. The four crew members were dressed in shirts and shorts for the low-level flight in the summer heat. When the camera-equipped aircraft dropped to 1000 feet to take its shots, it met heavy ground machine gun fire which pierced its main starboard fuel tank which began to leak. The observer, Lieutenant Mitchell, promptly climbed onto the wing and stopped the leak by holding his thumb over the hole. The escort aircraft suffered even worse: its engine was put out of action by ground fire and the pilot was forced to land. A Bolshevik cavalry force closed in but the observer managed to keep it at bay with fire from the disabled plane's Lewis gun. Seeing the escort crew's plight, the reconnaissance plane pilot, Captain Anderson, immediately decided to come to the rescue by landing alongside it. Lieutenant Mitchell then joined in the firing against the cavalry with his Lewis gun. The captain of the crippled aircraft then set fire to it, and both crew members scrambled across to the other plane and managed to squeeze into the second cockpit, Lieutenant Mitchell resuming his position on the lower wing stemming the leak. The overloaded plane then took to the air again for its unsteady 50 minute flight back to base where it succeeded in landing safely. The exhausted Mitchell was painfully burned by the exhaust gases which had played on his bare legs throughout the flight. Both captain and observer were awarded DSOs for their courage and daring in this astonishing exploit. Their squadron commander believed it would have earned them VCs on the Western Front, 'rather than in such an obscure backwater as South Russia'. The political sensitivity of the squadron's operations might well have been another factor.[23]

Important though such operations were in support of the Whites' offensive, they did nothing to restore the fighting power of the White Russians' own air crews. The promised aircraft were so long in arriving from UK that Maund eventually managed to get a consignment from British units demobilising in the Middle East. With these, after such a long delay, he was able to make a little progress in equipping four Russian Air Service flights which went to the front in June and July. But this was something of a false start; like so much of the British-supplied equipment, the machines were old and lacked spare parts. In addition there was much apathy and resistance on the part of the Russians to familiarisation training on the new machines. This continued, indeed worsened, when the first consignment of brand-new RE8s finally arrived. This model was designed for observation and artillery spotting rather than bombing or aerial combat; it was slow, lacking in manoeuvrability and somewhat unforgiving of pilot error. It is surprising that the Air Ministry should have chosen it for the Russians. Its evil reputation, first recounted by Russian pilots who had transferred from Archangel, quickly spread among the trainee pilots. Collishaw quotes one report of a RE8 training unit in which only six of the ten designated pilots turned up for the course. Of these one was sent away for disobedience, one refused to fly after his first solo attempt, one crashed on his second solo flight and was confined to hospital, while a further pilot was disabled by injury. There remained two, the report concluded, and 'we are not very hopeful of ever making either an RE8 pilot'. Similar reports came from the other training sections with the result that the instructors fast became demoralised and asked to transfer to 47 Squadron, where they considered 'their work will be appreciated and where they will live in more friendly surroundings'. Eventually a British-crewed flight of RE8s became an adjunct of 47 Squadron. Even when more suitable aircraft arrived, Maund complained that they were 'without tools, spares, equipment, transport or hangars'.[24]

Maund, who was promoted brigadier general before the campaign ended, also had difficulties with the senior Russian officers. His opposite number as head of Denikin's Air Service was Major General Kravtsevitch. Whilst Kravtsevitch seemed to appreciate the operational efforts of 47 Squadron, so far as training was concerned, Maund found him obstructive, jealous and rank-conscious, to the point of encouraging his officers to ignore British advice, sometimes with disastrous consequences. Maund was also in dispute with Denikin's Chief of Staff Romanovsky over the allocation of flights to the armies, with the Russian favouring the Tsaritsyn–Volga front and not the Kharkov region which Maund felt was undersupported. The British air training effort, like many other areas of the mission's work, was also hampered by the poor quality of instructors. This was a particular point made by Holman who later wrote, 'Such carelessness in the RAF's process of instructor selection for South Russia was astounding and a portent of tragedy for the Russian Air Service'. But this was a general failing; the home authorities were quite unable to find sufficient personnel of the necessary calibre prepared to volunteer for service in south Russia.

A further factor was beginning to undermine the morale and efficiency of the mission even as Holman was trying to improve them. A message from Mission

HQ to the War Office in early June 1919 put the matter succinctly: 'Personnel of the Royal Navy in Novorossisk are being paid in sterling while military personnel at the same port are paid in roubles at official rate of 80 to one pound. Navy sell to natives their sterling at 250 roubes to one pound.' In fact, in south Russia army officers were paid in sterling too, which made the other ranks even more keenly aware of their disadvantage. The consequence was obvious: discontent and resentment grew as the campaign wore on and inflation soared uncontrollably. It was, perhaps, only to be expected that some of the other rank staff resorted to selling stores in their charge in an effort to make up for their hardship. At no stage did the official rate of exchange even begin to catch up. Eventually, arrangements were made to allow the rate to be determined locally, but this happened much too late to affect matters; by then, as in Siberia, the campaign was lost.[25]

Once Denikin was able to take and hold ground the railways became of supreme importance. The advance was taking place over vast tracts of open country and the control of railway lines dominated tactics. If the line could be cut on each side of a town it would often be unnecessary to fight for it, since the defending army would retreat until it regained its rail communications. Perhaps it was this factor which led to one airman's laconic comment, 'There was very little actual fighting at this time, but as soon as one side heard that the other was likely to advance, the other side promptly retreated'. Armoured trains became an important weapon. Formation commanders and military units often had their own trains permanently allocated, or at least commandeered. These could range from a very basic set of carriages and wagons to well-appointed trains complete with kitchens, sleeping quarters and mess rooms. 47 Squadron travelled about the front by train: one of the squadron aircraft would make a reconnaissance flight and select a tactically suitable landing area close to the front and near the railway. The train would then move forward with the part-assembled aircraft on flat cars with wings strapped to their fuselages; it would be positioned in a suitable siding which would then become the base for operations, the crews living aboard the trains. Railway engines were always in great demand and these valuable machines, often Swindon- or Derby-built, seemed to be in constant operation without any servicing or rest for their crews. The moment the battle moved away from the railway was often the time when some senior officers lost control and interest. One Russian corps artillery commander told his British liaison officer that he 'never thought of visiting the batteries [at the front], as he could not get a special train and could not spare the time'.

Trains reflected status in a deeply rank- and class-conscious White Russian Army where the attitude to senior commanders was almost feudal. Captain Kennedy describes the preparations for General Mai-Mayevsky's journey to Belgorod: 'his magnificently appointed *train de luxe* lying opposite the special carpeted entrance by which he would come into the station. Scores of staff officers and sentries, armed to the teeth, stood on the platform awaiting the great man. What a contrast this scene of luxury formed to the condition of the miserable peasants, huddled up asleep on the platforms and in the great waiting rooms'. Captain Williamson added to the picture of the train subculture: 'places on trains which should have been given up to the wounded were sometimes occupied by women who had no right to be there, living in comparative luxury under some general's protection, while injured men dragged themselves along on foot. Whole trains were occcupied by influential officers'. The peasants themselves made their journeys often clinging to running boards, on carriage roofs or anywhere they could find space. 'Thirty-odd people dismounted from the engine alone, sliding down from buffers, body and boiler as soon as the train stopped', another officer recorded. As for the mission officers themselves accompanying trains of supplies to the front, their accommodation was generally comparatively modest and sometimes much worse. One group found that, although a special coupé had been set aside for the mission party, it was a 'filthy, flea-bitten carriage with canvas (rotten sacking) upholstery, with springs burst through the seats ... no lighting – we are prepared with candle dips – and what personal conveniences are available in such a deplorable condition as to be nauseating'. This experience came after a lecture from General Holman on the 'prestige' of the British and the importance of keeping it up by insisting on high standards.[26]

The fall of the city of Kharkov, the major industrial centre of the Ukraine, in late June 1919 was a great coup for Denikin, though the actual date of its capture remains a matter of debate. Lieutenant Colonel De Wolff gives us an explanation for this. He claims that the advancing Volunteer Army managed to cut off the city on both sides, and then sat down for three days, letting the enemy melt away, whilst sending back tales of a bloody battle for its capture. General Holman, De Wolff declares, became restless at the delay and decided to capture Kharkov himself. He walked towards the city, found a cab and drove to the city centre where he received a great ovation. There was a huge banquet and an exchange of swords with the City Commandant. When General Holman returned, apparently highly pleased with himself, he found Denikin speechless with rage as the capture was not on the programme until the next day! There was a frightful row and the upshot was that Holman had to get his sword back and hand over the one he had received from the Commandant. This account lacks corroboration, but would have been entirely in keeping with the antique tactics of the armies and with Holman's growing inclination to be at the front whenever possible, a proclivity which did nothing to aid the smooth operation of his Mission or arrest the developing indiscipline of some of its members. By late July Holman was asking the War Office for 'some means of controlling the acts and the behaviour of some undesirable elements belonging, I regret to say, to this Mission'. He asked for a provost marshal and some military policemen for the Mission HQ itself and for its two bases.[27]

The fall of Tsaritsyn was of great significance for the White Russian cause and came after the most bitter fighting. Tsaritsyn lay on the mighty Volga, which flows into the Caspian Sea. Also on the Volga north of Tsaritsyn was Saratov, the city at which Denikin had hoped to make a junction with Kolchak. He had earlier written to the Supreme Commander, 'Please God we shall meet at Saratov and decide the question for the good of the Motherland ... At present we are receiving ample assistance and supplies from the British and ample opposition on the part of the French'. Unfortunately, the letter fell into the hands of the Bolsheviks when its bearer was captured while crossing the Caspian Sea. The Reds published it and Clemenceau was incensed. It mattered little, however, since Kolchak's southern thrust was checked almost as Tsaritsyn fell. Holman wired home, 'After heavy fighting, tanks and British aeroplanes cooperating, Tsaritsyn occupied 30th, over 10,000 prisoners, enemy cavalry retreating'. The capture of the city, which the Bolsheviks had fought so hard to prevent (and which was the focus of one of the major quarrels between Stalin and Trotsky) was followed by the feasting with which the Cossacks invariably celebrated such victories. The CIGS sent Denikin his 'most hearty congratulations' on his 'magnificent successes' and hoped that he would now pause to consolidate his gains, particularly as Britain was intending to withdraw its forces from the Caucasus and the Caspian, which would leave open Denikin's right flank. Baron Wrangel, the victor of Tsaritsyn, and General Sidorin also argued for consolidation, and Wrangel advised particularly against a widening of the front. Denikin, however, wished to capitalise on the defeat and disorganisation of the Bolsheviks by keeping on their heels and making a broad-front drive for Moscow. He hoped to take the capital before the winter set in, believing that the people of the territories he reoccupied would have had enough of Bolshevism and follow the lead of the Volunteer Army.[28]

It was in the summer of 1919, with Denikin's armies on the advance and their prospects apparently good, that Britain decided to hand over the Caspian Flotilla to Denikin's navy and to withdraw its forces from Baku and Tiflis. Regular troops were badly needed elsewhere and others were long overdue for demobilisation. Holman, however, opposed the withdrawals, arguing that 'the political conditions of the Caucasus were so unstable that unless the Armed Forces of South Russia dominate the coastline after the departure of the British, Denikin's right flank will be exposed'. But Denikin had done nothing to secure the cooperation of the border states beyong insisting they return to his control. The Caspian Flotilla had done its best to support him, as had the RAF squadrons, even flying demonstration missions over the towns and villages of Daghestan to keep the people in order – the people whom Denikin's recruiting methods were doing so much to antagonise. Captain Bilney of 266 Squadron had even been sent on a bizzare mission to the small town of Guryev on the north Caspian coast in the belief that the town was anti-Bolshevik and had some military personnel who might be trained to fly seaplanes against the Bolsheviks. Despite local ignorance of his mission and the language barrier (he finally engaged the services of the only English speaker, the son of the composer Rachmaninov), Bilney and his small team did manage to provide some rudimentary training before they were withdrawn when the Bolsheviks began to advance in September. Commodore Norris, commanding the flotilla, also opposed the withdrawal, believing the Russians were too inexperienced to take over, that there was serious animosity between the White navy and army and that the Red ships in the sanctuary of the Astrakhan delta should be captured first. But the ships and the naval stores were handed over and the British left via Baku and Novorossisk. The flotilla's valedictory was appropriately spoken by Lieutenant J.D. Snow RNR, commanding *Allah Vardi* (God's Gift), a captured Russian merchantman at Baku: 'We sank most of their ships and those that got away had the wind up to such a tune that they have disappeared and nothing can be found of them ... But as far as I am concerned I'd see us in the remotest corner of Hades before I'd voluntarily stay one hour in their beastly country.'[29]

During July and August Denikin's armies continued to advance, but their preponderant gains were in the wrong direction. In the central and eastern sectors the front remained relatively static. Wrangel managed to push up the Volga about halfway towards Saratov, but under pressure from superior Red forces he ultimately fell back towards Tsaritsyn. In the centre, Sidorin made slow progress, apart from one spectacular, large-scale cavalry raid by General Mamontov in August which helped break up a Bolshevik counter-offensive, but failed in its main objective of cutting the Bolshevik army's communications. On the left, however, in the Ukraine, where partisan and anarchist movements were preoccupying the Bolsheviks, General Mai-Mayevsky's Volunteer Army was making sweeping gains, taking Poltava at the end of July and Kiev a month later, with Odessa, the scene of the earlier, spectacular French débâcle, also falling to his troops. This thrust, however, was taking his army away from Moscow rather than towards it and into an area notoriously difficult to control as both the Bolsheviks and the French had discovered. But the thrust of his other corps was directly north along the railway which led to Moscow. He took Kursk on 20 September and on 13 October entered Orel on the direct road and rail route to Moscow, now only 250 miles distant.

Denikin's armies now stretched from the Volga to the Roumanian border, but the front was thinly held and there were no reserves. Behind them the country festered with increasing unrest and disorder. The Ukrainian nationalists, well aware that Denikin, the ardent believer in 'one undivided Russia' would never agree to their independence, were soon in open revolt. The authorities in

Daghestan, now under Denikin's control, were bitterly resentful at their treatment at the hands of the Volunteer Army. A telegram from the General Assembly of Daghestan described the situation: 'On pretext of fighting the Bolsheviks our mountain settlements have been burnt, our cattle carried off and homes looted … Population is fleeing from the country and hiding in forests and caves … Volunteer Army are carrying off everything out of the country, not even sparing medicines left behind after Turkish evacuation.' Everywhere the armies were living off the land, generally feeding well in the front line in the rich agricultural region through which they passed; many post-battle meals turned into feasts with much drinking and many toasts in the commandeered houses occupied by the headquarters; but the compaigning life was harsh. Atrocities were as common in the Whites' treatment of their prisoners and the civil population as they were under the Bolsheviks. Some commanders allowed their troops to plunder indiscriminately. As to prisoners, their routine treatment was as one mission liaison officer recorded after the capture of Orel: 'Colonel P. told me he had taken 10,000 prisoners at Ariol [sic], had shot the officers, taken all overcoats and arms, and released the men'; but the peasant-soldier prisoners were as frequently pressed into service with the Whites. Baron Wrangel's practice was to shoot all the Bolshevik NCOs as well. Any identified commissars shared the fate of the captured officers. After the capture of Orel, another liaison officer recorded, 'A number of Jews and others, who were denounced as Bolshevik commissars, were summarily shot in the streets. Their bodies were left to lie on the pavements for days and were gradually stripped of clothing by the passers-by'.[30]

Even worse were the anti-Jewish pogroms for which the White forces were responsible in many of the territories they captured. Anti-Semitism was very pronounced in all the White Armies. The British Chief Rabbi later wrote of 'no less than 150 pogroms carried out by Denikin's Army'. Another account, based on Red Cross investigations, concluded that 'Retirement of the Soviet troops signified for the territory left behind the beginning of a period of pogroms with all their horrors'. When General Briggs was tackled on the issue by a meeting of MPs at Westminster, he declared that 'he had never heard of any excesses by Denikin's men'; but then he had been replaced before the White's advance had really got under way. Churchill tried several times, through staff channels, to have these outrages curtailed and on 18 September he wrote personally to General Holman asking him to urge Denikin to do everything in his power 'to prevent a massacre of the Jews in the liberated districts' and to issue 'a proclamation against anti-Semitism'. The Jews were very powerful in England, he declared, and it would make his task easier if Denikin could be shown to be protecting them; not the most altruistic expression of concern, it must be said.

Later, Lloyd George himself became involved in the matter when a prominent British Jew, Sir Alfred Mond (subsequently the founder of ICI and a prominent

Liberal MP) sent him details of the anti-Jewish atrocities in South Russia. Lloyd George forwarded the correspondence to Churchill under a strong covering letter which began sarcastically, 'I wish you would make some enquiries about this treatment of the Jews by your friends'. Churchill quickly wrote personally to Denikin emphasising the importance of 'preventing by every possible means the ill-treatment of the innocent Jewish population'; but since this was the last, rather than the first, topic in a long letter largely concerned with the supplies Britain was sending, its gravity was hardly emphasised. He also wrote an explanatory letter to Lloyd George in which he wrote of the 'solemn assurances' he had received from Denikin, whose 'bona fides on this matter are endorsed by General Holman'. It is not clear whether Churchill's letter had much effect: by the time Denikin received it his armies had largely ceased capturing fresh territory in which new pogroms could be conducted. Denikin, however, had already formally refused to declare Jews equal before the law. Nor, according to one mission member's diary, does it seem likely that ending the pogroms was an issue about which Holman would have badgered him: 'Cragg [a military chaplain] saw Holman this morning', noted Captain Kennedy, 'and says the latter is obsessed by the idea of wiping out the Jews everywhere and can talk of litle else, and Holman asked him why the English church did not start a crusade against them'. Numerous other contemporary military accounts wrote disparagingly of the local Jews as, for example, did Commander Goldsmith: 'A Russian Jew is quite the most loathsome type of humanity, as a rule, and they are the curse of Russia at this moment'. During 1919 more than 100,000 Jews were murdered in south Russia, many, no doubt, by partisan forces and bandit groups, but the majority, it seems, by Denikin's armies.[31]

The administrative side of Denikin's army remained hopelessly inefficient and corrupt. The signs of this and of the failure to make the best use of the British weapons and supplies were everywhere. One gunnery sergeant major in the mission reported that 'The Russians did not understand our guns, and did not try to learn about them. If a small part of a gun went wrong, they would ask for a complete new gun, to save the trouble of repair'. In the front-line batteries, the horses were in a poor state and the guns badly maintained. Another liaison officer reported during a tour of fighting units, 'This battery is in a very bad state chiefly owing to the fact that they have never received any oil for their guns ... the battery has practically no spares at all ... they say they have never received them'. One journalist reported that nearly every petty bureaucrat and official in south Russia wore a British uniform, while only 25 per cent of the troops had them. Officers in the rear often drew a double issue of clothing and sold the surplus at a lucrative price. This witness saw 'Girls who were emphatically not nurses, walking the streets of Novorossisk wearing regulation British hospital skirts and stockings'. Hospital beds and bedding also found their way into the homes of officers and officials. Holman's attempts to get Denikin to end these practices produced little result, particularly when his armies were enjoying such unparalleled success. After one interview with the Russian commander he left a brutally candid note with him which read: 'At a time when between 150,000 and 200,000 complete sets of clothing and equipment had been issued to your supply service and armies, I found not a single Russian soldier with a complete set of British equipment; soldiers barefoot and in rags, fighting on cold nights without greatcoat, blanket, or waterproof sheets, and on hot days without a water-bottle.' On another occasion he wrote to the War Office about the Russian officers at the fighting front, 'It is no exaggeration to say that at least 60 per cent of the officers have nothing beyond what they are wearing, and even these shabby uniforms are worn over the bare skin; they have no underclothing'. He asked for 25,000 sets of officers' clothing, underclothing and boots. Another young mission officer had his official joining interview with the Inspector General of the Artillery of the Volunteer Army, at the conclusion of which the general asked him to get a pair of braces for himself and some chocolates for his wife.[32]

On one tour of the front General Holman inspected a platoon of a Don Army regiment just out of the front line to see how they were equipped. Major Williamson, who was accompanying him, described the scene: 'Twelve men were paraded straight from the trenches and I have never seen such a miserable sight in my life. They had only five boots among the lot, one man had no rifle, and that of another was clogged up with dirt. Their clothes were hanging in rags, one man had no trousers and wore woollen underpants, and they looked half-starved. How could men so ill-equipped fight?' At the time they were not only fighting, but winning. Their divisional commander had previously admitted bitterly, 'We are very low in strength and we have no British uniforms at all, nor any British artillery or machine guns'. Both Holman and Williamson later did their best to remedy the situation for this division which was distant from the railhead. Of course, Denikin's control of equipment and supplies gave him a degree of leverage over the not-always cooperative governments of the Cossack states. Only when his offensive had run its course did Holman finally manage to get Denikin to issue an army order leaving all British equipment and supplies in the hands of the mission staff until it reached the forward fighting units.[33]

Meantime the mission itself was growing, as further officers arrived from Britain and elsewhere. Some had waited several weeks for their voyage to Novorossisk and took as many more to get there. Few of the newcomers were impressed with General Milne's headquarters at Constantinople through which many passed on their way to Novorossisk. 'General Milne's regime is too soft', wrote Lieutenant Colonel Lister, 'there is an atmosphere of "drift" about the way everything here is done.' Constantinople was 'a sink of iniquity', in the view of another new arrival, who believed that 'it would be well to burn the city down, and rebuild it, and repeople it'. Hardly encouraging impressions, since the links between Milne's headquarters and Holman's were most important for the success of the mission, whose supplies of weapons and equipment came generally from the headquarters stocks under Milne's control. When Lister finally arrived at the Novorossisk base, he heard from the Base Commandant of 'all the lack of cooperation between the War Office, the Ministry of Shipping, the RN and GHQ here'. What the newcomers found when they finally took up their mission appointments did not always impress them. Captain Kennedy commented, 'The officers of the Mission we have come across so far are of the lowest type, and obviously inefficient and the last people to be representing us here ... in fact we began to think that the scum of the Salonika forces had collected here'. Later, at Kharkov, he attended his first dinner with the Volunteer Army at which a number of mission officers got out of control. 'Why do we choose such people to represent us?' he asked himself. He subsequently discovered that the Chief of Staff of the Volunteer Army's 1st Corps did not want the British artillery liaison officers to use his corps mess. 'This must be due to the behaviour of our officers up here', Kennedy concluded, 'and their drunken brawls with the Russians – it is a thousand pities'. Another officer gave his candid view of mission headquarters: 'Am beginning to doubt any justification for the presence of several of the Mission personnel judged by the amount of asssistance they are giving to the Russians ... present appearances however seem to point to the Mission being in existence merely to run itself: the number of people employed in this glorious and heaven-sent job of running ourselves, comprising what appears to be the majority of the personnel present. To help the Russian seems to be the last consideration for most of 'em.'[34]

13

The Evacuation of Archangel

On each occasion the War Cabinet met in July 1919 it seemed to be given seriously unwelcome news from Archangel. On 9 July it received the extraordinary report that Ironside's advance on Kotlas, which it had so recently sanctioned, was to be abandoned. The abnormally low water in the Dvina, the Bolsheviks' improving morale and stronger flotilla, together with the mutiny in the Slavo-British Legion were the reasons Churchill gave for the decision. By 23 July it was digesting the shock of the Onega mutiny and the defections along the railway front, as well as General Yevgenii Miller's admission that it would be impossible for him to hold Archangel over the winter if the British withdrew. This was an astonishing reversal of the recent optimistic reports. Lord Curzon expressed concern because the Cabinet had been led to believe that the Kotlas offensive was necessary to secure the safe evacuation of our troops. Were they no longer safe? Churchill admitted that, though the retirement would now be more difficult, he still believed it would be possible to observe the agreed timetable. H.A.L. Fisher asked why it was not possible, as he had earlier suggested, to keep the river sufficiently mined to enable the evacuation to take place at an earlier date. The First Sea Lord pointed out that, as the river was now only two feet six inches deep, nothing could be done at present. He presumably meant that this was too shallow for mining to be possible, but could easily have added that much of the flotilla could neither move up nor down river. What had been planned as the main firepower and chief transport for the Kotlas offensive was temporarily stuck in a small stretch of deeper water.[1]

According to Sir Henry Wilson, the War Cabinet's meeting of 29 July 1919 was the first occasion on which it 'examined the Russian question as a whole'. It did not, however, spend very much time on north Russia. It heard from Sir Henry of the alarming *démarche*: the British north Russian representatives, Mr Hoare and Generals Ironside and Maynard, were now all suggesting an armistice with the Bolsheviks. In discussing the process of the withdrawal, Ironside even went so far as to suggest that it would be necessary to 'disarm all the forces not being evacuated with the Allies, this being practically the whole Russian National Army …' Churchill immediately commented that 'it would be disastrous for any British Government to ask the Bolsheviks to grant an armistice'. He 'could not conceive that we could sink so low'. In any case it was not a step we could take without consulting the Allies. Lloyd George, at last freed from his Peace Conference commitments and now presiding at the meeting, did not believe it was a matter for the Allies at all, but nevertheless agreed that the Bolsheviks could not be trusted 'not to indulge in massacres'. The CIGS, appearing to take a rather more conciliatory line, asked if, before any evacuation, the local authorities 'were to be allowed to pass through our lines to negotiate with the Bolsheviks'. Churchill's view was that this was most undesirable 'until all the arrangements for the withdrawal were complete'. Although it was far from clear exactly what this statement meant, no one else spoke. The minutes of the meeting declared simply, 'In this view the Cabinet agreed'. So serious did the situation suddenly seem to have become that the Cabinet even authorised the despatch of such further reinforcements as might be 'essential for the withdrawal'. 'If reinforcements are needed', Churchill later solemnly told the House of Commons, 'reinforcements will be sent to them; if they wish to manoeuvre in this direction or that ... so as to secure the best and safest possible circumstances for embarkation, they shall have the fullest liberty to do so ...' But the Cabinet also confirmed that after the British withdrawal no military mission would be left with the White Russians at either of the north Russian ports.[2]

In fact, the position of General Miller, and of the army he was attempting to put in the field before the British withdrawal, was made even worse by other decisions taken in London. Ironside had earlier been told to 'work on the assumption that all stores, including arms and equipment not necessary during the evacuation, will be left for the Russian troops'. Following the 29 July Cabinet meeting this instruction was revoked. Anything likely to be of any military value to the enemy was to be either removed or destroyed. Ironside was to leave behind only foodstuffs. The authorities were now so certain of the rapid collapse of Miller's force that they were to deny him the means of any prolonged resistance. It was a complete volte-face from the firm assurances which Ironside had given to Miller as recently as 2 July in his lengthy discussions with the Russian commander. After the Armistice, the determination 'not to let down the friends who had stood by us' had been the central rationale for keeping troops in north Russia at all. But the Cabinet's emergency reaction to the Russian mutinies was to turn this justification on its head.

In view of the worsening situation, the Cabinet agreed the CIGS's recommendation to appoint General Sir Henry Rawlinson as Supreme Commander to supervise the withdrawal from both Murmansk and Archangel. Rawlinson had managed emergencies before and was a 'safe pair of hands'. Such an appointment had long been needed: there had never been much sense in attempting to coordinate the operations of two separate but interdependent commands from the desk of the DMO in the War Office. In the difficult circumstances of a withdrawal, precise coordination would be vital. 'North Russia is a nasty job, but

I have decided to accept it', Rawlinson wrote, 'The Government is in a hole, and I consider it my duty to go and try to help them out of it … I accepted on condition that they sent me reinforcements and some tanks, and this both H. Wilson and Winston promised to do … Winston thanked me profusely for going, saying it was a very sporting thing to do.' The size of the hole which the government had dug for itself may be judged from the considerable fresh resources it was now prepared to put at Rawlinson's disposal. He was given a very substantial separate heaquarters staff of seventeen officers (soon increased to twenty-one), headed by two brigadier generals and supported by fourteen clerks, seventeen batmen and thirty other soldiers, and was also promised two more infantry battalions, one of marines, two machine gun companies, two field batteries and a detachment of tanks. A smaller second echelon of fighting units was to be available if he needed it. Had they been offered this mouth-watering level of manpower at an earlier stage of their time in north Russia, Maynard and Ironside would have been delighted. Yet Rawlinson's orders were merely 'to coordinate' the moves of Ironside and Maynard; otherwise they were to have 'a free hand'. There was more than an element of panic in these Cabinet decisions. Neither Ironside nor Maynard was pleased at the idea of being superseded. The Murmansk commander wrote that it was his 'firm conviction that, had Ironside and myself been left to complete our respective tasks, the evacuation of both theatres would have been effected without hitch of any kind'. They were somewhat mollified by a letter from Churchill explaining that this move did not imply any lack of appreciation or confidence in them, and noting that each was being granted a knighthood. For taking on the 'nasty job', Rawlinson was to receive a baronry.[3]

Before he set sail, Rawlinson had a long discussion with Churchill about the general policy for north Russia. Churchill was of the view that they should 'let the Russians fight it out for six months and then withdraw all political and financial support'. Rawlinson was more bullish, arguing for the possibility of retaining Murmansk and persuading General Miller to make his stand there with British material support. This would menace the Bolsheviks with the possibility of the renewal of the offensive the following spring. But Rawlinson developed this optimistic scenario in the quiet of Whitehall before he had seen the state of the White Russians. Churchill was immediately attracted by the idea. Strangely, in view of Ironside's explicit instructions to the contrary, Rawlinson was also 'authorised to give the North Russian Government all possible assistance … all military equipment, arms, ammunition, stores and supplies may, at your discretion, be handed over … before your departure'. He arrived at Murmansk on 9 August, where he received General Maynard's report on the situation on his front, which he read as his ship sailed across the White Sea to the more important front at Archangel. Maynard himself was further south at Kem, directing the last phase of his advance.[4]

The decision to send even more troops to North Russia, still under the pretext of covering the withdrawal, heightened the suspicions of the left-wing press, as well as the sturdily independent *Daily Express*. Lord Beaverbrook had kept Churchill's Russian policy under the most critical scrutiny throughout the development of the campaigns in the north. Curzon had already brought Sir David Shackleton, the Permanent Under-Secretary in the Ministry of Labour, to one of the earlier Cabinet meetings to explain how violently opposed the trade unions were to the Russian involvement. There was, Shackleton told the ministers, even the threat of a general strike over the issue. Such industrial action over political matters would have been unprecedented in these early days of union industrial power. The approaching TUC autumn conference was viewed with some apprehension: casualties in North Russia had to be avoided at all costs. OUR POLICY IN RUSSIA was the *Express* headline above the warning that, should disaster occur, 'it will be due to Mr Winston Churchill's passion for gambling adventures, which his colleagues seem totally unable to restrain'. After Rawlinson's appointment was announced, the paper asked, 'What is General Rawlinson doing in the Russian galley? Why a full general?' The editorial declared, 'This Russian expedition is a bad egg'. Churchill has had a Cabinet instruction to withdraw. 'We shall insist he obeys it.' Deprived of inside information, Beaverbrook was now barking up the wrong tree, but this in no way reduced the virulence of the attacks on his erstwhile close friend as the news came in of the size of the reinforcements Rawlinson was to have available. THE CHURCHILL ADVENTURE. PREPARING FOR A NEW CAMPAIGN IN RUSSIA?, his paper queried suspiciously.[5]

On the Archangel front things were not going well. A joint Russian-British attack to retake Onega was not successful, though heavy shelling by a British monitor practically destroyed the town. Ironside's main thoughts, however, were now on the preparations for the limited disengaging attack to break the Bolshevik front on the Dvina and enable him to withdraw in safety. Compared with the ambitious Kotlas adventure, this was to be a modest, single-brigade operation limited still further by the diversion of the Australians of 45th Fusiliers to the Railway Front. It was to be an advance of roughly twenty miles on both banks of the River Dvina, taking the brigade to positions only ten miles deep into the Bolshevik lines. Any thought of a two-brigade attack had been abandoned: Ironside dared not risk using a separate Russian force in brigade stength while the other brigade of his Relief Force was busy elsewhere. The planning was in the hands of the flamboyant and enthusiastic Sadleir Jackson, who proposed to use roughly one battalion group, supported by detachments of White Russians, on each bank, in an operation aimed to inflict maximum damage on the Boshevik lines based in the riverside villages. Most of the Bolshevik army was based there; there were no other significant troop concentrations between them and the Kotlas base. The attacks were planned for 10 August with the hope that the whole force could complete its withdrawal from the forward positions on the river by the end of the month. The idea was that the White Russians of General Maroushevsky would then take over the prepared positions a little further back at Bereznik which had been the army's winter front line. The worry for Ironside was whether the late summer rains would come early enough to enable the flotilla and river transport for the troops to get back to Archangel safely after their attack. Already there were concerns that the heavier monitors, which the lack of an armed alternative had forced Altham to use, would have to be left behind, stranded like beached whales on the sandbars of the shrunken Dvina.

The attacks were to take much the same form on each bank: one column from each force attacking the well-fortified forward positions frontally with artillery support from the flotilla and land batteries, while two columns advanced secretly through the forest to take the next village positions in flank and rear. Precise timing, secrecy and good communications were of the essence. These were assured by meticulous preparation, careful reconnaissance and close coordination between the land and river sectors of the force; but no walk-over was expected: all the positions were strongly held and fortified. Blockhouses, protected by wire and supported by artillery, fronted many of the villages. Sergeant Pond, the unwilling 'volunteer', found himself a key element in the communications set-up, in charge of the signal post atop Troitsa church.

On the right bank, the strongest column, a two-company mixed force of Russians and 46th Fusiliers, was led by Major A.E. Percival, who had already had the experience of commanding two different battalions on the Western Front. (A couple of decades later he was to achieve notoriety by leading the doomed Army of Malaya in the campaign which ended in the surrender of Singapore to the Japanese.) His objective on the Dvina was the middle village of Gorodok, the key to the Bolshevik defences. All columns had great difficulty with their approach marches across the marshy ground and over the muddy lateral rivers which ran into the larger Dvina, but all met the carefully timed programme. The speed and unexpectedness of the Gorodok column's attack 'sprung a complete surprise on the Bolo in the village', Percival later wrote, 'It was Sunday morning and he was just having his midday meal'. After an hour and some brisk fighting the village was in the hands of the column, and by 1 p.m. 300 prisoners had been taken. Later there was a more difficult fight to take a battery of 4.2 inch guns which the Bolsheviks had in action against the flotilla. On capture, it was found to be manned by German gunners. The Gorodok position was then reorganised in preparation for the large numbers of enemy expected to withdraw from the position attacked by the first column at Selmenga. These began to arrive at 3.45 p.m. and tried desperately to fight their way through the position, but came under heavy small arms and machine gun fire. Many men threw down their weapons and surrendered; some fled into the woods. By 10 p.m., still bright as a London noon in the northern summer, the fight was over. The Bolsheviks had been completely routed: large quantities of weapons and ammunition were captured and 750 prisoners taken. Percival's column, White Russians included, had but twelve casualties. The other right-bank columns were similarly successful, though without the dramatic speed of the Gorodok operation. The sector commander's report makes clear than the diversion of resources caused by the recent mutinies complicated his column's tasks. The southernmost Bolshevik position at Borok proved particularly difficult to subdue, its defenders being alert and well entrenched. The village itself was not occupied until the following day.[6]

The left-bank attack followed a similar tactical pattern, though apparently without the precision of its fellow. 'Everything to do with this coming show is very vague, and a good deal is left to chance', was Major Allfrey's verdict. In the first column, the untried Second Lieutenant Arderne led the point platoon of the company advance guard. This heavy responsibility in his first live action did not seem to nonplus him in the least: 'I had done a similar exercise at Sandhurst only a few months previously', he noted with some satisfaction. Undetected, the platoon was soon within sight of its entrenched objective. The only doubt in Arderne's mind was whether, when he blew his whistle, his platoon of hard-bitten veterans would actually charge. He had had trouble with them in training when they refused to go on a cross-country run. His first encounter with a real enemy armed with live ammunution is worth recalling:

> Suddenly a soldier climbed out of the trench, walked to a tree, opened his fly and peed. I don't think anything could have given me more joy. I stood up, shouted, blew my whistle and my Platoon broke cover and came forward at the double with fixed bayonets. When we reached the Russian position most of the men were standing up half-dressed. They looked very frightened, and were holding their hands well above their heads. A few were racing away unarmed and in different stages of undress. I don't think we fired a shot; you can hardly shoot a man running away and holding up his trousers with his hands.

The rest of the company soon closed up and moved on to the village itself which the Bolshevik trench line had been protecting. It was situated on a low escarpment overlooking an open plain and the river. The villagers were no less startled than the front-line troops:

> In the village was absolute chaos. All the inhabitants, women, children, old men and soldiers were racing down the escarpment and over the plain in mixed groups. They were heading for the next village which we had already occupied. The only order I remember giving was 'hold your fire', but even this was not necessary, our men were just sitting watching and laughing at the amazing scene below. The Russian propaganda had been good and the villagers expected to be killed on the spot.[7]

Major Allfrey recorded comparable surprise and demoralisation among his opponents: 'My men were digging the Bolos out of all sorts of extraordinary places such as up chimneys and underneath mattresses.' But not all columns of 45th Fusiliers were as successful. Sergeant Mouat was brutally frank about his experience:

> Our company was a complete failure. No organisation as usual. The Captain had not the faintest idea what to do and nearly got us wiped out. We found ourselves facing four strong block-houses defended by numerous machine guns and barbed wire six yards deep which we could not possibly have got through. The fire we had to endure was hellish and worse than anything I met in France. We found out later the enemy were using explosive bullets. The company had thirty-five casualties including the Captain who paid for his mistakes poor fellow.[8]

'The attack', Ironside noted later of the overall operation, 'was duly made at dawn on the 10th and went through practically without a hitch ... It was exactly what we needed for our peaceful evacuation.' This judgement, of course, gave the lie to the public rationale for the larger Kotlas and Viatka operations, now abandoned. In fact there was serious consternation for a time about the progress of the left-bank attack. Movement over the marshy ground there was very difficult, particularly in getting the light mountain guns forward. Meanwhile the Bolsheviks were landing reinforcements from their gunboats and organising a counter-attack. A second column commander was killed and the commander of the whole sector and his staff were, for some time, cut off by enemy movements; coordination became impossible. One desperate action occurred when a column was attempting to cross the hundred yards broad River Shika – not flowing water in the summer heat but a deep marsh crossed by a rudimentary, single plank bridge laid on logs. The column came under heavy fire and three men fell into the swamp. They were rescued by an Australian, Corporal A.P. Sullivan, under fire throughout his exertions, in an act of great heroism for which he was awarded the Victoria Cross.

Ultimately, however, all the objectives were taken. In the whole operation the greater part of six Bolshevik battalions were killed, captured or dispersed; 2000 prisoners were taken and eighteen field guns were captured together with many machine guns, rifles and a large quantity of ammunition. The elated Major Percival wrote, 'We have scuppered practically the whole of the Bolshevik Army on this front'. The only concern was the casualties incurred in the left-bank attack and the number of Bolsheviks there who had been merely 'dispersed'. Ironside lists the casualties as 145 killed and wounded: minimal by the standards of France and Flanders, despite including a disproportionate number of officers; but serious in a campaign of small numbers and so bitterly opposed by many at home. Besides, Ironside did not mention the casualties among the crews of the flotilla, which totalled more than those suffered by 45th Fusiliers and included almost as many officers as in both battalions put together. The Bolsheviks on the left bank continued to follow up the withdrawing 45th Fusiliers, though without any great enthusiasm and posing little risk to the withdrawal as a whole. A further minor action near the junction with the River Vaga was required finally to halt them.[9]

Lieutenant Colonel Sherwood Kelly was now in command on the railway front as part of Brigadier General Turner's Vologda Force. Kelly had a very mixed force: two companies of his own Hampshires and also detachments from both battalions of Sadleir Jackson's brigade, the small Polish Legion, and two 'special companies' of 6th and 13th Yorkshires, men who had volunteered to stay on for the extra pay after their battalions had returned home, as well as a large force of the White Russian Army, part of which was manning three armoured trains. Kelly was being his usual argumentative and difficult self. One major serving under Kelly found him 'overbearing' and 'very theatrical', touring his command asking 'Is you blockhouse bullet-proof?' and then emptying a rifle magazine into the timber walls to make sure. After Kelly's Troitsa failure Brigadier General Turner had written to his old friend Ironside, 'What a disappointment regarding Kelly – but the best thing you can do is get rid of him, he is only a swashbuckler'. Now Turner had the problem of commanding the man.

By this stage in the campaign news of the use of gas in North Russia had already leaked to Churchill's parliamentary opponents. In May, Colonel Wedgwood was asking in the House 'whether poison gas or plant for the making of it has been sent to Russia for use against the revolutionary Russians?' He received the reply that, as the Bolsheviks had already used it, preparations were being made to retaliate. But while Bolshevik use had been tiny, the preparations for a reply were massive. Ironside's command had large quantities of materials for the 'new gas': 50,000 ground generators, 10,000 respirators and a specialist team of gas officers led by a Major Davies, as Churchill had promised. These were now busy experimenting with delivery systems in the difficult local conditions. Ironside had hoped to use the gas in support of an attack by the Russians on the Railway Front, but Davies found the conditions quite unsuitable. He was arranging an experimental ground discharge trial with the M Device generators, when a fresh obstacle was put in his way. As a trial for the new weapon, Sherwood Kelly was ordered to carry out a raid on the enemy under cover of a substantial ground discharge of the gas. He objected. His opposition seemed to be less against the use of gas than the idea of the raid itself, whose purposes, he believed, could be achieved by other means. 'If the proposed operation is left to my discretion, I shall not carry it out', he wrote to Turner in his usual emollient way, 'I am continuing to make all preparations in case you order me to carry out the raid'. He was so ordered. Special demonstrations of the device were given, fifty men of the Hampshires were trained in its use and on the day selected, 17 August, two platoons 'staggered up with loads of smoke canisters to a point 500 yards fom the enemy position'. But the gas raid never took place: as so often on the Archangel front, the wind was not strong enough. This was the last attempt to employ the new gas as a ground-discharge weapon. It was also Sherwood Kelly's last day as a commanding officer.[10]

Kelly was abruptly replaced in command of 2nd Hampshires, ordered down to GHQ at Archangel and, after interviews with both Ironside and Rawlinson, sent back to Britain. The manner and mechanics of his relief are still somewhat unclear and were later publicly challenged by Kelly as unfair to him; but the formal reason was that he had written a private letter to a friend in England 'remarking adversely on matters of military import', criticising his superiors and divulging military secrets. The letter was but one of a series he had injudiciously penned and their despatch was, of course, a court martial offence. But just as important may have been the adverse report submitted on him by Ironside. This alleged that he was 'a very hot-headed and quarrelsome man who has had rows with practically every one with whom he has come in contact'. It was no less than the truth. The report considered him 'unsuitable for the command of a regular battalion under the present conditions' and recommended his removal. This came hard for an officer who, although not himself a regular, had commanded, as he later noted, nothing but regular battalions in France and Russia, and whose present battalion was universally regarded as well disciplined and trained. The career vicissitudes of the hot-blooded Kelly were soon to become subsumed within the larger political struggle between the Secretary of State for War and his opponents over the conduct of his Russia policy.[11]

After numerous hazardous experiments, the gas warfare specialist, Major Davies, managed to perfect the design of a bomb to deliver the new gas from the air and gained Ironside's permission to use aircraft to deliver it, thus largely eliminating the need for a favourable wind. Ironside had hoped to use the bombs during Sadleir Jackson's offensive, but the weather proved unsuitable for flying. Thus it was that the onus of using the new gas weapon for the first time, and in an undeclared war against the Bolsheviks, fell not to him but to the new Commander-in-Chief, General Rawlinson. Although the Dvina offensive had put an end to the Bolshevik threat on that flank and enabled the withdrawal there to proceed in relative safety, the Railway Front had yet to be cleared. Here the offensive was to be formally in the hands of General Miller's Russians, the first significant operation of which they would have operational control. Its success was to be assured, first by being spearheaded by the two companies of Australians who had been diverted there during the mutiny earlier in the summer, and secondly by being preceded by the first major use of the new M gas weapon. The Bolsheviks were well established on the railway in the town of Emptsa and the defended villages around it. The aircraft began their gas attacks on Emptsa station, fifty-three gas bombs being dropped in a first wave at 12.30

p.m. and sixty-two in a second at 7.30. The RAF reported the attack as successful, with smoke obscuring the town and panic-striken troops fleeing into the woods. Further gas attacks were made on Emptsa and Plesetskaya the following day and all seemed to have the desired effect. One Bolshevik prisoner who had been about forty yards from the nearest drop later reported that the smoke caused his eyes to water, he coughed badly, suffered head pains and 'was walking about as if drunk'. A second man, even closer to a gas drop, had worse symptoms, breathing difficulties and copious vomiting. He could not rest owing to sickness and coughing. Both men later surrendered. Other gas victims were described as 'lying practically helpless on the ground and the usual symptoms of bleeding from the nose and mouth'. Forty-six prisoners questioned later by Major Davies declared that their officers attributed the successful Allied advance to the M bombs. 'Dropped gas on enemy at Emptsa – said to be effective', Rawlinson wrote in his diary on the day of the attack, also recording later, 'Went round hospitals and saw Bolo prisoners who had been gassed. Good gas'.[12]

The ground attack on the Railway Front began in the late afternoon of 29 August. Some of the blockhouses put up stern resistance, but others were taken completely by surprise by the bayonet attack of the Australians which broke the Bolshevik line. In one part of the action an Australian, Sergeant Pearce, cut through the enemy barbed wire under very heavy fire and then, single-handed, attacked a blockhouse and knocked it out with hand grenades. Minutes later he was cut down by machine gun fire and killed. He was posthumously awarded the second Australian Victoria Cross, the only ones to be gained in the entire campaign. The Bolsheviks finally fell back across the Emptsa river, blowing the steel railway bridge behind them. Nearly a thousand prisoners were taken in the action and much material was destroyed. In this offensive, Ironside recorded, the White Russians seemed 'to have been completely changed from the men who had been mutinying with such regularity'. It seems that the spirited attack of the Australians and the effectiveness of the M gas bombs may have been the principal determinants of the change.[13]

The 'M gas' was used again on the railway front and as a preliminary to other actions in the last stages of the withdrawal to the inner defences of Archangel, when the White Russians were playing a larger part in the operations. 'Gas bombing from aeroplanes proved highly successful and materially assisted the Russian Operations', Ironside confirmed. Its usefulness appears to have been limited only by its very localised effect when there was no wind, or where the number of bombs dropped was small. So great had dependence upon gas bombing become that Brigadier General Grogan actually abandoned one attack when insufficient aircraft were available for the preparatory gas assault. Rawlinson reported to the War Office that the M bombs were mainly responsible for the success of the operations around Archangel. This was not simply a consequence of their serious if only temporary physical effects, but also of the widespread demoralisation and panic which they caused. The apparent revival of the Russians' morale and battlefield success continued when, on 10 September, they recaptured Onega, which had resisted earlier Allied efforts to retake it. This victory also seems to have been attributable to preliminary bombing with the new gas. A captured commissar said that it had caused them to vacate the entire Onega valley. The day before this Russian 'victory' Rawlinson's diary recorded 'Onega empty'. Such widespread use of the new gas weapon receives not a single mention in Ironside's published account of the campaign.[14]

10 September, when Onega was reoccupied, was also the day when Sadleir Jackson began withdrawing his brigade from the forward base at Troitsa. Although the late summer rains had started, it was some time before the river level showed any sign of rising. The troubles of the flotilla were continuing. On 26 August an ammunition barge caught fire and blew up; twenty-seven men, including the commander, were lost from the crew of the nearby gunboat *Glow-Worm*. The original withdrawal date of 1 September had been put back to the 10th by General Rawlinson in the hope that the water would rise sufficiently to get all the river craft away. The last of the gunboats left the upper Dvina on 29 August, but, after a week of 'toiling and straining', two Monitors, *M25* and *M27*, together with Sadleir Jackson's yacht *Kathleen*, were still blocked by several sand bars. Even when a channel through two of these was cleared by depth charges, the monitors still could not get through and had to be destroyed *in situ*. 'As soon as the tail of the convoy had passed, these poor, stout little craft, which had done such good work, were blown to atoms by skilfully-placed gun-cotton charges', wrote the flotilla commander. Conditions for the crews of the flotilla were hard throughout the hot summer. The men on one of the steel transport barges, working upriver in intense heat and with poor food, finally rebelled against their treatment. They 'struck work' and demanded to see their commanding officer. The result was that the barge's commander was relieved of his post and sent home on the next available boat. Of the sailors' tribulations some of the soldiers remained blithely unaware. 'We were able to drift back to Archangel with the river current behind us', wrote Second Lieutenant Arderne, 'another very pleasant and quiet journey.'[15]

Lieutenant Colonel Sherwood Kelly had now arrived back in Britian. His return was rapidly followed by a series of letters from him to the *Daily* and *Sunday Express*, the first of which appeared on Saturday 6 September. Virtually the entire front page was devoted to the north Russian situation, to Kelly's astonishing letter and to editorial comment supporting it. The burden of Kelly's attack, which Beaverbrook clearly masterminded against Churchill, his former Cabinet colleague, was borne in the successive headlines, DUPLICITY OF CHURCHILL'S POLICY TOWARDS RUSSIA – THE PUBLIC HUMBUGGED – FAMOUS VC

APPEALS TO THE NATION. Sherwood Kelly's letter charged that the Relief Force had not been sent to Russia to rescue its weary and embattled comrades but for 'offensive purposes, on a large scale and far into the interior, in furtherance of some ambitious plan of campaign the nature of which we were not allowed to know.' Furthermore, Kelly asserted, 'the much-vaunted "loyal Russian army" was composed largely of Bolshevik prisoners dressed in khaki', it was utterly unreliable, ever disposed to mutiny, and 'always constituted a greater danger to our troops than the Bolsheviks opposed to them'. Since this revelation was followed by a short editorial piece detailing Kelly's outstanding military career, wounds and decorations, the validity of his attack seemed thoroughly authenticated for the paper's readers.

The letter touched an already raw political nerve: the previous year the Director of Military Operatons, Major General Sir Frederick Maurice, had posed a similar challenge with a letter to the press questioning the government's statement of the army's strength on the Western Front. On that occasion the Liberal opposition had divided the House of Commons against the government for the only time during the entire war. Maurice was forced to resign. The Prime Minister later wrote of 'General Maurice's grave breach of discipline, which set a most subversive example to the Army at large'. That judgement now seemed particularly apt. Sherwood Kelly hardly had the eminence of the Director of Military Operations, but gainsaying the account of a Victoria Cross holder might not be a simple matter.

With Lloyd George out of the country, Churchill on a visit to Scotland (though not too distant to be unable to order that Kelly be placed immediately under open arrest, an order rescinded the following day) and with Parliament in recess, the reply to Sherwood Kelly's challenge came from a War Office spokesman whose attempt to answer the charges was printed in full in the *Express*. Unfortunately for the government, Beaverbrook had more bullets to fire. Cleverly juxtaposed with the War Office response, the *Express* editor printed another 'scoop' headed 'GEN IRONSIDE GIVES MR CHURCHILL AWAY', which summarised Ironside's unfortunate interview printed in June in the *G.A.F* which had been so hurriedly withdrawn. One copy at least had escaped suppression and the *Express* had got hold of it, no doubt from Sherwood Kelly himself. The full extent of Britain's role in the planned strategic reorientation of the White Russian forces, which the Kotlas and Viatka operation was to have made possible, was now plain for all to see.[16] Unsurprisingly, it was in the days following these revelations that Lloyd George's strictures on Churchill's 'obsession' with Russia became most severe.

There was much popular support for Kelly at home, particularly from the trade union movement, which was already involved in trying to prevent military *matériel* from being sent to North Russia. Kelly's appeal to the TUC appeared in the *Daily Herald*, just as the TUC Congress was meeting in Glasgow. Two days later the Congress passed unanimously a resolution calling for all troops to be withdrawn from Russia. Some troops themselves also backed him. Three wounded Fusiliers wrote to the *Express* from their London military hospital, 'on behalf of a ward of patients just returned from Russia', to say that they were prepared 'to swear that the facts that he has already stated are perfectly true' and that Kelly 'has the firm support of the Russian force in the work of revealing the truth to the British public'. Another just returned, a lance corporal, 'wearing five wound stripes' the paper pointedly noted, wrote, 'What I dislike about the business is that we are said to have been volunteers. There is not a man in Grogan's brigade who volunteered'.

The news of Kelly's public campaign soon reached Archangel via copies of the *Express*. Rawlinson's diary entry offered only the curt comment, 'Kelly being nasty in London'; but in the ranks others reacted quite differently. Seaman Jowett, who was involved in the the naval preparations at Archangel for the general withdrawal, wrote:

> Lieutenant Colonel Sherwood Kelly's scathing indictment of the Government's policy and general conditions in this area ... is causing a good deal of comment here, as we all know how true it is ... All the men who have been up-river are unanimous in declaring that the conditions spoken of by Lieutenant Colonel Kelly in his articles in the Press are absolutely so. I wonder how the High Official at the War Office would answer all these witnesses ... To those who have been here, his statement against Kelly simply makes him look foolish.'

The ever forthright Major Allfrey, writing as his battalion was making its final preparations for the return home, was forced to admit, 'There is of course a good deal of truth in Colonel Kelly's report, and it is the kind of thing that will appeal to the British public'.

When the withdrawing troops were safely within the inner defences of Archangel, a parade was held at which Ironside presented various medals and decorations. 'After the parade', wrote Major Allfrey, 'he made an awfully lame speech in answer to Colonel Kelly's attack in the English Press. He held out as the two things in favour of operating in this country (1) That they have evacuated 7000 women and children from Archangel; (2) Twenty shiploads of timber have been shipped from Archangel to England'.[17]

There was clearly a case for Churchill to answer, and he did so the following Thursday in a robust defence of his policy which, he was careful to explain, had the full approval of the War Cabinet. He attempted to draw some of the sting from Kelly's case by pointing out that the officer had been sent back from Russia 'for a serious offence under the Army Act' which had now been compounded by 'an offence of a different character against the King's Regulations'. This impugning of his honour impelled Kelly to a fresh bout of letter-writing to the *Express*, with strong editorial support, and to demand that he be court martialled so that he could put his case publicly. Churchill was able to deflect criticism and postpone an answer to Kelly's challenge by claiming operational secrecy. He promised that 'when it is certain that the lives of British soldiers will not be endangered by publicity or the interests of the National Russians prejudiced, a full account of the measures taken and the military reasons for them will be prepared by the General Staff and presented to Parliament by the Secretary of State'. That undertaking was given on 12 September 1919. Churchill's conditions were met when the Allied forces had withdrawn and General Miller's regime had collapsed in February 1920. But although the Blue Book, *The Evacuation of North Russia*, had been prepared by that time, it did not appear until the following July, by which time Lieutenant Colonel Sherwood Kelly had long since been court martialled and passed from the military scene.* [18]

General Rawlinson had arrived in Archangel in time to learn of Sadleir Jackson's successful offensive along the Dvina. If that good news restored his confidence in Ironside's position, little he heard or saw of the White Russians caused him to repose any faith in them: 'Their troops won't fight alone and their officers are hopeless', he wrote prophetically as the Relief Force celebrated its victory. He had his first formal meeting with the Russian commander on 12 August. General Miller was accompanied by his new Chief of Staff General Kvietsinsky, one of a clutch of generals recently arrived at Archangel. Also present was General Marushevsky, now relegated to a supernumerary appointment as Miller formally took over as Commander-in-Chief. The Russian commanding officers from the front were also present. Lord Rawlinson had both Ironside and Maynard with him for the meeting, since Murmansk was administratively within the Archangel government's purview, now run, since Chaikovsky's departure to represent Archangel as the White Russian Council in Paris, directly by General Miller. His Russian force had grown from very modest beginnings to a well-equipped army 25,000 strong, but he realised how brittle it was, despite the apparent success of the thousand men who took part in the Sadleir Jackson offensive, in the attack on the Railway Front and in retaking undefended Onega. There were still many men in the ranks who could not be trusted and were merely biding their time. The Russians had yet to operate on their own in testing battlefield conditions and Miller had grave doubts, shared by the meeting of commanding officers which he had called earlier, as to their ability and willingness to fight on alone. Some of his commanders believed that, once the British left, there would be widespread mutiny and the murder of officers, in the wake of which the whole front would collapse. Nevertheless, Miller had been in touch with the Supreme Commander, Admiral Kolchak, whose orders were that he should fight on at Archangel. He

---

* The details of the court martial are given at Appendix 3.

decided to overrule his officers and obey, despite his own misgivings.

Miller told Rawlinson of his decision to remain and of his doubts about being able to hold out without Allied assistance. Rawlinson and Ironside both argued that to remain at Archangel would expose the Russian officers and some of the population to almost certain slaughter. They suggested that Miller should move his force to Murmansk, which was easier to defend, could be supplied by the Royal Navy and presented better offensive opportunities towards Petrograd. At this stage there was still the possibility of a small British Mission remaining at Murmansk. Four days later, however, Sir Henry Wilson telegraphed Rawlinson to say that this would not be sanctioned. In any case, Miller obdurately refused to consider the move: it would have been in direct disobedience of Kolchak's orders. Besides his soldiers were all from the Archangel district and he knew they would never forsake their homes and families for the empty wastes of Murmansk. It was no doubt at this point that Rawlinson was confirmed in the resolve not to give the Russian any further supplies of weapons and military stores. It was a hard decision but the only one which made any military sense, whatever the earlier promises of the politicians and Ironside.

It was a policy which the CIGS now certainly supported. Sir Henry Wilson had already given up on the Archangel White Russians. 'Their inclination', he told Churchill, 'is to throw in their lot with the enemy and assassinate their British officers.' Churchill disagreed; he retained a great deal of sympathy for, if rather less faith in, the army of the Miller regime. Even if they refused to move their centre of defence to Murmansk, he argued, 'Rawlinson will have in honour no other choice but to leave them certain munitions and supplies, even though these will probably fall into Bolshevik hands in the end'. Despite the recent spate of mutinies, Churchill 'did not find in it sufficient grounds for withdrawing all sympathy from the great body of this army of more than 20,000 men which we have called into being and are now leaving to its fate'.[19] That negotiation with the Bolsheviks, proposed by both the local military and diplomatic leaders, might have been a better means of mitigating the worst excesses of that fate was an argument Churchill could never accept.

General Miller spent the next few weeks trying to persuade the Allied diplomatic representatives to get the British to reverse their decision to withdraw. He also took steps to widen the democratic representation of his administration in an effort to appease European opinion and particularly to increase the chances of continued British support. The Archangel bourgeoisie were at last beginning to take a real interest in their own defence; this had been lukewarm while the Allies were doing the job for them. The local businessmen's organisation passed resolutions to collect five million roubles for the Commander-in-Chief's use, to enforce conscription and to have all passports withdrawn. The local doctors appealed to their colleagues in Britain for their support in pressing for the retention of the Relief Force. The monks of Solovetsky Monastery telegraphed the Archbishop of Canterbury in similar terms. Chaikovsky travelled from Paris to London to intercede with Churchill himself. There was even a delegation to Churchill from the *zemstvos* and towns of the region, led by the archpriest of Archangel, representing the priests and laity of the town. Churchill received them and made a short speech in which he declared that 'with the weapons that will be available and the stores and munitions that will be at your disposal … you will be able if you stand together, to succeed in maintaining yourselves'. Whether he believed his words is another matter; neither Ironside nor Miller himself believed they had a chance.. The working-class suburbs of Archangel seem to have preserved a sullen silence as the anti-Bolshevik measures were tightened; but anti-Allied agitation and propaganda had been a constant feature of life in Archangel throughout the occupation. Now, as the British grip apparently slackened, agitators were preparing more overt action: a general strike timed to coincide with Miller's railway offensive. In the event it was as much a failure as the railway attack was a success. Rawlinson's had already arranged to bring one of his battalions of reinforcements, the Highland Light Infantry, across to Archangel in case of trouble in the town, where, as he put it, there were worrying 'signs of Boloism among population'.[20]

The morale of the White-supporting population was further shaken when the British Evacuation Bureau at Archangel issued a proclamation on 5 September inviting the people to take advantage of the steamship facilities to leave the northern region and warning them of the dire perils which awaited them when the British left. In the event only 6500 of the expected 18,000 chose to leave – a sign, no doubt, of the extent to which people were prepared to accept the return of the Bolsheviks, rather than their faith in Miller's ability to resist them. There was also a spate of soldier weddings in the last few weeks of the occupation, and local war brides joined the refugees. A mutiny in the prison camp on Mudyug Island in the estuary which allowed the escape of over fifty Bolshevik captives did nothing to help matters. Meanwhile, in another major blow to locale morale, the British garrison went methodically about the task of destroying vast amounts of military supplies, weapons and equipment: 'motor trucks, artillery guns and millions of rounds of ammunition' were sinking in the Dvina 'before the very eyes of the Russian authorities and of the population of Archangel', wrote one of the men. 'It was shocking, the waste', commented another, 'I turned a bind eye if an old fellow gave his wife a spade or something to smuggle home. Sandbags, barbed wire and tools etc. went as well.' Much of the redundant ground-delivery M gas equipment, produced and shipped north at considerable cost, was also dumped in the White Sea. After deliberating with the War Office, Rawlinson at last acceded to Miller's pleading and let him have two of his five tanks; but they were not unloaded at Archangel until 17 September, leaving little time for training the

Russians in their use. 'Miller came to beg another tank', wrote Rawlinson on 25th, 'I refused.' From a general whose army had deployed over 530 tanks at Amiens on the Western Front a year earlier, this seemed cheeseparing parsimony.[21]

Despite Sir Henry Wilson's pessimistic appraisal of the Russian general's chances, embodied in his emphatic signal to Rawlinson, his chief, Churchill, was still optimistic about the situation, at least in Murmansk, and continued to favour a mission remaining in North Russia. 'I consider Rawlinson is quite at liberty to put forward a proposal to leave a Mission of moderate size at Murmansk, if he thinks such a measure indispensable to keeping the North Russian Government alive', he wrote to Sir Henry Wilson. He also wished to continue supporting them at Archangel, believing that, if Miller remained obdurate, honour would compel Rawlinson to 'leave them certain munitions and supplies, even though many of these will probably fall into Bolshevik hands in the end'. Rawlinson's judgement was the more pragmatic.

By 23 September the entire British force was in its appointed positions in Archangel's Inner Defence Line, preparing to leave. All the local fronts were quiet as the troops boarded ship. The final departure took place on 27th. 'It was a lovely day, clear and bright. Trees clothed in gorgeous, burning, autumn tints', observed Seaman Jowett. The repair ships, store ships and other auxiliaries had already sailed. The huge transports, *Tsar* and *Tsarina*, loaded with troops, now followed, slipping past the bar into the White Sea. The admiral's yacht, with General Ironside aboard, followed the last transport out of the deserted harbour. A curfew was in place in the town. A short while earlier, the lone figures of General Yevgenii Miller and his ADC had walked to the yacht's mooring and had been piped aboard for the Russian commander to bid a formal farewell to Ironside and Admiral Green. A short and rather strained conversation took place on the quarterdeck. The Russian thanked them for what they had done for Russia. Ironside in turn wished Miller luck in his future campaign.

General Miller was then piped over the side and returned to Russian soil. He walked off without a backward glance past the silent quayside buildings. Two days later he was telegraphing urgently to Sablin, the White Russian chargé d'affaires in London, for flour, canned meat, cereals and butter for the army before the winter set in. These were needed, he said 'because the British High Command had left insufficient amounts of food supplies' and that 'this was known to General Ironside'. A week after this he was asking Chaikovsky in Paris for 30,000 shells for his French-supplied artillery pieces and Sablin in London for shells and ammunition. Both governments declined on the grounds that their agents had left sufficient supplies before their withdrawal.[22]

Nevertheless, the White Russians were not wholly disappointed to see the British go. 'Now at last we are back in Russia', one senior officer commented to a colleague as the ships left the quay. The Archangel schoolgirl who had recorded the arrival of General Poole's armada a year earlier, witnessed the departure of General Rawlinson's from her parents' riverside house. 'One morning', she wrote, 'a chain of ships, half-hidden by the early mist, slowly stole past our shores and vanished behind the island on its way to the White Sea. Only a year earlier these ships had been met with great rejoicing and now they were slinking away in silence. We watched them from our windows. Only Seryozha passed the bitter comment, "Why did they come at all? We shall pay a heavy price for this".'[23]

14

Crisis at Murmansk

General Maynard's urgent plea of late July for the promised reinforcement of a battalion of marines from the French was never met, though the Royal Navy was all prepared to ship them to Russia. It seemed, however, that other marines would soon be available from a different quarter. When the War Cabinet discussed the crisis in north Russia, on 23 July, the First Lord of the Admiralty remarked that 'the best men that could be sent to General Ironside's assistance would be a fine battalion of marines, which it had been proposed to send to Schleswig-Holstein, but had been retained in England for the present on account of the Labour situation'. This last remark reminds us of the disturbed industrial relations situation in Britain which formed the background to these campaigns. In fact Ironside had no need of further troops; but sure enough, even before Lord Rawlinson arrived at Murmansk with his large staff and two battalions of reinforcements, the marines, the 6th Royal Marine Light Infantry (6 RMLI), had already landed, transported in the ship that had been reserved for the French regiment. Whether this was a 'fine battalion', as the First Lord commended it to Churchill, is quite another matter: a force put together in considerable haste and trained only for ceremonial occupation duties in one of the most pleasant parts of Europe was hardly one ready for combat in a remote and unfamiliar theatre.[1]

6 RMLI had been formed in mid-June 1919. Its four companies, one of Royal Marine Artillery and three of light infantry raised from the Portsmouth, Chatham and Plymouth port divisions, included many young recruits, some old soldiers and even some ex-prisoners of war who had only recently been repatriated. They started training together for their ceremonial duties on 8 July; good drill, smart turnout and police work being particularly emphasised. Their most warlike duty was to be the supervision of polling stations and the prevention of intimidation. On 27 July these plans were abruptly changed and on 31st the battalion embarked for north Russia without pay or embarkation leave, lest either might encourage men to go absent. Their orientation for the new theatre consisted of a single lecture aboard ship; indeed, it was not until 6 August that they discovered they were bound for Murmansk rather than Archangel. Once the battalion arrived on 8 August, numerous men, generally the old soldiers, were commandeered for duties at the base, as barmen, clerks and the like, so that the companies were already somewhat reduced in strength and experience before they began their

journey across the tundra of north Russia towards the enemy. Their commanding officer, Lieutenant Colonel Kitcat, had thirty-one years of service behind him, much of it afloat, but no experience whatsoever of land warfare. Nevertheless, he seemed in cheerful vein as his battalion, already split into three separate parts, began the long and unnerving rail journey south. The warm rains of the season had melted the surface ice of the tundra and undermined the tracks so that 'the whole line swayed at the train staggered over the marshes', one young marine subaltern recalled. 'Everything was very peaceful there', Colonel Kitcat noted, 'and the prospect of any serious scrapping in the front was openly scoffed at. At a station much further south some wag is reported to have said that if there were any casualty due to fighting then there ought to be a court of enquiry held!'[2]

The reinforcements which accompanied General Rawlinson to Murmansk brought no significant increment to Allied numerical strength in the theatre, which had been haemorrhaging manpower since May when the French detachment left. In June the entire Italian contingent of 1200, long unreliable, had been withdrawn, followed by the troubled Royal Marine detachment and the US railway troops. Finally, following Churchill's promise of a return home before the harvest was gathered in, there was a general exodus of men of all corps and departments of the original British expeditionary force. They sailed for England on 10 August aboard the ships which had brought the new Commander-in-Chief and his men. The valuable contingent of Canadian gunners followed on 22 August. One of Rawlinson's fresh battalions was soon sent to Archangel to take charge of the city and port in case of trouble from the local population. With the Murmansk port to be secured and the 500 miles of railway to be protected there was not a great deal left to stiffen the offensive force itself; but at least Maynard now had dependable British troops with which to operate before the withdrawal left the defence entirely to the Russians, many of whom were scarcely trained and some thoroughly unreliable.

The Murmansk commander had become increasingly exasperated with the way the strategy in North Russia had been developing. He naturally resented the lower priority which was given to his theatre compared with Archangel and the rejection of his ideas for an advance on Petrograd, particularly since General Yudenitch was being supported for the same purpose. But he was also unhappy and worried at the way decisions taken in Archangel were likely to affect his own situation. If Ironside were to disarm all his Russians during the withdrawal, as he declared he was minded to do after the mutinies, the news of this would soon be known by the Russian forces at Murmansk. In consequence there was, Maynard emphasised to the War Office, 'no chance whatever of them [his Russians] being willing to continue serving'. Furthermore, he complained, with the Archangel withdrawal scheduled to take place first, 'for a month or six weeks the few Allied troops remaining here will be in a position of extreme peril'. Galled beyond measure by the situation in which he was likely to find himself, Maynard rounded on the War Office planners: 'It seems madness from the military point of view, putting aside possible naval considerations, not to permit my withdrawal to be carried out at the same time as that from Archangel.' Finally in his telegram came the suggestion which he, Ironside and Mr Hoare had all separately advocated: 'I recommend strongly that an attempt be made to negotiate with the Bolshevik Government ... Of course there is a risk that they would not abide by their agreement, but we stand to lose nothing, and, as we contemplate such a huge climbdown, this small addition is nothing.' When Rawlinson met Maynard for the first time a fortnight later, the Commander-in-Chief found him, perhaps unsurprisingly, 'rather windy'. Of course, Churchill would not hear of any negotiation with the Bolsheviks, and Ironside did not, in the event, disarm his Russians, although they had been, in the words of the straight-talking Major Allfrey, 'full of sedition for ages'.[3]

The Murmansk equivalent of the Sadleir Jackson offensive at Archangel was a much less spectacular affair and, furthermore, one of which the Bolshevik leadership was already forewarned by what had occurred at Archangel. It was to be a continuation of the advance down the corridor between Lake Onega and the Finnish frontier to the line of the River Suna, a distance of some thirty-five miles. There was some prospect of the White Russians holding the relatively narrow front there, though the first attempt to give them independent action – a drive to take Siding 10 on the railway and push on to link up with the rising against the Bolsheviks further down the Shunga peninsula – had failed, even though it had air and artillery support from the British. Maynard did not want to give the Bolsheviks their first taste of victory at this crucial stage in the campaign and so brought his British infantry back into the line in support of the Russians, in defiance of the wishes of the War Office. At the next attack the position fell and the Russians went on to clear the peninsula, after some heavy fighting and resolute defence by a Bolshevik force which turned out to be composed largely of Red Finns. Almost a decade later General Maynard was to write of the local Russian army, by this time between six and seven thousand strong and including two field batteries and engineer units, as being 'a force with which the Bolsheviks would have to reckon seriously'. This, however, was a rose-tinted memory, somewhat different from what he thought and wrote at the time. Even as he was making his plans for the final offensive, one of the new Russian infantry battalions which had completed its training at Maselga was refusing to entrain for the front.

Maynard's withdrawal plan turned on his final attack being delivered with as much force and violence as he could muster, to cause maximum casualties to the Bolsheviks and disruption to their positions, so that the British force could make the long move back to Murmansk undisturbed. This 'huge climbdown', as he called it, would seem less like pure funk if the Whites could make some semblance of a defence whilst his men got away, and might even enable the politicians at home to claim that they had 'stood by their friends' in north Russia. When Lord Rawlinson reviewed Maynard's plan, he agreed its main element – an advance to the line of the Suna river – with the proviso that the British troops would not advance beyong the line of the River Nurmis, leaving the last ten miles of the drive to the Suna to be undertaken by the Russians themselves, but with artillery and bombing support from the British. It seemed a wise modification. The offensive was planned for mid-September.

One further reinforcement was now in the hands of Murmansk Command – the new M gas. Rawlinson had been very impressed with the results of gas bombing during the withdrawal to Archangel. 'The Chief is very anxious for you to use this Gas', Rawlinson's Chief of Staff told Maynard, and on 9 September six gas specialists were sent across the White Sea with 250 M bombs. Unfortunately, the gas specialist, Major Davies, was not immediately available to the Murmansk commander; he had been incapacitated when demonstrating the weapon to the Archangel Russians. With the offensive due to start on 14 September, it was arranged for it to be preceded by bombing with high explosive and M gas bombs by planes carrying up to forty M bombs each. High winds on both 12 and 13 September limited the effectiveness of the exercise but it seems, nevertheless, to have done almost all that was expected of it. A strong position on the Chorga line and the important railway towns of Mikheeva Selga and Lijma all fell with minimal resistance after they had been gas-bombed as a preliminary to the ground attack. A subsequent investigation at the captured positions, which included the questioning of Bolshevik prisoners, seemed to confirm the bombing's effectiveness: troops had retreated in disorder, abandoning strong positions and discarding rifles and equipment. None of the prisoners, however, showed symptoms of gassing; so the bombing may well have produced demoralisation and panic rather than physical incapacitation.[4]

There were to be three thrusts in the final Murmansk offensive, one down the railway, one to its east and the third much further west, clear of the main belt of lakes. All three involved turning movements; the object being the destruction of the Bolshevik forces, rather than simply pushing them back. Maynard's fresh troops were taking the lead, supported by the long-suffering Serbs, as well as Russians of the new White Army. It was planned that the widest turning movement would be performed by the westernmost of the thrusts, aiming first at the destruction of the Bolshevik villages of Koikori and Ussuna before moving, on D Day itself, to take Konchozero, the hub of the routes from the south, located where the River Suna flowed from one of the smaller lakes. If this attack were successful, the force would then, as Maynard planned it, 'roll up the left flank of the enemy's forces, should they make a stand on the line of the Suna and convert defeat into rout'. 6RMLI was to take the lead in this vital thrust.

The marines' battalion headquarters and C Company made their slow progress south from Murmansk to Kandalaksha, taking over accommodation from units going home, while the other companies went on to Kem. There, one of their junior officers noted how 'the barrack-like routine has made the troops tired of Russia already'. They were also dispirited by never having volunteered for this Russian service, by the lack of pay, and the prospect that after the Armistice with Germany they might have to risk their lives for Russia. It was rumoured that they and the other reinfocements were to be ordered to force their way over two hundred miles of territory to capture Petrograd. Finally, after journeying across lakes to the west of Lake Onega, Lieutenant Colonel Kitkat and his force arrived at the front-line village of Syatnavolok, where the commanding officer was briefed on the company task: an attack on the village of Koikori, which was to be destroyed, after which the other villages were to be similarly treated once the battalion had closed up. 'Everything was to be perfectly plain sailing', Kitkat wrote to a friend, 'The Bolo were to run as we showed ourselves and we had visions of samovars galore in the way of loot.'[5]

They started their approach march to their objective shortly after midnight on 29/30 August, but came under sniper fire after about eight miles. One man from the accompanying unit of Serbs was killed before the snipers fled. Then, as they approached the village objective, the marines were halted by machine gun fire from trenches to their front and were sniped at from both flanks. 'Then I tried to think what I ought to do and found I couldn't think at all', confessed Kitkat. Despite more sensible options being available, he weakly took the advice of an enthusiastic subaltern for an immediate flank attack towards the village church. The attack came under heavy machine gun and rifle fire which the artillery failed to silence; an officer was wounded and the attack came to a halt. Whilst Kitkat was forward with the company, trying to organise a second effort, he was shot through the foot. The attack had stalled completely and Kitcat, now incapacitated, told his adjutant to order a withdrawal: 'the men were pretty well dead beat and had had a rotten experience'. Kitcat was disconsolate. 'So ended my first and probably only experience of active service … I am obviously no use as a soldier, the sooner I leave masquerading as one the better', he wrote later to a friend. From the ambulance train, where he had no doubt heard of the company's subsequent misfortunes, Kitkat wrote to his Royal Marine chief in England with disarming frankness:

> I do not think I could have made such a hopeless mess of things. I suppose I was suffering from 'wind up' but I did not realise it. One thing stands out perfectly clear is that I am not fit to command troops either in the field or out of it. I feel I ought to be court martialled and at least cashiered but if I am to be spared that humiliation I must at least retire from the service. I have served so badly.[6]

The company ended up back at its midnight start point. The men had covered about twenty miles all told, four of the force had been killed and fifteen wounded. They had achieved nothing. The men were tired, demoralised and hungry. No food had been issued since the previous night. In the afternoon the local infantry commander, Major Strover of the Machine Gun Corps, asked the marine company commander to form an outpost on the Koikori road. The men refused and the company commander apparently weakly accepted their refusal and reported it to the commander citing their reasons. They had not been asked to volunteer for Russia; they had done all the fighting to date and it was time the other companies did some; they wanted proper hospital arrangements before they went on fighting; and there were Germans among the Bolsheviks fighting on the other side and Britain was at peace with Germany. It was not an auspicious start to front-line service for 6RMLI.

'Everyone is satiated with Russia already', wrote a subaltern in B Company, which was now coming south to the front. The news of C Company's failure and the casualties they had taken had got back to the men who heard that the 'Bolo was getting very unpleasant and that our troops up the line had "the wind up"'. The feeling that the campaign was not worth casualties – a general attitude in north Russia: specific instructions had been issued about keeping casualties down – was also evident among the marines. 'In B Coy we heard, I do not recall how, that the men were anxious that the officers should not try to win any medals. They feared that officers might do something rash when in action and their men might become unnecessary casualties.' This seemed to be the mood on 8 September as D Company left Svyatnavolok for their attack on Ussuna and as B Company, which had practised for an attack on Koikori the previous day, moved forward with C Company in support for the second attempt on the village defences. The command arrangements were distinctly odd. Major Ridings, the second-in-command and now the acting battalion commander, together with the adjutant, went off with the one-company force to Ussuna, leaving the two-company group at Koikori in the charge of its own company commanders but apparently under the overall command of the army man, Major Strover. They had local Russian guides for their advance through the difficult wooded terrain and had been briefed that an officer with a party of partisan fighters would catch the Bolos in rear as they tried to escape from the village when the attack went in.[7]

B Company bumped an enemy patrol before they got near their objective and were clearly under observation when they came within range of it. A confused and strongly contested action followed during which the company commander and a machine gun sergeant were both wounded. At one stage the forward platoons were being fired on from the front and from both flanks. One platoon was ordered to cease fire when it was told that it was firing on another. It became clear that the enemy was operating in rear of them as well. The company second-in-command ordered a retirement and subsequently suffered a psychological collapse and was put under arrest. Command devolved upon Lieutenant Smith-Hill, the senior subaltern. Accounts of exactly what happening on the battlefield are confused and conflicting. Major Strover, clearly angry with the failure to take the village, got involved in giving orders, via his own Machine Gun Corps officers, directly to the demoralised men of the two companies in the action, as he did personally on the road back to Svyatnavolok, exacerbating the confusion and the developing indiscipline. The young acting company commander, Lieutenant Smith-Hill, later recorded that:

> I reorganised the Coy and manned outposts on the Koi-Svy road at about 15 ½ V.P [Verst Post]. On my return from speaking to Major Strover DSO (M.G. Corps) I found the company collected on the road. On asking why they had left their positions they informed me that a major in the M.G.C. had told them to leave their L.G's and 'Get to hell out of it' as they were not needed and that he would find someone 'who was some use to man the positions'. The word had also been passed to them that men who did not wish to fight could march back to 12 V.P.

Some did just that whilst Smith-Hill was away checking the orders. He later discovered that the Machine Gun Corps major apparently intended his outburst only for C Company. The remainder of B Company slept out where they were that night, without blankets or greatcoats, before being marched back the following day for about three miles. Both B and C Companies were then addressed by the C Company commander who called for volunteers to man the outpost line. An insufficient number came forward. Later about fifty men of B Company quit the position and made for Svyatnavolok.[8]

The War Office passed a brief explanation of the whole affair to the Admiralty:

> Apparently they lost direction whilst attacking a village and became demoralised under fire and refused to obey orders. The majority of the men in two companies then went back to camp despite the orders of their officers. Their total casualties were two officers and fourteen other ranks in two strong companies. Lord Rawlinson attributes this firstly to indifferent officers and secondly to panic of troops in action for first time.[9]

The verdict of a naval officer who made a study of naval mutinies was that:

> The discipline of the Chatham [B] and Portsmouth [C] companies broke down completely ... The men either refused to advance, or if they did, retired as soon as they were fired on; Lewis gun sections threw down their guns in the presence of foreign troops, and, in short, the Royal Corps went through the blackest day in its history.[10]

The evidence seems to suggest that, aside from battlefield panic resulting from surprise at the very aggressive defence at Koikori, the worst indiscipline occurred not when the troops were in action but during the demoralisation and acrimony of its immediate aftermath.

The attack which D Company mounted on Ussuna similarly ended in failure. The company came under fire as soon as they were within sight of the village, and an attempted outflanking attack led by the adjutant was unsuccessful: fire from supporting Vickers machine gunners could not shift the enemy. A patrol probed to investigate the defences and found that they had well-built trenches fully manned and with plenty of wire defending them. The attack was renewed the following day but without success. The company was finally withdrawn. It was another failure, but one unmarred by the indiscipline and disorganisation seen at Koikori. The battalion adjutant who led the flank attack was killed whilst engaged in a sniping duel with the enemy. A brave officer without doubt; but neither flank attacks nor sniping duels were the adjutant's responsibility in a company at full strength, any more than leading the first company attack had been an appropriate responsibility for Lieutenant Colonel Kitcat.[11]

Lord Rawlinson travelled to Kem on 10 September. He had spent much of the previous two weeks supervising the last operations of the troops on the Archangel front but was already concerned about the Murmansk commander. 'Sent Tom H. to see Maynard and quiet him down – he worries', the Commander-in-Chief recorded. That the Murmansk commander was increasingly anxious and irritable in the final weeks of his isolated and overstretched command had been clear from the recent barrage of telegrams he had addressed to the War Office. Now Rawlinson was to see the general for himself in the aftermath of the marines' failure. 'Not happy about Maynard', he wrote.[12] Within days Maynard had nearly died of a serious heart attack; he was transported back to Murmansk seriously ill, at last free of his unending concerns. One is reminded that he was still convalescing from an illness when he had first been selected for the Murmansk appointment. The medical board had never declared him fit and he had been appointed despite their misgivings. Maynard's experience in command was the epitome of all that was wrong with the decision to stay in north Russia after the Armistice.

'Marines seem to have behaved very badly. Panic and no fight in them', was Rawlinson's immediate verdict on the Koikori affair. He ordered a court of enquiry and got the victorious Sadleir Jackson over from Archangel to conduct it. It lasted three days and confirmed all his blackest suspicions. 'Spent all morning reading the Marines' Court of Enquiry', he wrote. 'It is the worst case I ever read. Court Martial opens tomorrow. It was the officers who did worst.' The rules for convening a field general court martial to try Royal Marines subject to the Naval Discipline Act but fighting on land under army officers was the kind of theoretical problem that used to be set for officers taking their military law promotion examinations, but such a problem was seldom met in reality.

Rawlinson had wisely taken advice of the Adjutant General when he first heard of the trouble and the disciplinary procedures were agreed and executed with some despatch. Brigadier General Grogan from Archangel presided over the court martial which had a Royal Marine lieutenant colonel as a member. The court of enquiry reported on 1 October, the main court martial sat on the 3rd and its findings were confirmed by Rawlinson on the 4th. A second court martial was held on the 7th. Rawlinson sailed for England on the 8th, admitting that he was 'very glad to be quit of North Russia'. The episode gives the appearance of a somewhat hasty trial with minds already made up. Before leaving Russia, Lord Rawlinson summoned the officers of 6 RMLI and gave them one of the severest dressings down it can ever have been the duty of a general officer to hand out.

He opened by exempting A Company from his remarks and then, at the request of its company commander, D Company as well. That he needed prompting to make this latter concession, but immediately agreed it, weakened his pitiless condemnation of the remainder:

> Throughout the whole of my experience, and after four and a half years continuous fighting in France, I have never come across so bad a case of indiscipline, insubordination and panic in the presence of the enemy. There is, as far as I can ascertain, no redeeming feature in the whole story of failure ... Discipline can only be created and enforced by the officers, by their example, by their strict attention to duty, by their care in the welfare of their men and, above all, by the high standard of honour and military efficiency which they observe amongst themselves and exhibit in the training and the leadership of the NCOs and men. From enquiries I have made, I gather that you officers have done none of these things, and, consequently, your battalion has been tried and found wanting ... in conclusion, it is my unpleasant duty to express censure upon the whole of you officers as a body and particularly on your Lieutenant Colonel who is your responsible head.[13]

Rawlinson did not add, of course, that soldiers also fight best and accept discipline most readily when they know what they are fighting for, believe in what they know and are appropriately trained for action, prerequisites which were present throughout Rawlinson's four and a half years in France but entirely absent from the situation of the Royal Marine battalion in north Russia, where, moreover, the exemplary purposes of courts martial were not nearly so compelling as they had been in France. Lieutenant Colonel Kitcat, somewhat recovered from his wound, subsequently assembled the battalion in a hollow square and read out the court martial verdicts to the accused men drawn up on the open flank. Two officers (the officer commanding C Company and the second-in-command of B Company) and ninety-four other ranks had been tried by the courts martial. Both officers and eighty-nine of the other ranks were found guilty.[14] The most serious charge was 'disobeying so as to show wilful defiance' for which an NCO and twelve marines were condemned to death. Lord Rawlinson commuted the sentence to five years' penal servitude. Most of the remaining other ranks received significant periods of imprisonment with hard labour or penal servitude. One officer was dismissed the service and the other was severely reprimanded. Kitcat himself was placed on half pay by the Lords of the Admiralty and subsequently resigned his commission. In addition, virtually all the other officers, NCOs and men of B and C Companies received a formal recorded rebuke from their Lordships. In sum, it was the most substantial and severe disciplinary verdict ever passed on Royal Marines. Thereafter 6 RMLI disappeared from the Royal Marine order of battle and the numeral '6' has not since been connected with any of its combat units.[15]

Lord Rawlinson declared that the case had no redeeming features. In fact, mitigating factors are not hard to find, both in the circumstances of the minor battles themselves and in the larger military background to them, starting with the First Lord's misdescription of a very ordinary, hastily assembled and ill-trained unit as 'a fine battalion'. It is particularly surprising that the Adjutant General Royal Marines allowed it to be sent to Russia in the circumstances of the time, especially after the performance and treatment of the earlier detachment about which the contents of the strained correspondence between War Office and Admiralty was still reverberating. The 'Marine Mutiny', as the 6 RMLI episode has become known, did not involve a single marine being convicted either of mutiny or cowardice and there was, as the senior subaltern and very temporary commander of B Company noted, 'no case of any men refusing to obey a direct order to return to the line'.[16] However unsatisfactorily the Marines performed in the fighting, the great bulk of the offences occurred not in the presence of the enemy but, after some confusing and contradictory orders, on the road back to Svyatnavolok. Many seem to have been no more serious that those committed earlier by the Royal Marine detachment which were allowed to go unpunished by General Maynard, whose chosen course of action was a complaint to London. This merely generated enquiries, argument and acrimony. Was Maynard disinclined formally to discipline the earlier detachment because he knew the men were long overdue for relief and had received a raw deal? The men of 6 RMLI knew about the actions of their predecessors from 'Glory III', as their Murmansk depot ship was known, that they 'had burnt their rifles and that nothing had happened to them'. Their own, and the local army attitudes were no doubt influenced by these earlier events. It also appears that the enemy at Koikori and Ussuna were not only well armed, determined and prepared, but also in possession of very good intelligence about their opponents' moves; hence their sniping and alert defence. There is good evidence to suggest that at least one of the Russian guides was in the pay of the Bolsheviks and in touch with the defenders at Koikori. The subaltern commanding the lead platoon of B Company noted that 'many of my men were shot in the back although they were facing the enemy'. By contrast, British intelligence was poor. Finally, at Koikori there was no M gas available in support of the marines.[17]

Koikori and Ussuna were attacked by the Russians and Serbs on 11 September without success, and once again as part of the final offensive on 14th, but the defences, which were manned mainly by Red Finns, held firm; the relatively strong natural positions had by then been fortified and nothing would shift them. The main part of Maynard's offensive went largely according to plan: 9000 troops, almost 6000 of them Russians, took part, with the Russians remaining in support for the first two days. Aided by the gas bombing, British troops had reached the line of the Nurmis river by 18 September. Bolshevik losses were heavy and in prisoners alone they lost a thousand, besides quantities of rolling stock, supplies and *matériel*. Time and again the defenders had been outflanked and surprised, forfeiting their chances of destroying the railway line before they retreated. But the complete failure of the right-flank attacks was a serious blow to the Russians who were to take over the line, despite the fact that the major bridge over the River Suna was blown, holding Bolshevik reinforcements back for some time.

By 22 September all the Allied troops had withdrawn to Medveja Gora, by the 25th the lake flotilla and aircraft had been transferred to the Russians. But the British withdrawal to Murmansk was not an unopposed affair. The port lay 500 miles away from the fighting troops; the vulnerable single-track railway line over which they had to travel crossed innumerable wooden bridges which were not difficult to destroy, whilst the limited population of the region had little for which to thank the departing army. Maynard, now *hors de combat*, had been concerned at the possibility of some attempt to disrupt his communications on the way back and had suggested that some troops might be taken off the line at Kem and returned to Murmansk by sea. Rawlinson thought at first that this was unnecessary, whilst Admiral Green was not keen on the idea. Ultimately the Commander-in-Chief did accept that it would be a wise precaution. The Red Finns, who been a thorn in the side of the Murmansk commander ever since the end of the war against Germany and who had put paid to the Koikori and Ussuna operations, continued to complicate the campaign even as it drew to its conclusion.

The high command received a report that a group of armed deserters from Maynard's long-disbanded Finnish Legion were preparing to sabotage the railway in the area of Kandalaksha. A British detachment was sent by boat along the White Sea coast to deal with them, but it was ambushed while still afloat and suffered numerous casualties. The Finns then built upon this success by burning down several of the railway bridges north of Kandalaksha. Momentarily, there was a serious risk of the departure programme being compromised, but the precautionary plan was implemented and some of the troops were withdrawn by sea whilst Russian engineers made repairs to the bridges allowing the rail traffic north to resume. In the end the overall departure programme was little affected. The flotilla of flat-bottomed river boats from Archangel was afforded time to complete their refitting at Murmansk, ready to tackle the daunting challenge of the journey home in open waters.

The first snow of the winter was falling as the convicted marines passed into the charge of the provost officers at the port where they were embarked under guard on SS *St Helena* for imprisonment at home. On 12 October the last troopship at Murmansk cast off her moorings and headed for the open sea as the long, dark Arctic winter began to close over the defenders of the region. Perhaps the last words on the campaign should be given to the man who commanded it, and to the senior provost officer who took charge of the convicted marines. 'To my mind', Maynard wrote, 'our action at Murmansk … can give rise to no feeling of self-reproach, and only to one of regret – namely, that the help we gave fell short of that required to throttle in its infancy the noisome beast of Bolshevism.' By contrast, the provost officer, Captain H.E. Ward, wrote home to his sister, 'Our force out here has been really practically useless. There never was any real Bolshevism here and most of the people here were only fisherfolk formerly, before the riff-raff drifted up here to Murmansk'.[18]

When many of the men from north Russia arrived back in England, a general strike was in progress. Whilst still on the voyage General Ironside was cabled by the War Office and told to hold his men in readiness for 'duties in aid of the Civil Power', a task which all soldiers dislike; but within a few hours the message was cancelled. There was no public reception as the ships docked and many of the troops had to unload their own baggage and stores. When Ironside disembarked at Liverpool the press campaign orchestrated by Beaverbrook over the Sherwood Kelly affair was at its height. The general was asked if he had any comment. No doubt regretting his earlier indiscretion with the *Gazette of the Archangel Expeditionary Force*, he replied simply, 'I think a damn sight too much has been said already'. On 10 October he reported to General Wilson, who recorded that day in his diary, 'I also saw Ironside just back from Archangel. He says if the Bolsheviks attack Archangel will fall'.

No news of the fate of 6 RMLI had reached the public at large when the convicted men began to serve their sentences in the naval prison at Bodmin; but over the succeeding weeks accounts began to seep out as prisoners, their families and servicemen's organisations addressed complaints, pleas and petitions to MPs, the Admiralty and even the Prime Minister himself. In mid-November questions began to be asked in Parliament, demanding the facts of the cases and calling for clemency. At first the questioners, who included those indefatigable opponents of the Russian intervention, Colonel Wedgwood and Lieutenant Commander Kenworthy, were fobbed off by Walter Long, the First Lord of the Admiralty. Ultimately, on 22 December, in response to a further question from

Kenworthy, Long made a long and carefully worded reply, announcing that 'We have given these cases our most careful and anxious consideration, and have decided to deal with them in what we believe the House will regard as a spirit of clemency'. He then proceeded to announce some remarkable reductions in sentence. Of those initially sentenced to death the great majority were to serve only one year; the fifty one men given five years' penal servitude or two years' hard labour were to be released after six months. Of the eight under-nineteens who had been convicted, six had already been released; the other two would serve only six months. The government thus defused what could have been another embarrassing consequence of its Russian involvement. By reducing sentences which the Admiralty had already confirmed, it was not simply acting in a 'spirit of clemency' on the matter, it was admitting its own responsibility for sending into battle such an ill-prepared force and one which contained both young soldiers and recent prisoners of war, both categories which were not normally required to face the enemy even in a legitimate war. There was, of course, no clemency for the marines who had died at Koikori.[19]

The resistance of the White Army in north Russia was not finally extinguished until 21 February 1920. That it held together as long as this is attributable less to the fighting qualities of the force of 25,000 men left to defend the whole huge region than to the fact that, with the Allied threat in north Russia at an end, its reconquest was not an urgent priority for the Bolsheviks. More pressing were the dangers which General Yudenitch presented to Petrograd and General Denikin to the heartland of Russia. The threat which Admiral Kolchak posed from Siberia might have temporarlily waned, but his forces had not been decisively defeated. The day after the British departed, the resistance at Archangel was much heartened by the sight of Russian ships steaming up the Dvina delta loaded with food supplies from Siberia sent by Kolchak via the mighty River Ob. The following day General Miller's forces began a successful offensive on the Railway Front. Another advance in mid-December, in the remote Pinega, Petchora and Mezen districts, was equally successful and brought vast new territories into non-Bolshevik hands. But it was a hollow victory since there was little resistance and it brought no fresh resources to the Whites, whilst adding the responsibility for feeding the scores of thousands who inhabited the region. An attack launched to recapture Shenkursk was a failure, producing only demoralisation.

At Murmansk there were not even initial victories to buoy up the defenders. The line of the Suna river was never reached and the Nurmis river line, which the British handed over to the Russians intact and unthreatened, was vacated within four days when the Bolsheviks steamed a strong flotilla up Lake Onega and landed a force behind them. This was a danger which had been evident from the moment the line of furthest advance had been selected: water is only an obstacle if the enemy has nothing to sail on it. The Bolsheviks were never deprived of their lake flotilla. Meanwhile the virus of political activism was spreading among the troops, stimulated by the wave of peace propaganda which the Bolsheviks directed at them. In pamphlets and leaflets secretly distributed, the soldiers were invited to lay down their arms and promised 500 roubles for a surrendered rifle, 1000 for a machine gun and 5000 for an officer, as well as two months' leave so that they could visit their families. Other leaflets told officers that the Allies had betrayed them and assured them that their counterparts in the Red Army were well paid and even had orderlies. One leaflet was signed by 160 officers of the Red Army and authenticated with their former ranks and positions in the Imperial Army. General Miller was meeting increasing demands for the democratisation of his regime and growing opposition from the welter of political parties in the region. Some wanted an armistice and direct negotiations with the Bolsheviks, the majority called for a truly democratic government to inspire the troops, and only a small group argued for some reorganisation and a continuing uncompromising fight against the Reds. On 4 February the Archangel front commanders complained to General Miller that the general concern with political matters was affecting the fighting spirit of their men. Their meeting with the general hastily broke up when it was heard that the Bolsheviks had opened their offensive on the Dvina and Railway Fronts. Within a few days the 3rd Infantry Regiment, believed to be one of the best in the region, mutinied and arrested or killed most of its officers, and opened its Onega valley positions to the enemy. This compromised the position of 6th Infantry Regiment, which was forced to withdraw. On 13 February units of 7th Infantry at Seletskoe went over to the enemy. Two days later, with the situation on the Railway Front becoming critical, Miller sent one of his officers to the Bolshevik headquarters at Vologda with an offer of peace and a request for the conditions of surrender. He also sent a secret cablegram to Lord Curzon, the British Foreign Secretary, asking for his mediation in the coming negotiations.

Meanwhile the Dvina Front had ceased to exist, broken by desertion and Bolshevik heavy artillery. The same was happening on the Railway Front, with some officers and the few remaining loyal troops making their way towards the long escape route to the Murmansk theatre. Unsurprisingly, the Bolsheviks' reply to Miller was a demand for unconditional surrender. Miller finally decided to take the step he had stubbornly refused to countenance hitherto – to evacuate Archangel and make for Murmansk. It was inevitably a hasty and disordered flight. The remaining loyal White forces, mainly officers, together with many civilians, began the long and hazardous overland journey, whilst Miller and a mixed body of his staff, some wounded officers, the Archangel government and some wealthy citizens – about 1100 people in all – left by icebreaker accompanied by an armed yacht.[20]

Once the news reached Murmansk that Archangel had been taken over by the Bolsheviks, the soldiers and workers in the township rose in revolt. They killed the assistant governor-general and a number of officers and declared Murmansk to be in the hands of the Soviet regime, leaving the troops in the field with no base to which to return. All effective resistance to the Bolsheviks was now at an end. This same day, 21 February 1920, Lord Curzon's telegram to the Commissar for Foreign Affairs, Chicherin, arrived in Moscow. After explaining that he was writing at the request of General Miller, who had asked that when the Soviet authorities assumed control in Archangel 'there should be no violence permitted against the representatives of the propertied classes of the population', Curzon's main message read as follows:

> You will readily understand that as His Majesty's Government were for over a year in a large measure responsible for the feeding and general well being of the population of the Northern Region it would make a peculiarly painful impression in this country if serious disorders occurred or severe reprisals were exercised by the Soviet authorities against the population which had resisted them for so many months.

The official who had drafted the minute for Curzon admitted that Britain was 'now powerless to affect Soviet behaviour in North Russia'. Since at the time of the telegram's drafting Miller had every intention of continuing to fight on from Murmansk, and Britain was actively supporting the Whites in other theatres, Chicherin had little incentive to cooperate. The situation might have been different if negotiations had taken place when Hoare, Ironside and Maynard had first suggested them, when Churchill had so forcefully rejected the proposal. The tide had since turned in the Soviets' favour on every front. Chicherin did pen an emollient reply, willingly agreeing that the lives of those who surrendered would be spared. But Moscow was a long way from Archangel and Murmansk, Chicherin's authority was incomplete, and disorder was already widespread in the two regions.[21] The White regimes in the north had been brutal in their repression of internal opposition. Hundreds of political prisoners were now released. There were many old scores to settle in the disorganised period as power was transferred. Miller's party never landed at Murmansk, the Soviets being already in power when his vessel approached. He took flight to Norway. The remants of General Skobeltsin's Murmansk command retreated to Finland when they heard Murmansk had fallen. The party struggling along the Onega trail from Archangel's Railway Front surrendered near Onega. The consequences were dire for most of the White officers who gave up the struggle; many were summarily slaughtered as the final traces of resistance in North Russia were extinguished.[22]

15

Petrograd Fiasco

In May 1919 General Gough had established his mission headquarters in a comfortable hotel on one of the islands in Helsingfors harbour. From there he travelled about the region aboard the light cruiser HMS *Galatea* which the Admiralty had provided for his use. Since the capitals of all the Baltic States were based on coastal ports, this was a convenient and speedy form of transport. The arrangement did present, however, an unfortunate metaphor for the operation of the Mission to the Baltic States – a general without an army and often at sea. Von der Goltz's truculence and prevarications continued, though after his army's defeat he presented, for a time, something less than a critical threat to the independence of the new states, which continued their struggle to rid themselves of both German and Russian influence. By the terms of the local armistice which the Allies arranged, the Germans had to evacuate Riga immediately and to withdraw from Latvia 'as soon as possible'. But by a mixture of trickery and delaying tactics von der Goltz managed to remain until the autumn, a seriously complicating factor in Gough's already complex task. Gough's own account tends to underplay the difficulties he continued to experience with the defiant German, but with the defeat of the attempted German march into Estonia and the success of Agar's CMB venture at Kronstadt, the mission was perhaps able to spend a little more time on the other element of Gough's instructions: examining the practicability of the Russian Northern Corps continuing its operations against Petrograd from Estonia, and considering the help it might need from Britain to sustain a renewed campaign.

In any event, the activities of the Balts and their German protector were only peripherally concerned with the intervention itself, which was Churchill's, if not the acting Foreign Secretary's, main concern. Yudenitch's thrust from Estonia, it will be recalled, was one element in the great strategic plan for the destruction of Bolshevism which Churchill had graphically outlined to Gough: great forces advancing on the Bolshevik heartland from all points of the compass. Unfortunately, there were many factors which this 'big hand – small map' approach to strategy failed to take into account. One was the attitude of the Estonians themselves. Gough found the Estonians keen to send the Germans packing, deeply mistrustful of the White Russians; but, while hostile to the Bolsheviks, without 'the least intention of invading Russia themselves'.[1]

Yudenitch had arrived in the Baltic about a month before General Gough, who much later wrote in his memoirs that he found the Russian to be 'a kindly person, simple and far more honest than his compatriots whom he had gathered round him'. At the time, however, while recommending that the Russians should be supplied separately from the Estonians, he noted in a message to Curzon, that 'Yudenitch seemed unpopular, both with the Estonians and the Russian Army'. *The Times* reported favourably on Yudenitch, calling him a man of 'iron will … not greatly interested in politics'. Few local observers, however, had a good word to say for the Russian. Marshal Mannerheim wrote that, in view of Yudenitch's reputation against the Turks, he had 'expected to meet a forceful personality, but to my surprise he struck me as physically slack and entirely lacking in those inspiring qualities which a political and military leader of his standing should possess'. The British Commissioner, Tallents, called him 'that tough and unattractive commander'. Far from being non-political, Yudenitch made his views on the local political situation abundantly clear. 'There is no Estonia', he once declared, 'It is a piece of Russian soil, a Russian province. The Estonian Government is a gang of criminals who have seized power, and I will enter into no conversations with it.' It was an attitude hardly conducive to good relations with the country that was hosting his army. His officers were of the same opinion, often boasting when in their cups that they would quickly crush Baltic independence once they regained power. Unsurprisingly, Lord Curzon regarded Yudenitch as a 'thoroughgoing reactionary' whom he knew to be bent on the recapture of the Baltic States. None of this did anything to reduce Churchill's enthusiasm for supporting the Russian's venture.[2]

It was not long after Gough's arrival that the question of Finland's possible support for the Yudenitch operation against Petrograd was raised. The Estonians' peremptory action in withdrawing support from the White Russians left Yudenitch desperately in need of both supplies and allies, and with another distasteful option to consider: to enter discussions with the Finns for their support and cooperation in the renewed advance on Petrograd. Finland was, in his view (as in that of Denikin and Kolchak) still a province of Russia, if one entitled to a certain degree of local autonomy, and it was clear that there would be a high political price to pay for its support. He began negotiations with Mannerheim. Gough was soon telegraphing the War Office reporting Mannerheim's terms for joining the operation. These included, and it would have come as no surprise to Murmansk's General Maynard to have learnt this, the ceding of Pechenga and the strip of territory leading to it, a plebiscite for the people of Karelia as to which state they wished to join, as well as the support of the Allies for the Petrograd venture with tanks, aircraft and other military supplies. Opinion in the Cabinet, as Gough realised from his pre-appointment interviews, was divided. Curzon was opposed to any Finnish involvement and decidedly lukewarm about the whole Yudenitch operation. Churchill, as he made clear to his colleagues and later in a public speech, was all for the Whites and the Finns cooperating to take Petrograd; indeed he thought that 'no great harm would be done' if the Germans joined in as well. Gough's own views, which he expressed in private to Curzon, were that nothing but trouble would come from Mannerheim's army, the best organised military force in the area, leading the occupation of the old Russian capital. This was also the general Foreign Office position. In any case, there was considerable domestic Finnish opposition to it. Britain intended to impose very strict conditions on the terms under which it would approve of the Finns taking part or, as was more likely given the shambolic character of the Russian force, leading the venture; these included the clear agreement of the Finnish Diet to whatever Mannerheim was proposing.[3]

As time went on the negotiations between Mannerheim and Yudenitch seemed to end in firm agreement and on terms which General Gough considered less 'exorbitant' than those Mannerheim had first proposed. They, nevertheless, included the recognition of Finland's independence. The Supreme Commander Kolchak was sounded for his views. 'Fantastic' he commented when the Finns' terms were put to him, 'One would suppose that Finland had conquered Russia'. Nevertheless, under pressure from Britain, he gave his approval, hedged about with important conditions which seemed to pass unnoticed by many of those concerned. Gough presented the various options for decision by Churchill and the Cabinet, emphasising the difference in view between Mannerheim and the Finnish government. The Cabinet, and indeed the Supreme Council in Paris, remained resolute in refusing direct support for the Finns' involvement. Churchill had to bow to the views of his colleagues when he wrote to Gough, 'We cannot promise the assistance in arms and munitions asked for by the Finns ... the difficulties of your Mission are fully recognised by us ...' This really settled the matter: without the approval and active support of the Allies, the Finns would not march on Petrograd. The activities of their unofficial, 'volunteer-only' force south of Lake Onega was another matter entirely.[4]

This left Yudenitch again in considerable difficulty. He was based in a country with which his relations were decidedly cool, denied the support of the only significant military force in the region, sustained only by gold from Kolchak and food from the Americans. His army, halted by his supposed ally's withdrawal of support, was in a wretched condition. In London, the representative of the long-defunct Kerensky regime complained to the Foreign Office of 'the piteous state in which the Russian forces of the North-Western Front find themselves today. They completely lack clothing, boots and equipment. They receive no pay and their food is most inadequate'. He might have added that the men were deserting in large numbers. Yudenitch had brought with him to the Baltic a collection of Russian civilian notables, forming a Political Council who were to advise him and form the administration of Petrograd once it had been delivered from the Reds, but they showed no interest in moving to the territory his troops had captured, apparently preferring the comforts of life in Helsingfors and Reval to any civic duties. Importantly, the supplies promised earlier by Britain had not arrived.

In late May, shortly after his arrival in Helsingfors, Gough telegraphed the War Office with the view that 'if given immediately 2000 tons of food and supplies and a sufficient quantity of arms and munitions to equip existing reserve of 5000 men, Yudenitch would be able to capture Petrograd'.[5] This was a most optimistic judgement, but no doubt music to Churchill's ears. The War Office quickly summoned a meeting of the relevant departments and a generous package was agreed: clothing, equipment and weapons for 7500 men, boots and medical stores for 10,000, together with lorries, artillery and ammunition. More would follow. But the supplies were slow to appear: it was not until the end of July that they arrived, only to be greeted, as in south Russia, with complaints as to the appropriateness and condition of some of the weapons and the absence of spares and essential parts. Nevertheless, they served to keep the Russians going and helped them to withstand the Bolshevik counter-attack, which was also weakened by a bombardment from Admiral Cowan's squadron offshore. The arrival of the military *matériel* also strengthened Gough's hand in his attempts to turn the North-Western Army not only into an efficient, but also a respectable force, something which Churchill was very much concerned about. If General Gough and the War Office seemed quite sanguine about the prospect of Yudenitch capturing Petrograd, *The Times* was even more optimistic, producing a series of encouraging news items culminating in one with the headline 'LENIN FEARS FOR PETROGRAD', quoting a third-hand report from Austria that Lenin believed the city was surrounded and that its capture was inevitable. These were not good days for rigorous and independent reporting at the 'Thunderer'.

Churchill was worried about the behaviour of Yudenitch's troops if Petrograd were captured.. He telegraphed Gough, 'Excesses by anti-Bolsheviks if they are victorious will alienate sympathy British nation and render continuance of support most difficult. This should be represented tactfully but strongly to Yudenitch and other leading Russians with whom you come into contact'. He emphasised fair public trials, no indiscriminate shooting and no pogroms. Since such excesses had been routine behaviour in the more distant White armies, as Josiah Wedgwood was making embarrassingly clear in Parliament, he did not want them repeated almost on Britain's doorstep. Given the indiscipline of Yudenitch's army and the reactionary views of its officers, he was effectively asking Gough to make a silk purse out of a sow's ear. Nothing daunted, Gough set about his task with a will.[6]

First, he wrote to Yudenitch admonishing him for the loose talk among his officers about the lateness and inadequacy of the British equipment (some were saying that they could have done better from the Germans) and enjoining him to clean up the whole White movement in the area in readiness for the creation of a democratic Russia. Furthermore, he declared, since the British arms and supplies were now available, the offensive on Petrograd should take place forthwith. If it did not, there would be no further Allied support. Realising, however, that more than a mere shipment of supplies would be needed to ensure victory for Yudenitch's still modest force, Gough next tried to re-establish cooperation between Yudenitch and his erstwhile allies and paymasters, the Estonians. He asked Yudenitch to put in writing to the Estonian Commander-in-Chief his full recognition of Estonian independence in return for the Estonian army's assistance in the forthcoming campaign.

Gough was already beginning to exceed his remit as head of a Military Mission. He then went further, taking the *Galatea* across to Reval on 8 August and summoning the principal members of the Estonian government to a conference with the leading Allied representatives. There he formally requested close cooperation between the Estonian and North-Western armies. The Estonians leaders were reluctant, fearing, quite understandably, that any new regime in Russia would deny Estonia's right to independence. By contrast, the Bolsheviks, hard-pressed on other battlefronts, were already offering to recognise Estonia's sovereignty, provided it ceased cooperating with the White forces. The Estonians' dilemma exposed the contradiction at the heart of Allied Baltic policy; it was an issue about which neither the British Cabinet nor the Supreme Council in Paris had been able to make up their minds. How could acceptance of the independence of the Baltic States be reconciled with support for the Whites who were determined to deny it? Gough told the assembled Estonian ministers of the guarantee he already had from Yudenitch, but they remained deeply mistrustful and wanted one from a properly constituted Russian government. The exasperated Gough then decided to take his cavalry sabre to this Gordian knot: he resolved to form a Russian government.[7]

That very day the members of Yudenitch's Political Council were summoned from Helsingfors to the Estonian capital. When they arrived on 10 August they were conducted straight to the British Consulate where they joined the British, French and American representatives, the Estonian statesmen and, a bizarre addition to the gathering, John Pollock, the correspondent of *The Times*. Whatever else might be said of the forthcoming diplomacy, it certainly seemed that it was to be open. Yudenitch was away on other duties and General Gough himself had returned to Helsingfors. The British Commissioner, Colonel Stephen Tallents, the only Briton in the Baltic who might have been considered remotely competent to conduct such negotiations, was also absent. The assembled council was therefore addressed by Brigadier General Marsh, an Indian Army officer, who headed the Helsingfors section of Gough's mission. Marsh spoke in fluent

Russian. His terse message was delivered at 6.15 p.m. The North-Western Army, he declared, was in a catastrophic state; to take Petrograd it needed Estonian support, in return for which the Estonians demanded Russian recognition. Shortage of time precluded consulting Kolchak on the matter. Therefore, Marsh asserted, the Russians in the room had to form a government which could provide the agreement the Estonians needed. It was now time for the Russians' love of talking to be replaced by action. According to one account, he then read out the agreement he wished them to sign. It was then 6.20 p.m., noted Marsh; if they had not formed a government by 7.00 p.m. they would receive no further Allied support. (One Russian account suggests that the words actually used translate as 'We will throw you aside'.) He urged them to put away their political differences for the sake of an anti-Bolshevik North-Western Russia. Leaving behind him the text of the agreement for their signature and a list of the suggested members of a Russian government, Marsh left the room. The exercise had all the finesse of a steam hammer.[8]

Needless to say, by 7.00 p.m. the Council had not achieved a great deal. Marsh permitted the Russians several adjournments in the subsequent days. He later apologised for 'any brusqueness in his manner. He was a simple soldier and had to get things done'. The result of this pressure was finally telegraphed to the Foreign Secretary on 14 August by Colonel Tallents's deputy: 'After negotiations lasting for four days during which pressure was constantly exerted by British Military and Diplomatic Missions and Representatives of France and United States, a North-West Russian Government for Provinces of Pskoff, Novgorod and Petrograd has been formed.' But Marsh's draft pact with the Estonian government was not agreed to. The pressurised Russians issued only a 'preliminary declaration' about recognising Estonia and expressed the pious hope that Kolchak would do likewise. Rodzianko begged Yudenitch to have nothing to do with the agreement. When Marsh heard that Yudenitch might repudiate it, he is said to have declared, 'We have another Commander-in-Chief all ready'. Similar, if less brutal, pressure was applied to the Estonians, who remained distrustful and decided to raise the stakes and demand full *de jure* recognition from the Allies as their price for cooperation. When Gough heard this he added upward pressure to Paris to the downward pressure of his deputy at Reval. He telegraphed Balfour (throughout this period Balfour in Paris was formally the Foreign Secretary, with Lord Curzon in London acting for him there) saying that the Allies must comply with the demand of the Estonians, otherwise 'disaster' was to be expected. In his quest for a concerted attack on the Bolsheviks, Churchill could hardly have asked for more determined, if ham-fisted, support than that provided by Gough and Marsh. The Foreign Office's Commission in the Baltic even chipped in, with Tallents's deputy reporting, by way of extra support, that he had given the Russians permission to buy some supplies in Germany.[9]

These developments were viewed by the Foreign Office ministers with surprise, rapidly turning to furious incredulity. Curzon's initial reaction referred to 'the Ruritanian experiment which General Gough and his Merry Men have been making in Estonia', but he was soon telling Balfour more soberly that they had acted without London's authority or even knowledge. Balfour's first response to the affair was a little more relaxed: he said that it read like 'the prospectus of a bubble company'. But before the Cabinet in London was even aware of this reaction, the ministers were taking their own actions. They heard from the Russian chargé d'affaires in London that he regarded the Reval business as 'most objectionable' and that Kolchak would never accept the agreement. What made things rather worse was the garbled account of these extraordinary negotiations which appeared in *The Times* from its Baltic correspondent. Pollock hailed the Russians' 'new government on democratic lines' as a 'milestone on the road towards victory'. It was neither of these things. The Cabinet first repudiated Gough's 'most irregular' action and the following day formally reprimanded all the British officers involved. Gough, the scheme's initiator, was sacked, as, subsequently, was Tallents's deputy, Pirie-Gordon. Strangely, Brigadier General Marsh, whose only previous experience in that rank had been three months commanding a brigade, was left in post. Lord Curzon subsequently tried to have him recalled, but he was protected by Wilson and Churchill.[10]

It is difficult to summon much sympathy for Gough; but he deserves a little. He was under pressure from Churchill and the CIGS to produce a White army capable of taking Petrograd and of playing its part in Churchill's 'converging armies' strategy. Churchill, moreover, was a personal friend who had recently arranged for Gough to be awarded the GCMG, much to Lloyd George's annoyance. Gough was also hoist to some extent by his earlier optimistic report of what Yudenitch's army might achieve if only it had arms and supplies. Even with them, Marsh had reported its condition as 'disastrous'. Gough's judgement had been undone to some extent by the Estonians' fears of Russo-German complicity which they believed would work against their wish for independence. To such complicity, it must be remembered, Churchill was not himself opposed, providing it were directed against the Bolsheviks. Fence-mending there had to be, but Gough no doubt considered he could not leave the exercise to Lieutenant Colonel Tallents, who, though now a senior civil servant, was in military terms vastly outranked by Gough. Furthermore, the general had little time for him, as he had earlier made clear to Churchill: 'Tallents, who has just arrived as Foreign Office representative, is not much of a man. He lacks force, and experience and is very much in the hands of the French, or Germans, whichever are nearest him at the moment.' At one point he even suggested that Tallents should be absorbed into the Military Mission. Exasperated by the squabbling and incompetence around him, Gough's military culture and command experience seem to have impelled him to decisive, if decisively fatal, action.[11] Churchill remained sympathetic, defending his friend to the Prime Minister and the Foreign Secretary, and claiming that he 'has had to make bricks without straw, and in my opinion it is remarkable that he should have succeeded to such a considerable extent'. This drew an excoriating response from Lloyd George which criticised Churchill's entire Russian policy, as well as his plans for Petrograd, and his 'injudicious' choice of Gough, who was 'utterly unsuited for a task requiring great judgement'. Lloyd George even subtly raised the possibility that Gough might have been acting under separate departmental orders. The Prime Minister wrote, 'unless secret instructions were given to him of which the Cabinet had no knowledge – and I cannot believe that – then General Gough ought to be reprimanded for taking upon himself a responsibility inconsistent with his orders'. He also declared that 'General Yudenitch never had a chance of taking Petrograd'.[12]

Churchill remained defensive and optimistic, believing, as he told the CIGS, that they should await Gough's return and hear his explanation before making any judgements. Gough later submitted a memorandum defending his action, which Churchill confirmed that he found 'in every way clear and satisfactory'. Yudenitch, however, did not. He condemned the mission's (and particularly Marsh's) interference in the internal affairs of his army and claimed that Marsh had foisted on him a government of 'men of doubtful character' in circumstances which he found deeply humiliating, and which made its recognition of Estonian independence 'utterly worthless'. Gough denied that any pressure had been brought to bear and gave his personal view of the White Russians in a private letter to Asquith: 'I think we are backing the wrong horse! All the émigré class of Russians are inefficient and untrustworthy and I do not think they will or could ever govern Russia again.' Back in England, he became an embarrassingly vocal opponent of the intervention. Much later he was to blame the White Russian émigrés in London and their influence on Lloyd George and Churchill for his peremptory recall. Another Military Mission, this time provided by France and headed by General Mangin, was eventually sent to the Baltic, though it was more concerned with dealing with the Germans than supporting the Whites.[13]

Despite the government's reluctance, Churchill of course excepted, to 'make war' on the Bolsheviks, Admiral Cowan at least now had firm Cabinet authority to engage the Soviet navy wherever he found it. Reinforcements had been flowing out to his Baltic squadron for some time. In mid-July he received a much-needed minesweeping flotilla. The seaplane carrier *Vindictive* (actually a converted heavy cruiser) with a scratch collection of obsolescent aircraft soon followed. For this valuable reinforcement, a rough, hazardous and barely practicable airstrip was hastily fashioned on a tiny peninsula close to Selskar. Henceforth photo-reconnaissance and air attacks on Kronstadt became a regular feature of Cowan's operations; but given the embryonic state of aerial bombing at the time, these were a more fruitful source of intelligence for Cowan than damage to the Bolshevik fleet. Most significantly, in early August a flotilla of large CMBs joined the admiral's now impressively large squadron. Lieutenant Agar's exploit having dramatically illustrated their potential, Cowan began to prepare for a much larger attack by CMBs on the Kronstadt main fleet within its base. He planned the operation for 18 August, when it was hoped that the local festival that marked the official end of the Russian summer might divert the defenders. To drown the engine noise of the powerful 55-foot CMBs which were to make the main assault, an air raid on the harbour was arranged to coincide with the attack. Eight of these large CMBs had been sent out from England, but one had been lost in the voyage across the North Sea, so the attacking force was completed by Agar commanding one of his smaller models. As with the earlier attack on the *Oleg*, the key to the operation was to be secrecy and surprise. Pollock of *The Times* had one brief interview with Cowan and departed disgruntled; on this occasion he was not to be privy to the key events. The minuscule force managed to clear the fort defences and get to the protected naval base itself with scarcely a response from its defenders.

The following day the Admiralty put out a blandly worded statement:

A report has been received from the British senior naval officer in the Baltic that a naval engagement took place in the Gulf of Finland early on August 18th. Two Russian battleships, the *Petropavlovsk* and the *Andrei Pervosanni* were sunk. A cruiser was also seriously damaged. The British losses were three coastal-motor boats.

These vapid, unemotional words disguised the high drama of the occasion for, once the boats had passed through the narrow entrance into the protected middle harbour, the Bolshevik reaction was violent. They also gave little hint of the scale of the achievement and the heroism of the crews of the CMBs, and of the aircraft who continued flying throughout the attacks in an effort to support the boats which were under shore fire throughout. Besides crippling the battleships, as the Admiralty statement noted, the attackers managed to sink the important Russian submarine depot ship (the 'cruiser' of the Admiralty statement); other warships escaped damage only because of inevitable mishaps in the dark confines of the protected harbour, the heavy fire of the defenders and sheer bad luck. Nor does the statement make clear what a costly exploit the raid was for the tiny force which carried it out: not only did only five of the eight CMBs return to Cowan's base, six officers and nine ratings were killed and nine were taken prisoner. The action of this little unit ensured that the threat from Kronstadt to the British Baltic force, and to the seaward flank of the White Army, was ended. Thereafter nothing larger than a destroyer ever advanced beyond the base's minefields. Soon the sea ice bottled up what remained of the Russian Baltic Fleet for the long and bitter northern winter.

The Kronstadt attack was also a significant benefit for the emerging Baltic governments: most of their major coastal settlements were dangerously exposed to possible hostile naval action. No doubt the spectacular action also played its part in Soviet decision-making: the month after the attack the Bolshevik government, hard-pressed on other fronts, made fresh approaches to Latvia and Estonia offering to end hostilities and recognise their independence. Further trouble from von der Goltz, however, and the development of Yudenitch's offensive from Estonia served to frustrate these peace approaches.[14] The possibility of the Baltic States negotiating with the enemy impelled the British government, and the Supreme Council in Paris, to a fresh bout of diplomatic activity in an attempt to manage the contradictions in its policy.

The Commander-in-Chief of the Grand Fleet, Admiral Sir Charles Madden, hailed the achievement of the CMB raid as ranking 'among the most daring and skilfully executed of the naval operations of this war. On no other occasion during hostilites has so small a force inflicted so much damage on the enemy.' Cowan's praise for the action was equally unstinting as he congratulated the survivors on their strike against the Bolsheviks, for 'the devastation you have wrought on their harbour – the strongest naval fortress in the world, ravished and blasted'. Two of the CMB officers were awarded Victoria Crosses for their exploit and three others (Agar included) Distinguished Service Orders, while all the ratings received Conspicuous Gallantry Medals. When the success of the attack was conveyed to the Cabinet, however, its members did not seem at all pleased by the news. Apparently the possibility of a negotiated withdrawal from Archangel was still in the air and this spectacular attack did not help matters. The First Sea Lord was 'so disgusted by this example of political opportunism that he tendered his resignation'. But Admiral Wemyss had done this too often in the recent past to be taken seriously.[15]

Nor did the surprise Kronstadt victory seem to attract much attention from the Whites, who continued to squabble among themselves. Yudenitch and Rodzianko quarrelled about everything from the army's needs and command appointments to the allocation of their two motor cars. Meantime the Provisional Government of North-Western Russia issued a stream of unenforceable democratic proclamations, though they had yet to base themselves on any of the territory which they claimed to administer, fearing that if they did so they risked being unseated by Yudenitch's reactionary officers. While the senior commanders were distracted by their squabbles, they managed to lose the Pskov area to a Bolshevik attack. Of the three provinces the government claimed to represent, one, together with the only significant town in the area, was now in Bolshevik hands.

The British Cabinet's interventionists were busy trying to paper over the cracks in their Russian policy which was brought under fresh scrutiny by the Baltic States' willingness to begin the peace talks the Soviets were offering. It was the same old problem. The Supreme Council in Paris concluded that it was generally agreed that the Baltic States deserved recognition, but that such recognition was incompatible with support for Kolchak and Denikin. Curzon advised Latvia and Estonia not to make peace, but could offer nothing tangible as an inducement. Churchill did his best to support him, writing, 'With regard to any of these little Baltic States, I can easily give them a consignment of weapons, if that makes the difference to their carrying on and if you ask me for them'. But the little states wanted rather more: *de jure* recognition and substantial material assistance. The Cabinet finally faced the facts. It decided that recognition was a matter for the Peace Conference and the League of Nations, and that the Baltic States had to decide for themselves whether to negotiate with the Bolsheviks. Churchill disagreed and presented a long memorandum to his colleagues predicting that the direst consequences would follow. If the Baltic States made peace, Finland and Poland might do the same, 97,000 Red troops would be freed to face Denikin, Petrograd would be left in despair, and Yudenitch would join up with the Germans in the Baltic. He then decided, without consulting either Curzon or the Cabinet, to try to twist the arm of the White leaders, Kolchak and Denikin, by getting the heads of mission in Siberia and South Russia to tell them of the Bolsheviks' peace proposals to the Baltic States and to persuade them to offer recognition. Generals Holman and Knox replied with firm refusals from the White leaders. Churchill's unilateral attempt to overturn a Cabinet decision initiated by the Prime Minister himself had failed. So pitiful did the War Office consider Yudenitch's chances that a paper was written recommending that his army be transferred to Denikin's front. As events turned out, Churchill's grim predictions went unfulfilled: the first domino did not fall. Still mistrustful, the Estonians did join with the Latvian and Lithuanian governments in informing the Soviet authorities that they would begin preliminary peace talks no later than 25 October; but earlier the same month the Estonians also agreed to join Yudenitch in his new offensive against Petrograd.[16]

Meantime Brigadier General Marsh was continuing with his efforts to kick-start the Yudenitch offensive, again by approved and unapproved means. A further consignment of weapons and equipment had been secured, including a detachment of six tanks, originally planned for Murmansk but diverted to Reval, where they arrived on 5 August. With the new weapons came twenty-two officers and twenty-six other rank instructors to train the Russians in their operation. Churchill received generous thanks from Yudenitch: 'On behalf of the Russian people, struggling to throw off the yoke of the Bolsheviki, I tender you the sincerest thanks for the timely assistance the munitions and supplies afforded to our army.'

By this stage the chronic troubles with von der Goltz were changing form. He had reluctantly begun to send his German soldiers home, but was enterprisingly recruiting Russian prisoners from Germany in their stead, as well as fresh German volunteers. He remained in occupation of a large tract of Latvia, but his real objective seems to have been a German-dominated Russia. Demands for his removal continued, but the only pressure brought to bear was Cowan's tight control of all German shipping visiting Latvia. The only ships allowed to dock were those repatriating Germans and their equipment. Realising that the Allies would never accept him as head of the new army, von der Goltz had now appointed a Russian adventurer who went under the assumed title of Colonel Prince Pavel Mikhailovitch Bermont-Avalov to lead an 'Army of Western Russia' on his behalf. Marsh seems to have played a part in approving the supply of men and materials from Germany for the renamed force (a practice which had been forbidden by the Allies in the summer), which appeared to conflict directly with what the navy was doing. He also tried to promote cooperation between Yudenitch and Bermont-Avalov for the attack into Russia. He much preferred Bermont-Avalov to Yudenitch, though few others did. Tallents believed Bermont-Avalov was 'an adventurer, suffering apparently from megalomania, highly theatrical and obviously envisages himself as a possible future Tsar of Russia.' The depredations of Bermont-Avalov's army on the countryside and population of Courland were severe enough to cause the Latvian premier to address a moving letter of complaint to Lloyd George. Churchill, however, was all in favour of letting this army operate, providing it helped to ensure that 'the Lenin–Trotsky regime is struck at effectively'. Marsh summoned the commanders of both armies and the Estonians to a conference in late August, at which plans were made for an offensive to begin in mid-September, but the Bolshevik peace proposals forced a delay.[17]

In early October events moved quickly. In Paris the Supreme Council at last decided to pressure Germany to get its troops out of the Baltic States by threatening to withhold food supplies. The reaction was speedy. The Weimar government told von der Goltz there would be no more money for his ventures. Within a week he had received his recall and an order forbidding Germans to enrol in any Russian force. But there was to be one last and very damaging foray by his force. Incidents increased between the Latvian troops and Bermont-Avalov's Russo-German occupiers. Bermont-Avalov therefore decided to march first on Riga to secure his base, rather than directly into Russia. In consequence Latvian troops left their frontier posts to counter the threat, enabling the Bolsheviks to transfer manpower to the threatened Petrograd sector. Yudenitch tried desperately to dissociate himself from what Bermont-Avalov, 'a traitor and enemy of the fatherland', was doing. Nevertheless, Estonians began to desert the White Russian's cause, unsettled by the threat to Riga. British support, too, began to be diverted. Though Cowan remained at Biorko, an increasing part of his squadron became involved in the struggle for Riga, which was fought along the banks and from the waters of the western Dvina on which the Latvian capital stood. The threat of Bermont-Avalov's operations spreading to Libau forced a further dilution of Cowan's resources supporting Yudenitch. To Bermont-Avalov's complaint that British ships were 'supporting Lettish insurgents to the detriment of Russian Army which is fighting for restoration of Russia', Cowan replied curtly, 'I recognise no Russian commander who fights under German direction or in opposition to General Yudenitch'. Bermont-Avalov's assault on the Latvians was a serious setback to the White Russians' cause, which its own commanders were themselves doing little to further, as Yudenitch and Rodzianko began to squabble about which of them would actually command the offensive. It was a dispute which split the officer corps and led to much bitterness and dissension.[18]

This was the moment at which the War Office was considering advising Yudenitch to call off his offensive and transfer his army to Denikin's front. Instead, despite not having a satisfactory agreement with the Estonians, but urged on by Brigadier General Marsh who threatened to withdraw his British supplies if he did not attack, Yudenitch opened his offensive on a wide front on 12 October. At the time many of his officers were still on leave in Stockholm and elsewhere. The battlefield commander, Rodzianko, refused to establish any effective liaison with the Estonians on his coastal flank, whilst Yudenitch was sufficiently heedless of the importance of their support as to appoint a Russian governor of Reval, a useless, reactionary gesture The North-Western Army was about 17,800-strong; it had fifty-seven heavy artillery pieces, a cavalry force of 700 and four armoured trains. It also had six tanks manned by British crews and the support of the guns of the British ships lying off the coast. The White Russians made rapid, almost spectacular, progress. One thrust, moving north along the railway with its armoured trains, retook Pskov and by 13 October had cut the Pskov–Petrograd railway at Luga. A second, advancing from the Estonian town of Narva, took Yamburg and then pressed on to take the railway town of Gatchina. This brought the army to within thirty-five miles of the glittering prize of Petrograd; but it was a similar distance from the arterial railway line from Moscow, a more immediately significant objective. The coastal thrust by the Estonians was being supported by British light cruisers and destroyers. 'They are fighting very hard for Krasnaya Gorka', Cowan reported, but the navy could get no further without sweeping the mines which lay ahead of them. A Russian detachment was landed on the coast under the cover of the British guns, but the massive coastal fortress which dominated the approaches to the Kronstadt base, the Neva estuary and Petrograd itself still held out. The main advance continued; by October 16 Yudenitch's force was only twenty-five miles from the city.[19]

The following day Churchill sent a secret and personal telegram of congratulations to Yudenitcht which began, 'I congratulate Your Excellency on the very remarkable measure of success which has attended the opening of your offensive'. It went on to promise to send further war supplies to the Russian 'with the utmost speed'. These would include rifles, clothing and equipment for 20,000 men; twenty 18-pounders, twelve 4.5-inch and four 6.0-inch howitzers and their ammunition. Churchill hoped to include 'some aeroplanes and a few more tanks', together with about 400 Russian officers who had been training in England. He also discussed with General Wilson sending out a senior officer 'to be at Yudenitch's side in the event of his entry into Petrograd'. His aim was to get early information, but also, an abiding concern as criticism of the Russian venture continued to mount, 'to prevent excesses in the event of victory'. General Sir Richard Haking, an experienced corps commander and able negotiator, was chosen and given carefully drafted instructions which included, as their last item, the return to England of Brigadier General Marsh as soon as he could be conveniently spared. Curzon had been pressing to get Marsh home for some time. It is a pity Churchill had not despatched an experienced general to head the mission when Gough was first recalled.[20]

Yudenich's advance continued until, by 20 October, his men were within ten miles of the centre of Petrograd, but misfortunes and mistakes were already dogging his progress. The destruction of a railway bridge by the Bolsheviks ended the assault of the British tanks which had been driving all before them. It also halted the progress of the two armoured trains. Krasnaya Gorka was still holding out despite the pounding it was receiving from the naval squadron. Without taking the fortress the Estonians could not advance; without clearing the minefields which they were now meeting, the navy could not support a further coastal advance to Kronstadt and beyond to the city itself. Naval support was nevertheless very effective: one bombardment from the British ships broke up a Bolshevik counter-attack in the coastal sector and determined their high command to lay a fresh minefield to halt the ships' progress. Four destroyers left Kronstadt on this mission in the early hours of 21 October only to run into a British minefield. Three of them struck mines and were lost with all hands. Balancing this success, Yudenitch's force was held up within two miles of the main Moscow railway line along which Bolshevik reinforcements and supplies were being despatched to the threatened city.

The Bolshevik response to the threat to the old capital was as decisive as the totalitarian regime could make it. Trotsky took command of the defences and the subsequent counter-attack, commanding from horseback and personally halting panicking soldiers and leading them back into the line. Discipline was restored; field tribunals did their gruesome work; factories turned out makeshift armoured vehicles – useless as attacking weapons but good for morale. Trotsky's orders were 'clear and precise, sparing nobody and exacting from everybody the utmost exertion', according to an eyewitness. By contrast, Yudenitch's failure, once the attack was launched, to control the subsequent operations, was a manifest shortcoming. The significance of his inability to subdue Krasnaya Gorka and threaten Kronstadt directly was underscored by Trotsky's switching of 11,000 volunteer seamen from the naval base to the defence of the threatened Peterhof district on which Yudenitch was advancing, and by the fire which the 12-inch guns of the dreadnought *Sevastapol*, already raised from the shallow harbour waters in which the CMBs had sunk it, was able to bring down on the land attack. Several destroyers, similarly immobile in the Kronstadt base, joined in the bombardment with their smaller weapons. Trotsky's line held. Yudenitch's army, once halted, could only retreat; its brittle morale and indiscipline could not withstand a check.

By 22 October Trotsky's force, about equal in numbers to Yudenitch's before the offensive began, was now far superior to it and counter-attacking. The North-Western Army fell back from the railway town of Gatchina on 3 November; it lost Gdov on the Soviet bank of Lake Peipus on the 7th, and Yamburg near the Estonian frontier on the 14th. Its tribulations were exacerbated by a severe outbreak of spotted typhus which struck the troops during the retreat. On the coastal sector the attempt to subdue Krasnaya Gorka had been continuing. After a desperate plea from Admiral Cowan, the Admiralty diverted the monitor *Erebus*, which was returning to home waters from duty in the White Sea, to assist in the siege. The monitor's formidable 15-inch guns may have done a little to hearten the attacking Estonians, but its heavy shells did not manage to dislodge the hard-pressed defenders of the fortress: it had arrived too late. Its bombardment did not begin until 27 October, by which time the cause of the Whites was lost. The Estonian commander, Laidoner, now in an awkward forward salient, decided to give up the attempt and retire to the frontier. General Haking arrived just in time to hear from the Russian commanders that the attempt on Petrograd had failed. Their plight could have been worse; Trotsky was anxious not to let the remnants of Yudenith's force get away and wished to pursue them across the Estonian frontier. Wiser Bolshevik counsels prevailed. Chicherin, supported by Lenin, thought that such action would simply serve to 'rouse the English Liberals and moderate Tories against us' and 'save a tottering Churchill'. The Russian regime demanded only that the White troops be disarmed and interned.

Admiral Cowan's verdict on the Yudenitch operation was brief and critical: 'It would be difficult to recall any offensive effort ever conducted', he reported, 'which has shown such an utter lack of intelligent leadership, or in which greater military mistakes have been made. Yudenitch thought that our tanks on land, and our ships off the coast, would do everything for him.' Colonel Hope-Carson, commander of the British tank detachment, was similarly censorious, criticising the indiscipline of the Russians, and the 'political and private intriguing among the commanders which robbed the army of much of its effectiveness'. He also blamed the lateness in supplying the British equipment, which left insufficient time for training the Rusians in its use. Much of it was unfamiliar to the Russians and, as has been noted, some of it was incomplete.[21]

The Estonians complied with the Bolsheviks' demands and gave the hapless ministers of the Government of North-Western Russia two weeks to leave their territory. The White troops were not interned in Estonia as an organised force but put to work in timber camps under harsh conditions. The sick and wounded were herded into a typhus-ridden camp at Narva where the disease inevitably spread. An American journalist claimed that the epidemic carried off 10,000 of them. Yudenitch stayed on in Reval, subsisting on the funds Kolchak had sent him. In early January 1920 he addressed a plaintive appeal to Churchill for assistance in securing his army's valuable military property and moving it and the remaining White troops to General Denikin's front. 'In these grave minutes of temporary failure,' he wrote, completely misappreciating the terminal condition of the White cause, 'I trust you will come to our assistance with all the power of your authority.' Churchill now had very little of either so far as Estonia was concerned. 'I do not see what action is possible', he wrote on Yudenitch's letter.[22] *The political and military threads of British policy in the Baltic had by this time become so separated that Curzon actually committed to paper in January 1920 the view that he welcomed the disappearance of Yudenitch's army from the scene. He received the inevitable caustic rejoinder from Churchill.[23]

On 31 October 1919, with Yudenitch defeated and Bermont-Avalov's depredations in Latvia coming to an end, the Cabinet decided that the British Baltic Squadron should be withdrawn. Even then Churchill pleaded for it to continue its bombardment until the ice rendered the Baltic impassable. The Prime Minister was against the idea. It was ultimately decided to leave behind a small nucleus simply 'to show the flag'. It had been a long watch for Admiral Cowan. His squadron had started as a couple of cruisers and half a dozen destroyers. Within twelve months it had grown to include every type of vessel except for capital ships. These latter the Admiralty was not prepared to risk in the confined and mine-strewn waters of the Baltic, despite the initial battleship threat from the Kronstadt base. With this significant exception, the Baltic Squadron became a large and multi-tasked force which merited a more senior commander than a rear admiral; yet their Lordships neither offered Cowan temporary promotion nor took the step of replacing him with a more senior and experienced commander

---

* A few days previously, on 31 December 1919, Estonia had agreed an armistice with the Bolsheviks. It concluded a peace treaty with Moscow in February 1920. By October 1920 Lithuania, Latvia and Finland had followed suit.

when his force and responsibilities grew so considerably.

It would be foolish to pretend that under Cowan the Baltic squadron was always a contented force. The sense that it was disadvantaged compared with other parts of the navy was first engendered when Alexander-Sinclair's cruisers had to forego their Armistice leave in order to proceed directly to the Baltic. This built upon other navy-wide grievances of longer standing, the most important of which concerned pay. The basic pay of an able seaman had been set at 1s. 6d. in 1852 and had only risen by a penny by 1912, when Churchill as First Lord secured a further 1d. rise. However adequate this might have been considered at the time (and many believed it was far from being so), the steep rise in the cost of living which came with the war soon made it appear meagre in the extreme, particularly for those seamen with wives and families to support. In recognition of this an increase of 10 per cent was made in 1917 when wives were also granted a separation allowance, but this was already quite inadequate given the dramatic wartime rise in costs and by comparison with civilian pay rates which had risen by about 80 per cent. By the time of the Armistice, those who continued to serve at these rates were simmering with resentment and discontent. In January 1919 committees were set up to review pay rates, whilst representatives of the aggrieved lower deck held their own pay discussions with newspaper reporters present. This latter development no doubt played its part in the government's decision to award a large interim increase before its committees had even reported. Ultimately able seamen were awarded an increase to 4s. a day with comparable rises for other ranks and similar improvements to allowances and pensions. 'An old scandal, which lay heavily on the nation, has at last been removed', declared the *Daily Telegraph* soberly. Officers did not fare quite so well and still did not receive marriage allowance, already granted to the other services. Even these increases, however, were not introduced fully until May. The recommendation that they should be backdated to October 1918 was rejected. The discontent rumbled on.[24]

Added to this long-standing injustice was the retention in the Royal Navy of the demobilisation scheme which had caused such resentment in the army and which Churchill quickly changed: the release first of those men with civilian skills which were needed to revitalise industry, often those who had served the shortest time. The deeply-detested 'last in, first out' effect of this policy was itself a sufficient cause of serious trouble. The navy, in any event, had great problems in arranging demobilisation, with its need to keep its post-war fleets fully manned whilst attempting to demobilise the 'hostilities only' men who often represented 80 per cent of a ship's crew. Then there were the difficulties of the Baltic watch itself. Service in the Gulf of Finland was hard: the winter cold was severe, the daylight was limited, and the comforts and diversions were few. The island anchorage at Biorko Sound was not a proper base with decent facilities, and the distribution of cigarettes, provisions and other canteen comforts was often faulty. There was much resentment that, despite their evidently arduous service, the men were not receiving the extra pay being issued to their colleagues, army and navy, who were fighting at Archangel and Murmansk, or even to the Merchant Navy operating in the Baltic. Then again, there was some disappointment at the absence of active 'scrapping' which some of the officers had expected when they volunteered for the Baltic service.

The result of these grievances was perhaps inevitable: mutiny. It was, however, mutiny at the milder end of the scale of the offence, on a par with the 'soldiers' strikes' on home soil of some months earlier. The First Destroyer Flotilla, returning to port from the Baltic for leave in August 1919, was declared by Admiral Cowan to be 'a model of discipline and cheerful high war spirits'; yet when the men returned for duty in October, and learnt that they were about to return to the Baltic, 150 broke out of their ships, leaving half the flotilla to have its crews made up from the Atlantic Fleet. Though most of the men soon gave themselves up or were arrested locally, forty-four made their way to London to present a petition to the authorities. They were arrested at King's Cross without much difficulty and taken off to Chatham. By late November, ninety-six men had been arrested and punished, ten by sentences of imprisonment. A second mutiny occurred on the aircraft carrier *Vindictive* at Copenhagen in November, when about forty men initially refused duty, although those who persisted with their disobedience were many fewer. The same month the 'hostilities only' crews of the minesweepers in the Baltic also refused duty, having reached the end of the year for which they had volunteered at the time of the Armistice, and because they were involved in hostilities, which they had been promised they would not be. They had a very reasonable case. Finally, there was a mutiny on Admiral Cowan's own flagship, the light cruiser *Delhi*. In this case the unpopularity of the ship's captain added to the list of local grievances. The final straw had been Cowan's order for the ship to proceed direct to Biorko, when the men had been led to expect that they would spend Christmas at Reval. One of the *Delhi*'s officers recalls the crew's response: 'Even the most loyal among the ship's company felt that this was "a bit 'ard." No Christmas shopping, no run ashore, nothing but an immediate return to bloody Biorko. So when the Commander ordered, "Both watches prepare for sea", the response was very poor; only about 25 per cent of the ship's company obeyed the bugle.'[25] Discipline was finally restored and off to Biorko they went.

There seems little doubt that the navy-wide grievances provided the necessary background, and the arduous circumstances of service on the Baltic station the immediate causes, for this rash of mutinies. Did Admiral Cowan himself bear any responsibility? The pocket-sized admiral was a strict disciplinarian; a field sports enthusiast when ashore, once at sea his concern with his operational responsibilities seemed to crowd out much else. Looking back at the end of a full career he was to write, 'When I commanded a squadron I made the mistake of expecting too high a standard of discipline'. It is indeed the case that he had discipline problems aboard ship before his time in the Baltic and after it. No doubt his hard-driving approach did play some part in exacerbating the unrest. He considered Baltic service sufficiently arduous, however, to justify extra pay and additional leave and had represented this view to higher authority, but whether early enough or with sufficient force is another matter.[26]

The ultimate responsibility for the unrest surely lies with the government for its failure to accord to what was essentially war service in the Baltic the same status as regards special pay, allowances and other concessions as was granted in the other theatres of the intervention. If the nation was, as Lloyd George finally admitted, 'at war' with the Bolsheviks, this surely applied as much to the Baltic theatre as to any other. Distaste for the idea of fighting an opponent with whom we were not formally at war no doubt played its part in the men's thinking when they refused duty. It had certainly caused considerable anxiety and frustration among their commanders as well as within the Admiralty. Some sailors could no doubt see that there was something a little more noble in supporting the Baltic republics' struggle for independence, than in other, rather grubbier, aspects of the intervention, but this was no reason for the government to treat the Baltic service as though it consisted of nothing more than none-too-exacting naval manoeuvres.

That the Baltic naval operations were considerable, costly and fraught with the risks that come with fighting a war is evident from the statistics. Up until June 1919 the Royal Navy had a daily average of twenty-nine warships and auxiliaries employed in the Baltic, and from July onwards this rose to an average of eighty-eight. This was a huge drain on naval resources and a costly venture for the impoverished nation to support. It was also very evident to all who took part that this was dangerous war service. A total of seventeen ships (including a light cruiser, two destroyers and a submarine) were lost to enemy action, mining and the stress of weather, with a further sixty-one damaged by mining, grounding, collision and the like, to the extent that they were unable, at least temporarily, to continue operations. One of the stricken ships had been the *Curacoa*, to which Cowan had transferred his flag only days before, only to have it mined beneath him while it was steaming fast in open seas. Several men were killed and numerous wounded. Another was a badly needed supply vessel bound for Selskar, but sunk instead, which reduced the crews based there to depending for a period on the indigent islanders for their victuals. A third was the submarine, sunk with its entire crew by a Bolshevik destroyer. In all thirty-three officers and 164 men became casualties in the campaign, 128 of them killed. Churchill was correct to claim, in regard to the Baltic effort, that we had kept 'anything from thirty to fifty thousand Bolsheviks' on the Petrograd front and away from Denikin, but it was absurd to suggest, as he did, that this was at practically no cost 'beyond one or two shipments of munitions'.[27]

16

Collapse

Captain Brian Horrocks viewed the approach of the first intake of Russian recruits joining the Anglo-Russian Brigade with mounting dismay: 'In front came the extremely smart band and drums of the Hampshire regiment followed by the filthiest and most unkempt mass of humanity I have ever seen in my life.' His suspicion was that the new brigade had been allocated the dregs from all the call-up depots in Siberia. Horrocks, later a notable lieutenant general and corps commander in the Second World War, had spent most of the First as a prisoner of the Germans after being wounded and captured at Ypres. Much of his incarceration had been spent with Russian prisoners and he had acquired a working knowledge of their language. This was to stand him in good stead when he volunteered for General Knox's Mission, which was very short of Russian speakers. His misgivings about the attitude of the Russians towards the new Anglo-Russian Brigade proved well founded: the civil authorities in Ekaterinburg were deliberately obstructive; the brigade's staff had to fight for everything they needed, even water, food and transport. The problems had started with accommodation, when the brigade was allocated a large block of what Sergeant Jupe described as 'dilapidated, rat-infested Russian barracks'. A couple of days later the recruits arrived, 750 on the first day and a thousand on the second. 'The first thing we have to do is wash them', the Hampshires' Colonel Johnson wrote to his wife, 'they are perfectly filthy and crawling with vermin – then entirely reclothe [them] from head to foot and burn their personal rags'. Despite these inauspicious preliminaries, Johnson remained optimistic as he set about his role in training the new recruits, 'It is up to us to set an example to these poor helpless Russians and show what just a handful of British can do'. The principle was a simple one, the same as had been applied in Archangel with the SBL: that firm but fair discipline, well-organised training and sensible man management would turn this ill-kempt mob into a loyal and effective fighting force. Captain Horrocks was soon transferred to the brigade's NCO School where the philosophy seemed to be working. 'As soon as they realised that we were doing our best to look after them,' he wrote later, 'to see that their food was properly cooked, that they really got their tobacco ration, and that they were paid regularly, they became very devoted.' Sergeant Jupe, however, took a broader view, 'We kept at it for some months … and it is possible they might have become a respectable force, though whether or not they had any belief in their cause, we had no idea'.[1]

The training continued at Ekaterinburg, and the other training centres, against a background of continuing difficulties with the Russian authorities. Sometimes these concerned training matters, as at Irkutsk, where the Russian programme for machine gun training consisted of eighty hours in the lecture room and only four hours of practical instruction, until the British took over; or at Tomsk, where the small British instructional staff found themselves responsible for building the range and other training facilities, besides clearing piles of manure from inside the training blocks. In all the training establishments there were too few British NCOs and many officers who were too young and inexperienced for their difficult role. As in south Russia all the officer training staff were promoted to the rank of captain and all the NCOs to sergeant, irrespective of their experience. The mission itself was similarly placed. 'Take our case', wrote Captain Savory at Vladivostok, 'we are carrying on with less than half the men we require to run a big show like this. We call for volunteers from home and get none, but officers, and it is very hard on the few men who are out here.' Everywhere there was a shortage of interpreters and training staff who spoke any Russian at all. General Gaida had promised interpreters for Ekaterinburg, but none ever arrived. Colonel Ward of the Middlesex commented that 'It was truly a stroke of genius for our War Office to flood us with officers and men as instructors for the new Russian army, scarcely one of whom could speak a word of Russian'. A further factor militating against efficiency and encouraging corruption was the practice, already much criticised in south Russia, of service pay being issued in local currency at rates which took little account of the rapid inflation of the rouble. Ward makes the point succinctly, 'It is not very satisfactory to receive your rouble at 6d. and spend it a 1d.' In Siberia the system seemed to apply to officers as well as other ranks, leaving, in Ward's somewhat exaggerated words, 'officers at the front in a state of poverty not one whit better than the people whose all had been destroyed by the Revolution'. The British servicemen at least received their food, clothing and accommodation free of charge; but the pay issue was, nonetheless, a serious shortcoming in their conditions of service.[2]

No doubt this factor played a part in the trouble Colonel Johnson was having with some of his men, not apparently his original territorials, but conscripts who had joined the battalion just before it left India. He also felt that his nine years in command had taken their toll and that he had lost some of his 'edge'. Some pilfering of government stores had been discovered and he had to take strong disciplinary action. 'As a result there was very nearly a mutiny incited by the draft men.' It seems that about a dozen men broke out of barracks, but returned soon after. 'It was touch and go for a short while', Johnson confessed, 'but we succeeded in averting anything really serious – about a dozen poor fools who have been severely punished.' The conscripts were in the same position as their fellows in North Russia: impressed for the war against Germany, but now involved in an undeclared war between different groups of their former allies. The conscripts, no doubt all private soldiers, would not have had any role in training the Russians. Johnson confessed that one of his great problems was keeping the men occupied. Amateur dramatics, ice skating and amateur boxing were all introduced successfully, but they did not solve the pay problem or answer the basic question in the minds of the conscripts: why they were there.[3]

That the Bolsheviks should so easily have lost the Urals, the only significant mountain barrier between their capital and the advancing Siberian forces, allowing the Whites access to the rich and populous steppe country to the west, was a matter of great concern to them. Futhermore, they already knew of the Allied deliberations concerning the recognition of Kolchak's regime. Trotsky feared that, once recognition took place, the Allies would 'go on and on' and flood Siberia with arms and men. The way to prevent this, he believed, was to treat the Eastern Front as the important one. The Red Army would assume the offensive, he declared, 'since any hesitation, let alone withdrawal on our part of the Eastern Front would create conditions favourable to the recognition of Kolchak'. Special levies drawn from the Communist Party itself and from the trade unions which it controlled were despatched to the threatened front; ultimately twenty-two provinces sent detachments to the four concentration points behind the Red front line, three of them opposite White General Khanzin's army in the centre. The Novgorod Provincial Committee mobilised half its members (imagine Kolchak's overstuffed *Stavka* doing this!); Penza provided a regiment of shock troops. All along the line the Reds were readying their move.

On 26 April Churchill told the Prime Minister that 'The advance of Kolchak's armies is the more remarkable in view of the fact that it is being conducted exclusively with Russian troops'. He explained that 'The whole credit of regaining this really enormous stretch of country rests with a purely Russian army of about 100,000 men', and went on to assure Lloyd George that there was another Russian army of 100,000 'in an advanced state of formation in Siberia, and five divisions from this army are expected to reach Admiral Kolchak during the course of the next three months'. In fact, the luxury of three months' preparation was not to be available to them; it was just three days later that the Bolshevik Commander-in-Chief Vatzetis's armies launched their blow. They struck in strength at the left flank of General Khanzin's thinly-spread army and broke through, whereupon a regiment of Ukrainian troops holding Khanzin's right flank seized their opportunity: they killed their officers and deserted, complete with their British uniforms, weapons and equipment. Red troops poured through the gap. Further north, General Gaida continued with his advance towards Glazov, midway between Perm and Viatka, perhaps believing that Khanzin's army would regroup behind the River Belaya and hold Ufa. It did not; Ufa, the starting-point of the earlier White offensive, fell to the Reds on 9 June. The extent to which Churchill was misreading the character of the Kolchak regime and basing his judgements on outdated information is made plain by his messages to Lloyd George at the time. On 5 May he was recommending that Kolchak's 'Omsk Government should at once be recognised as the National Provisional Government of all Russia'; on 7th, a week into the Red offensive, he was advising that, on the basis of Kolchak's advances, 'we have a tremendous chance of securing the future of Russia as a civilised democratic state'.[4]

Trotsky and Vatzetis favoured a halt after Ufa had fallen to them. A greater threat was developing from Denikin in South Russia and Kolchak's reserves had yet to be brought into play; little did they know that he had virtually none. Lenin, however, insisted that the Ural territory was the vital theatre and that the offensive should continue.This precipitated a major crisis in the Soviet High Command; Vatzetis resigned and Trotsky was only with difficulty dissuaded from doing the same. A new commander, Kamenev, was appointed and the eastern offensive went on, now veering towards the north east, threatening to cut off Gaida's army from its supplies. Gaida was forced to withdraw, and his army's retreat rapidly turned into a disorderly rout as the Reds took the railway towns of Perm and Kungur. All hopes of a junction with Ironside, whose reinforcements were now readying their own offensive, disappeared. Two subordinate attacks were also made in the centre and south of the line. After a series of defeats, the White Southern Army was finally caught between the Red forces moving directly eastwards and another group moving northwards from Turkestan. It was forced to surrender, thus putting paid to all hopes of the other anticipated strategic junction, that between Kolchak and Denikin. By the end of June the Bolsheviks were within sight of the foothills of the Urals. In these early defeats the Whites lost great quantities of equipment which had been sent to the front but which, General Knox reported, the staffs 'had failed to distribute though the troops were starving and naked'.

Part way through the Red offensive, Churchill had the bright idea of trying to persuade the Czechs to re-enter the fray by offering 'to repatriate them all, or as many of them as care to go, via Archangel before the winter ice closes in in November ... provided that they for their part will cut their way through as a definite part of the operations which are contemplated to secure the junction between Kolchak's right wing and the Archangel force'. His idea was that the Czechs, in conjunction with the Anglo-Russian Brigade, would initially bolster the right flank of the White forces and then push on to Viatka. This notion took little account of how opposed to the Kolchak regime the Czech political leaders had become, and of how hostile and unruly the Legion's troops now were. Besides, the idea was already being outpaced by events. The other potential reinforcement, the Anglo-Russian Brigade, was having its own troubles. Whatever regard Kolchak and Gaida might have had for it, the White officers in general were jealous of the brigade; they resented this attempt by the British to create a Russian army in their own mould. Captain Horrocks declared that 'every conceivable difficulty was put in our way' and that 'the better the brigade became the more the Russian officers came to hate us'. Its recruits were openly criticised in the streets for saluting in the British fashion and for serving under British officers. Its NCOs and soldiers were often beaten up. There were other problems. The idea that the brigade would go into action commanded by British staff from the mission and the Hampshires had to be abandoned owing to language difficulties and the dissatisfaction of the Hampshire NCOs with their terms of service. There were also concerns about going into action while having to rely on the incompetent Russian battlefield administrative system. In the event, the possibility was never put to the test. The advance of the Bolsheviks was now threatening Ekaterinburg, which gave the Russian officers, who, in General Knox's view, 'hated to see our fellows making a success of what they had so conspicuously failed at', the opportunity to break up the brigade and use its men as drafts for the front. That Knox should subsequently have discussed with Kolchak the idea of raising a fresh Anglo-Russian Brigade on Russian Island at Vladivostok, rather than at Omsk where he 'would not be able to fight intrigue and propaganda ... under present conditions', is eloquent of the great gulf in understanding between the British and the bulk of Kolchak's officers, whom the British were doing their best to support.[5]

The Red offensive continued, principally along the two branches of the Trans-Siberian Railway leading, in the case of the northern branch, to Perm and Ekaterinburg, and of the southern, to Chelyabinsk, beyond the Urals. Perm fell on 3 July and on the 14th the victorious Red troops occupied Ekaterinburg, the capital of the Ural territory. The Hampshires had quit the place a few days earlier. A British training officer who remained a little longer, artillery Lieutenant Colonel Steel, remarked, 'The departure of the Hampshire Regiment from here has been the signal for a general exodus, and a stream of carts pours down to the station all day and night ... any night now the whole [Russian] staff may disappear without saying a word to anyone. So we are all on the *qui vivre* [sic] ... The Russian Army is simply trekking backwards because they've started and no one can stop them'. Brigadier General Jack, head of the Railway Section of the Mission, was living in his carriage on the railway at Ekaterinburg, doing his best to organise the trains, and with steam up ready for a quick departure. Steel wrote of him, 'General Jack managed to get nearly everything away from Yekaterinburg [sic] before the Bolsheviks took possession – a great feat as the Russians were quite off their heads. Train after train went out with nothing but officers and women and the whole Siberian Army has disappeared for the time being'.[6]

After this series of defeats Kolchak decided to dismiss Gaida. He accused the Czech of 'excessive ambition', suspected him of left-wing views, and in a fit of rage sent him back to Vladivostok. Gaida was replaced by General Dieterichs, a veteran Tsarist staff officer, but the real influence on Kolchak remained the confident and optimistic but incompetent Lebedev. The nominal Allied Commander-in-Chief, General Janin, had earlier advised that a general defence system should be prepared, based on Ekaterinburg and Chelyabinsk, but nothing had been done to get it ready. Lebedev persuaded Kolchak to allow the Reds to take Chelyabinsk, so that he might outflank them from high ground to the west, cut them off and destroy them. In accepting this over-ambitious proposal, Kolchak may have been influenced by the fact that the US Ambassador to Japan was visiting at the time – a result of the Allied decision in Paris to support, but not to recognise, Kolchak. In any event, the complex plan, incapable of execution by half-trained and ill-supplied levies, failed utterly, while absorbing Kolchak's only reserves. Altogether the Whites lost 15,000 men in this action, the climax to the loss of the whole of the Ural industrial region. Kolchak was now left with only Asian Russia: the vastness of Siberia.

The two branches of the Trans-Siberian Railway followed separate but converging courses over the 500 miles which lie between the Ural mountains and the city of Omsk, where they joined to form the single line running on for thousands of miles across Siberia to Vladivostok. Omsk, the base of Kolchak and his *Stavka*, was also the major city of western Siberia and a crucial railway artery for the whole region. Three great rivers, the Tobol, the Ishim and the Irtish, all flowing south–north, crossed the plain between the Urals and Omsk, each offering a natural line of defence. Dieterichs pulled the remnants of his forces back behind the Tobol, reformed them into three 'armies', though none truly merited the title, and then conducted a more orderly withdrawal to the River Ishim, where a defensive line was established. Many of the men recruited from the western steppes had long since melted away from the White ranks; they had been offered no realistic training, they were short of supplies and were being driven far from their homelands. The White rear areas were becoming a seething mass of discontent and deprivation. Civilian railway traffic, on which Siberia depended, was disrupted by military demands. Horses were requisitioned and young men conscripted at the very time they were needed on the land. There were brutal reprisals if the requirements of the military were not met. Ataman Krasilnikov, leader of the coup which had brought Kolchak to power, 'is completely inactive,' a report to the *Stavka* declared, and 'devotes himself exclusively to drinking and disorderly conduct'. His officers were the same; meanwhile his soldiers looted, robbed and raped. 'The whole population is eager for Bolshevism', the report concluded. Bolshevik guerrilla bands provided a further disruption. In early June, Captain Savory, a staff officer organising the despatch of supplies from Vladivostok, complained, 'The Bolsheviks keep on raiding the railway line … one of the horse trains I sent up country recently lost 2 killed, 68 wounded, 18 horses killed and 18 trucks smashed'. He noted that 'another playful trick' of the Reds was to put sand in the axle-boxes of the trucks so that the axles became red hot and the trucks caught fire. At the end of May, in Vladivostok itself, Bosheviks managed to set fire to a large shed of American YMCA stores, gutting the place.[7]

As late as mid-June 1919, the War Office's optimism about the Siberian situation remained unshaken. It commented on reports from Siberia that it was 'difficult to believe situation is so black as depicted [by General Knox] since Denikin is doing well and the internal situation of the Bolsheviks is bad'. That view might have been correct about Denikin, but it was quite wrong about Siberia and the Bolsheviks. By early July, Knox was reporting grimly, 'Russian Command have ... proved so incompetent that it is difficult to recommend supplying them with any more material unless the Allies are guaranteed effective control of operations'. He already knew that such control was impossible; he had not even managed to control recruit training, even that of the Anglo-Russian Brigade. The dismissed Gaida had told him that 'the *Stavka* had all through been against the Anglo-Russian unit' and had twice given him secret orders to draft it into other regiments. He added the telling judgement that 'the Bolshevik direction of operations is far superior to ours now, and they have some units that fight with conviction while we have just at present none'. On the matter of supplies Churchill and the War Office soon agreed with General Knox: in future supplies were to be concentrated on Denikin, with a small quantity going to Yudenitch in North-West Russia. On 2 August Kolchak's *Stavka* had the gall to ask the Allies (effectively Britain) for 600,000 fresh sets of equipment. Knox told the Director of Military Operations that he had replied by saying that 'if I were to ask you for this after the scandalous misuse of the 200,000 we had already given, you would telegraph to me not to be "a damned fool"'.[8]

By this time, the Middlesex Regiment had already withdrawn from Omsk and the War Office had decreed that it and the Hampshires were to sail for home as soon as shipping became available. Only volunteers were to remain in Siberia after the summer. General Knox published the terms for volunteering which included generous additional leave at the end of the Russian service and substantial allowances to be paid locally in sterling or dollars; a great advance on the previous arrangement. Quite a number of the mission members volunteered but of the 1800 men of the two departing regiments only one officer and thirty-five other ranks came forward. Before Colonel Ward left Omsk, he took part in a special parade organised by the 2nd Siberian Cossack Regiment to thank him and his men for their help.Ward was invested as an honorary Ataman of the Siberian Cossacks and presented with their badge and a Cossack sword. Admiral Kolchak even took the trouble personally to visit Ward in his railway carriage and thank him for his services to the Russian cause. This very unusual Labour parliamentarian, the 'Navvies' MP' as he was known, then made his way back to London where he resolutely defended Churchill's Russian policy and the White cause generally on the floor of the House of Commons. All this despite knowing, as he subsequently recorded, that 'Russia has no ideas about labour at all … The officer class, that forms so large a proportion of Russian life, never gave the subject five minutes' consideration.'[9]

The return to England of Colonel Johnson of the Hampshires was more bizarre. His efforts to have his wife 'pull strings' in Westminster seem to have paid off. In early June a telegram arrived asking for his early release to take up an important civilian post. Johnson hesitated to leave his men, then still at Omsk, and put the matter, as only a Territorial could, to his sergeants for decision. They urged him to go. He left with twelve of his married soldiers who had priority for demobilisation. They went not by the orthodox route – rail to Vladivostok and then on by sea, but in an epic overland journey which achieved the feat which had eluded Gaida: they travelled to Archangel just before the Bolshevik advance closed off that possibility. In fact, the journey was largely by river: first a tributary of the Kama, then the Pechora, with many miles of trekking in between, and in the final stage, when their plans were almost frustrated, by the still ice-blocked Barents Sea. The Royal Navy finally picked up the party and took them round the coast to Archangel. Despite their remarkable and arduous odyssey, Johnson and his twelve men arrived home months before their battalion, for while they travelled across the empty spaces of northern Russia, the battalion was making its way eastwards to UK, first to Vladivostok, then across the Pacific to Vancouver, and finally across both North America and the Atlantic. The Hampshire Territorials had completed a full circuit of the globe by the time their war service ended and they arrived at Southampton on 5 December.[10]

The war was also now over for the Royal Marine detachment aboard their river boats, *Suffolk* and *Kent*. These had formed an important part of the Kama River Flotilla and rendered excellent service to the White cause until the Red advance on Perm drove them from the river. They bombarded Red troop concentrations, protected bridges with their fire while White units withdrew across them, provided direct fire support to army actions and took part in operations against the Bolshevik flotilla – in one action sinking the Red flotilla flagship and putting a second gunboat out of action. At Sarapul, already captured by the Bolsheviks, they helped keep the bridge free whilst the outflanked flotilla ran the gauntlet beneath it to make good its escape. One White naval officer, admiring the marines' gunnery, remarked, 'They used their guns like revolvers and it was a heartening sight'. The Bolshevik authorities were sufficiently impressed by the detachment's performance to issue a radio report stating that 'Our naval manoeuvres on the River Kama are being seriously hampered by the British destroyers'. Captain Jameson and his crews also saw at close hand the state of the retreating army. The *Suffolk*'s diary records seeing 'White troops in a filthy condition and their equipment in a deplorable state. The men seemed to be in anything resembling uniform and quite unfit to go into action.' Jameson wrote that 'It was hardly surprising that these conscripted and illiterate Siberian peasants, lacking both training and leaders, had little enthusiasm for the cause for which they were fighting. Their rations and clothing were inadequate to the point of destitution.' The detachment received particular thanks from Admiral Smirnov and numerous decorations from Admiral Kolchak. These, unfortunately, had to be returned at the orders of Sir George Eliot – since Britain 'supported' but had not 'recognised' Kolchak's regime – a distinction which those who had fought for it must have found difficult to understand. The detachment set numerous records. It advanced further westwards than any British unit in the Siberian campaign and, at 4350 miles, served further from its parent ship than any naval unit had done previously. Its little campaign also included the first occasion when a Russian admiral had flown his flag at the topmast of a British man-of-war, as Admiral Smirnov did for a time aboard the gunboat *Kent*.[11]

During August and September 1919, there was something of a pause in the Siberian war: the Whites were temporarily exhausted and the Bolsheviks were giving priority to dealing with Denikin, who had made such spectacular advances. Although the British Military Mission was to remain in theatre for some months yet, its main contribution to the White cause had already been made. At the beginning of August, General Knox's wrote from Omsk to the Director of Military Operations at the War Office: 'Our equipment effort is about drawing to an end. I hope to issue most of the stuff we have here within the next fortnight.' Back at Vladivostok, there were still some items of equipment, odds and ends left by the Canadians and ammunition which intended to go forward to dumps at Irkutsk and Krasnoyarsk. It had been a very significant contribution to the White cause, but much of it had been wasted by them, as Knox had made clear to Kolchak in a very blunt letter some weeks earlier. 'The situation at the front renders it necessary to write plainly', he warned the Supreme Commander. 'I hope you will remember that I am a soldier and not a diplomat and forgive my frankness.' He went on to list the aid Britain had supplied and his staff had struggled to deliver: 132 field guns, 58 light howitzers, 500,000 grenades, 170,257 Russian rifles and almost one and a half million round of small arms ammunition; adding that 'Since about the middle of December every round of rifle ammunition fired at the front has been of British manufacture, conveyed to Vladivostok in British ships and delivered at Omsk by British guards'. Then there were the 200,000 sets of uniform and equipment. Thirty thousand sets had been given to Kappel's corps. Kappel, able, enthusiastic and loyal, was one of the few Russian commanders for whom Knox had any respect. 'I consider it is my duty to inform you that in my opinion the material given to Kappel's corps has been wasted.' The expanded corps had been thrown into the fight in driblets, without training or discipline. Knox told Kolchak that 10,000 sets of British uniforms were now being worn by Bolsheviks: 'some so arrayed have already attacked our units south of Kama'. The mission had already equipped three newly-recruited divisions, 11th, 12th and 13th, and Knox was fearful that, if they were not allowed to complete their training, 'it will be the equivalent of handing over their rifles, uniforms and equipment to the enemy'. After this litany of complaints and criticisms, Knox went on to make suggestions for improving things. That his list should have included the recommendation that 'adequate arrangements sould be made at once to feed and pay the men regularly', and this to the commander who had the entire imperial gold reserve in his control, bespeaks the depth of incompetence and unprofessionalism in Kolchak's inflated *Stavka*. 'We want to help if we are allowed and to save time,' Knox's letter concluded, 'but we are only being made fools of'.[12]

This was but one of numerous letters Knox had written in similar vein to Kolchak and his subordinates over the months, all filled with good military sense and all to no avail. His efforts, however, did not prevent Churchill becoming disenchanted with Knox as the defeats mounted. He criticised his reports as being too concerned with political rather than operational matters, and as 'sloppy, piecemeal and amateurish productions' compared with one he had seen written by Janin. He believed Knox to be 'lacking in both military knowledge and mental force' and considered replacing him with 'a more adequate officer'. It was a harsh judgement. Apart from Churchill himself, there could have been no more committed anti-Bolshevik and supporter of Kolchak than Knox. But as *Chef de l'arrière* at Vladivostok, while Janin was nominal Commander-in-Chief at Omsk, Knox was bound to be less well versed in operational matters; training and supply were his responsibilities. For operational information he had to rely on Captain Steveni liaising at the Stavka. Steveni had good relations with the Russians and spoke the language well but felt he was being deliberately squeezed out because 'the Admiral does not altogether approve of giving our Mission the information'. Steveni was quite junior in rank; but then Lieutenant Colonel Nielson had been removed from his liaison post against Knox's wishes. Knox was a far from perfect operator, but as Brigadier General Jack noted, 'He is quite often wrong, is full of prejudices and flies off at tangents without much thought, but he works like a trojan, keeps in touch with everything and everybody and does his best to direct a most difficult situation on sound lines according to his lights'.[13]

Towards the end of September, Dieterichs had managed to rally his troops sufficiently to launch a counter-offensive. They drove forward from the River Ishin and pushed the Reds back along the railway and across the Tobol river. It proved to be a desperate last success, short-lived because of shortage of supplies and reinforcements. By mid-October the Bolsheviks were on the march again, or rather on the armoured train, for this campaign was essentially a struggle for the railway. By the thirtieth they had retaken all the lost ground, while the demoralised White troops had lost all will to fight and ceased to be a significant factor in the way the campaign was developing. General Dieterichs, now Chief of Staff after the sacking of the useless Lebedev, ordered the evacuation of Omsk, the Siberian capital. Kolchak challenged the decision and replaced Dieterichs with another young incompetent, Sakharov, who cancelled the order. Two days later he changed his mind: the River Irtish had suddenly frozen over, allowing his troops across to the city, but ending its protection from the advancing Reds. Troops and refugees streamed eastward, demoralised and fearful of Boshevik retribution. As one mission member put it, it was 'Just a thoroughly demoralised army legging it, for all it is worth'. The sight of the *trains de luxe* waiting with steam up to carry away the Allied Missions cannot have helped morale. Thereafter the thousand-mile retreat to Lake Baikal in the depths of the Siberian winter was less a campaign than a horror story. Both 'up' and 'down' lines of the railway were now crammed with eastbound traffic; even then blockages, sabotage and the icy cold caused stoppages lasting several days. Many of the troops of the Siberian Army and thousands of refugees had no choice, despite the bitter Siberian winter, but to make their flight on foot along the track which ran parallel to the railway.

Before Omsk was evacuated, however, a crisis developed in the British Military Mission between its Omsk and Vladivostok elements. The complex and unstable Siberian political situation was never an easy one for the military decision-makers to read and react to. It had become complicated by the worsening military state of affairs, Kolchak's growing unpopularity, and fact that the High Commissioner at Vladivostok, Sir Charles Eliot, had left to become Ambassador to Japan. Kolchak had little formal control in Vladivostok, though he had a garrison there. The Japanese, however, had 30,000 troops in the town which, though largely anti-Bolshevik, was increasingly anti-Kolchak. General Gaida was also in the town, stripped not only of his appointment but also of his rank, personally bitter, increasingly angry at Kolchak's reactionary rule and certainly more popular locally than the admiral. He had made peace with his fellow Czechs, who were also in the town in some strength. There was a strong left-wing but non-Bolshevik grouping in the town supported by the local workers and led by one Yakushev. When Gaida and Yakushev's group met, plotting began for the overthrow of Kolchak's dictatorship. General Knox had moved to Omsk, where there was a newly-appointed consul, Mr Hodgson. At Vladivostok was the new acting High Commissioner Mr O'Reilly and Brigadier General Blair, in charge of the British contingent training the Russian young officers and NCOs on Russian Island in Vladivostok Bay. The British leaders were in touch with all the parties, Gaida, Yakushev and Colonel Butenko, the commander of the Vladivostok garrison. Gaida told Blair that he had hitherto been totally loyal to Kolchak but now intended to do all in his power to overthrow him and his government. The telegrams flew between Vladivostok, London and Omsk. With the battalion of Hampshires still available, what was Blair to do in the event of a rising in Vladivostok? What role should he allow the Russian trainees to play? O'Reilly was sympathetic with the plotters, believing they had Czech and American support and a better chance than Kolchak's regime of keeping the people out of the arms of the Bolsheviks. Blair's view was that both the British and their trainees should remain neutral in the event of a rising.

When General Knox heard of Blair's views he was outraged. He ordered him to put the Russian trainees at the disposal of the Kolchak authorities and to urge the Allied Military Council at Vladivostok to employ the British battalion similarly. In fact the Council proved rather more sympathetic to the plotters, since the regime's reaction to the unrest was to make use of Kalmykov's brutal Cossack squadrons. Knox finally removed Blair from his command. It was an unfortunate end to Blair's fine record as a trainer in the difficult circumstances of Siberia. The Gaida-led coup at Vladivostok took place on 17 November with the insurgents capturing the railway station, the terminus of the Trans-Siberian line, by evening. Warrant Officer Ivens, a member of the Railway Mission in Vladivostok, witnessed the rising and made clear where his sympathies lay, the Social Revolutionary Party behind the coup attempt representing, in his view, 'the nearest approach to the common English people that it is possible to find in Russia ... clamouring for Parliamentary Government as against the present dictatorship of Admiral Koltchack [sic]'. The following day, a counter-attack, strongly supported by the Japanese, put an end to the attempted revolution. Ivens attempted to sum it all up: 'both government troops and insurgents were wearing British clothing and boots and firing British ammunition out of American rifles and Canadian machine guns ... There you have in a nutshell the result of Allied "help" to Russia.'[14]

Before his own departure back to Vladivostok, Knox had ordered several young officers to remain based at Omsk to liaise with the retreating Siberian Army and send back daily reports. Captain Horrocks was one; another was a Captain Hayes (also to become a general in the Second War). These young men were able to see at first hand the progressive collapse of the Whites. 'The trouble was', wrote Horrocks, 'that as soon as a White Russian battalion arrived at the front – having been trained and equipped by us – it almost invariably deserted *en bloc* to the Red workers' paradise on the other side of the lines.' They also saw some of the agonies of the winter retreat from Omsk, which they left on one of the last trains to quit the city. To the cold, hunger, frostbite and discomfort which the troops had to endure were added the horrors of typhus, whose death rate was over 10 per cent in the last stages of the retreat. At Tiaga, 150 miles east of Omsk, Czechs, Poles and Russians were fighting for the control of engines.

It was at this town that Horrocks received the message, 'If the situation seems to warrant it, do not hesitate to take complete control'. Horrocks's response was that 'It would have taken a well trained British division to enable this to happen'. Many of the railway stations along the line were turned into emergency hospitals, each with a pile of frozen corpses nearby: the bodies of those who had succumbed to the disease. There were reported to be 30,000 cases of typhus in Krasnoyarsk alone. This railway town was as far as the young liaison officers got, for there a Bolshevik formation cut across the line ahead of them and they became prisoners, in the case of Horrocks for the second time. This unfortunate officer also had the misfortune to contract typhus in the desperately crowded town. He was not released from captivity until October the following year, at the Finnish border.[15]

Kolchak left Omsk on 14 November, some hours before the Bolsheviks occupied the city, but it was not until 15 January, after numerous delays, some lasting several days, that his train reached Glazov, still some miles short of Irkutsk where, some years earlier, he had been married. There, after weeks of confusing diplomacy between the Allied High Commissioners, General Janin, the Czechs who were guarding Kolchak, and the anti-Kolchak factions along the line who were now powerful and threatening, the decision was taken to hand Kolchak over to the newly established Irkutsk government. This happened at a siding in Irkutsk station where the admiral's Czech guard was withdrawn. Kolchak's incarceration, extended interrogation and execution at Bolshevik hands soon followed. The key decisions in surrendering Kolchak were taken by General Janin and General Syrovy, the Czech commander. Whether their action was necessary is very much open to debate. Surrendered with the admiral was the Russian imperial treasure his train was carrying. This consisted of gold bricks to the value, at the time, of sixty-five million pounds: a welcome present for the Bolsheviks. This was very considerably more than the cost of all the aid that Britain had supplied to Siberia throughout the intervention, and which seventy-nine ships had sailed half way around the world to Vladivostok to deliver.[16]

After the collapse of the Kolchak regime, conditions in easern Siberia dissolved into near anarchy from which a Far Eastern Republic, democratic, non-Bolshevik but radical, began steadily to assert its authority over much of the region. The Bolsheviks were content to let this state of affairs exist until, in 1923, they were secure and powerful enough to extinguish it and incorporate this huge area into the Soviet empire. When the DMO came to write his covering summary to General Knox's final report, he attributed the failure of the White cause in Siberia principally to 'the innate rottenness of the Russian officers and officials themselves'. He also criticisd the 'jealous stupid opposition to any professional ideas by all but a few rare patriots' among the Whites. Besides these failings it seems invidious to add the inability of the Allies to agree a policy for the theatre or to provide it with any substantial measure of economic assistance. The two British battalions there and the mission itself had done their best, but, as General Knox explained, 'The British Mission was never allowed to organise. It could only give advice and its advice was disregarded.'[17]

The events of early October 1919 seemed, to Churchill, to provide a complete vindication of the almost ten months of incessant and passionate effort that he had devoted to the anti-Bolshevik cause. Lloyd George had been opposed to Churchill's intervention policy all through, trimming his disapproval when domestic political circumstances demanded or the Whites armies were successful; as Churchill chided him in one exchange of views, 'you have had one policy in your heart and have carried out another'. The Cabinet members were growing tepid or indifferent to the White cause, with Lord Curzon, though very much an anti-Bolshevik, wearying of it to the point of declaring, 'We shall never satisfy WO [the War Office]. Anyone who does not bend the knee to Denikin and Kolchak is looked upon as a double-dyed traitor.' The Commons were still generally supportive, except for some Labour members and the ever-combative 'Three Musketeers', Kenworthy, Malone and Wedgwood. The right-wing press was broadly sympathetic, but the left-wing papers were whipping up popular opposition to Churchill's policy, with Max Aitken's independent *Express* papers also a constant irritant. Their recent exploitation of Sherwood Kelly's revelations had become more than an embarrassment; it was now playing a role in massing Trade Union opinion against the Secretary of State's interventionism.

Churchill's policies, however, were now being sustained by substantial successes on the battlefields. In mid-October, Kolchak's armies, though evidently in retreat, were still masters of huge tracts of territory and, Churchill believed, reserves were in training to support them. Churchill had written personally to the Supreme Commander, in a letter whose implicit personal recognition of Kolchak's regime infuriated Lloyd George, rejoicing 'beyond words that the supreme effort of Your Excellency's Army has at last been attended with so great a measure of success'. All this had been achieved by the Russians alone, Churchill emphasised to Lloyd George; the British battalions were on their way home, only a mission of 500 men remained in Siberia. The same was true of North Russia, from which, by 15 October, all British troops had been withdrawn. Yet 'the Russians left behind', Churchill emphasised, 'are holding their own well both at Archangel and at Murmansk'. In the north west Yudenitch's offensive had taken his army to within thirty miles of its Petrograd objective, a feat for which Churchill again wrote personally to congratulate the commander. There, however, British ships and tanks were a powerful support for quite the worst of the White Armies. It was in south Russia, now the coping stone of Churchill's strategy, that the greatest measure of success was being achieved. There Denikin had reached Orel, ready for his drive on Moscow. His armies controlled regions holding thirty-five million European Russians, including the country's third, fourth and fifth largest cities. By the time Orel fell to him, Denikin had taken a quarter of a million prisoners, 700 guns, 1700 machine guns and thirty-five armoured trains. British supplies were pouring into the port of Novorossisk; indeed, Churchill had just secured Cabinet approval for a 'final packet' of supplies for Denikin valued, he told the Russian, 'at fourteen and a half million pounds sterling including shipping charges'. On 18 October, in a private letter to the CIGS, General Holman, the mission commander, declared, with quite inappropriate precision, that he hoped to see Denikin in Moscow by 15 January 1920. Against such a background of success, Churchill was tempted to believe that, despite domestic misgivings and mounting opposition, ultimate victory for the Whites was on the horizon. As the south Russian offensive surged to its peak, he wrote optimistically to Lord Curzon, 'Out of all this Russian tangle it is, I think, possible to see very definite decisions emerging. The Bolsheviks are falling and perhaps the end is not distant. Not only their system but their regime is doomed.'[18]

Within a month of penning these words Churchill was witnessing the cracks in his strategy turn into great fissures, and the entire edifice begin to crumble. On 14 November Yudenitch was back at the start point of his brief, chaotic offensive, his army in total disarray. Trotsky had managed to beat off the threat to the old capital without even needing to divert troops from any of his other threatened fronts. On the same day, Omsk fell to the Bolsheviks and the long and horrific retreat of Kolchak and his disintegrating Siberian Army began. Further north, General Miller's Archangel Command was relatively quiet, the Whites even making small though insignificant gains; but the Bolshevik High Command had little interest in this unimportant sideshow now that the British had left. It could be reoccupied at leisure, if it did not implode first.

In the south, however, the really significant changes were taking place. A week after taking Orel, the Whites lost it again. They were driven out by a Bolshevik offensive which did not pause until the White forces had been driven far south behind the line of the River Don. The Red successes were now every bit as spectacular as Denikin's had been. In the early stages, the Volunteer Army resisted stubbornly; this strange mixture of officers serving in the ranks, young cadets from the military colleges and loyal NCOs from the old army was not easily pushed aside. But in the triangle of territory between Orel, Kursk and Voronezh it was effectively destroyed. The Red reserve of shock troops was instrumental in forcing the Whites to quit Orel, whilst further south east Budenny's Red cavalry routed Mamontov's, together with his Kuban horsemen. Voronezh fell and within a few days Kursk as well. Denikin dismissed General Mai-Mayevsky as commander of the Volunteer Army and replaced him with the abler Baron Wrangel from the Caucasian Army, but the change came too late and, while necessary, was not popular with the troops. Before Wrangel could take up his new command, Kharkov had fallen. The British training school there had been hastily dismantled and the instructor sergeants sent back down the line. Captain Woods, who had helped set up the school, spent the next three months on reconaissance duties and in a struggle to get stores back to the base at Taganrog. He and his colleague lived off bully beef and biscuits and spent the cold nights sleeping folded in Cossack *bourkas*. The subsequent dismissal of Mamontov, the Don Cossack cavalry commander, also served to alienate many of his men. With both infantry and cavalry broken, the Volunteer Army streamed back in disorder. After the fall of Kursk there was no serious resistance until Denikin's men reached the Don at Rostov, almost 300 miles to the rear.

The reasons for these rapid reverses are not hard to find. Denikin's armies were seriously overextended, without any reserves and much diluted by unwilling and unreliable conscripts. Unrest and discontent behind the front forced Denikin to withdraw troops from the forward areas to re-establish control. There was also the ever-present inefficiency and corruption of his military administration, which left units short of supplies and the wherewithal to continue fighting. In allowing pillage and orgies, as the drunken Mai-Mayevsky had done, popular discontent grew as his soldiers' morale declined. Denikin's 'Great Russia' policy – the refusal to concede independence to any of the aspiring nations of the old empire – robbed him of much support. It meant, for example, that Roumania, hoping to retain Bessarabia, would offer him no assistance, while Poland's nationalist aspirations precluded what could have been valuable cooperation for the Russian leader. During the decisive months of the Bolsheviks' offensive the strong Polish armies observed a *de facto* armistice with them. It was a repeat of the situation in the Baltic: Yudenitch had only minimal support from the Estonians and none from the other Baltic states and Finland during his abortive offensive. The result was inevitable. 'The White troops are everywhere overpowered by force of numbers and superior strategy', declared Captain Kennedy from the British base at Taganrog.

These critical reverses, inevitably greatly telescoped in the account above, were not calculated to improve morale in the British Military Mission. In June, General Holman had attempted to improve its efficiency by purging his staff of some of its worst elements, but the replacements were not much better. 'Here one might almost be in London', commented Kennedy of the Mission Headquarters, 'The Mission has set up a sort of small War Office, and many more officers are arriving from England ... many of the officers in the mission are useless weeds. It would be an excellent thing if a clean sweep could be made of these latter. We ought to be represented abroad by specially picked men.' Despite the urgency, some of the replacements insisted on taking their full entitlement of post-war leave before they left England. Lieutenant Colonel Lister was one such;

appointed in October to one of the liaison groups attached to Denikin's army, he did not arrive in Constantinople until mid-December when the retreat was unstoppable. He travelled out with Brigadier General Percy who, very late in the day, was going out to be Holman's Chief of Staff. They travelled via the Crimea, where preparations were already being made to set up a British base. Lister was not impressed: 'A Colonel Chichester is in charge. I was not much struck by his officers; the drinking habit is evidently as pronounced here as it is in Odessa from all accounts. It looks as though our officers copy the Russians in their vices instead of shewing them an example. Drink and inefficiency are most marked.' This was a sad reflection on the expansion of the mission, whose objective had been to provide Denikin's force with a 'moral stiffening' and 'more tangible proof of support'. Lister moved on to the port of Novorossisk where he, too, was struck by the pay disadvantage which the British other ranks continued to suffer as rip-roaring inflation slashed the value of the rouble. Whilst, in late December, Lister was able to get 2300 roubles for a £1 note, the soldiers at the base were being paid in roubles at 400 to the £1. 'Naturally there is much discontent among the men', wrote Lister, 'who know that the officers' pay is credited in sterling … it is simply robbing the men of four-fifths of their pay.'[19]

As the retreat continued, General Holman spent more and more time at the front. As early as 22 October he and Maund, the mission's Air Commander, were up making bombing flights over the front. Holman indulged his small force of aviators and ensured that their mobile mess was well supplied with liquor, not the wisest policy since 47 Squadron was already something of a disciplinary problem for Maund. The unforgiving RE8 aircraft, however, despite being brand new, were continuing to demonstrate their unsuitability for the Russians. 'Accidents which have occurred within this country with RE8s', the Mission told the War Office, 'have shaken confidence of Russians in RE8s which I am convinced are not suitable for them and will serve no useful purpose in their hands ... It is perfectly clear to me that Russian pilots will not fly these planes in action.'[20] Holman seemed to wish to make up for any Russian shortcoming by his own actions and those of his troops. When a cavalry force was later assembled to defend Kharkov, Holman gave it a stiffening of his own men in tank and aircraft detachments for first-line repair and maintenance. Later still, when Rostov was threatened, he offered to take an armoured train there himself and blow the vital bridge across the Don. Early in the retreat, General Briggs, Holman's predecessor and now an adviser to Churchill on Russian matters, arrived in Taganrog and gave Holman details of the 'final packet' of British material assistance.

On 8 November, Prime Minister Lloyd George made a key speech at the Guildhall in London expressing his desire to cease British support for the Whites altogether and favouring a negotiated settlement of Russia's civil war. Acording to Captain Lever at Novorossisk, the speech offended Russians and English alike, 'the former because they are existing on our help and the latter because they fear losing their occupations'. Churchill's responded with a long and detailed Cabinet memorandum defending the decision to keep supplying Denikin and noting that with the onset of winter and denied the food, coal and oil of South Russia, 'the Bolsheviks will have great difficulties in living through it'. He laid out a plan of action, much of which involved stimulating the involvement of other states in the anti-Bolshevik struggle, but also recommending economic and political aid for Denikin. Now, at the eleventh hour, the proposal for a British High Commissioner for the region was finally agreed: something similar had been first suggested by Captain Blackwood almost a year earlier. Sir Halford Mackinder, a Unionist MP newly knighted for the purpose, stepped ashore at Novorossisk on 1 January 1920, much too late to be of any assistance to Denikin's ailing regime. This was also the day on which Taganrog was evacuated by Denikin's headquarters and the accompanying headquarters of the British Military Mission. Taganrog, the main base for the entire southern front and also the location of the important British tank training school, was abandoned amid scenes of chaos and confusion as troops, refugees and supplies poured through the town. The tank school did not reopen elsewhere.[21]

The list of British supplies which were abandoned at Taganrog occupies four pages of General Holman's final report: everything from aircraft and field artillery to stores of personal equipment had to be left behind. One officer commented, 'All stores reported looted first by our troops and then by civilians'. There had apparently been 'elaborate arrangements for the Christmas festivities' at Taganrog, despite the fact that the British advance party planned to leave the place on 26 December. Captain Lever, the Senior Wireless Officer, forced to abandon his precious wireless equipment in the mud alongside the railway, left the town in a cattle-truck with twenty-six of his fellow officers 'variously distributed over a mass of official despatch boxes, personal kit, Mess stores, food and cooking utensils, etc.' Much of the chaos resulted from the *sauve qui peut* attitude of the Whites, though some of the mission officers were inclined to blame their own chief. 'I cannot think why General Holman persists in staying up at the front when he is so urgently wanted here to settle big questions', wrote Captain Kenedy four days before the pull-out. Lieutenant Colonel Lister wrote at Ekaterinodar, 'I gather his [Holman's] presence at Taganrog might have made all the difference in our getting our various aeroplanes and ordnance stores away ... I don't think he appreciates always the real seriousness of the situation'. Apparently Holman had been having 'the hell of a time' for a fortnight with 2 Detachment RAF's bombing aircraft, whilst the Reds closed in on his headquarters.[22]

If the gravity of the situation escaped Holman, it was now very clear to both Denikin and the authorities in London. On 28 December, Sir Henry Wilson recorded, 'Poor Denikin wires to Winston to say he *must* have Allied troops to help him even "if only one or two Corps". Three days later Churchill was admitting to Wilson, 'There seems to be very little doubt of the complete victory of the Bolsheviks in the near future'. By 8 January Holman was wiring Churchill with his reasons for the great defeat, which included the view that Mackinder had arrived eight months too late. He said that he would do all in his power to keep things going, and that Denikin was 'full of courage and not shaken', but wanted a British assurance for the safety of his officers' wives and families. Halford Mackinder was able to give him this pledge, but little else; after a brief stay in the theatre Mackinder returned to England, 'highly disgusted' according to Captain Kennedy. His plan to provide broad economic, political and military support to Denikin was rejected by the Cabinet.[23]

Sir Henry Wilson was now becoming concerned about the safety of the mission itself. On 14 January he ordered General Milne from Constantinople to go directly to the mission, now with its headquarters and base at the port of Novorossisk, to assess the situation. Although Holman was able to persuade Milne that his men were in no immediate danger, the decision was soon taken that British support for Denikin was to come to an end. Holman was told that the Mission strength would be gradually reduced from 30 March and terminated altogether by 30 June. Meanwhile the retreat continued amid scenes of horrific distress. Colonel Lister described the state of Tikhoretskaia junction, an important railway artery on the line of retreat to the Kuban capital Ekaterinodar and Novorossisk: 'The station here is a pitiable spectacle. Filth, mud, pools of unspeakable water.' Eighteen thousand people were thronging the place, a third of them were deserters. 'Typhus and enteric are raging everywhere', he wrote. Holman seemed to attribute some of the chaos of the Taganrog withdrawal to his own mission members. He wrote what one of them described as 'a fierce insulting letter' addressed to 'all officers'. He accused them of 'dereliction of duty', but his scattergun approach was bitterly resented by those who were doing their level best in difficult circumstances. Brigadier General Cotton, the chief artillery officer in the mission was said to be demanding a court of inquiry over the letter's uncomplimentary terms. Captain Lever expressed his reaction very pointedly, 'Twould be better if the General stayed occasionally at the base and made some attempt at running his show instead of spending the whole of his time sculling about in an aeroplane at the front doing spectacular stunts in the way of bomb-dropping. Most of us have never had a glimpse of the man …'[24]

Only at Rostov was there any serious attempt to halt the triumphal progress of the Reds. There, the line of the River Don was held for two months before infiltration behind the White positions forced a retirement. The Ukraine front presented a depressing spectacle of the lack of the will to fight on the part of the local commander, Lieutenant General Shilling, and his army. Captain Lancaster, an intelligence officer in the liaison group attached to Shilling's army, reported that Kiev was given up on 11 December without a fight, and without any guns, military *materiél* or supplies being saved from the place, although many trainloads of barley and sugar were sent to Odessa for shipment to the Crimea. His clear and valuable report went on, 'From that date up to the fall of Odessa, there was never any real intention of defending the Ukraine. From Kiev to Odessa, roughly a matter of 200 miles, the armed forces of South Russia retreated without putting up any fight or being engaged in a single action – in fact, it is certain that Lieutenant General Shilling began making preparations for the evacuation of Odessa immediately he was notified of the fall of Kiev.' Such proved to be the case. Shilling resigned his appointment and left the defence of Odessa in the hands of some ill-disciplined Ukrainian nationalists. In fact, the only men in the defence line were a Captain Macpherson and the men of the mission's Kiev machine gun school which had been operating at Odessa, together with a small body of White Russians. When all was lost, this small force and the Mission detachment staff were able to withdraw from the port in good order under the guns of British warships, taking a hundred sick and wounded Whites with them. Since some planning attended this withdrawal, it was not quite the débâcle the earlier French exodus had been. This did not mean, however, that there were not scenes of panic and horror as thousands of refugees, many women and children among them, struggled in a heaving mass to get aboard. 'Ships slowly listed under the weight of people clinging to the deckrails and scrambling aboard. Sailors and soldiers tried to keep them out, but were pushed and borne down …' Many were, inevitably, left behind.[25]

The only haven now available to the Whites was the Crimea which, almost a island, was readily defensible. From the port of Novorossisk and the Taman peninula to the north of it, which only a narrow strait separated from the Crimea, easy withdrawal routes to the Crimea were available; but White apathy, indiscipline and their total lack of planning enabled the Bolsheviks to seize the peninsula, leaving only Novorossisk as an escape route. The role of the Mission now changed: it was to protect British personnel and stores, defend the Russian wives and families prior to their evacuation, as guaranteed by Mackinder, and act as a rearguard during their evacuation. Holman and the whole mission were now put under the orders of General Milne. All the Mission detachments were ordered to concentrate at Novorossisk. Lieutenant General Bridges was sent by General Milne to Novorossisk to mastermind the evacuation. He did not relish the task, writing that it was 'a thoroughly unsatisfactory operation for us to be mixed up in'. Holman chafed at the change of role and his own subordination to Bridges. Lieutenant Colonel Lister, now heading the General Staff section at the mission, wrote of Holman's attitude, 'He will not speak seriously on the subject of retirement. His usual reply if you mention such unpleasant facts is "Let's take an aeroplane and a tank and bomb the blighters" or something to that effect.'

Apparently, General Bridges had almost to give Holman a direct order to get him down from Ekaterinodar where he had remained with Denikin. 'We do not, of course, see eye to eye', wrote Bridges, with studied understatement, 'Holman's preoccupation is the success of Denikin's movement, mine to extricate the mission and stores with as little loss as possible.'[26]

Surrounded by low hills and backed by the sea, Novorossisk had a naturally strong defensive position. Trenches had long since been prepared along the hills and the mission staff had developed defence plans to hold the positions. Bridges was planning an orderly evacuation spread over several weeks, with naval transports making several journeys to the Crimea or Constantinople. Denikin, however, had no plans for the port and could not get his demoralised troops to man the defences. In view of this Bridges felt unable to recommend that British troops should hold them or that they should take any responsibility for the evacuation of the Volunteer Army. He wanted to withdraw the mission direct to Constantinople and leave Denikin to fend for himself in the Crimea. Holman disagreed: he wished the mission to stay with Denikin and the British to take responsibility for evacuating the Volunteer Army to the Crimea. Holman appealed directly to Churchill, who supported him. Thus an orderly, planned evacuation became a hurried, disorderly one. It was decided that a reduced mission, commanded by Holman's Chief of Staff, Brigadier General Percy, would move to the Crimea in support of Denikin. 'To me on the spot', wrote General Bridges, 'the whole affair was a degrading spectacle of unnecessary panic and disorder, and I urged the Government by cable to dissociate themselves from the White Russians who had no prospects and little fight left in them.' No such action was taken and the agony was prolonged.[27]

Bridges had brought the 2nd Royal Scots Fusiliers to act as a rearguard while the evacuation from the quay took place. On 22 March he organised a great parade of all the British forces he could muster to buoy morale, prevent panic and quell any possible rising. The disciplined lines of sailors, marines, the battalion of Scots, the mission staff, some small field guns and even a field kitchen unit were an impressive sight as they marched through the streets of the port to the martial tunes of the military pipes and drums and a naval band. All merchant ships sailing in the Black Sea under Allied or Russian flags were collected at Novorossisk, their rigging clothed in ice, together with the warships *Empress of India* and *Waldeck-Rousseau*, which lobbed shells at the roads along which Budenny's Red cavalry was approaching the port. General Bridges managed to evacuate a total of 40,000 White troops to the Crimea, together with all the dependent families who were registered with them. He managed to salvage most of the guns, but had authority to destroy all the stores he could not get away. Huge quantities were left behind. One mission member wrote of 'all the paraphernalia of an army lying on the quays to be abandoned', including 'thirteen aeroplanes in a line meeting the onslaught of a tank whose last office on our behalf, before it too is abandoned, is the joy-ride reducing many thousands of flying material to mere matchwood'. Much equipment was simply dumped in the sea. Since famine was now stalking the Kuban, Bridges could not bring himself to destroy the food, clothing and boats, which were left as a present to the Bolsheviks. These included over a million pairs of socks and vast quantities of winter clothing. Throughout the night of 26 March 1920 General Holman stood on the mole of the harbour, personally supervising the embarkation of his beloved Don Cossacks, now driven from their home river valley. On the last day in Novorossisk, some Cossacks even had to swim their horses out to the ships and clamber on as best they could, leaving their wretched mounts to drown alongside.[28]

Captain M.H. Jenks was adjutant to the base commandant at Novorossisk. He wrote at the time of the evacuation that the town 'was crammed wth refugees from all over the Don. Not often can one have seen people dying of wounds, typhus, starvation, exposure, drowning or just plain despair all at the same time and place'. Major Williamson, who had formed and led the Don Army liaison group, himself about to succumb to the typhus which was sweeping the port, captured the scene in the final hours of the evacuation.

> The waterfront was black with people, begging to be allowed on board the ships ... Conditions were appalling. The refugees were still starving and the sick and the dead lay where they had collapsed. Masses of them even tried to rush the evacuation office and British troops had to disperse them at bayonet point. Women were offering jewels, everything they possessed – even themselves – for the chance of a passage. But they hadn't the ghost of a chance. The rule was only White troops, their dependants and the families of men who had worked with the British were to be allowed on board.

Midshipman Basil Jones, aboard the *Empress of India*, wrote of the ship's departure: 'In no time we were full of starving, lice-ridden men and women, and as night fell we sailed away for Constantinople'. In the final stampede, thousands of troops and civilians were left behind.[29]

When Sir Henry Wilson learnt that General Bridges's difficult task had been successfully completed, he confided to his diary, 'Wires from Milne say that he has got all Holman's Mission safely shipped from Novorossisk. Denikin has come to the Crimea. So ends in practical disaster another of Winston's military attempts. Antwerp, Dardanelles, Denikin. His judgement is always at fault, and he is hopeless when in power.' A couple of days later all support for Denikin was formally withdrawn. Wilson's diary again: 'Cabinet at 6 p.m. We decided, Curzon leading, finally to tell Denikin to wind up affairs and come to terms with Soviet Government. Great joy. Winston fortunately absent. Beatty relieved at decision.' The ships of the First Sea Lord, Admiral Beatty, had been supporting the White Russians as best they could throughout the campaign. Believing that he had lost the confidence of his men, Denikin decided to resign his post in favour of Baron Wrangel in April 1920. He left for Constantinople with his Chief of Staff, General Romanovsky, and accompanied by General Holman. Within half an hour of their arrival, the much-hated Romanovsky had been shot dead by one of his brother officers.[30]

Even Churchill now accepted that the White cause was lost, though it gave every appearance of improved prospects of survival once General Wrangel took charge in the Crimea. A couple of days before he replaced Denikin, both commanders had read the letter from the British High Commissioner in Constantinople in which Britain offered to negotiate an amnesty for the people of the Crimea and the Volunteer Army based there. Since both Denikin and Wrangel refused to countenance this, the new commander could have been under no illusions that British support was at an end and that the struggle would be difficult to continue. Wrangel, a tall, slim Baltic aristocrat, always immaculately turned out in his Cossack uniform, was not a professional soldier but had a fine record as a fighting cavalry commander. As one young officer of the now-shrunken British Mission later recalled, 'General Wrangel with driving energy set about the task of reorganising the army and establishing a sound and corruption-free civil administration. To an astonishing extent he was successful ... Although the towns were overcrowded with refugees, a semblance of law and order appeared and was gradually reinforced; trains started to run on time; shops and markets operated more or less normally; as did the postal and other services.' The Volunteer Army similarly recovered its morale. The smaller, but still substantial, British Mission comprised 150 officers and 450 other ranks, headed by Brigadier General Percy, who took a much more realistic view of the Whites' chances than his predecessor. He saw Wrangel's problems as being as much political as military, writing to his friend Lister, now confined to a hospital ship with typhus, 'I've asked dozens of times for a political representative to be sent here as I consider it absolutely necessary that the Russians should have someone to whom they can open their hearts. No result so far.'[31]

Much military equipment had been saved and transferred to the Crimea, including all the artillery saved from Novorossisk. With its base established at Sebastopol, the mission soon resumed its training and liaison duties. Captain Wood was again organising Vickers and Lewis machine gun training at a battalion school near Theodosia on the south-east coast, which he found 'not unlike Lyme Regis'; Captain Ashton-Wade was setting up communications between the various mission detachments; Captain Lever was again the Senior Wireless Officer for the mission and Captain Kennedy remained to cast his critical eye over mission affairs. He found General Percy 'a much finer soldier' than Holman, 'and a gentleman, which Holman is not'. There were, however, still problems with some mission members: officers bouncing cheques, petty misdemeanours by other ranks and a general slackness of dress in the RAF detachment at their base in the north. Nevertheless, when he visited the mission, General Milne found both it and the Volunteer Army 'greatly improved'.[32]

The Whites repulsed repeated Bolshevik attacks on the narrow Crimean isthmus at Perekop, and then in April, the Polish army, in cooperation with the Ukrainian nationalist leader Petlyura, attacked the Bolsheviks in the Ukraine. The Polish offensive quickly made considerable gains and the Soviets' preoccupation in dealing with it created Wrangel's opportunity. His army had been reorganised and was ready for action, moreover the mountainous and arid Crimea could not feed its normal population, let alone the great influx of refugees and the Volunteer Army as well. On June 6, therefore, Wrangel struck north, hoping to replenish his granaries from the rich agricultural region in the south Ukraine. With some cooperation from Poland, Wrangel even managed to land troops in the Kuban and also in Don Cossack territory, but once the Soviet government made peace with Poland in October, all its strength was turned against Wrangel, whose forces were inevitably defeated after very heavy fighting in the defence lines of the isthmus. Finally, Wrangel ordered a withdawal to the south Crimean ports from which a successful evacuation took almost 150,000 troops and civilians into exile around the world.

When Wrangel launched his offensive, in defiance of Curzon's wish that he cooperate in seeking a negotiated settlement, the Cabinet finally withdrew all support from his regime. The Military Mission began its retirement from the Crimea. General Percy left Sebastopol with the final contingent aboard SS *Rio Negro* on 29 June 1920. The British intervention in Russia's civil war – costly, disputed and finally unsuccessful – was at an end. This did not, of course, bring an end to Chuchill's opposition to the Bolsheviks. He continued to urge support for all who tried to oppose them; but he was increasingly a lone voice. The Prime Minister had already determined that, with the Whites all but defeated, he now had the political strength to open discussions with the Soviets, negotiations which were to cover not only trade matters but also the many issues in dispute between the two governments in different parts of Europe and the East. The negotiations began even before the last members of the mission had left the Crimea and while British troops were still at Batum and Enzeli in the Caucasus. On 31 May Lloyd George led the strong Cabinet team which that day held their first meeting with Leonid Krassin, the senior Soviet government representative, initiating a policy departure which the Secretary of State for War and Air had so long opposed.[33]

17

Failure

When General Bridges, the officer who oversaw the withdrawal of the Military Mission from Novorossisk, came to record his evaluation of the British intervention in Russia's civil war, he expressed himself with simple clarity. 'From time immemorial the classic penalty for mixing in a family quarrel had been a thick ear, and our ill-staged interference in the Russian civil war cost us some thousands of British soldiers' lives and £100,000,000 in money, while we earned the bitter enmity of the Russian people for at least a decade ... On the credit side I can think of nothing.'[1] While it is possible to debate the general's calculation of the human and financial cost, it is difficult to challenge his conclusions. As to casualties, there are 526 burials recorded in the British military cemeteries in north Russia; many hundreds more were wounded in action or maimed by frostbite. There were also those killed in the Transcaspian campaign against the Tashkent Bolsheviks, though land casualties elsewhere were relatively few. This, however, is far from being the grand total. To be added are, as we have seen, the Royal Navy's losses in the Baltic and there were others elsewhere. Finally, no account was taken of the men who died of influenza and typhus contracted in the confines of ships, trains and crowded stations, a fate which they might well have avoided but for the intervention. Despite these caveats, the human cost remained a modest one compared with the slaughter of the Great War itself; but it was a cost which was hard to bear in an undeclared war after so great a sacrifice.[2] As to the Bolshevik casualties, we can only hazard that thousands were killed by the direct action of the British forces themselves, and many thousands more as a result of the aid which Britain provided to the Whites. Most were not Bolsheviks at all but merely conscripted peasants.

Bridges is probably nearer the mark on financial costs. During the course of the intervention, the government published two White Papers covering the cumulative cost of the intervention from the Armistice onwards. It issued a third, the most complete, in July 1920, in which Churchill's department argued, not very effectively, that many of the stores and munitions supplied to the Whites should be regarded as 'non-marketable' and given an extremely low estimated value, rather than their cost of production. There was some justification for this, in view of the condition of some of the goods supplied, but hardly to the extent the War Office was arguing. The total given by General

Bridges, one hundred million pounds, is the broad figure which Lloyd George, Churchill and Mackinder subsequently used and which covered all theatres of the intervention and all forms of support for the Whites. Of this amount about a half went to support Denikin in south Russia. Altogether, it was a huge sum in the circumstances of the time.[3]

As to the 'bitter enmity of the Russian people', there is no doubt some truth in the claim, though there are historians who believe it is overplayed. In fact, the intervention did serve some useful purposes for the Bolsheviks. It enabled them to assert that they were fighting, not a simple civil war, but a larger struggle to defend 'Holy Mother Russia' against the invaders. Thus they were able to introduce measures of coercion and control that might have been more difficult in other circumstances; but this hardly offset the benefits of the great material support the Whites received. The intervention also served enduring propaganda purposes for the Communists, as the case of the Twenty-Six Commissars illustrates. Much later, in 1957, Nikita Khrushchev was to use the Allied intervention for his own propaganda ends when, on a visit to the United States, he declared 'All the capitalist countries of Europe and America marched on our country to strangle the new revolution ... Never have any of our soldiers been on American soil, but your soldiers were on Russian soil. Those are the facts.'[4] Is it not possible also to imagine that the memories of the bitter struggles of 1919 for Tsaritsyn, attacked by British tanks and bombed by British aircraft, lay behind the dark Georgian eyes of Joseph Stalin as he negotiated with his allies of convenience, Churchill and Roosevelt, at Yalta, making promises that he would subsequently break?

Considering the intervention in the larger alliance context, Captain Stephen Roskill, the naval historian, is as critical as Bridges, writing that 'the War of Intervention may well stand for all time as an example of unrivalled futility in the conduct of military and diplomatic affairs by four nations who, in that context, worked for disparate and often conflicting aims and could by no stretch of the imagination be described as Allies'.[5] Certainly the limited accord that was achieved between Britain, France, Japan and the United States before the Armistice did not endure beyond it. Japan was never particularly interested in installing or unseating any particular regime in Moscow. Providing the Russian governments remained relatively weak, it could more easily achieve its imperial purposes in eastern Siberia. America's intervention forces were committed to an ill-defined but broadly 'defensive' policy in Russia. This was applied rigorously in Siberia, and although the US force in North Russia was unconfined, for a time, by its rather nebulous terms, the men were withdrawn as soon as possible in 1919. Despite France's ideological commitment to the anti-Bolshevik cause, two unsteady and mutinous battalions in North Russia, one in Siberia and a disastrous expedition to Odessa, were the total of her contribution. Churchill's account in *The Aftermath* of what 'twenty or thirty thousand resolute, comprehending, well-armed Europeans' might have achieved must remain in the realms of fancy. No such force intent on overthrowing the Bolsheviks was to be found in the circumstances of 1919, despite Churchill's efforts to get the Allies to assemble one. His great mistake was to imagine that such a thing was possible or that it would have achieved his purpose.

It is difficult to find very much with which British policy-makers could console themselves in the outcome of the entire intervention, except perhaps, twenty years of relative freedom for Estonia and Latvia. The initial motives for the invasion of Russian territory, the re-establishment of the Eastern Front to keep German divisions contained there and to prevent submarine base facilities and military supply dumps from falling into German hands, were born of understandable anxieties caused by the increasingly desperate situation on the Western Front. In each case, however, the assumptions underlying their efforts were shown to be largely false and often confused. Churchill was to claim that 'From the time we landed there [Archangel] not another division was sent from the Eastern front'. In fact the westward flow of German divisions had ended in May 1918, while the Archangel landing did not take place until August, the very month when the westward flow resumed.[6]

Since the Allies could not themselves provide substantial forces for it, the re-creation of the Eastern Front rested on the assumption that large numbers of 'loyal' Russians were prepared to take up arms again against the Central Powers. But the Russian Army had been a broken reed long before the Bolsheviks sued for peace. The million casualties it suffered in the Brusilov Offensive, loyally launched in April 1917 in support of the Entente, saw to that. By the winter of that year another million men had deserted the ranks, most of whom lived quietly at home untroubled by the failing authorities. Having suffered greater losses than any other belligerent and than all her Allies put together, Russia would no longer fight for the Entente. As the British liaison officer at the Caucasus headquarters had cabled gloomily to London long before the intervention began, 'The old Russian army is dead, quite dead. Our efforts, therefore, to resuscitate it stand useless'.[7] George Lansbury's *Daily Herald*, virtually alone among the British dailies, realised this truth as early as the first week after the Revolution, when he rebuked his colleagues in the British press who had 'never to this day faced the plain fact that Russia is physically unable to continue the war without self destruction'. It was Churchill's misjudgement to suppose it was; a misjudgement compounded by labelling the Russian collapse as 'treachery'. The other effort at resuscitation, that from Vladivostok, was even more fanciful. Even if the Japanese had been willing to participate, and they were not, the idea of sustaining a substantial army, sent along 6000 miles of railway to Europe, across country whose control was disputed by many factions was ludicrous in the extreme.

Similarly, the threat posed by the White Finns, and von der Goltz's German troops who supported them, to the Russian ports of Murmansk and Pechenga assumed greater proportions in the minds of the military planners than the reality warranted. Having assisted in installing Marshal Mannerheim's regime, the Germans were called to more urgent tasks elsewhere. It was much the same story with the military equipment delivered by Britain to Archangel and Murmansk; much had been spirited away by the Bolsheviks before the tiny Allied force landed ostensibly to secure it. In Siberia, at Vladivostok, there were substantial military stores, but the Americans kept such tight control of them that, in the early stages of the intervention, they positively hampered the British efforts.

It was in the post-Armistice phase that Churchill assumed centre stage in an effort to transform the modest Allied intervention effort into a major offensive, coordinated with the White armies, to unseat the Bolsheviks His attempts, pursued at times by methods that were less than respectable, were unable to expand the modest room for manoeuvre which Cabinet, press and public were prepared to grant him, and they were never significant enough to overcome the serious shortcomings of the White forces and the advantages which the Bolsheviks enjoyed and were able, hard-pressed though they were at times, to create for themselves. That Churchill was unable or unwilling to see this is the reason why his policy must be considered a significant and costly misjudgement.

The Bolsheviks held the central industrial and agricultural heartland of European Russia with its ethnically cohesive population, the military arsenals of the old Tsarist army and an extensive rail network centred on Moscow. They thus operated from 'interior lines' and were able to transfer troops from one threatened sector to another, a benefit denied to their opponents operating from the fringes of the old empire. As Bruce Lockhart had warned, but no one seemed to believe, the Reds also enjoyed more popular support than their opponents. The troops on the ground were not slow to see this. The Bolsheviks' promises of peace, land reform and a reformed social order were all popular cries, as was the slogan 'Down with the Foreign Invader', which came with the intervention. Despite all the horrors of War Communism, with its arbitrary arrest of 'class enemies', armed requisition squads and the terror tactics of the Cheka, the population remained broadly supportive or at least quiescent, whilst the regime applied all its zeal, determination and control mechanisms to supporting the war against the Whites and the intervention forces. 'Most of our energy at present', wrote Pavlovitch, the President of the Committee of State Constructions in February 1919, 'has to be spent mending and making roads and railways for the use of the army. Over 11,000 versts of railways are under construction ... hampered as we are, we have been able to beat the counter-revolutionaries, concentrating our best troops, now here, now there, wherever the need may be ...' This top-ranking Bolshevik wrote later, 'We have been working here in overcoats and fur hats in a temperature below freezing point. Why? Wood was already on its way to us, when we suddenly had to throw troops northwards.' The wood was immediately discharged from the wagons and reinforcing troops were put in its place and sent to the threatened north. 'The thing had to be done,' continued Pavlovitch, 'and we have had to work as best we could in the cold.' No such priorities were ever determined and observed in the White camp.[8]

The Bolsheviks' other great advantage lay in the personality and policy of Trotsky himself. The Commissar for Military Affairs was everywhere, travelling in his special train of twelve carriages to whichever front was most threatened. With him went a a staff of about 250 included a Latvian bodyguard, a machine gun unit, a group of agitators and a team of drivers and specialist track repairmen. There was also a communication crew, in a purpose-built compartment, which kept him in constant touch with Moscow. At each sector of the front, Trotsky would make a visit to ascertain the needs of the local force, hold a conference of all concerned, including members of the lower ranks, local civil representatives and trade union officials, and decide what was to be done. Perhaps the local administration would be ordered to produce more supplies for the army, a group of dedicated Communists would be added as stiffening to an unreliable unit, or Lenin would be wired and asked for more armaments. Besides ensuring the best possible rations and support for the fighting troops, Trotsky also made certain that the terror weapon was always available, telegraphing Lenin on one occasion, 'The absence of revolvers creates an impossible situation at the front. It is impossible to maintain discipline without a revolver.' On another he declared, 'the command will always be obliged to place the soldiers between the possible death at the front and the inevitable one in the rear'. With Moscow's approval he introduced 'blocking units' for this purpose, with orders to shoot the culprits if withdrawals took place without authority. Conscious of the importance of propaganda, Trotsky later had a printing press added to his train for the production of newspapers for the troops. If this brief account of the War Commissar's methods suggests a clockwork precision throughout the Red forces, it is wildly misleading. Many units remained indisciplined, at times supplies did not arrive, Stalin continually interfered with Trotsky's arrangements, and strategic misjudgements were undoubtedly made, but the Red war effort was a model of ruthless efficiency compared with the performance of its opponents.[9]

The Whites presented a sorry spectacle. The patrician General Yevgenii Miller worked a full day in his office at Archangel, writing long, rambling orders of the day about the importance of not drinking to excess, the impropriety of women serving in the army, and ('the most extraordinary document I have ever read', declared Ironside) the shame of a dead soldier not being buried quickly and with due ceremony. At Omsk, Admiral Kolchak attempted to make sensible decisions about land warfare which he little understood and made tours of the front where he was seldom allowed to see an ordinary soldier, while the administration around him degenerated under officers chosen not for their skill but their loyalty. In the south, General Denikin issued the British armaments and supplies via a system whose inefficiency and corruption was the despair of his mission paymasters. He and the other senior commanders fought inflexibly for 'one Russia, great and indivisible', incurring the enmity and opposition of the new nation states freed from the old empire. Both he and Kolchak were quite unable to institute sensible training systems and produce discipined fighting forces.

Whilst many of the officers in the British Military Missions retained some respect for the White Commanders-in-Chief (Yudenitch, perhaps, excepted), whom they found, despite their manifest shortcomings, brave, patriotic and possessed of a certain idealism, this sentiment did not extend to the generality of their subordinates. 'The Russians seem incapable of doing anything', declared Lieutenant Colonel Steel (later to die of influenza in Omsk), 'Everything is "Never mind it doesn't matter". We call it the "Land of Tomorrow".' Lieutenant Colonel Johnson in Siberia quickly came to a similar conclusion: 'I am getting to regard the situation here as pretty hopeless ... their army is useless ... I never saw such an incapable lot ...the army has no discipline. The regimental officers are useless'. The terse judgement of Lieutenant Ker, a mature and educated (Rugby and Balliol) Highland Light Infantry signals officer at Archangel, was that 'The Rusian officers here are almost all duds'. He had no more respect for their civilian counterparts: 'As for the Bourgeoisie, I have met no Englishman or American at Archangel who has any use for them. Their present plight seems to be due to their own dishonesty and greed and incompetence.' Captain Kennedy in South Russia denounced the White officers at greater length: 'Hundreds and thousands of useless old officers occupy staff and administrative sinecures in rear, with their families, without giving value in return. Everyone wants someone else to do the fighting ... and the disorganisation and confusion and corruption and speculation increase every day.' Even during the crisis of the retreat in the south it was the same story, according to Major Williamson, with 'Russian officers ... still busily engaged in exchanging and selling loot ... those employed on equipment work had enormous sums of money'. Even General Knox, loyal to Kolchak to the point of even being prepared to use his own troops to keep the admiral's regime in power, believed that 'the officer class and the Intelligentsia generally have lost all sense of discipline' and that 'not one of the chief military and civil figures in Siberia has shown any sign of organising ability'. Ultimately, despite his own reactionary sentiments, his disgust with the Whites' incompetence led to the recommendation that support for them be discontinued. The uncomfortable fact was that, although the British intervention forces had no love for the Bolsheviks, they came to despise the majority of the Whites, military and civilian.[10]

Yet throughout the intervention the Whites enjoyed Churchill's enthusiastic and, all too often, uncritical support. He mentioned, from time to time, the setting up of a democratic system in Russia following a White victory, even that of the arch-reactionary, General Yudenitch, but the improbability of such an outcome ever deriving from the regimes he was supporting seemed not to detain him. The White leaders, too, made mildly democratic pronouncements. Kolchak declared to General Knox on more than one occasion that 'he regarded the peasant class as the future rulers of the country', while Denikin spoke about recalling the Constituent Assembly after the White victory. But the officer corps which surrounded them had both aspirations and intentions that were almost wholly reactionary. Lieutenant Colonel John Ward took the view that 'The Russian officers are Royalist almost to a man, and will remain so, for they are almost childlike in their adherence to this principle'. Captain Kennedy was more emphatic: 'Personally I consider we are making a big mistake in continuing to support Denikin ... The cause is purely Royalist.'[11]

Whilst in England Churchill was denouncing the Bolsheviks in the most dehumanising language, likening them to bloodsucking vampires, plagues of locusts, baboons, a bacillus or a phial of typhoid or cholera, and deploring their atrocities as 'incomparably more hideous, on a larger scale, and more numerous than any for which the Kaiser is responsible', the British troops in Russia were finding that the Whites were no better. In the south, the pogroms reached horrific proportions. With *The Protocols of the Elders of Zion* still rolling off the European presses,[12] and Jews predominating in the Bolshevik leadership, the wave of anti-Semitism was perhaps understandable; but pogroms were not.[13] There was, however, no trace of anti-Semitism in Churchill's make-up and he opposed the wholesale executions on political and moral grounds. As to more general barbarities, Captain Horrocks remarked that 'We were always being shown photographs of atrocities being committed by the Reds. But it was six of one and half a dozen of the other, because after being captured we were shown identical photographs as examples of atrocities committed by the Whites'. Commander Goldsmith had come to a similar conclusion as early as April 1919 when he wrote, 'Both sides are equally barbarous and the torture commonly applied to prisoners is so inhuman that I cannot write about it here'. Commissars and local Communist officials were shot without a second thought. Both sides executed captured officers out of hand and torture was employed by both sides.[14]

The Whites neglected their own troops and treated them with brutal severity. Captain McCullagh, in the mission at Omsk, gives an example: 'A regiment was sent from Tomsk to the Front in the middle of 1919, but at Omsk the men sent a deputation to their CO to say that they had no boots or clothing, and could go no further; and, as a matter of fact, they had been swindled of their pay, rations and clothing by their own officers. The CO had several members of this deputation shot and the remainder brutally flogged, with the result that the whole regiment passed over to the Reds a few months afterwards.' McCullagh declared that every

British officer in Siberia could give lots of similar examples. Denikin's magistrates and police were equally culpable; they were largely pre-revolutionaries, imbued with old ideas, unpopular with the people and, according to Captain Kennedy, they 'oppressed and even tortured peasants in order to extract money for them'. Commander Goldsmith confessed, 'I have no soul for this business and dislike the Volunteers for their lives and their habits quite as much as I do the Bolshevik for theirs'.[15]

Churchill claimed correctly that the key intervention decisions had been taken by the Cabinet and Supreme War Council before he came into office. There is no doubt, however, that he strove, and managed at times, to extend, revise or circumvent them. If the British forces were to remain in north Russia, he argued sensibly, then Lloyd George should allow specialist reinforcements there to ease the local problems, despite the earlier commitment not to send any. But then he attempted to turn Prinkipo, arranged as an effort at a negotiated settlement between the warring sides in Russia, into a planning conference for a much expanded intervention. His was the central role in alarming the public about the apparent plight of the troops in north Russia, so that a 'Relief Force' might be despatched. It was he, with the connivance of the CIGS, who planned the 'punch towards Viatka' and persuaded the Cabinet (Lloyd George having already unwisely assented) to accept it. Thus the Relief Force was turned into an offensive task force responsible for a substantial thrust into the heart of Russia, on the pretext that this was necessary for a safe withdrawal. If some members of the Cabinet were able to see through this pretence, the 'volunteers' for the Russian campaign, recruited by means of this artifice, were taken by surprise. This was the reason for Sherwood Kelly's outburst. Churchill's quid pro quo for the withdrawal from the Caucasus was the expanded mission and the extra packet of supplies for Denikin. Breaching the conventions of Cabinet government and departmental management in his communications with White leaders and his own commanders were other indiscretions born of Churchill's self-belief and fixation on destroying the Bolsheviks. It was, as his biographers generally acknowledge, a performance which added little lustre to his name.

Of the main British military leaders of the intervention, three, Generals Ironside, Maynard and Knox, were already in post when Churchill took over at the War Office. He cannot, consequently, be blamed for any of their shortcomings. Both Ironside and Maynard, however, suffered the consequences of the War Minister's excessive enthusiasm for using the northern port of Archangel as the fulcrum for a proposed strategic reorientation of the White forces. Both proposed a negotiated withdrawal from north Russia, only to have the suggestion rejected by Churchill. General Knox, formerly a trusted adviser to Lloyd George, was not Churchill's choice for Vladivostok, though he was as pro-White as his minister could have wished, but even he advised abandoning the Kolchak cause. General

Briggs seems to have been Henry Wilson's choice to head the Mission to south Russia, selected in some haste to counteract French competition to influence Denikin. Churchill was soon dissatisfied with him, perhaps because of Briggs's depressing, but sound, early reports which emphasised the deplorable condition at the White base in south Russia. Churchill was prone to regard gloomy or unfavourable reports as 'defeatism' on the part of the writer. Briggs's sensible recommendations were frequently ignored. Generals Gough and Holman were a different matter; both were selected by Churchill, but neither was a great success. Holman seemed ideally suited for the appointment, speaking Russian fluently and having high-level administrative experience, yet his penchant for leading operations in person against the Bolsheviks rather than managing the work of his mission, and his undimmed optimism concerning Denikin's cause, seem to have clouded his judgement, besides demoralising many in his mission. Gough was not a suitable choice for the difficult mission to the Baltic States. One can sympathise with his political problems in the Baltic tangle, but not with the serious error of leaving Brigadier General Marsh in charge of crucial political negotiations which the Foreign Office later claimed were carried through 'almost with violence'; nor with the military misjudgement over General Yudenitch's qualities and prospects. As David Footman concludes, 'it is hard to see how any real hopes could have been set on a venture so small, so divided, so ill-equipped and so precariously based'. Neither Holman nor Gough seem to have helped Churchill to make realistic judgements, but, given the virulence of his anti-Bolshevism, he might well have ignored or sacked them if they had.[16]

What then was the root of Churchill's unremitting hatred of Bolshevism and his determination to destroy its Russian practitioners, which so distanced him from the Prime Minister and many of his Cabinet colleagues? Was it a class detestation of the Reds, as Lloyd George unkindly suggested, when he declared that Churchill's 'ducal blood revolted at the wholesale elimination of Grand Dukes in Russia'? Churchill seemed to have abandoned such class interests in 1904 when he crossed the House to become a radical Liberal. Indeed, a speech he delivered a year later might almost have been drafted by a Bolshevik, as he declared the Tory Party to be 'a party of great vested interests, banded together in a formidable confederation, corruption at home, aggression abroad ... dear food for the millions, cheap labour for the millionaire'. But his views had changed a good deal since those days. Was it rather that Churchill alone saw something uniquely threatening in Bolshevism with its global aspirations and Machiavellian determination to use any means to attain them? Perhaps so, though this is difficult to reconcile with his earlier draft plan to guarantee the Reds the 'permanent fruits' of their revolution in return for their continuing support of the Allied cause. Perhaps he did truly fear the latent power of the masses whom the Bolsheviks wished to mobilise and who were already flexing their industrial muscle in Britain. Some suggestion of this is evident in Churchill's reaction to a report he received from General Macready in Ireland in which the general explained that some measure or other 'would not be tolerated by the proletariat'. 'Who does he mean by the "*proletariat*" and where are they to be found?' demanded Churchill, 'How is their opinion to be elicited? Who speaks in their name?' Perhaps the answer, trembling at the back of Churchill's mind, was 'the Bolsheviks'.[17] By 1919 Churchill was feeling increasingly uncomfortable in the ranks of the Liberals. The chief support for his anti-Bolshevik crusade came from the Conservative backbenchers, who were keener to back him than their own leaders. They and the right-wing press were his mainstay, not his own party or the Liberal *Manchester Guardian*. At a dinner in January 1920, where Frances Stevenson noted that 'Winston [was] still raving on the subject of the Bolsheviks', Lloyd George commented, perhaps only half jocularly, that 'Winston is the only remaining specimen of a real Tory'.

The singularity of Churchill's position in 1919 was only partly that he seemed to see the Bolsheviks as a unique threat to the ordered, structured and civilised society in which he occupied an important and privileged position.[18] It also lay in his judgement that a military response to that threat was the appropriate one; that full-scale 'regime change' should be its purpose; that the means for embodying this response were to be found in Britain or among her allies, and in supporting the White side in Russia's civil war. In this belief he persisted long after his colleagues had wearied of the business. Though communications were slow and uncertain throughout the intervention, Churchill did not lack information, overt and covert, in making these judgements. Like many decisive men, he had the ability to brush aside or reinterpret information which did not suit his purposes. What Lord Attlee wrote of him in regard to the Second World War, might equally apply to the intervention: 'Rather than have access to information that might cause him to change his mind about something, Winston would sometimes prefer to be left in ignorance.'[19] Isaiah Berlin, however, offers an alternative interpretation: 'He has an immense capacity for absorbing facts but they emerge transformed by the categories which he powerfully imposes on the raw material.'[20] Altogether, Churchill's policy represented a major political and strategic misjudgement whose consequences were very significant for his future. It underscored his already popular reputation as a reckless military adventurer; it led Lloyd George to distrust his judgement and decline to offer him the promotion to Chancellor for which he was hoping; and it widened the gulf between him and the trades union movement and Labour Party, whose animosity he never entirely assuaged. No doubt it also played its part in the loss of his Dundee seat, by a considerable margin, in the 1922 election.[21]

Churchill's anti-Bolshevism continued unabated, with rhetoric just as extreme ten years later in *The Aftermath* as it had been throughout 1919; but his support for the White cause did finally wane. It is difficult to pinpoint the moment when this began. Perhaps it was 3 November 1919, the day when General Briggs arrived at Taganrog to give General Holman the details of the 'final packet' of miltary assistance to Denikin that the Cabinet had sanctioned. By this time north Russia had been vacated, Kolchak had been defeated, Yudenitch was on the point of being trounced and Denikin, the heart of the White resistance, was in full retreat. That day, the first of the White Papers was published showing the cost of the intervention. The following morning, the *Daily Express* seized on the information in a bitterly critical piece headed ENORMOUS WASTE IN RUSSIA. On the evening of this disclosure, Churchill and Beaverbrook, who had not spoken for months, were induced to dine together with their young friends, the newly-married Duff and Lady Diana Cooper. Lady Diana, a favourite of Beaverbrook, who had given the couple a motor car as a wedding present, had long been anxious to effect a reconciliation between him and his erstwhile close friend and colleague. 'The two shook hands', Duff Cooper's diary recorded, 'They were both obviously nervous, Max more so than Winston.' Russia was discussed at length, with one of the other guests acting as arbiter; but the debate did not become unduly heated. After the dinner was over and the guests had departed, Duff Cooper was relieved to record, 'They ended perfectly good friends and both said they had enjoyed themselves tremendously.' The *Daily Express* campaign steadily subsided and Churchill's attention became increasingly diverted to Ireland, where the first IRA campaign was gathering intensity.[22]

For many of the British officers and soldiers of the intervention, their involvement in a war in the strange and exotic land of Russia remained one of the most intense experiences of their lives: a profound cultural and military shock in a war without boundaries, fixed fronts, trustworthy allies or noble causes; where White officers despised their men and thousands of them declined to take any part in the fighting at all. This is why, no doubt, so many British soldiers chose to record, in diaries and letters, their participation in the strange drama. For the Americans, the experience was, if anything, even more profound, for they had the added trauma, in north Russia, of undergoing their first taste of battle while serving under British commanders. One American, Lieutenant Cudahy, a young lawyer who commanded a small force in the bitter little fight for the village of Toulgas on the banks of the Dvina, reflected the vividness of his recollection of the occasion rather oddly: by choosing to give his only daughter the strange name of 'Toulgas'. Field Marshal Lord Ironside had a varied and eventful military career after the intervention which took him to the pinnacle of his profession. Yet, when he was ennobled in 1941, he chose the style 'Baron of Archangel and of Ironside', recalling his Scottish birthplace but also the setting for his first and most testing general's command. Lieutenant Colonel John Ward returned home from Siberia to a long and distinguished career in politics and the trade union movement. When he came to name his house in the leafy Hampshire village of Weyhill, he chose to call it 'Omsk', incongruous in its rural English setting but marking his vivid recollections of his time in Siberia when he had stood at the centre of momentous events. Others had little more tangible than the white polar star from their tunics and some fading memories to represent their unusual experiences in Russia. Some had not even that, but only pale headstones in the Archangel and Murmansk military cemeteries or their names merely recorded on other distant memorials. Britain did not strike a medal to commemorate its servicemen's campaign service in the undeclared war. Instead the authorities extended the entitlement to the Great War's campaign and victory medals, 'Mutt and Jeff' as they were popularly known, to those whose first war experience was in the distant Russian theatres. This decision acknowledged the fact that the intervention had a tenuous connection, though it was never very much more than that, with the First World War.

Appendix 1

The Twenty-Six Commissars

The commissars who had formed the Bolshevik administration of Baku before they were deposed and imprisoned, shortly before General Dunsterville's arrival, were no ordinary local officials. Twenty-six in number and led by Stepan Shaumian, they had been appointed by Lenin to form the government of Russian Central Asia, an area as big as India, and had only recently taken power. According to General Malleson, they included 'men of the first importance' who had been sent to sort out the situation in the Caucasus before moving on to Central Asia. When they escaped from Baku in the panic as the Turkish troops attacked, it had been Shaumian's intention to take a ship for Astrakhan, the only Caspian port still firmly in Bolshevik hands. The ship's crew, however, fearing their own arrest there, pleaded shortage of fuel and headed across the Caspian to Krasnovodsk. There the commissars were arrested by the town commandant, Kuhn, a Caucasian Cossack with a pitiless reputation.

Neither the Ashkabad Committee of Social Revolutionaries who formed the government at the western end of the Central Asian Railway, nor General Malleson at Meshed, where the Committee also had an envoy, wished to have the commissars remain in Transcaspia. With a Bolshevik army ahead of them, the Committee had no wish to keep a group of Bolshevik agitators in their rear. For his part, Malleson saw the commissars' potential usefulness as hostages for British prisoners and others at risk in Central Asia. He met the Committee's envoy, an ex-railway ticket collector named Dokov, and asked that the commissars should be handed over, alive, to the British for safe custody and transport to India. He even offered to send a delegation to collect them. Dokov demurred and only when Malleson threatened the withdrawal of his support from the Ashkabad regime did the Russian relent and say he would press his government to agree to Malleson's wishes, though he feared that it might already be too late and the commissars might no longer be alive. To reinforce his appeal, Malleson telegraphed his own representative in Ashkabad, Captain Teague Jones, and ordered him to press the case for the commissars to be handed over to the British, 'if not too late'. Teague Jones was a Punjab police officer by training but spoke Russian fluently.

In Ashkabad, the Committee was being pressed by town commandant Kuhn at Krasnovodsk to take the commissars off his hands. His jail was not large enough to accommodate them and he feared an attempt by local Bolsheviks to set them free. The Ashkabad Committee met to consider the matter. Teague Jones was asked to attend the meeting. The committee president, Funtikov, arrived the worse for drink and argued that, since the local jails were overcrowded and Malleson had declined to take charge of the commissars, they should be shot. Other committee members, however, disagreed and a long argument followed. Teague Jones left before the meeting ended. Only the following evening did he learn from Funtikov that the Committee had decided to have the commissars killed. They had been bundled onto a train at Krasnovodsk, apparently on Funtikov's orders, taken off into the desert and shot.

It was not until the following March that the news of the executions reached Moscow via an article in a Baku newspaper which asserted that the British had been responsible for bringing the commissars to Krasnovodsk, where they had been secretly shot under the orders of Teague Jones and certain members of the Ashkabad Committee, in fulfilment of the wishes of the British Mission. It may be that Funtikov, whom the Baku reporter interviewed, concocted the story to save his own skin. General Malleson suggests that Teague Jones showed his telegram to the Committee and that the words, 'if not too late', may have influenced their decision. It could be that town commandant Kuhn ordered the executions on his own authority. What is clear is that the British did not order the executions; on the contrary they were keen, for very good reasons, to have the commissars kept alive. The actions of Teague Jones, however, remain something of a mystery. In the subsequent furore which the executions caused, Teague Jones wrote a forceful defence of his position for the Foreign Office, but his letter did not make clear whether he had disputed Funtikov's account to the Committee of General Malleson's wishes, whether he had shown the Committee Malleson's telegram, or why he left the Committee's meeting before the crucial decision on the fate of the Commissars was taken.

Moscow took the story at its face value and extracted the maximum propaganda value from it, not simply in the days immediately following the news of the executions, but for years afterwards. It became a *cause célèbre*. In 1919 Stalin denounced the 'lawlessness and savage debauchery with which English agents settled accounts with the "natives" of Baku and Transcaspia, just as they had with the blacks of Central Africa'. A well-known artist depicted the execution with the heroic commissars, fists clenched in Communist salutes, defying the firing squad behind whom stand British officers, apparently directing the proceedings. In 1963, *Pravda* marked the forty-fifth anniversary of the executions with an item praising 'the twenty-six commissars of the Baku commune' who were 'shot by the English interventionists and their Social Revolutionary servants'. Munuments were raised to the heroes in Baku and Erivan. In Tiflis, the capital of Georgia, a station on the local underground was even given the name 'The Twenty-Six Commissars'; inventive memorialising perhaps, but a bit of a mouthful for those in a hurry for a ticket.[1]

Appendix 2

Churchill's Letter of 8 March 1919

My dear Prime Minister,

I send you the following notes on our conversation this morning.[1]

(1) It is your decision and the decision of the War Cabinet that we are to evacuate Murmansk and Archangel as soon as the ice melts in the White Sea. Russians (including women and children) who have compromised themselves through working with us are to be transported, if they desire it, to a place of refuge.

    If reinforcements are required to cover the extrication of our forces and the withdrawal of the aforesaid Russians, they may be taken for this purpose from the volunteers now re-engaging for service in the army. It will be made clear to these men that they are only going to extricate their comrades and not for a long occupation of North Russia.

    Subject to the above, I am to make whatever military arrangements are necessary to carry out your policy.

(2) It is also decided by you and the War Cabinet that we are to withdraw our army fom the Caucasus as quickly as possible. This will certainly take 3 or 4 months, as the detachments which have been thrown out as far as Kars to the Southward and the troops on the other side of the Caspian have also to be withdrawn, and our lines of communication from Hamadan to Enzeli have to be wound up.

Denikin will be compensated for the loss of the support of this army (a) by arms and munitions and (b) by a military mission, which may if necessary amount to 2000 in all of technical assistants and instructors. This military mission is to be formed of officers and men who volunteer specially for service in Russia and not by men of the regular volunteer army ordered to proceed there. In return for this support, we should secure from Denikin undertakings not to attack the Georgians and others South of a certain line which the Foreign Office are tracing; and later instalments of arms and munitions will be dealt out to him as he conforms to this agreement. If he fails to conform to this agreement, it will be open to us to withdraw our mission. The limits of our assistance to Denikin will be clearly stated to him, and it will be open to him to accept or reject our conditions and our help.

(3) You have also decided that Colonel John Ward and the two British battalions
    at Omsk are to be withdrawn (less any who volunteer to stay) as soon as they
    can be replaced by a military mission, similar to that to Denikin, composed
    of men who volunteer specifically for service in Russia.

(4) On these lines and within these limits, I should be prepared to be responsible
    for carrying out the policy which you and the War Cabinet have decided. It
    will be necessary to inform the Allies of our intention, and this I presume
    will be done by yourself or Mr Balfour.

If, however, I have wrongly interpreted your decisions in any respect, I hope
you will let me know what you really wish, in order that I may see whether it
can be done.

Yours very sincerely

Winston S. Churchill

The Court Martial of Lieutenant Colonel J. Sherwood Kelly VC, CMG, DSO

After the first letter written by Sherwood Kelly appeared in the *Daily Express* on the morning of Saturday 6 September, there were urgent discussions among Churchill's closest military advisers as to whether he should be court martialled, and if so, on what charge. A court martial would be an unusual disciplinary procedure for an officer, rare for one of Kelly's rank, unprecedented for one so well decorated, four times wounded (twice gassed) and three times mentioned in despatches. Reports were called for which revealed his outstanding bravery and his qualities as a battalion commander, but also his chequered military career off the battlefield and very mixed record in north Russia. 'He is not normal', the Adjutant General wrote to Churchill, 'and suffers from an ungovernable temper.' Both the Director of Personal Services and the Adjutant General initially recommended against a court martial and in favour of Kelly being removed from the army administratively for misconduct, as permitted by an article of the Pay Warrant. This would be quick and straighforward: the facts were clearly established and he would be deprived of the opportunity for further advertisement – a particularly important consideration, the Adjutant General advised Churchill, since 'the *Daily Express* is using his letter as a weapon against you'. Besides there was the precedent. Major-General Sir Frederick Maurice had written to the papers the previous year criticising the government's military policy but had suffered no financial penalty beyond his premature retirement. Then came Kelly's second letter. Opinion hardened. Churchill now favoured a speedy court martial, kept as simple as possible. There was to be no mention of Russia in the charges: none of Kelly's alleged misconduct there which had occasioned his adverse report from Ironside, nor even of the letters in which he 'gave away everything about forthcoming operations that it was possible to give away' and for which he was sent home, but simply for writing to the newspapers. By this means it was hoped to deprive Kelly of a platform for his complaints since the letters to the Press could hardly be denied.[1]

Sherwood Kelly was placed under open arrest on 13 October 1919 and his court martial took place in Westminster Guildhall on the 28th. It aroused considerable press and public interest and was widely reported. For the *Daily Express* it was front-page news. The charge was simply the writing of three letters to the press on 5 September, 12 September and 6 October, on his return from Russia. Under

King's Regulations an officer was 'forbidden to publish in any form whatsoever or communicate, either directly or indirectly, to the Press any military information or his views on any military subject without special authority'. Kelly had plainly done both and pleaded guilty to what he considered a 'purely technical' offence. During his plea in mitigation he spent most time in defending himself against the adverse report which Ironside had rendered on him and which he considered to be most unjust. Kelly presented various documents in support of his case. He also inveighed against the way in which those who had volunteered for service in Russia had been misled as to the purpose of their mission. 'I plead with you to believe', he concluded, 'that the action I took was to protect my men's lives against needless sacrifice and to save the country from squandering wealth it could ill afford.' He was found guilty and severely reprimanded. Two weeks later 'Fearless Kelly of Cambrai' relinquished his commission 'on completion of service'. He was allowed to retain the rank of lieutenant colonel.[2]

Out of uniform, Sherwood Kelly was a sad and uncomfortable figure. Pursued by a neglected wife and sundry creditors, he made many unsuccessful efforts to re-enter the service, but failed even to secure a recommendation for a place in the French Foreign Legion when enquiries were made of the War Office. Later he stood unsuccessfully as a Conservative parliamentary candidate, achieving a little more notoriety by thrashing a heckler who insulted him. Finally, he went to Bolivia on some commercial business and was said to have opened contact for the first time between Buenos Ayres and the Great Paraguayan River. A spell in Tanganyika followed, where he unfortunately contracted the malaria from which he subsequently died in London in August 1931. He was granted a full military funeral and buried in Brookwood Military Cemetery. A most courageous if unruly and difficult officer whose Russian experiences provided a small but important footnote to the political history of the British intervention.[3]

Notes

Notes to Introduction

1   Roy Jenkins gave but seven paragraphs to it in the 900-odd pages of his major biography *Churchill* (2001); Geoffrey Best gave it five paragraphs in his 300 page reflective study *Churchill: A Study in Greatness* (2001). John Keegan's 170-page introductory biography *Churchill* (2002) and Richard Holmes's 300-page work, *In the Footsteps of Churchill* (2005), each allot it a single paragraph.

2   H.W. Massingham to Winston Churchill, 16 March 1919, M. Gilbert, *Winston S. Churchill*, iv, *CV*, pt 2, p. 587.

3   Kennan to Michael Kettle in a letter commenting on the draft of the latter's *Churchill and the Archangel Fiasco*.

4   They were Major Generals Ironside at Archangel, Knox at Vladivostok, Malleson in Transcaspia, Maynard at Murmansk, Poole in the Caucasus and Thomson at Baku.

5   There are over two dozen unpublished diaries of young officers who later rose to the rank of general or its equivalent. Some display a commendable candour and maturity of judgement.

6   The expression is Geoffrey Best's: see his *Churchill and War* (London, 2005), chapter 14.

7   J.M. Kenworthy, *Sailors, Statesmen – and Others* (London, 1933), p. 163.

8   Roy Jenkins, *Churchill* (London, 2001), p. 345.

Notes to Chapter 1: The Eastern Front

1   C.R.M.F. Crutwell, *A History of the Great War, 1914–1918* (Oxford, 1936), pp. 79–80.

2   B.H. Liddell Hart, *The Real War, 1914–1918* (London, 1930), p. 244.

3   Crutwell, *The Great War*, p. 430.

4   This abortive effort had enjoyed the bizarre support of a British armoured-car squadron under Commander Oliver Locker-Lampson MP, which had travelled to Russia to support the imperial cause.

5   R.H. Bruce Lockhart, *The Two Revolutions: An Eyewitness Study of Russia, 1917* (London, 1957), p. 110.

6   These are the Reichsarchiv figures quoted in Giordan Forg, 'The Movement of German Divisions to the Western Front, Winter 1917–18', *War in History*, 7 (2000), p. 26.

7   A. Agar, *Footprints in the Sea* (London, 1959), pp. 74–76.

8   Martin Gilbert, *Winston S. Churchill*, iv (London, 1975), pp. 219–20; David Carlton, *Churchill and the Soviet Union* (Manchester 2000), p. 5.

9   Poole to Colonel Byrne, 4 December 1917 quoted in Michael Kettle, *The Allies and the Russian Collapse* (London, 1981), p. 146.

10 Poole to Ratcliffe 16 February 1918, quoted in J. Bradley, *Allied Intervention in Russia* (London, 1968), p. 19.

11 Bradley, *Allied Intervention in Russia*, p. 20.

12 Martin Gilbert, 'Churchill and the European Idea', in R.A.C. Parker (ed.), *Winston Churchill: Studies in Statesmanship* (London, 1995), p. 203. Churchill's unusual proposal apparently involved his offer to go to Moscow as a sort of 'Commissar for the Allies'. Gilbert to the author.

13 Martin Gilbert, *Winston S. Churchill*, iv (London, 1975), pp. 219–20; David Carlton, *Churchill and the Soviet Union* (Manchester 2000), p. 5.

14 *War Memoirs*, vi (London, 1936), p. 3157.

15 Russia's Czech scouts were useful in encouraging disaffected Czechs to desert the Austrian lines. One force of nine scouts 'brought across' practically a whole regiment – sixty officers, two thousand men and thirty-two machine guns – in this way. J. Swettenham, *Allied Intervention in Russia, 1918–1919*, p. 89.

16 'The Czechoslovaks, perfidiously abandoned at Tarnapol by our infantry, fought in such a way that the world ought to fall on its knees before them', Brusilov declared. J. Swettenham, *Allied Intervention in Russia, 1918–1919* (London, 1967), p. 90.

17 Imperial War Museum, 93/23/3, Colonel C.B. Stokes, 'Pages from Life'.

18 Swettenham, *Allied Intervention in Russia*, p. 48.

19 The best account of the exploits of Dunsterforce and the defence of Baku is given in Dunsterville's own words, *The Adventures of Dunsterforce* (London, 1920), pp. 218–317.

20 Imperial War Museum, Papers of Paymaster Commander M.C. Franks; Air Vice-Marshal C.H. Bilney, 'A Seaplane Pilot's Wanderings'.

21 Richard H. Ullman, *Intervention and the War* (London, 1961), chapter 11, passim; John Silverlight, *The Victors' Dilemma* (London, 1970), pp. 209–13; Major General Sir W. Malleson, 'The Twenty-Six Commissars', *Fortnightly Review*, 133 (1933), pp. 333–48.

Notes to Chapter 2: Arctic Danger

1   Stephen Roskill, *Naval Policy between the Wars*, i (London, 1968), pp. 131–36.

2   Richard H. Ullman, *Intervention and the War* (Princeton, 1961), p. 116; John Silverlight, *The Victors' Dilemma* (London 1970), p. 32.

3   This important telegram later became a key part of the Stalinist indictment of Trotsky as an 'enemy of the people'.

4   National Archives, ADM 137/170, Admiralty telegram 178, 17 April 1918.

5   National Army Museum, 8403–30, Papers of Lieutenant Colonel Godfrey.

6   Major General Sir C. Maynard, *The Murmansk Venture* (London, 1928), ch. 2; Imperial War Museum, 73/9/21, Sturdy Papers, comments on *The Murmansk Venture*.

7   National Archives, WO 106/1161.

8   Maynard, *Murmansk Venture*, ch. 2.

9   Ibid.

10   Imperial War Museum, P/76, Lieutenant Colonel A.G. Burn, 'The Jottings of a Dugout in North Russia'.

11   Quoted in Silverlight, *The Victors' Dilemma*, p. 42.

12   Imperial War Museum, 78/24/1, P.J. Woods, 'Karelian Diary'.

13   National Archives, ADM 116/1161, Geddes Memorandum for the Imperial War Cabinet and War Cabinet, 'Murmansk and North Russia'; Roskill, *Naval Policy*, pp. 135–37.

14   St. Antony's College, Oxford, D. Footman, 'Murmansk and Archangel' (unpublished, 1957).

15   Balfour to Lord Reading 11 July 1918, quoted in Ullman, *Intervention and the War*, p. 233.

16   R.H. Bruce Lockhart, *Memoirs of a British Agent* (London, 1932), p. 305.

17   A.W. Abbott, 'Lapland, 1918–19: The British Army's Farthest North', *Army Quarterly*, July 1962.

18   Ibid.

19   A.H. Macklin, quoted in Roland Huntford, *Shackleton* (London 1985), pp. 665–66.

20   National Archives, WO 32/5664; Huntford, *Shackleton*, pp. 649–72; G. Schuster, *Private Work and Public Causes* (Cowbridge, 1979), pp. 16–34; W.K.M. Leader, 'With the Murmansk Expeditionary Force', *RUSI Journal*, 66 (1921).

Notes to Chapter 3: Archangel

1   Captain E. Altham, 'The Dwina Campaign', *RUSI Journal*, 470 (1923), pp. 231–32.

2   Altham, 'The Dwina Campaign', pp. 233–34.

3   Eugenie Fraser, *The House by the Dvina* (London, 1986), p. 241.

4   Fraser, *The House by the Dvina*, p. 242.

5   R.H. Bruce Lockhart, *Memoirs of a Secret Agent* (London, 1974), pp. 212–13.

6   Richard H. Ullman, *Intervention and the War* (Princeton, 1961), p. 236.

7   Fraser, *The House by the Dvina*, p. 240.

8   National Archives, WO 106/1161.

9   Quoted in C. Dobson and J. Miller, *The Day We Almost Bombed Moscow* (London, 1986), p. 130.

10   National Archives, WO 106/1161.

11   War Office to Poole, 10 August 1918, quoted in Ullman, *Intervention and the War*, p. 240.

12   National Archives, WO 95/5419.

13   The *aide mémoire*, a three-page diplomatic document, contained little in the way of explicit military instructions. It is quoted in full in John Swettenham, *Allied Intervention in Russia, 1918–1919* (London, 1967), pp. 145–47.

14   E.M. Halliday, *The Ignorant Armies* (London, 1961), p. 44.

15   Louis De Robien, *The Diary of a Diplomat in Russia, 1917–1918* (London, 1969), p. 289.

16   Ullman, *Intervention and the War*, pp. 247–48; Halliday, *The Ignorant Armies*, pp. 39–42.

17   Liddell Hart Centre for Military Archives, King's College London, Poole Papers, Poole to DMO, 10 September 1918.

18   National Archives, CAB 23/7, meetings 470 and 473.

19   Liddll Hart Centre, Poole Papers, Poole to DMO, 10 September 1918.

20   National Archives, WO 106/1163.

21   Ibid.

22   National Archives, WO 95/5419.

23   According to the memoirs of the waspish young French diplomat, Louis de Robien, a certain Baroness Accurti at Archangel had 'awakened the somewhat extinguished ardours of the good general' and their 'far too much publicised affair is the subject of a great deal of gossip'. L. De Robien, *Diary*, pp. 305–6.

24   J. Powell, 'John Buchan's Richard Hannay', *History Today*, August 1987, pp. 32–39. The best known of Buchan's Hannay adventure stories, *The Thirty-Nine Steps*, was published in 1915.

25   Edmund Ironside, *Archangel, 1918–1919* (London, 1953), p. 13.

26   Imperial War Museum, 92/21/1, G.E. Cormack, 'War Times in Russia'.

27   Altham, 'The Dvina Campaign', p. 239; Major General Sir Edmund Ironside, 'The North Russian Campaign', *Royal Artillery Journal*, 53 (1926), pp. 309–10; Ironside, *Archangel*, p. 35.

28   Halliday, *The Ignorant Armies*, passim.

29   Ironside MS diary, 6 October, quoted in Ullman, *Britain and the Russian Civil War*, p. 23, footnote.

30   D. Volkogonov, *Trotsky: The Eternal Revolutionary* (London, 1996), pp. 126–34.

31   Commissar Pavlovitch, President of the Committee of State Security, and Commissar Krasin, quoted in Arthur Ransome, *Six Weeks in Russia, 1919* (London, 1992), pp. 110, 136–37. It may be that the British authorities already had this information since Ransome was known to be in contact with MI6. National Archives, KV2/1903 and 1904.

Notes to Chapter 4: Siberia

1   Richard H. Ullman, *Intervention and the War* (Princeton, 1961), pp. 98–100; Josiah C. Wedgwood, *Memoirs of a Fighting Life* (London, 1940), p. 141.

2   John Swettenham, *Allied Intervention in Russia,1918–1919* (London, 1967), p. 131.

3   Ullman, *Intervention and the War*, pp. 156–59.

4   Peter Fleming, *The Fate of Admiral Kolchak* (London, 1963), pp. 17–25. Fleming gives a valuable account of the Cheliabinsk incident and the subsequent actions of the Czech Legion.

5   C.F. Horne, *Source Records of the Great War* (New York, 1923), vi, p. 239, quoted in Swettenham, *Allied Intervention*, p. 123.

6   National Army Museum, AM 7603–93, Papers of Lieutenant General Sir Reginald Savoury; Fleming, *Kolchak*, p. 92; G. Blaxland, *The Middlesex Regiment* (London, 1977), pp. 96–99; J. Ward, *With the 'Diehards' in Siberia* (London, 1920), passim.

7   Ullman, *Intervention and the War*, p. 263. Others give a total about a thousand lower.

8   Ward, *Diehards*, chs 1–4; Blaxland, *The Middlesex Regiment*, pp. 66–68; National Archives, WO 95/5433.

9 Lloyd George to Lord Reading in Washington, 17 July 1918, quoted in Ullman, *Intervention and the War*, p. 221.

10 W.S. Churchill, *The World Crisis: The Aftermath* (London, 1929), p. 94; General I.A. Denikin, *The White Army* (Cambridge 1992), p.123.

11 Ward, *Diehards*, p. 200; Ullman, *Intervention and the War*, pp. 264–76.

12 Swettenham, *Allied Intervention*, pp. 125–36.

13 Many of the Canadians were conscripted illegally under the Military Service Act which stipulated that they could be used only for the defence of Canada.

14 Knox to Emsley, 6 November 1918, quoted in Swettenham, *Allied Intervention*, p. 142.

15 Michael Kettle, *Churchill and the Archangel Fiasco* (London, 1992), p. 11; Ullman, *Intervention and the War*, p. 282.

16 Ullman, *Intervention*, p. 277–78, based on Boldyrev's diary account: John Silverlight, *The Victors' Dilemma* (London, 1970) p. 226.

17 National Archives, WO 32/5676, Ward Report of 18 November 1918; Fleming, *Kolchak*, p. 105.

18 Kettle, *Archangel Fiasco*, pp. 12–13.

19 Silverlight, *Victors' Dilemma*, pp. 227–31; Kettle, *Archangel Fiasco*, pp. 15–19; Ward, *Diehards*, pp. 128–45.

20 National Archives, WO 32/5676, Ward Report of 20 November 1918.

21 Kettle, *Archangel Fiasco*, pp. 20–23; Fleming, *Kolchak*, pp. 114–16.

22 National Archives, WO 32/5707, Knox, 'Report on the Work of the British Military Mission to Siberia, 1918–1920'; Ward, *Diehards*, p. 197.

Notes to Chapter 5: Armistice

1 Imperial War Museum, 74/65/1, Papers of Private F. Hirst; L. Brayshaw, 'Adventures on a Troopship', *Green Howards Gazette*, 81 (1974), pp. 11–13; H.C. Wylly, *The Green Howards in the Great War* (Richmond, 1926), passim; National Archives, WO 33/966, Ironside to War Office, 8 March 1919.

2 National Archives, CAB 24/73, paper GT 6662; Richard H. Ullman, *Intervention and the War* (Princeton, 1961), pp. 296–300; Michael Kettle, *Churchill and the Archangel Fiasco* (London, 1992), pp. 1–2.

3 Lord Beaverbrook, *Men and Power* (London, 1956), p. xxvi.

4 C.R.M.F. Crutwell, *A History of the Great War, 1914–1918* (Oxford, 1934), p. 501.

5 National Archives, CAB 24/70.

6 National Archives, CAB 23/8.

7 Richard H. Ullman, *Britain and the Russian Civil War* (Princeton, 1968), pp. 10–16.

8 Ullman, *Britain and the Russian Civil War*, pp. 66–81.

9 National Army Museum, diary of Field Marshal Sir Henry Wilson, 13 December 1918.

10 Ullman, *Britain and the Russian Civil War*, pp. 59–64.

11 J.M. Kenworthy, *Sailors, Statesmen – and Others* (London, 1933), p. 157; Josiah Wedgwood, *Memoirs of a Fighting Life* (London, 1940) p. 146.

12 Issues of 11 January 1919 for both newspapers.

13   Martin Gilbert, *Winston S. Churchill*, iv (London, 1975), p. 175.

14   National Army Museum, Wilson Diary, 16 and 19 December 1918.

15   *Hansard*, cxxiii, 191 (15 December 1919); Winston S. Churchill, *The World Crisis: The Aftermath* (London, 1929), p. 263; Connaught Rooms speech, April 1919; House of Commons, May 1920; Kerr to Lloyd George, 15 February 1919.

16   26 November 1918, quoted in Gilbert, *Churchill*, iv, p. 227.

17   Kenworthy, *Soldiers, Statesmen – and Others*, p. 153; National Army Museum, Wilson Diary, 17 January 1919.

18   Andrew Rothstein, *The Soldiers' Strikes of 1919* (London, 1980), passim.

19   Churchill, *The Aftermath*, p. 61; Rothstein, *The Soldiers' Strikes*, p. 165.

20   Churchill College Archive Centre, Cambridge, CHAR 2/106, folio 178.

Notes to Chapter 6: *General Denikin*

1   Richard H. Ullman, *Britain and the Russian Civil War* (Princeton, 1968), pp. 90–94.

2   Ullman, *Britain and the Russian Civil War*, pp. 95–98.

3   In the preparation of this chapter, I am indebted to J. Ainsworth, '"A Friend in Need": The British Military Mission to South Russia, 1919–1920', unpublished PhD thesis, University of Queensland (1991).

4   Michael Kettle, *Churchill and the Archangel Fiasco* (London, 1992), p. 36.

5   National Archives, WO 106/1191, Blackwood Report.

6   National Archives, FO 371/3962, Bond Report, 'Mission to the Don Country Southern Russia', pp. 174–206.

7   Poole was to have had Brigadier General A.P. Wavell as a member of his mission, but the future Second War Supreme Commander was not in the end available.

8   National Archives, CAB 24/69.

9   General I.A. Denikin, *The White Army* (Cambridge, 1992), p. 197.

10   Ainsworth, 'A Friend in Need', p. 87, quoting Denikin.

11   Denikin, *Ocherki*, iv, p. 71, quoted in Ainsworth, 'A Friend in Need', p. 86.

12   National Archives, WO 157/765, South Russia Intelligence January 1919.

13   National Archives, WO 33/965 ; Ainsworth, 'A Friend in Need', pp. 110–26.

14   Kettle, *Churchill and the Archangel Fiasco*, p. 39.

15   Kettle, *Churchill and the Archangel Fiasco*, p. 106.

16   Denikin, *The White Army*, p. 209.

17   National Archives, WO 33/965.

18   Liddell Hart Centre for Military Archives, Poole Papers. The general's papers contain a copy in Russian of the Ekaterinodar notary's documents authorising this gift.

19   National Archives, CAB 29/2, Poole Report.

20   Kettle, *Churchill and the Archangel Fiasco*, pp. 119–21.

21   Ullman, *Britain and the Russian Civl War*, pp. 90–121; Silverlight, *The Victors' Dilemma* (London, 1970), pp. 136–152; Kettle, *Churchill and the Archangel Fiasco*, pp. 100–24.

22   Churchill, *The World Crisis: The Aftermath* (London, 1929), p. 173–74.

23   Kettle, *Churchill and the Archangel Fiasco*, p. 129, quoting the Lloyd George Papers.

24 Kettle, *Churchill and the Archangel Fiasco*, p. 132.

25 Ainsworth, 'A Friend in Need', p. 87.

26 Denikin, *The White Army*, pp. 199, 206.

27 G. Nicol, *Uncle George* (London, 1976), p. 206.

28 Imperial War Musem, 90/37/1, De Wolff, 'Odd Notes'.

29 Ibid.

30 National Archives, WO 0149/7530.

31 Kettle, *Churchill and the Archangel Fiasco*, p. 102; Silverlight, *Victors' Dilemma*, p. 274; Denikin, *White Army*, p. 202.

32 National Archives, WO 33/971, Holman Final Report.

33 'Odd Notes', p. 50, IWM.

34 National Archives, WO 158/748, Briggs Report, 15 March 1919.

35 Ainsworth, 'A Friend in Need', ch. 6; John Harris (ed.), *Farewell to the Don* (London, 1970), p. 43.

36 National Archives, WO 33/967A.

37 Harris, *Farewell to the Don*, pp. 23–24; Nicol, *Uncle George*, p. 206.

38 Liddell Hart Centre, Papers of Admiral Sir Malcolm Goldsmith; De Wolff, 'Odd Notes'; Ullman, *Britain and the Russian Civil War*, p. 213.

39 Liddell Hart Centre, diary of Captain G.H. Lever; Harris, *Farewell to the Don*, pp. 14–15; Imperial War Museum, Major-General Ashton Wade, 'A Life on the Line', pp. 55–61; 78/31/1 Major General G.N. Wood, 'A Subaltern in South Russia, 1919–20'.

40 National Archives, WO 33/965; Wade, 'Life on the Line'; Lever, diary.

41 Ainsworth, 'A Friend in Need', ch. 6 ; Major General Ashton Wade, 'Military Missions to South Russia', *Army Quarterly and Defence Journal*, October 1981.

42 National Archives, WO 33/971, Holman Final Report.

43 Nicol, *Uncle George*, pp. 202–8.

44 Richard H. Ullman, *Intervention and the War* (London, 1961), pp. 325–29.

Notes to Chapter 7: The Winter War

1 Major General Sir C. Maynard, *The Murmansk Venture* (London, 1928), p. 64.

2 A. Soutar, *With Ironside in North Russia* (London, 1940), p. 28.

3 Ibid., p. 27.

4 National Archives, WO 33/966, 3 February 1919.

5 W.K.M. Leader, 'With the Murmansk Expeditionary Force', *RUSI Journal*, 66 (1921).

6 A.W. Abbott, 'Lapland, 1918–19: The British Army's Farthest North', *Army Quarterly*, 84, July 1962.

7 National Army Museum, 6302–61, Trevor Barlow, 'Letters from Murmansk'.

8 Major-General Sir Edmund Ironside, 'The North Russian Campaign', *Journal of the Royal Artillery*, 53, October 1926.

9 Roland Huntford, *Shackleton* (London, 1985), pp. 667–72.

10 Maynard, *Murmansk Venture*, p. 168.

11 H.C. Wylly, *The Green Howards in the Great War* (Richmond, 1926), pp. 208–9; G. Powell,

The Green Howards (London, 1992), p. 165; Nationl Archives, WO 95/5427; Edmund Ironside, *Archangel, 1918–19* (London 1953) pp. 110–11.

12   The diary of Private J. Grogan, quoted in J. Maddocks, *The Liverpool Pals* (London, 1991), pp. 199 and 201.

13   Imperial War Museum, 80/28/1, A.E. Thompson, 'North Russian Diary'.

14   John Swettenham, *Allied Intervention in Russia, 1918–1919* (London, 1967), pp. 5–6.

15   E.M. Halliday, *The Ignorant Armies* (London, 1961), pp. 125–28; Ironside, *Archangel*, pp. 98–100.

16   Halliday, *Ignorant Armies*, pp. 128–39; Swettenham, *Allied Intervention*, pp. 196–98.

17   Ironside, *Archangel*, pp. 102–4; Halliday, *Ignorant Armies*, 198–99; Swettenham, *Allied Intervention*, pp. 140–46.

18   Martin Gilbert, *Winston S. Churchill*, iv, pp. 507–8 and 515–16.

19   National Archives, WO 158/714.

20   Imperial War Museum, Papers of W.C.T. Roeber, R.H. Gilmore, 'With the North Russian Expedition'; National Archives, WO 106/1530, GOC Archangel to War Office, 2 February 1919; WO 33/966, War Office to GOC Archangel 2 February 1919; WO 106/1153, GOC Archangel to War Office, 3 February 1919, War Office to GOC Archangel, 7 February 1919.

21   Quoted in Gilbert, *Churchill*, iv, p. 105.

22   For example Kettle, *Archangel Fiasco*, pp. 77 and 317; Ullman, *Britain and the Russian Civil War*, p. 181.

23   Royal Artillery Archives, Woolwich, Turner Papers, Turner to Ironside, 17 April 1919.

24   National Archives, WO 33/966; Halliday, *Ignorant Armies*, p. 186; *Times*, 3 February 1919; S. Jones, 'The Right Medicine for the Bolshevist', *Imperial War Museum Review*, 12 (1999), pp. 78–88.

25   Bentley Historical Library, University of Michigan, R.S. Clark, 'What Ails the ANREF?'

26   National Archives, WO 106/ 1153, Ironside to War Office, 19 February 1919.

27   Imperial War Museum, P352, diary of Captain Roeber, pp. 41–42.

28   National Archves, WO 106/1153, Ironside to War Office, 27 February 1919.

29   National Archives, WO 106/1153; WO 95/5427; Ironside, *Archangel*, pp. 112–14.

30   General Maruchevsky, quoted in L. James, *Mutiny in the British Commonwealth Forces, 1797–1956* (London, 1987), p. 134.

31   National Archives, WO 106/1153, Ironside to War Office, 27 February 1919. The court martial records, however, WO 213/29, show only six Yorkshires convicted of mutiny in north Russia.

32   The records show three men of 17th Liverpools court martialled for mutiny on the same day as some of the Yorkshires.

33   Imperial War Museum, diary of Private Riley Rudd RAMC. Rudd was a stretcher-bearer whose duties took him between the front line and the Seletskoe hospital.

34   WO 95/5427. There is, of course, no mention of the mutiny in the unit war diary.

35   Imperial War Museum, A.E. Thompson, North Russian Diary.

36   National Army Museum, 6602–68, Sergeant E.S. Virpsha, 'The Archangel Expedition'.

37   Imperial War Museum, Roeber Papers; E.H.Gilmore, 'With the North Russian Expedition, 1918–19'.

38 Ironside, *Archangel*, p. 84.

39 G.Fraser, *The House by the Dvina* (London, 1986), p. 253; Ironside, *Archangel* pp. 557–58, Ironside, 'The North Russian Campaign', p. 317.

40 National Army Museum, AM 8202, Beavan Papers. There was, however, some delay in getting the necessary officers and NCOs. Posts in the SBL were still being advertised in Sector Orders as late as mid-April 1919.

Notes to Chapter 8: The Baltic Knot

1 St Antony's College, Oxford, D. J. Footman, 'Civil War in the Baltic Area: II. The North Western Army' (unpublished, 1959).

2 S. Roskill, *Naval Policy between the Wars* (London, 1968), pp. 143–45; John Silverlight, *The Victors' Dilemma* (London, 1970), pp. 293–96.

3 Admiral Sir Bertram Thesiger quoted in G. Bennett, *Cowan's War* (London, 1964), p. 59; General Sir Hubert Gough, *Soldiering On* (London, 1954), p. 195.

4 L. Dawson, *Sound of the Guns* (Oxford, 1949), p. 158; Martin Gilbert, *Winston S. Churchill*, *CV*, iv, pt. 1 (London, 1977) pp. 641–42.

5 Gough, *Soldiering On*, pp. 190–92.

6 Sir Stephen Tallents, *Man and Boy* (London 1943), pp. 343–44.

7 This account of Lieutenant Agar's exploits is based on his autobiography, *Footprints in the Sea* (London, 1959), pp. 87–147, and his more detailed account, *Baltic Episode* (London, 1963).

8 National Archives, CAB 23/15, War Cabinet Minutes, 4 July 1919.

Notes to Chapter 9: Plan of Attack

1 Michael Kettle, *Churchill and the Archangel Fiasco* (London, 1992), p. 134.

2 Richard H. Ullman, *Britain and the Russian Civil War* (Princeton, 1968), p. 136–48; Kettle, *Archangel Fiasco*, pp. 134–35, quoting the US Senate hearings on the Bullitt Mission.

3 National Archives, WO 0149/6324.

4 Edmund Ironside, *Archangel, 1918–19* (London, 1953), p. 123.

5 *Hansard*, Commons, cxiii.

6 Martin Gilbert, *Winston S. Churchill* (London, 1975), iv, pp. 275–76.

7 National Archives, WO 32/6582, Churchill to Generals Harington and Radcliffe, 5 March 1919.

8 National Archives, WO 0149/ 6399.

9 Gilbert, *Churchill*, iv, p. 270.

10 Ironside, *Archangel*, p. 56.

11 John Silverlight, *The Victors' Dilemma* (London, 1970), pp. 136–37 and 197.

12 Ullman, *Britain and the Russian Civil War*, p. 180.

13 Gilbert, *Churchill*, iv, p. 274.

14 Quoted in John Swettenham, *Allied Intervention in Russia, 1918–1919* (London, 1967), p. 217.

15   Churchill College Archive Centre, Cambridge, Churchill Papers, CHAR 16/22.

16   Ibid.

17   Churchill to Beaverbrook, 12 February 1918, quoted in Kenneth Young, *Churchill and Beaverbrook* (London, 1966), p. 47.

18   HMSO, Cmd 8 (Russia No 1 [1919]), April 1919.

19   Ullman, *Britain and the Russian Civil War*, p. 141; Silverlight, *The Victors' Dilemma*, p. 191.

20   F.R. Harris in a Foreign Office minute cited in Ullman, *Britain and the Russian Civil War*, pp. 142–43.

21   Silverlight, *Victors' Dilemma*, p. 192, emphasises this point.

22   Ironside, *Archangel*, p. 106.

23   Gilbert, *Churchill*, iv, p. 271; Ullman, *Britain and the Russian Civil War*, pp. 143–44.

24   Ullman, *Britain and the Russian Civil War*, pp. 144–51; Kettle, *Archangel Fiasco*, pp. 211–12, 223–24; Silverlight, *Victors' Dilemma*, pp. 156–60.

25   Riddell Diary, quoted in Ullman, *Britain and the Russian Civil War*, p. 153.

26   *Hansard*, Commons 16 April 1919, col. 2945.

27   Ibid., col. 2973.

Notes to Chapter 10: Maynard's Offensive

1   John Swettenham, *Allied Intervention in Russia, 1918–1919* (London, 1967), pp. 200–2.

2   National Archives, WO 33/966; Sir George Schuster, *Private Work and Public Causes* (Cowbridge, 1979), pp. 22–23.

3   Imperial War Museum, DS/Misc/97, autobiography of Group Captain R.J. Bone.

4   Imperial War Museum, Colonel P.J. Woods, 'Karelian Diary'.

5   Schuster, *Private Work and Public Causes*, pp. 28–29; National Archives, WO 33/966.

6   National Archives, WO 33/967A, Maynard to War Office, 24 June.

7   National Archives, WO 33/966.

8   National Archives, WO 33/967A.

9   Major V.M. Bentinck, *Mutiny at Murmansk*, ch. 2 and annex C, Royal Marines Historical Society, 1999; Imperial War Museum, PP/MCR/99, Commander Drage, 'Some Modern Naval Mutinies'; National Archives, ADM 137/1721.

10   National Archives, ADM 137/1721, telegrams of 4, 12, 18 and 21 June, 21, 23 and 27 July.

Notes to Chapter 11: The North Russian Relief Force

1   *The Times*, 9 April 1919.

2   Imperial War Museum, 86/86/1, Major E.M. Allfrey, 'Five Months with 45th Battalion Royal Fusiliers in North Russia'.

3   Quoted in Michael Kettle, *Churchill and the Archangel Fiasco* (London, 1992), p. 269.

4   G.R. Singleton-Gates, *Bolos and Barishnyas* (Aldershot, 1920), p. 2.

5   Allfrey, 'Five Months', pp. 1–2; Kettle, *Archangel Fiasco*, p. 542.

6 Allfrey, 'Five Months', p. 5.

7 National Archives, WO 95/5422.

8 Imperial War Museum, PD/MCR/182, Papers of Major General D. Wimberley; 78/27/1, Major B.A. Pond, 'A Sergeant in North Russia'; J.E.H. Neville, *History of 43rd and 52nd Light Infantry in the Great War, 1914–19* (Aldershot, 1938), p. 309.

9 Richard H. Ullman, *Britain and the Russian Civil War* (Princeton, 1968), p. 181.

10 National Army Museum, DS/Misc/80, Wilson Diary.

11 Edmund Ironside, *Archangel, 1918–19* (London, 1953), p. 208.

12 Allfrey, 'Five Months', p. 1.

13 Captain E. Altham, ' The Dwina Campaign', *RUSI Journal*, 470 (1923), p. 241.

14 Altham, 'The Dwina Campaign', pp. 240–43.

15 National Archives, WO 32/5749, Price to Churchill, 16 April 1919.

16 National Archives, WO 32/5749.

17 Ironside, *Archangel*, pp. 126–27; John Swettenham, *Allied Intervention in Russia, 1918–1919* (London, 1967), pp. 218–19.

18 National Archives, WO 106/1153, Ironside to War Office, 18 May 1919 (three separate telegrams).

19 Twenty years earlier, as a young officer, Churchill had written *The River War*, a 250,000 word, two-volume account of the reconquest of the Sudan via its great river, the Nile.

20 Altham, 'The Dwina Campaign', pp. 243–44; Kettle, *Archangel Fiasco*, p. 355.

21 Kettle, *Archangel Fiasco*, pp. 356–67.

22 Major V.M. Bentinck, *Mutiny in Murmansk*, Royal Marines Historical Society (1999), p. 46.

23 Imperial War Museum, Papers of Commander T. St V. Tyler; 76/114/2, Papers of Commander J.H. Bowen.

24 P. Burgess, 'The Australians in North Russia, 1919', *Sabretache*, August 1976, pp. 266–78; Imperial War Museum, 94/11/1, Diary of Sergeant R.S. Mouat; Allfrey, 'Five Months', p. 15.

25 Imperial War Museum, Brigadier E.A. Arderne, 'An Army Life, 1918–1944', p. 6.

26 Imperial War Museum, P 352, Roeber Papers, *G.A.F.*, Issue 1, 7 June 1919.

27 Martin Gilbert, *Winston S. Churchill*, iv, *CV*, pt 1 (London, 1977), p. 679.

28 Ibid., pp. 679 and 680.

29 Ibid., pp. 685–86.

30 Ibid., pp. 699–704.

31 Ironside, *Archangel*, pp. 151–52; National Army Museum, 6112–637, Graham's Brigade Order No. 1 and War Diary; R. Hampshires Museum, 2nd Hampshire's War Diary.

32 National Army Museum, Graham's Brigade Operation Report; Ironside, *Archangel*, pp. 152–53.

33 National Archives, WO 33/967a, Ironside to War Office, 22, 23 and 27 June; WO 95/5419; National Army Museum, Graham's Brigade Operation Report; WO 339/13469; Kettle, *Archangel Fiasco*, p. 504, WO 95/5422; Imperial War Museum, Papers of Brigadier J.B. Gawthorpe.

34 Imperial War Museum, 74/29/1, Letter of Lieutenant M.S. Moore, 25 June 1919.

35 National Archives, WO 33/967A, Ironside to War Office; Imperial War Museum, 74/29/1,

Moore letter 6 August 1919; Hampshire Regimental Journal, March 1920, p. 45; National Archives, WO 95/5422, WO 339/13469.

36 Gilbert, iv, *CV*, pt 1, p. 705–6.

37 Ullman, *Britain and the Russian Civil War*, p. 190; Kettle, *Archangel Fiasco*, p. 520; Altham, *Dwina Campaign*, pp. 238–39.

38 Gilbert, *Churchill*, iv, *CV*, pt 1, pp. 715–19.

39 Ironside, *Archangel*, pp. 155–56.

40 Ironside, *Archangel*, pp. 157–58.

41 Papers of Commander Tyler; Allfrey, 'Five Months', p. 76; Kettle, *Archangel Fiasco*, pp. 541–43. Ironside's figure for the extent of the defection varied in his writings over time: 'about 150' in his first despatch, 300 in 1926, 100 in 1953, WO 0149/6399; Ironside, 'The North Russian Campaign', p. 158; Ironside, *Archangel*, p. 158.

42 Ironside, *Archangel*, p. 158; National Archives, WO 0149/6399, WO 32/9545.

43 *Times*, 25 July 1919; A. Soutar, *With Ironside in North Russia* (London, 1940), pp. 137–39; National Archives, WO 35/9545; Allfrey, 'Five Months', pp. 76–79; Kettle, *Archangel Fiasco*, p. 544.

44 Singleton-Gates, *Bolos and Barishnyas*, p. 55; Altham, 'Dwina Campaign', pp. 246–47.

45 Once again Ironside's published account is erroneous: he writes of only two being shot. *Archangel*, p. 159; Allfrey, 'Five Months', p. 81; J. Putkowski, *British Army Mutineers, 1914–22* (London, 1998); National Archives, WO 213/32/58–9, WO 33/967; Eugenie Fraser, *The Dvina Remains* (Edinburgh, 1996), p. 146.

46 Allfrey, 'Five Months', pp. 75–84.

47 National Archives, WO 32/9545.

48 Ironside, *Archangel*, pp. 160–61; Ullman, *Britain and the Russian Civil War*, pp. 193–94.

49 L. I. Strakhovsky, *Intervention at Archangel* (Princeton, 1944), p. 210; Ironside, *Archangel*, pp. 161–64; M. Hudson, *Intervention in Russia, 1918–1920* (Barnsley, 2004), pp. 5–8; St Antony's College, Oxford, D. Footman, 'Murmansk and Archangel' (unpublished, 1957).

50 National Archives, WO 95/5419; Kettle, *Archangel Fiasco*, pp. 550–51; Imperial War Museum, 84/52/1, Papers of Seaman R. Jowett, Papers of Commander Tyler.

51 Altham, 'Dwina Campaign', pp. 247–48; Ullman, *Britain and the Russian Civil War*, pp. 194–45; National Archives, WO 33/967.

Notes to Chapter 12: The White Advance

1 C.T. Atkinson, *The Royal Hampshire Regiment* (Winchester, 1952), ii, p. 444; Royal Hampshire Regiment Archives, Winchester, A.A. Jupe, 'Round the World with the PBI'.

2 J. Swettenham, *Allied Intervention in Russia, 1918–19* (London, 1967), pp. 172–78 and 186.

3 Swettenham, *Allied Intervention*, pp. 176 and 186.

4 National Archives, WO 32/5707, 'Report on the Work of the British Military Mission to Siberia, 1918–19'; R.H. Ullman, *Britain and the Russian Civil War* (Princeton, 1968), pp. 35–637; Swettenham, *Allied Intervention*, pp. 160–62.

5 T.H. Jameson, *Expedition to Siberia, 1919*, Royal Marine Historical Society (1987).

6   Swettenham, *Allied Intervention*, pp. 160–62; M. Kettle, *Churchill and the Archangel Fiasco* (London, 1992), pp. 25–26.

7   National Archives, WO 32/5707, Knox Final Report; Ullman, *Britain and the Russian Civil War*, p. 32.

8   J. Ward, *With the 'Diehards' in Siberia* (London, 1920), pp. 172–97.

9   National Archives, WO 106/1320, Peacock Report.

10   Jameson, *Expedition to Siberia*, pp. 13–15.

11   National Archives, WO 33/977, Narrative of Events in Siberia, p. 30.

12   P. Knightley, *The First Casualty* (London, 1975), pp. 157–62.

13   Martin Gilbert, *Winston S. Churchill*, iv, *CV*, pt 1 (London, 1975), pp. 624–66.

14   National Archives, WO 32/5707, Knox Final Report; C. Dobson and J. Miller, *The Day We Almost Bombed Moscow* (London, 1986), p. 238.

15   Gilbert, *Winston S. Churchill*, iv, *CV* pt 1, p. 650; iv, pp. 288–93.

16   Liddell Hart Centre for Military Archives, Papers of Admiral Sir Malcolm Goldsmith.

17   Imperial War Museum, P/400, Papers of Engineer Rear Admiral P.J. Shrubsole; 87/20/1, Diary of H.A. Hill.

18   Imperial War Museum, Papers of Air Vice-Marshal C.N.H. Bilney.

19   Imperial War Museum, C.E. De Wolff, 'Odd Notes', p. 44; John Harris (ed.), *Farewell to the Don* (London, 1970), pp. 33, 81.

20   Liddell Hart Centre, J. Kennedy, 'South Russian Diaries'; De Wolff, 'Odd Notes'; J. Ainsworth, 'A Friend in Need', ch. 6; John Silverlight, *The Victors' Dilemma* (London, 1970), pp. 332–34.

21   National Archives, WO 33/967A; B. H. Liddell Hart, *The Tanks* (London, 1959), pp. 211–12.

22   R. Collishaw, *Air Command: A Fighter Pilot's Story* (London, 1973); Ainsworth, 'A Friend in Need', ch. 7.

23   Collishaw, *Air Command* pp. 185–87; H.A. Jones, *Over the Balkans and South Russia: 47 Squadron RAF* (London, 1923), pp. 149–50.

24   Ainsworth, 'A Friend in Need', ch. 8; Collishaw, *Air Command*, p. 190.

25   National Archives, WO 32/5687, Denmiss to War Office.

26   Kennedy, 'South Russian Diaries'; Harris, *Farewell to the Don*, p. 82; Lever, Diary.

27   De Wolff, 'Odd Notes', pp. 45–46; National Archives, WO 95/4959.

28   General I.A. Denikin, *The White Army* (Cambridge, 1992), p. 224.

29   National Archives, WO 95/4959; Imperial War Museum, Air Vice-Marshal C.N.H. Bilney, 'A Seaplane Pilot's Wanderings'; Papers of Lieutenant J.D. Snow.

30   National Archives, WO 33/975; Harris, *Farewell to the Don*, p. 144; J.N. Kennedy, 'The Anti-Bolshevik Movement in South Russia, 1917–1920', *RUSI Journal*, 67 (1922), p. 611.

31   W.R. and Z.K. Coates, *Armed Intervention in Russia, 1918–22* (London, 1935), pp. 288–91; Gilbert, *Churchill*, iv, pp. 330, 341–43; Gilbert, *Churchill*, iv, *CV*, pt 2, pp. 906–7, 912; Kennedy, 'South Russian Diaries'; Papers of Admiral Sir William Goldsmith.

32   Kennedy, 'South Russian Diaries'; Imperial War Museum, Pole-Evans Papers; J.E. Hodgson, *With Denikin's Armies* (London, 1934), quoted in Ullman, *Britain and the Russian Civil War*, p. 213; National Archives, WO 95/4959, Holman Interim Report, 21 July 1919.

33   Harris, *Farewell to the Don*, pp. 141–42.

34 Liddell Hart Centre, Lieutenant Colonel F.H. Lister, 'Diary of a Journey to South Russia'; Kennedy, 'South Russian Diaries'; Lever, Diary.

Notes to Chapter 13: The Evacuation of Archangel

1 Martin Gilbert, *Winston S. Churchill*, iv, *CV*, pt 2 (London, 1977), pp. 736–39 and 752–56.
2 Gilbert, *Churchill*, iv, *CV*, pt 2, p. 766–74; Imperial War Museum, DS/Misc 80, Wilson Diary, 29 July 1919; Natinal Archives, WO 33/967A.
3 Gilbert, *Churchill*, iv, *CV*, pt 2, p. 777.
4 National Army Museum, 5201–33, Rawlinson Diary, 31 July 1919; National Archives, WO 95/5419, Rawlinson Terms of Reference dated 2 August 1919.
5 Glbert, *Churchill*, iv, *CV*, pt 1, pp. 716–19; *Daily Express*, 26 July, 1 and 2 August 1919.
6 Imperial War Museum, P/19, Papers of Lieutenant General A.E. Percival; G.R. Singleton Gates, *Bolos and Barishnyas* (Aldershot, 1920).
7 Imperial War Museum, Brigadier E.A. Arderne, 'An Army Life, 1918–1944'.
8 Imperial War Museum, 94/11/1, Diary of Sergeant R.S. Mouat.
9 Edmund Ironside, *Archangel, 1918–19* (London, 1953) p. 168; Percival Private Papers; Singleton-Gates, *Bolos and Barishnyas*; Allfrey, p. 170; Mouat Diary.
10 S. Jones, 'The Right Medicine for the Bolshevists', *Imperial War Museum Review*, 12 (1999); Michael Kettle, *Churchill and the Archangel Fiasco* (London, 1992), pp. 316–17.
11 National Archives, WO 339/13469.
12 Jones, 'The Right Medicine for the Bolshevists' p. 83; Rawlinson Diary, 27 August and 7 September.
13 P. Burness, 'The Australians in North Russia, 1919', *Sabretache*, August 1976.
14 Imperial War Museum, 73/9/2 Sturdy Papers, Ironside, Report on Operations May–October 1919; Jones, 'The Right Medicine for the Bolshevist' p. 84–85; Rawlinson Diary, 9 September.
15 Captain E. Altham, 'The Dwina Campaign', *RUSI Journal*, 470 (1923); Imperial War Museum, 84/52/1, Papers of Seaman R. Jowett.
16 *Daily Express*, 10 September 1919.
17 *Daily Express*, 10 September 1919; W.P. and Z.K. Coates, *Armed Intervention in Russia, 1918–1922* (London, 1935), p. 172; Rawlinson Diary; Imperial War Museum, Papers of Seaman Jowett; Major E.M. Allfrey, 'Five Months with 45th Battalion Royal Fusiliers in North Russia', p. 179–80.
18 HMSO, Cmd 818, 1920.
19 Gilbert, *Churchill*, iv, *CV*, pt 2, Churchill to Wilson, 30 August 1919, p. 825.
20 Leonid I. Strakhovsky, *Intervention at Archangel* (Princeton, 1944), pp. 213–30; Gilbert, *Churchill*, iv, CV, pt 2, pp. 834–35.
21 Imperial War Museum, 86/30/1, Papers of J.M. Cordy; National Archives, WO 95/5419; St Antony's College, Oxford, D. Footman, 'Murmansk and Archangel' (unpublished 1957); Rawlinson Diary.
22 Strakhovsky, *Intervention at Archangel*, pp. 231 and 232, quoting Russian sources.
23 Eugenie Fraser, *The House by the Dwina*, p. 262.

Notes to Chapter 14: Crisis at Murmansk

1   Martin Gilbert, *Winston S. Churchill*, iv, *CV*, pt 2, p. 753.
2   Imperial War Museum, 65/38/1, Papers of Brigadier P.R.Smith Hill; PP/MCR/99, Commander C.H. Drage, 'Some Modern Naval Mutinies'; Major E.M. Bentinck, *Mutiny in Murmansk*, Royal Marines Historical Society (Portsmouth, 1999).
3   National Archives, WO 33/967A; National Army Museum, 5201–33, Rawlinson Diary.
4   Simon Jones, 'The Right Medicine for the Bolshevist', *Imperial War Museum Review*, 12 (1999), pp. 65–66.
5   Smith-Hill Papers; Drage, 'Naval Mutinies'.
6   Letter of 3 November quoted in Bentinck, *Mutiny in Murmansk*, pp. 63–69.
7   Smith-Hill Papers.
8   Bentinck, *Mutiny in Murmansk*, pp. 32–34; Smith-Hill Papers.
9   National Archives, ADM 137/1721, MO5 to Ops Div Admiralty, 15 September 1919.
10 Drage, 'Naval Mutinies'.
11 Julian Thompson, *The Royal Marines* (London, 2000), pp. 210–11.
12 National Army Museum, 5201/33, Rawlinson Diary; WO 33/967A.
13 The speech is given in full in Bentinck, *Mutiny at Murmansk*, pp. 72–73.
14 One of the officers, Captain Watts, was sentenced to be dismissed the service for 'using words calculated to create alarm and dispondency'. He had been wounded at Gallipoli, had a permanently disabled arm and a record of subsequent accidents and illnesses. During the battle he had personally spent time under fire bandaging the wounded. The Admiralty later quashed his conviction and sentence.
15 Smith-Hill Papers; Bentinck, *Mutiny at Murmansk*, annex G.
16 It is notable that the Royal Marines' own publication on the incident employs the term.
17 Smith-Hill Papers; Bentick, *Mutiny at Murmansk*, ch. 3; Jones, 'The Right Medicine for the Bolshevists', p. 86.
18 Major General Sir C. Maynard, *The Murmansk Venture* (London, 1929), p. 311; Imperial War Museum, Papers of Major H.E. Ward.
19 *Hansard*, Commons, 19 November and 22 December 1919; Bentinck, *Mutiny at Murmansk*, annexes I and L.
20 Leonid I. Strakhovsky, *Intervention at Archangel* (Princeton, 1944), pp. 240–54.
21 Reports coming to the Foreign Office indicated that the bulk of the excesses were committed, not by the Red Army, but by civilian irregulars and partisans, Ullman, *Britain and the Russian Civil War* (Princeton, 1968), p. 201.
22 Ullman, *Britain and the Russian Civil War*, pp. 200–1; Strakhovsky, *Intervention at Archangel*, pp. 240–54.

Notes to Chapter 15: Petrograd Fiasco

1   General Sir Hubert Gough, *Soldiering On* (London, 1954), p. 126.
2   John Silverlight, *The Victors' Dilemma* (London, 1970), pp. 306 and 316–17; G. Bennett, *Cowan's War* (London, 1964), p. 105; Gough, *Soldiering On*, p. 194; St Antony's College,

Oxford, D.J. Footman, 'The North Western Army' (unpublished, 1959).

3   Richard H. Ullman, *Britain and the Russian Civil War* (Princeton, 1968), pp. 258–62; Martin Gilbert, *Winston S. Churchill*, iv, *CV*, pt 2 (London, 1977), p. 726.

4   Silverlight, *Victors' Dilemma*, pp. 308–9, Martin Gilbert, *Winston S. Churchill*, iv, p. 292.

5   National Achives, WO 32/5692.

6   Gilbert, *Churchill*, pp. 292–93.

7   Silverlight, *Victors' Dilemma*, 6 p. 310; Ullman, *Britain and the Russian Civil War*, pp. 266–67.

8   W.P. and Z.K. Coates, *Armed Intervention in Russia, 1918–22*, pp. 183–84; Ullman, *Britain and the Russian Civil War*, p. 268, uses both Russian and British sources for the account of this extraordinary meeting. They largely agree.

9   Footman, 'North-Western Army'.

10 Silverlight, *Victors' Dilemma*, p. 310–12; Ullman, *Britain and the Russian Civil War*, p. 273.

11 Gough to Churchill, 14 June 1919, Gilbert, *Churchill*, iv, *CV*, pt 1, p. 696; Churchill to Lloyd George et al., 24 August 1919, Gilbert, *Churchill*, iv, *CV*, pt 2, p. 816; Sir Stephen Tallents, *Man and Boy* (London, 1943), p. 318.

12 Memorandum dated 30 August, Gilbert, *Churchill*, iv, *CV*, pt 2, p. 827.

13 Gilbert, *Churchill*, iv, *CV*, pt 2, pp. 818 and 825; Ullman, *Britain and the Russian Civil War*, p. 272; Gough, *Soldiering On*, p. 120.

14 L. Dawson, *Sound of the Guns* (Oxford, 1949), pp. 164–69, Stephen Roskill, *British Naval Policy between the Wars* (London, 1968), p. 150.

15 Bennett, *Cowan's War*, pp. 157–58.

16 Silverlight, *Victors' Dilemma*, pp. 316–20; Ullman, *Britain and the Russian Civil War*, pp. 274–81.

17 Ullman, *Brtain and the Russian Civil War*, p. 282; Bennett, *Cowan's War*, p. 143; Silverlight, *Victors' Dilemma*, p. 320–22; Churchill to Balfour 23 August 1919, Gilbert, *Churchill*, iv, *CV*, pt 2, p. 813.

18 Bennett, *Cowan's War*, pp. 172–80; Silverlight, *Victors' Dilemma*, p. 323; Footman, 'North Western Army'.

19 Ullman, *Britain and the Russian Civil War*, pp. 283–84; Bennett, *Cowan's War*, pp. 181–82.

20 Gilbert, *Churchill*, iv, p. 348; Gilbert, *Churchill*, iv, *CV*, pt 2, pp. 923, 931–34.

21 Bennett, *Cowan's War*, p. 187; Lieutenant Colonel E. Hope-Carson, 'British Tanks in North-West Russia', *Royal Tank Corps Journal*, vol. 9, no. 98.

22 Gilbert, *Churchill*, iv, *CV*, pt 2, p. 995.

23 Ullman, *Britain and the Russian Civil War*, p. 286–87; Gilbert, Churchill, iv, *CV*, pt 2, p. 990.

24 Bennett, *Cowan's War*, p. 197–98; J. Wells, *The Royal Navy: An Illustrated Social History, 1870–1922*, pp. 125–26.

25 Quoted in Bennett, *Cowan's War*, p. 202.

26 Gough, *Soldiering On*, p. 195; Roskill, *British Naval Policy between the Wars*, p.153; Bennett, *Cowan's War*, pp. 203–4.

27 Bennett, *Cowan's War*, appendix A; Churchill to Curzon 5 January 1920, Gilbert, *Churchill*, iv, *CV*, pt 2, p. 990.

Notes to Chapter 16: Collapse

1   B. Horrocks, *A Full Life* (London, 1960), pp. 44–46; Johnson Papers, quoted in C. Dobson and J. Miller, *The Day We Almost Bombed Moscow* (London, 1986), pp. 238–39; Royal Hampshire Regiment Archives, Sergeant A.A. Jupe, 'Round the World with the PBI'.

2   National Archives, WO 32/5707, Knox, Final Report; National Army Museum 7603–93, Papers of Lieutenant General Sir Reginald Savory; J. Ward, *With the 'Diehards' in Siberia* (London, 1920), pp. 216–22.

3   Dobson and Miller, *Moscow* pp. 235–37.

4   Martin Gilbert, *Winston S. Churchill*, iv, *CV*, pt 1, pp. 624–25, 640 and 645.

5   Gilbert, *Churchill*, iv, *CV*, pt 1, pp. 680, 693; National Archives, WO 32/5707, appendix I, Blair Report; WO 106/1272.

6   A.E. Steel, *A Memoir of Lieutenant Colonel A.E. Steel* (London, 1921), pp. 154–55.

7   John Silverlight, *The Victors' Dilemma* (London, 1970), p. 258; National Army Museum, 7603–93, Papers of Lieutenant General Sir Reginald Savory.

8   National Archives, WO 106/1272.

9   National Archives, WO 95/ 5433, War Diary, British Military Mision Siberia; J. Ward, *With the 'Diehards' in Siberia* (London, 1920), pp. 170 and 225–32.

10   Royal Hampshire Regiment Archives, A.A. Jupe, 'Round the World with the PBI'; Dobson and Miller, *Moscow*, pp. 240–41.

11   T.H. Jameson, *Expedition to Siberia, 1919*, Royal Marine Historical Society (Plymouth, 1987), pp. 26–38.

12   National Archives, WO 32/5707, Knox Final Report, appendix C.

13   Gilbert, *Churchill*, iv, *CV*, pt 1, p. 694; National Archives, WO 106/1272, enclosure A; Imperial War Museum, Jack Papers, Jack to Brigadier General Mance, 23 July 1919.

14   Imperial War Museum, 88/46/1, Papers of T.E. Ivens.

15   Horrocks, *A Full Life*, pp. 47–60; Francis McCullagh, *A Prisoner of the Reds* (London, 1920), passim.

16   Swettenham, *Allied Intervention in Russia*, pp. 239–43; Peter Fleming, *The Fate of Admiral Kolchak* (London, 1963). A full acount of Kolchak's *via dolorosa* to his Irkutsk execution is given in chapters 15–20.

17   National Archives, WO 32/5707, Knox Final Report.

18   Gilbert, *Churchill*, iv, *CV*, pt 2, pp. 896, 904–6 and 911.

19   Liddell Hart Centre for Military Archives, Lieutenant Colonel F.H.Lister, 'Diary of a Journey to South Russia, 1919–20'.

20   National Archives, WO 32/5711.

21   National Archives, AIR/1/2375; Dobson and Miller, *Moscow*, pp. 23–24; Liddell Hart Centre, Diary of Captain G.H. Lever; Gilbert, iv, pt 2, p. 954.

22   National Archives, WO 33/971; Liddell Hart Centre, Lever Diary; Kennedy Diary; Lister Diary.

23   National Archives, WO 33/971; IWM P/358, Lieutenant H.W. Sedgewick, 'Journey to South Russia'; Liddell Hart Centre, Lever Diary; Gilbert, Churchill, iv, CV, pt 2, pp. 986–87, 993–94.

24   Liddell Hart Centre, Lister Diary; Lever Diary.

25   Imperial War Museum, Report of Captain J.W.C. Lancaster; K. Paustovsky, *Into That Dawn* (1967), quoted in Silverlight, *Victors' Dilemma*, p. 355.

26   National Archives, WO 158/746; Liddell Hart Centre, Lister Diary.

27   National Archives WO 158/746; Sir Tom Bridges, *Alarms and Excursions* (London, 1938), pp. 287–94.

28   Liddell Hart Centre, Lever Diary; National Archives, WO 158/76.

29   Imperial War Museum, 79/45/1, Papers of Wing Commander Jenks; J. Harris (ed.), *Farewell to the Don* (London, 1970), p. 280; Liddell Hart Centre, Captain Basil Jones, *And So To Battle* (privately published).

30   Gilbert, *Churchill*, iv, *CV*, pt 2, pp. 1059 and 1061.

31   Liddell Hart Centre, Lister Diary, Percy to Lister, 9 May 1920.

32   Major General Ashton Wade, 'Military Missions to South Russia', *Army Quarterly and Defence Journal*, October 1981, pp. 417–18; Lieutenant J.N. Kennedy, 'The Anti-Bolshevik Movement in South Russia 1917–20', *RUSI Journal*, 67 (1922), pp. 617–18.

33   Martin Gilbert, *Winston S.Churchill*, iv (London, 1975), pp. 399–400.

Notes to Chapter 17: Failure

1   Sir Tom Bridges, *Alarms and Excursions* (London, 1938), p. 295.

2   Records of the Commonwealth War Graves Commission.

3   HMSO, Cmd 307, 395 and 772; Winston S. Churchill, *The World Crisis: The Aftermath* (London, 1929), p. 256.

4   *New York Times*, 20 September 1959, quoted in John Silverlight, *The Victors' Dilemma* (London, 1970), p. 368.

5   Stephen Roskill, *British Naval Policy between the Wars* (London, 1968), p. 180.

6   Speech on Army Estimates, 29 July 1919, reproduced in Cmd 818, *The Evacuation of North Russia*, p. 3; *Daily News* 31 July 1919, letter of Major General Sir Fredrick Maurice.

7   F.J. Moberly, *History of the First World War: Mesopotamia* (London, 1927), iv, p. 44.

8   Quoted in Arthur Ransome, *Six Weeks in Russia, 1919* (London, 1992), pp. 110–11.

9   D. Volkogonov, *Trotsky: The Eternal Revolutionary* (London, 1996), pp. 164–79.

10   A.E. Steel, *A Memoir of Lieutenant Colonel A.E. Steel* (London, 1921), p. 148; Lieutenant E. Ker, Letter to Mother, 14 February 1919 (private collection); Liddell Hart Centre, Papers of Major General Sir John Kennedy, 2/2, 'South Russian Diaries'; John Harris (ed.) *Farewell to the Don* (London, 1970), p. 256; National Archives, WO 32/5707, Knox Final Report.

11   Colonel John Ward, *With the 'Diehards' in Siberia* (London, 1920), p. 160; Kennedy, 'South Russian Diaries'.

12   An entirely fictional account of a supposed Jewish plan for world domination, plagiarised from an earlier satire and published in Europe as support for the anti-Jewish policies of the Romanov dynasty.

13   Hadassa Ben-Itto, *The Lie That Wouldn't Die: The Protocols of the Elders of Zion* (London, 2005).

14   B. Horrocks, *A Full Life* (London, 1974), p. 51; Liddell Hart Centre for Military Archives, Papers of Admiral Sir Malcolm Goldsmith.

15 Francis McCullagh, *A Prisoner of the Reds* (London, 1921), p. 324; Kennedy, 'South Russian Diaries'.

16 National Archives, FO 608/200; St Antony's College, Oxford, D.J. Footman, 'The North Western Army' (unpublished, 1959).

17 Martin Gilbert, *Winston S. Churchill*, iv, *CV*, pt. 2, p. 1153.

18 Geoffrey Best, *Churchill: A Study in Greatness* (London, 2002), p. 97.

19 Lord Attlee, 'The Churchill I Knew', in *Churchill by his Contemporaries* (London, 1965), p. 30.

20 Quoted in David Stafford, *Churchill and the Secret Service* (London, 1997), p. 9.

21 Roy Jenkins, *Churchill* (London, 2001), pp. 351–53.

22 Duff Cooper, *Old Men Forget* (London, 1979), pp. 98–99; Diana Cooper, *The Rainbow Comes and Goes* (London, 1979), p. 171.

Notes to Appendix 1: The Twenty-Six Commissars

1 Major General Sir W. Malleson, 'The Twenty-Six Commissars', *Fortnightly Review*, 133 (1933), pp. 332–48; Cmd 1846 (Russia No. 1 [1923]), Correspondence between H.M. Govt. and the Soviet Govt. respecting the murder of Mr C.F. Davison in Jan. 1920, pp. 6–11; R.H. Ullman, *Intervention and the War* (London, 1961), pp. 30–25, and John Silverlight, *The Victors' Dilemma* (London, 1970), pp. 210–13.

Notes to Appendix 2: Churchill's Letter of 8 March 1919

1 Churchill Papers, quoted in Gilbert, *Churchill*, iv, *CV*, pt 1, p. 581.

Notes to Appendix 3: The Court Martial of Lieutenant Colonel J. Sherwood Kelly VC, CMG, DSO

1 National Archives, WO 339/13469.

2 *Times*, 29 October 1919 and 19 August 1931; *Daily Express*, 19 August 1931.

3 National Archives, WO 339/13469; I.S. Uys, *For Valour* (Johannesburg, 1973), pp. 261.

Bibliography

PUBLIC DOCUMENTS

Cmd 8 (Russia, No. 1, 1919), *A Collection of Reports on Bolshevism in Russia*, April 1919.

Cmd 307, 1919, *Cost of Naval and Military Operations in Russia from the Date of the Armistice to 31 July 1919.*

Cmd 395, 1919, *Cost of Naval and Military Operations in Russia from the Date of the Armistice to 31 October, 1919.*

Cmd 772, 1920, *Statement of Expenditure on Naval and Military Operations in Russia from the Date of the Armistice to 31 March 1920.*

Cmd 818, 1920, *The Evacuation of North Russia, 1919.*

BOOKS

Agar, A., *Footprints in the Sea* (Evans Bros, London, 1959).

—, *Baltic Episode* (Conway Maritime Press, London, 1963).

Albertson, R., *Fighting Without A War* (Harcourt, Brace and Howe, New York, 1920).

Bailey, F.M., *Mission to Tashkent* (OUP, Oxford,1992).

Beaverbrook, Lord, *Politicians and the Press* (Hutchinson, London, 1925).

—, *Men and Power* (Hutchinson, London, 1956).

Bennett, G., *Cowan's War: The Story of British Naval Operatios in the Baltic, 1918–20* (Collins, London, 1964).

Bentinck, V.M., *Mutiny in Murmansk* (Royal Marines Historical Society, Portsmouth, 1999).

Best, G., *Churchill: A Study in Greatness* (Hambledon and London, London, 2001).

Blaxland, G., *The Middlesex Regiment* (Leo Cooper, London, 1977).

Bradley, J., *Allied Intervention in Russia, 1917–20* (Weidenfeld and Nicholson, London, 1968).

Bridges, T., *Alarms and Excursions* (Longmans, Green, London, 1938).

Brogan, H., *Signalling from Mars: The Letters of Arthur Ransome* (Cape, London, 1997).

Bruce Lockhart, R.H., *Memoirs of a British Agent* (Macmillan, London, 1974).

—, *The Two Revolutions: An Eyewitness Study of Russia, 1917* (Phoenix House, London, 1957)

Carlton, D., *Churchill and the Soviet Union* (Manchester University Press, Manchester, 2000).

Chronicler, A, *The American War with Russia* (McChurg, Chicago, 1924).

Churchill, W.S., *The World Crisis: The Aftermath* (Thornton Butterworth, London, 1929).

Coates, W.P. and Z.K., *Armed Intervention in Russia, 1918–22* (Gollancz, London, 1935).

Collishaw, R., *Air Command: A Fighter Pilot's Story* (William Kimber, London, 1973).

Conquest, R., *Stalin: Breaker of Nations* (Weidenfeld and Nicholson, London, 1991).

Cooper, Diana, *The Rainbow Comes and Goes* (Michael Russell, London, 1979).

Cooper, Duff, *Old Men Forget* (Rupert Hart-Davies, London, 1954).

Dawson, L., *Sound of the Guns* (Pen-in-Hand, Oxford, 1949).

De Lisle, Lieutenant-General Sir B., *Reminiscences of Sport and War* (Eyre and Spottiswoode, London, 1939).

Denikin, A.I., *The White Army* (Ian Faulkner Publishing, Cambridge, 1992).

Dobson, C. and Miller, J., *The Day We Almost Bombed Moscow* (Hodder and Stoughton, London, 1986).

Doolen, R.M,. *Michigan's Polar Bears* (University of Michigan, Ann Arbor, 1965).

Dupuy, R.E., *Perish By The Sword* (Military Service Publishing Co., Harrisburg, 1939).

Egremont, M., *Under Two Flags: The Life of Major General Sir Edward Spears* (Weidenfeld and Nicholson, London, 1997).

Fleming, P., *The Fate of Admiral Kolchak* (London, Hart Davis, 1963).

Fraser, E., *The House by the Dvina* (Mainstream, Edinburgh, 1984).

—, *The Dvina Remains* (Mainstream, Edinburgh, 1996).

Gilbert, M., *Churchill: A Life* (Heinemann, London, 1991).

—, *Winston S. Churchill*, iv, *1916–22* (Heinemann, London, 1975).

—, *Companion Volume*, parts 1 and 2 (1977).

Gough, Sir Hubert, *Soldiering On* (Arthur Barker, London, 1954).

Haffner, S., *Churchill* (House Publishing, London, 2003).

Halliday, E.M., *The Ignorant Armies: The Anglo-American Archangel Expedition, 1918–19* (Weidenfeld and Nicholson, London, 1959).

Harris, J. (ed.), *Farewell to the Don: The Journal of Brigadier H.N.H. Williamson* (Collins, London, 1970).

Horrocks, B., *A Full Life* (Leo Cooper, London, 1974).

Hudson, M., *Intervention in Russia, 1918–1920* (Leo Cooper, Barnsley, 2004).

Huntford, R., *Shackleton* (Hodder and Stoughton, London, 1985).

Ironside, E., *Archangel, 1918–19* (Constable, London, 1953).

Jackson, R., *At War with the Bolsheviks* (Tom Stacey, London, 1972).

James, L., *Mutiny* (Buchan and Enright, London, 1987.

Jameson, T.H.J., *Expedition to Siberia, 1919* (Royal Marines Historical Society, Portsmouth, 1987).

Jenkins, R., *Churchill* (Macmillan, London, 2001).

Jones, H.A., *Over the Balkans and South Russia* (Edward Arnold, London, 1923).

Katkov, G., *The Kornilov Affair* (Longman, London, 1980).

Kenworthy, J.M., *Sailors, Statesmen – and Others* (Rich and Cowan, London, 1933).

Kettle, M, *The Allies and the Russian Collapse* (André Deutsch, London, 1981) —, *Churchill and the Archangel Fiasco* (Routledge, London, 1992).

Knightley, P., *The First Casualty* (Harcourt Brace Jovanovich, London, 1975).

Liddell Hart, B.H., *The Tanks*, i (Cassell, London, 1959).

Luckett, R., *The White Generals* (Longmans, London, 1971).

Lukacs, J., *Churchill* (Yale University Press, New Haven, 2000).

Macpherson, W.G., and Mitchell, T.J., *Medical Services General History*, iv, (HMSO, London 1924).

Maynard, Major-General Sir C., *The Murmansk Venture* (Hodder and Stoughton, London, 1928).

McCullagh, F., *A Prisoner of the Reds: The Story of a British Officer Captured in Siberia* (John Murray, London, 1921).

Jahns, L.E., Mead, H.H., and Moore, J.R., *The History of the American Expedition Fighting the Bolsheviki* (Detroit, Michigan, 1920).

Muirden, B., *The Diggers Who Signed On For More* (Wakefield Press, Kent Town, South Australia, 1990).

Neville, J.E.H., *History of the 43rd and 52nd Light Infantry in the Great War 1914–19* (Gale and Polden, Aldershot, 1938).

Nicol, G., *Uncle George: Field-Marshal Lord Milne of Salonika and Rubislaw* (Reedminster Publications, London, 1976).

Parker, R.A.C. (ed.), *Winston Churchill: Studies in Statesmanship* (Brassey's, London, 2000).

Pelling, H., *Winston Churchill* (Wordsworth, London, 1999).

Perrett, B., and Lord, A., *The Czar's British Squadron* (William Kimber, London, 1981).

Ponting, C., *Churchill* (Sinclair-Stepheson, London, 1994).

Powell, G., *The History of the Green Howards* (Arms and Armour Press, London, 1992).

Putkowski, J., *British Army Mutineers, 1914–22* (Francis Boutle, London, 1998).

Ransome, A., *Six Weeks in Russia, 1919* (Redworks, London, 1992).

Robien, L. de, *The Diary of a Diplomat in Russia, 1917–18*, trans. Camilla Sykes (Michael Joseph, London, 1969).

Roskill, S., *Naval Policy Between the Wars*, i (Collins, London, 1968).

Rothstein, A., *The Soldiers' Strikes of 1919* (Journeyman Press, London, 1985).

Schuster, G., *Private Work and Public Causes* (D. Brown, Cowbridge, 1979).

Silverlight, J., *The Victors' Dilemma* (Barrie and Jenkins, London 1970).

Singleton-Gates, G.R., *Bolos and Barishnyas* (Gale and Polden, Aldershot, 1920).

Soutar, A., *With Ironside in North Russia* (Hutchinson, London, 1940).

Stafford, D., *Churchill and Secret Service* (John Murray, London, 1997).

Stakhovsky, L.I., *Intervention in Archangel* (Princeton University Press, Princeton, 1944).

Steele, J.P., *A Memoir of Lieutenant Colonel A.E. Steele* (Simkin, Marshall, Hamilton, Kent and Co., London, 1921).

Swettenham, J. A., *Allied Intervention in Russia, 1918–1919* (Allen and Unwin, London, 1967).

Tallents, Sir Stephen, *Man and Boy* (Faber and Faber, London, 1943).

Taylor, A.J.P., *Beaverbrook* (Hamish Hamilton, London, 1972).

Thompson, J., *The Royal Marines* (Sidgwick and Jackson, London, 2000).

Uys, I.A., *For Valour* (Ian Uys, Johannesburg, 1973).

Volkogonov, D., *Trotsky: The Eternal Revolutionary* (Harper Collins, London,1996).

Ward, J., *With the 'Die-Hards' in Siberia* (Cassell, London, 1920).

Wedgwood, J., *Memoirs of a Fighting Life* (Hutchinson, London, 1940).

Wells, J., *The Royal Navy: An Illustrated Social History, 1870–1982* (Allan Sutton, 1994).

Wylly, H.C., *The Green Howards in the Great War* (Richmond, Yorks, 1926).

Young, K., *Churchill and Beaverbrook* (Eyre and Spottiswoode, London, 1966).

Young, K. (ed.), *The Diaries of Sir Robert Bruce Lockhart, 1915–1938* (Macmillan, London, 1973).

Index

For individual British and Allied units, see under British and Allied units